Progress in Communication Sciences

Volume X

edited by

Brenda Dervin

The Ohio State University

Melvin J. Voigt

University of California, San Diego

ABLEX Publishing Corporation
Norwood, New Jersey 07648

Copyright © 1991 Ablex Publishing Corporation

Printed in the United States of America.

ISBN:0-89391-645-5   ISSN:0163-5689

ABLEX Publishing Corporation
355 Chestnut Street
Norwood, New Jersey 07648

Contents

Contributors

William L. Benoit (1), Department of Communication, University of Missouri, Columbia, MO 65211

Charles R. Berger (21), Department of Communication Studies, Northwestern University, Evanston, IL 60208–1340

Mary Anne Fitzpatrick (67), Professor and Director, Center for Communication Research, University of Wisconsin, Madison, WI 53706

William B. Gudykunst (21), Department of Speech Communication, California State University, Fullerton, CA 92634

Thomas R. Lindlof (103), Associate Professor, Department of Telecommunications, University of Kentucky, Lexington, KY 40506–0042

Douglas W. Maynard (143), Department of Sociology, University of Wisconsin, Madison, WI 53706

Mary-Jeannette Smythe (173), Associate Professor, Department of Communication, University of Missouri-Columbia, Columbia, MO 65211

Robert S. Taylor (217), School of Information Studies, Syracuse University, Syracuse, NY 13215

Frank Tutzauer (257), Department of Communication, State University of New York, Buffalo, NY 14260

Preface

Volume Nine of *Progress in Communication Sciences,* like its predecessors, is published to provide scholars and students in the diverse specializations within communication and information studies with definitive reviews of advances in theory, research, policy, and practice.

The selection of reviews in this volume reflects, as have past volumes, both the diversity and commonality within and between the different sub-fields which bring to bear their attention on communication and information issues. On a surface level, it is the diversity which is most apparent—a diversity of focus, vocabulary, and reference networks. Yet, at a deeper level closer examination shows a redundancy in fundamental issues being addressed and an increased, although not usually documented in references, intermingling of framings.

Throughout these chapters one finds, for example, evidence of a series of what might be called "turns"—the cognitive turn, the critical turn, the interactional turn, the micro-macro turn, the multiperspective turn. In terms of calls or mandates for attention, these "turns" call for increased attention to: cognitive processes in all arenas of study, the ways in which individual behavior is constrained or defined by larger societal processes, the interrelationships of micro-level and macro-level considerations, the understanding of communicative processes of interactional rather than transmissional, and the bringing to bear on specific phenomena multiple perspectives and research approaches.

Even more apparent throughout these reviews, however, is something which might be called the self-reflexive turn—a way of framing these reviews which is reaching for attention at a higher abstraction level while at the same time being more self-critical and analytic.

Taking these "turns" as the major threads in a larger fabric, they yield a series of state-of-the-art reviews which are theoretically exciting far beyond their individual emphases, while simultaneously being as useful as ever in their individual specificities. There is meat here, therefore, for the individual wanting to get a quick and accessible update on research and thought in specific arenas of study as well as the person reaching for improved understandings and approaches generally.

There are eight chapters in this volume—presented in alphabetical order based on the first letter of the senior author's name. The chapters are focused as follows:

Chapter 1: Benoit's "A cognitive response analysis of source credibility" adopts a cognitive view of communication and social influence in explaining how credibility functions to mediate the relationship between persuasive communications and attitude change. Human goals, motives, purposes, and intent are seen as cognitions that shape both the production of and the interpretation of messages. Using this model, Benoit concludes that for credibility to influence attitude change from a persuasive message it must affect the cognitive processing of the message by suppressing counterargument—by rendering the audience as less likely to question the message. Benoit then identifies factors which may limit this impact.

Chapter 2: Berger and Gudykunst's "Uncertainty and communication" focuses on the processes of the creation and reduction of uncertainty as a grand theory. To this end, the authors explicate the construct of uncertainty and examine research in interpersonal and intercultural communication to demonstrate the construct's utility and ability to transcend contexts. The authors also examine other research which has used uncertainty as a central construct.

Chapter 3: Fitzpatrick's "A microsocietal approach to marital communication" focuses on theoretical and methodological advances and issues relating to the study of communication in marriage. A major focus of the chapter is that understanding marital communication requires attention both at the individual and interactional levels. The individual focus is required because conversation involves cognitive activity by each spouse. The social focus is necessary because conversation involves the sending of messages between spouses. Fitzpatrick reviews major theories and approaches within both foci.

Chapter 4: Lindlof's "New communications media and the family: Practices, functions, and effects" presents a review of what is known or hypothesized about the role of new communication media in the functional processes of family life. The review is based on the rationale that the social setting in which most mediated communication is situated and in which acculturation to the practices of media usage normally takes place is the family. Lindlof reviews the available literature and sets forth an agenda for improving research by presenting three research perspectives from different traditions which suggest ways in which new media influence audience formations and activity. The three perspectives—critical, rationalist, and accommodative—all focus on the extent to which autonomy of choice devolves from the acquisition and use of new media, although they differ in the ways in which they situate the locus of control for information seeking and use behaviors.

Chapter 5: Maynard's "Bearing bad news in clinical settings" starts by reviewing the literature regarding the disclosure of information in clinical settings and then proceeds to a discussion of how communication must be understood strategically if it is to handle the complexities of the delivery and receipt of diagnostic news. Maynard details three arenas where understanding is needed—how one defines communication effectiveness, how one looks at the nature of intervention, and what one defines as disclosure. Maynard emphasizes the need for focusing on the diagnostic situation as an interaction rather than a transmission.

Chapter 6: Smythe's "Gender and communication behaviors" is organized thematically in four sections which examine gender differences in: (a) language production, (b) perceptions of language, (c) gestures, and (d) self-presentation. The review is then set in the context of four alternative explanatory frameworks which account for the presence and/or absence of gender differences by focusing on sociocultural factors, context-centered factors, self-presentational strategic factors, or androgenous factors.

Chapter 7: Taylor's "Information use environments" calls for information institutions to free themselves of the assumption that user behavior can be understood by starting from the system. To this end, Taylor explicates an approach to the study of information transfer that looks at the user and the uses of information, and the contexts within which those users make choices as to what information is useful to them at particular times. Taylor emphasizes that users make choices that are based not only on subject matter but on other elements of the context within which a user lives and works. He describes various approaches to structuring research taking this approach, discussing strengths and weaknesses, and illustrating with examples.

Chapter 8: Tutzauer's "Bargaining outcome, bargaining process, and the role of communication" reviews recent literature relevant to four functions of communication in bargaining and negotiation settings: (a) the transmitting and accepting of offers, (b) the conveying of information about bargainer's preferences and expectations, (c) the shaping of relationships between the bargainers, and (d) the uncovering of new outcomes. Particular themes and issues covered include: the dynamics of offers and counteroffers, the role concessions play, the processing of uncovering new outcomes, the role of argument, and the coding of communicative behavior.

Brenda Dervin
Columbus, Ohio
July 1990

Contents of Previous Volumes

1

A Cognitive Response Analysis of Source Credibility

William L. Benoit
Department of Communication
University of Missouri
Columbia, MO

I. INTRODUCTION

The concept of *source credibility* received scholarly attention in studies as early as 1936 in social psychology (Lorge & Curtis, 1936) and 1949 in communication (Thompson, 1949). This makes it one of the earliest and longest-lived areas of inquiry in persuasion. Nor is it one we can ignore today, for messages and their effects are intimately tied to their sources. It is common knowledge that a given remark would be (and should be) interpreted differently if it were attributed to different sources. For example, we tacitly share the presumption that *reluctant testimony* (evidence given against one's self-interest) should be valued highly, while *biased testimony* (evidence which happens to further one's selfish interests) should be discounted. Similarly, we realize that we must consider the source of a complaint (or a compliment) along with the nature of the remark itself to fully appreciate it. Furthermore, interactants naturally form assessments of others (*impression formation*) while seeking to create favorable impressions with others (*impression management*), further evidence of the pervasive influence of source in communication. No theory of communication is complete without a treatment of this concept; no experimental inquiry can safely ignore the possible effects of source on communication. Despite the long history of the concept of source credibility and the plethora of research conducted on it, despite the indubitable importance of source in communication generally and persuasion specifically, we lack a clear understanding of how source factors, even in the more limited area of persuasion, actually influence communication.

Two competent literature reviews assess the available data on this important topic in persuasion through the beginning of the 1960s and 1970s (Andersen & Clevenger, 1963; Littlejohn, 1971). What we need at this point, however, is not another exhaustive catalog of individual studies on credibility. Instead, this chapter advocates a new conceptualization of this concept, in order to explain the way in which this variable influences the process of persuasion.

This review adopts a cognitive view of communication and social influence in order to advance a novel explanation of how credibility functions to mediate persuasion. This is an appropriate choice at this juncture, for the cognitive approach is beginning to pervade our understanding of social behavior. In social psychology, this perspective so pervades the literature that Markus and Zajonc observe that "the cognitive approach is now clearly the dominant approach among social psychologists, having virtually no competitors" (1985, p. 137). This viewpoint is becoming increasingly influential in communication theory and research as well (see, e.g., Craig, 1979; Greene, 1984; Hample, 1980; Planalp & Hewes, 1982; or the recent special section of *Western Journal of Speech Communication* devoted to "Consciousness and Communication," [Nofsinger, 1986]).

The cognitive perspective is gaining popularity for a variety of reasons. It attracts those who view human beings as active contributors to the communication process, for it views humans as processors of information contained in (and around) messages. It eschews a "black box" view of communicators who react to and generate messages (but who knows how!). Generally, this approach views goals, motives, purposes, or intents—while not necessarily singular or clearly known in all cases to either interactant or analyst—as cognitions that shape both interpretation and production of messages. Furthermore, we are coming to see that people have limits on their cognitive processes, on their ability to interpret, recall, and make use of information in their communication activities. These limitations on capacity force people to use their cognitive resources carefully, influencing communication. In short, many scholars believe that our cognitive system significantly influences both production and reception/interpretation of communication, and that we therefore ignore the cognitive aspects of communication at our peril.

An important cognitive approach to communication and persuasion is the cognitive response model (Greenwald, 1968a; Perloff & Brock, 1980; Petty, Ostrom, & Brock, 1981b). An indication of this approach's timeliness is that one particular variant of this model, the *Elaboration Likelihood Model of Persuasion* (Petty & Cacioppo, 1986a, b), recently generated controversy in the communication literature (see Stiff, 1986; Petty, Kasmer, Haugtvedt, & Cacioppo, 1987; Stiff & Boster, 1987; Petty, Cacioppo, Kasmer, & Haugtvedt, 1987). The cognitive response model conceived broadly provides the theoretic framework for the subsequent analysis. Accordingly, the next section of this chapter explicates the cognitive response model, which will then be employed to explain how source credibility influences the processing of information contained in persuasive messages.

II. THE COGNITIVE RESPONSE MODEL

This section provides the necessary background for this review, addressing the nature of the cognitive response model, data available to support it, its advantages and disadvantages, and its relationship to prevailing perspectives on attitude change. The fundamental assumption of this perspective on persuasion is that auditors are active participants in social influence attempts, producing cognitions (thoughts) in response to the stimulus of the persuasive communication. These cognitive responses may be irrelevant, or they can be arguments which either support or refute the persuader's position. Just as the notion of "attitude" is a mediating variable between persuasive communication and behavior, so too "cognitive response" is a mediating variable between persuasive communication and attitude change. Thus, this theory is essentially a description of how individuals process messages. It makes the assumption that human beings are not influenced by unmediated messages, but by what they think about the message (their cognitive responses to it).

Greenwald (1968b; cf. Love & Greenwald, 1978) observes that, in previous research, only low correlations have been found between retention of message content and attitude change. Love and Greenwald's (1978) study confirms this finding, and also reports that the audience's cognitive responses correlate with both immediate and delayed assessments of persuasion. Other research also reinforces the claim that receivers' cognitive responses to persuasive communication are a determinant of attitude change (see, e.g., Petty & Cacioppo, 1979a, b). Cacioppo, Harkins, and Petty (1981, p. 49) call attention to a variety of evidence which supports the cognitive response approach:

> (1) high correlations exist between polar and cognitive responses and the amount of persuasion produced; and the more important the topic of the persuasion attempt is to the recipient, the stronger the relationship between the cognitive responses elicited and the amount of attitude change that results (Petty & Cacioppo, 1979a, 1979b); (2) manipulations that affect cognitive responses also affect persuasion (Calder et al., 1974; Petty et al., 1976; Roberts & Maccoby, 1973); and (3) implementation of statistical procedures to assess causal orderings of cognitive responses and persuasion has indicated that cognitive responses may have mediated yielding to persuasion (e.g., Greenwald, 1968b; Osterhouse & Brock, 1970) but that the reverse causal ordering was not operating. (Cacioppo & Petty, 1979a, 1979b; Petty & Cacioppo, 1977)

Thus, audience-produced supportive and refutative arguments (receiver-generated cognitive responses to persuasive messages) play an important role in the persuasion process, more so than simple comprehension and retention of message content.

This does not mean, of course, that arguments or message content do not influence attitude change. The persuasive message stimulates the receivers' cognitive responses (supportive and counter arguments) and supplies materials for developing supportive and refutative thoughts. Messages provide the focal points that stimulate favorable or unfavorable audience reactions in the form of cognitive responses. Petty and Cacioppo (1979b) find that, under high involvement conditions, strong message arguments create more supportive and fewer refutative thoughts (audience arguments) than weak message arguments, so content can be important. While some studies indicate that audience thoughts that cannot be directly traced to the message are the most effective in producing persuasion (Greenwald, 1968a; Roberts & Maccoby, 1973), others report that audience responses which can be traced to the message are the most significant influences on attitude change (Calder, Insko, & Yandell, 1974; Insko, Turnbull, & Yandell, 1974). Cacioppo, Harkins, and Petty (1981) offer the plausible suggestion that, when subjects have information about the topic, the receiver-generated thoughts might be the most influential, and when the audience has little information on the topic, they have no choice but to think about the arguments present in the message. In either case, much social influence through communication is mediated through receivers' cognitive responses to persuasive messages.

Research on the effects of distraction on persuasion illustrates the data that is accumulating in support of the cognitive response model on a variety of topics. Petty and Brock (1981) observe that 20 of 22 studies on distraction report that, at least under certain conditions, distracting receivers increases attitude change. This finding is somewhat difficult to reconcile with perspectives on persuasion that assume that persuasion occurs simply (or exclusively) through learning of message content. On this view, distraction should interfere with learning, reducing persuasion rather than facilitating it. However, considered from the cognitive response perspective, the result that distraction can enhance attitude change is perfectly explicable. In studies that included measures of cognitive responses, the distraction functioned to decrease the audience's cognitive response production. Since the dominant cognitive response during reception of a counterattitudinal message is likely to be unfavorable, distracting the audience during such messages inhibits the audiences' ability to develop counterarguments to the speaker's position. The relative lack of critical thought under distracting conditions permits greater persuasion. On the other hand, since a proattitudinal message is likely to encourage favorable thoughts, distraction has been found to reduce persuasion from those messages. Hence, distraction hampers thought production. On counterattitudinal topics, the distraction interferes with unfavorable thoughts, facilitating persuasion; on proattitudinal topics, it inhibits favorable thoughts, reducing persuasion (cf. Buller, 1986).

Involvement (the importance or salience of a topic to a person) is an important aspect of the cognitive response approach to persuasion. As involvement increases, they are more likely to carefully scrutinize messages (critically evaluate, generate cognitive responses) on that topic. On the other hand, people are not very motivated to closely examine the content of messages of little importance. Instead, they defer to other factors, such as source cues, or possibly the opinions of others. This effect is a result of the limited processing capacity of human mind, for carefully scrutinizing a persuasive message can be very effortful. Hence, when a message is important, we are more likely to devote significant portions of our limited cognitive processing capacity to thinking about that message. This is an important place in which the motives, goals, or purposes of auditors (which determine a topic's importance to them) influence their information processing.

The cognitive response model has several important advantages. First, for those who reject the "hypodermic needle" conceptualization of attitude change (i.e., advocates "inject" receivers with persuasive messages, which persuade them), it posits an important and active role for the receiver. Receivers are not persuaded by unmediated persuasive messages, but by what they think about them. Second, it provides attractive explanations for results that are difficult to account for otherwise, for example, the finding that distraction can increase persuasion, just discussed. Third, because it introduces a new mediating variable (cognitive response) into the process of attitude change—rather than positing new relationships between or orientations toward existing concepts—it is compatible with existing approaches to persuasion. Petty, Ostrom, and Brock (1981b) explain how the cognitive response model is congruent with the four major orientations to attitude change:

> Each of the four traditional approaches can be discussed in cognitive response terms, although the focus of each is different. For example, a learning theorist would propose that a persuasive communication is effective to the extent that the recipients adopt the message's argument as their own cognitive responses. Perceptual theorists would be interested in how a person's pre-existing repertoire of cognitions influences the meaning given to a message. Functional theorists would expect people to have different cognitive responses to the same communication depending on how the communication relates to underlying needs. Consistency theorists would focus on the consistency or inconsistency between the responses elicited by the message and already existing cognitions. (p. 14)

The major disadvantage to the cognitive response model is that it complicates the process of persuasion by introducing another mediating variable. However, the fact that it is somewhat less parsimonious is more than offset by the gain in explanatory power that it offers to persuasion theorists.

Thus, cognitive responses are receiver-generated reactions to persuasive messages. These cognitions can either support or refute the arguments of those messages (they can, of course, be irrelevant as well). Message content stimulates production of these thoughts, and makes available materials for auditors to think about in developing their cognitive responses. These thoughts mediate attitude change, which is correlated with cognitive responses but not with recall of message content. With this understanding of the cognitive response model, we can turn now to the subject of this essay, the effects of source credibility on persuasion.

III. A COGNITIVE RESPONSE PERSPECTIVE ON SOURCE CREDIBILITY

Even a cursory examination of the literature on source characteristics reveals a plethora of approaches to conceptualizing communicator characteristics. This area has undoubtedly attracted the attention of researchers not only because source characteristics are important in communication generally and persuasion specifically, but also because they are relatively easy to study. It is much simpler, for example, to study communicator credibility by writing a single persuasive message and attributing it to different sources than to study message variables by constructing several different messages. Use of a single message also provides greater experimental control than use of several different messages (a simple illustration is that when message content is varied, message length often changes). Faced with the amount of research on source characteristics such as similarity, attractiveness, and expertise, it makes sense to limit the purview of this discussion. Accordingly, this essay will limit its review to credibility operationalized specifically as expertise. Furthermore, rather than rehearse current understandings about credibility and persuasion, this chapter (a) advances an explanation of how credibility mediates attitude change, and, based on that account, (b) explores the limits of this important phenomenon by discussing five factors limiting the persuasiveness of high credibility sources. Finally, the implications of this conceptualization of source credibility in persuasion are discussed.

Only one essay has presented a discussion of credibility from the cognitive response perspective (Hass, 1981; cf. also Perloff & Brock, 1980, pp. 71–72, and Sternthal, Phillips, & Dholakia, 1978, for brief discussions). While Hass provides a solid beginning, its treatment of credibility is incomplete because it fails to consider some of the issues addressed here (e.g., intrinsic vs. extrinsic credibility, superiority of moderate credibility courses, discrepancy and credibility).

Perhaps the most fundamental question regarding source credibility is, "How does it work?" Why are highly credible or expert sources generally more persuasive than neutral or disreputable sources? For example, source credibility and message content could be additive in their persuasive effects. In other words, the persuasiveness of a favorable source may be added to that of the message, while an unfavorable source may subtract some from the effect of the message. This could be symbolized with a formula like this: P (persuasion) = S (Source credibility) + M (Message content). Or, perhaps the audience's perceptions of the source influence the persuasiveness of the message multiplicatively: P = S x M. This conception is suggested by everyday remarks like, "You have to take what he says with a grain of salt" (i.e., the other should partially devalue the message content because of the nature of the source). However, the cognitive response model takes a quite different tack, arguing that credibility mediates persuasion by influencing the way in which a persuasive message is cognitively processed.

Given the claim advanced earlier that the recipient's thoughts (supportive and counter arguments) on the topic are responsible for attitude change—and not simply message content as measured by recall—then, for credibility to influence attitude change, it must affect the cognitive processing of that message. According to this view, a source of high credibility effectuates attitude change by suppressing counterargumentation—that is, an expert source renders the audience less likely to question a message (or generate unfavorable cognitive responses) than a disreputable one. Furthermore, auditors who develop fewer unfavorable cognitive responses to persuasive messages should experience greater attitude change than other listeners.

In line with this analysis, Gillig and Greenwald (1974) report that more counterarguments are produced in response to a message attributed to a low than a high credibility source. This is consistent with Cook's (1969) finding that persuasive messages attributed to sources of high credibility stimulate fewer counterarguments that communications with no source identified, and that no-source messages stimulate fewer counterarguments than messages from low credibility sources. Thus, source credibility mediates persuasion by making the audience less (or more, in the case of disreputable sources) likely to carefully scrutinize the message (i.e., generate counterarguments). Thus, it appears that source credibility is analogous in its effect to the cognitive response explanation of distraction: distraction reduces auditors' ability to counterargue the message, while expert sources reduce their motivation to counterargue it.

One approach to describing a concept is to sketch its boundaries. That approach will be employed here, as five limitations on the effectiveness of high credibility sources will be explicated on the basis of this cognitive perspective on persuasion. They are: timing of source identification, audience involvement, extrinsic vs. intrinsic credibility, superiority of moderately credible sources, and discrepancy and credibility. This review will simultaneously provide support for the cognitive response explanation of source credibility and persuasion and map the key limitations on the effectiveness of this variable.

A. Timing of Source Identification

This analysis of source credibility effects from the standpoint of the cognitive response model readily accounts for the finding that more attitude change occurs when the source is identified before the message than after. Ward and McGinnies (1974; and Greenberg & Miller, 1966) found no difference in attitude change between messages attributed to high and low credible sources when the sources were identified after the speech. By that time it is too late for the knowledge that the speaker is highly credible to suppress counterarguing in the high credibility condition: the message and its attendant cognitive responses have already been processed. Similarly, early mention of noncredible sources was less persuasive than late mention of noncredible sources. In this situation, receivers did not have the information that the source was questionable until after the message, after it has been processed and unfavorable thoughts have already occurred to the receiver. Similarly, Sternthal, Dholakia, and Leavitt (1978; as well as Greenberg & Tannenbaum, 1961) report that credibility has no effect on persuasion when the source is identified after the message. Husek (1965) and Mills and Harvey (1972) also found that expert (but not attractive) sources produce more attitude change when identified before than after the message. The fact that attractive sources are just as persuasive when identified after as prior to the speech can be explained by suggesting that attractive sources are persuasive because of *who* they are, whereas credibility influences persuasion by affecting how critical we are likely to be of *what* they say (see Kelman, 1958, 1961).

So the cognitive response model suggests that knowledge that a source is highly credible facilitates persuasion by reducing the production of unfavorable cognitive responses (counterarguments). Knowledge that a source is disreputable inhibits persuasion by encouraging the audience to scrutinize a message, i.e., to produce unfavorable thoughts. However, neither of these effects can occur if the source is not identified until after the message has already been processed. Notice that conceptions of credibility as additively or multiplicatively related to message content would find it difficult, if not impossible, to account for these findings of timing of source identification. The persuasiveness of the source could be added to or multiplied by the persuasiveness of the message, regardless of when the source is identified. Only if knowledge of the source's credibility influences processing of the message as it is received can these results be explained, and a cognitive perspective opens up information processing to our theories and research (cf. O'Keefe, 1987).

B. Audience Involvement in Topic

Audience involvement in the topic is an important variable in the cognitive response model, and it influences the effectiveness of source credibility appeals. Petty, Cacioppo, and Goldman (1981) report that, on highly involving topics, message arguments produced significant attitude change, while source credibility did not. On uninvolving topics, both source credibility and message arguments create attitude change, but credibility is more effective than arguments. Chaiken (1980) found that number of arguments influenced attitude change on involving but not on uninvolving topics, while likability of sources influenced persuasion on uninvolving but not on involving topics. In a study of high and low credibility sources on high and low involvement topics, Johnson and Scileppi (1969) report that more attitude change occurs with high credibility sources on low involvement topics than with any other combination. Finally, Benoit (1987) discloses that expert sources were no more persuasive than nonexperts on an involving topic. It should not be surprising that receivers would carefully scrutinize a message on a highly salient topic (deferring less to the opinions of any source, even a highly credible one), and expend less effort examining a message on a nonsalient topic (choosing instead to defer to the judgment of a source they respect, consequently generating fewer unfavorable cognitive responses, or refutative arguments).

Hass (1981) makes somewhat different predictions, using slightly alternate terminology (he refers to *commitment* rather than *involvement*). He suggests that, when receivers are uncommitted, more counterargument should be expected for low than high credibility sources, but when receivers are highly committed to their position, more counterargument is expected for high than low credibility sources (because high credibility sources are more threatening to their position). His study reports that more counterarguments were produced under low commitment conditions, in response to the message attributed to low than high credibility sources, than would be expected from the discussion of involvement.

However, the prediction that there would be a significant difference in counterargument production between high and low credibility sources under high commitment conditions—which would not expected from the analysis presented here—was not confirmed in his study (Hass, 1972). So the available evidence indicates that source credibility may only (or primarily) influence attitude change on less salient or involving topics, as the cognitive response model would predict.

There might be exceptions to this rule, however, which have yet to be explored. For example, the best course of treatment for a serious illness ought to be a highly involving topic. Given the complexity of modern medicine, it is possible that few patients would believe themselves qualified to evaluate messages from health care personnel. In such cases, auditors might well defer to those perceived to be experts, despite the high involvement of the listeners in the topic. This is a area ripe for further investigation. Still, extant research suggests that the persuasiveness of a high credibility source may be limited to less involving topics.

C. Extrinsic vs. Intrinsic Credibility

The cognitive response analysis of credibility advocated here can also shed light on the suggestion that extrinsic credibility studies are more consistent than those employing the intrinsic credibility paradigm. The first, and more common approach to manipulating source credibility (which Andersen & Clevenger, 1963, label *extrinsic* credibility) attributes a single message to several sources with different levels of credibility. Since the actual message and its presentation remain constant, any differences in attitude change must be a function of variations in the sources' credibility. The second paradigm (Andersen & Clevenger's *intrinsic* credibility) prepares different messages and/or presentations of a message, assuming that those differences will generate varying degrees of perceived credibility, which in turn should mediate attitude change.

Support for credibility effects on persuasion using the extrinsic approach is generally positive (see, e.g., Brewer & Crano, 1968; Choo, 1964; Haiman, 1949; Horai, Naccari, & Fatoullah, 1974; Hovland & Weiss, 1951; Koslin, Stoops, & Loh, 1967; Lorge & Curtis, 1936; Maddux & Rogers, 1980; McGinnies & Ward, 1980; Miller & Basehart, 1969). Messages attributed to sources of higher expertise are generally more persuasive than those from less credible sources. There are exceptions, to be sure (e.g., in forced compliance studies, as Zimbardo, Weisenberg, Firestone, & Levy, 1965), but the literature is generally quite consistent in finding that high credibility sources are more effective than less credible ones (see also the previous literature reviews of credibility by Andersen & Clevenger, 1963; Littlejohn, 1971).

However, support for the superiority of high credibility sources in research employing the latter, less common approach, is mixed. Use of metaphor (Bowers

& Osborn, 1966) and evidence (McCroskey, 1967, 1970), fluency and organization (McCroskey & Mehrley, 1969), rate (Miller, Maruyama, Bealer, & Valone, 1976), and language diversity (Bradac, Courtright, Schmidt, & Davies, 1976; Bradac, Konsky, & Davies, 1976; Bradac, Desmond, & Murdock, 1977) have all been found to enhance both credibility and attitude change. However, Thompson (1949) found that a speech might increase a speaker's credibility without increasing attitude change. Studies on style (Bowers, 1965; Miller & Hewgill, 1964; Pearce & Brommel, 1972), perceived organization (Baker, 1965), and fluency (Sereno & Hawkins, 1967) report that these variables enhance credibility but not persuasion (McCroskey & Mehrley, 1969, report the lack of significant attitude change in Miller & Hewgill's study).

The cognitive response model suggests that source credibility mediates attitude change by influencing favorable and unfavorable audience thoughts in reaction to the message. Hence, credibility induction must take place early enough in the message to influence processing of the message. This is precisely why an expert source must be identified as such prior to the message to have persuasive impact, and why knowledge that a source is not credible does not significantly reduce persuasion if that information is withheld until after the speech. That is to say, if variables such as content, style, or delivery induce perceived credibility increases early in the message, the audience will soon become less motivated to be critical of the message. On the other hand, if credibility is not enhanced until near the end of the message, the audience will already have produced sufficient counterarguments to inhibit persuasion. Thus, the results that support the persuasiveness of the intrinsic credibility approach may well come from studies in which the source's credibility was increased early enough to inhibit much of the audience's counterarguments, while results which do not support it may have occurred in studies in which credibility was increased, but not early enough to stop the audience from producing substantial counterarguing.

Although it is convenient to suggest that there is a point at which the source's credibility is enhanced, in most cases this is probably a gradual process (e.g., with each use of evidence the audience's opinion of the speaker rises a bit), although no research has examined this process. Furthermore, although the claim that credibility induction must occur "early enough" is vague, it is unlikely that more specificity is possible. If there is nothing that is very controversial, say, in the first half of the speech, there is likely to be little counterarguing, and no need for enhanced credibility at that point in the speech. On the other hand, if the beginning of a persuasive message is extremely controversial, it may not be possible to induce higher perceived credibility early enough to stop the audience from developing effective counterarguments. Thus, credibility must be enhanced early enough in the reception of the message to significantly inhibit unfavorable cognitive responses. This can explain the consistent effectiveness of extrinsic credibility as well as the inconsistent results of intrinsic credibility.

D. Superiority of Moderately Credible Sources

Another limitation on the persuasiveness of high credibility sources that is amenable to explanation by this perspective on the process of persuasion is that sources of moderate credibility are, in some circumstances, more persuasive than ones of high credibility (Dean, Austin, & Watts, 1971; Bochner & Insko, 1966; Bock & Saine, 1975; Sternthal et al., 1978). These results only occur when the speaker advocated a position close to the audience's own attitude (i.e., one of low discrepancy, or a proattitudinal topic). High credibility sources have been found to decrease argument production, as discussed earlier. However, the predominant type of cognitive response to a *pro*attitudinal message (advocating minimal discrepancy from the audience's attitudes) should be *supportive* arguments, or favorable cognitive responses (rather then unfavorable thoughts or counterarguments generated by a counterattitudinal message). Just as a decrease in unfavorable thoughts should enhance attitude change, so too should fewer favorable cognitive responses reduce persuasion. Therefore, moderate credibility sources permit the supportive argumentation necessary for attitude change on proattitudinal topics. In line with this analysis, Sternthal et al. (1978) report that more supportive arguments are produced in the moderate credibility condition than in the high credibility condition. Disreputable sources, which incite suspicion in receivers, should increase unfavorable thought production and not be very persuasive.

The parallel drawn earlier between distraction and credibility can usefully be reiterated here. Distraction enhanced persuasion from counterattitudinal messages by interfering with the dominant response, unfavorable. It reduced persuasion from proattitudinal messages by interfering with their likely response, favorable thoughts. Similarly, high credibility sources reassure the listener, decreasing cognitive processing. On proattitudinal messages this reduces favorable thoughts and lessens persuasion. While disreputable sources would increase scrutiny, moderate credibility sources neither trigger suspicion nor encourage shallow processing, permitting productions of supportive thoughts and hence optimum persuasion on such topics.

E. Discrepancy and Source Credibility

Several studies investigate the relationships among discrepancy (between message and audience attitude), source credibility, and persuasion. Cognitive consistency theories (e.g., Abelson, Aronson, McGuire, Newcomb, Rosenberg, & Tannenbaum, 1968; Brehm & Cohen, 1962; Feather, 1967; Feldman, 1966; Festinger, 1957, 1964; Heider, 1946; Wicklund & Brehm, 1976) tend to predict that discrepancy is directly related to attitude change. However, research in congruity theory supports the common-sense notion that a message that is too extreme will be ineffective, if not counterproductive (Osgood & Tannenbaum,

1955; Tannenbaum, 1967). It is possible that credibility and discrepancy interact, so that highly credible sources permit greater effectiveness than less credible ones at high levels of discrepancy.

In 1963, Aronson, Turner, and Carlsmith reported that discrepancy is directly related to attitude change for high credibility sources, but that the relationship is curvilinear for moderately credible ones. Bochner and Insko (1966) confirm these results. Rhine and Severance (1970) report similar results with an uninvolving topic (attitude change significantly related to discrepancy, credibility effects approaching significance), but not on involving topics. They observe that "the low-ego-involvement curves. . . are close to those of Aronson et al. (1963), who used an issue that was probably not very involving" (p. 182). Exceptions to these findings include Choo (1964), who failed to replicate results with trustworthiness manipulations (not expertise), and two studies which report curvilinear results but did not employ persuasive messages (Brewer & Crano, 1968; Koslin et al., 1967). Hence, it appears that on less involving topics, high expertise permits more persuasion at higher levels of discrepancy.

Let us first consider discrepancy, and then discuss the effects of expertise and involvement on discrepancy and attitude change. Highly discrepant messages are likely to provoke greater audience counterarguing than moderately discrepant ones. Hence, there should be a curvilinear relationship between discrepancy and attitude change. Slightly discrepant messages provide little motivation to change (yielding little persuasion), while highly discrepant ones stimulate counterarguments (again yielding little persuasion). The most persuasive messages are moderately discrepant, ones that provide enough discrepancy to motivate change without evoking strong counterarguing.

As suggested earlier, expertise interacts with the audience's involvement in the topic. On involving topics, the cognitive response model suggests that expertise does not mediate attitude change. Thus, the relationship between discrepancy and persuasion should be curvilinear, regardless of source credibility. However, on uninvolving topics, highly credible sources decrease the audience's motivation to counterargue. This permits highly discrepant messages to provide greater motivation to change attitudes without evoking counterarguing. On such topics, with expert sources, discrepancy is directly related to persuasion.

IV. CONCLUSION

The cognitive response model suggests that receivers produce supportive or refutative thoughts in response to the stimulus of persuasive messages. These arguments mediate attitude change, and in fact correlate more highly with persuasion than recall of message content. Receivers are more highly motivated to carefully scrutinize and produce counterarguments in response to messages generated by low credibility sources. On the other hand, receivers are less likely to be critical of sources they respect. This perspective can be employed to satisfactorily explain several limitations on the persuasiveness of high credibility sources—timing of source identification, audience involvement, extrinsic vs. intrinsic credibility, superiority of moderately credible sources, and discrepancy and credibility—as well as to argue generally for the importance of receivers in social influence. Furthermore, the success of the analysis developed here argues for the desirability of the cognitive approach to communication generally and persuasion specifically.

What are the implications of embracing this perspective? As suggested earlier, the cognitive response model adds an additional mediating variable to our conceptualization of persuasion. Hence, one obvious result is that theories which adopt this perspective will be somewhat more complex than other theories. We must consider, not only the construct of *attitude,* but additionally that of *cognitive response.* However, for those who see people as active information processors, who are influenced by what they think about (how they interpret) incoming persuasive messages, this is a necessary addition to these theories. Source credibility can influence the way a persuasive message is processed, making the person less (in the case of an expert source) or more (in the case of a disreputable source) likely to scrutinize the message. Furthermore, this cognitive activity is influenced by a person's goals or motives, for if the topic is highly involving to the audience, source cues are unlikely to affect message processing. Hence, a cognitive perspective would be a useful addition to our theories of persuasion.

This perspective also encourages the theorist to adopt a more holistic approach to persuasion. We must consider how the various aspects of the persuasion situation interact. This view of source credibility illuminates several points of interaction. For example, expert sources decrease motivation to scrutinize messages carefully (at least on uninvolving topics), so source variables are viewed as influencing how messages are processed. Disreputable sources motivate receivers to carefully scrutinize persuasive messages attributed to them, again affecting how receivers process the message. The auditor's goals, as they affect involvement, are important as well (for the persuasiveness of expert sources may be limited to less involving topics). Here, one part of the auditor's cognitive system (goals, which influence topic involvement) influences message processing and determines whether credibility is likely to significantly affect the persuasion process. Furthermore, credibility interacts with message content (e.g., discrepancy). Hence, this perspective links the audience's preexisting cognitions (goals/topic involvement), credibility, and message content.

This perspective holds implications for research as well as theory. First, studies could profitably assess cognitive responses to persuasive messages (see, e.g., Benoit, 1987). This will continually test the cognitive response model, while providing insights into what auditors think as they process persuasive messages. Cacioppo and Petty (1981) and Miller and Baron (1973) offer useful discussions concerning procedures for measuring cognitive responses.

Furthermore, this perspective encourages persuasion researchers to take into account the auditor's cognitions (involvement), perceived expertise, and message content. As mentioned before, these variables interact, so they must each be varied or controlled in studies. Persuasion is a complex process, and this perspective recognizes the interplay among several important variables in the persuasive situation.

Finally, persuasion research has typically been oriented toward the speaker and the speaker's message, despite the fact that the key dependent variable here (attitude change) occurs in receivers (social judgment involvement theory was an exception, but it failed to generate the research of, say, cognitive dissonance theory; see, e.g., Sherif & Hovland, 1961; Sherif & Sherif, 1967; Sherif, Sherif, & Nebergall, 1965). A cognitive approach to persuasion, like the one advocated here, while not ignoring speaker and message, places emphasis on receivers and how they construe, or respond to, influence attempts. This is a much needed shift in focus, one facilitated by this approach to credibility in persuasion.

REFERENCES

Abelson, R. P., Aronson, E., McGuire, W. J., Newcomb, T. M., Rosenberg, M. J., & Tannenbaum, P. H. (Eds.). (1968). *Theories of cognitive consistency: A sourcebook.* Chicago, IL: Rand McNally.

Anderson, K., & Clevenger, T. (1963). A summary of experimental research in ethos. *Speech Monographs, 30,* 59–78.

Aronson, E., Turner, J. A., & Carlsmith, J. M. (1963). Communicator credibility and communication discrepancy as determinants of opinion change. *Journal of Abnormal and Social Psychology, 67,* 31–36.

Baker, E. E. (1965). The immediate effects of perceived speaker disorganization on credibility and audience attitude change in persuasive speaking. *Western Speech, 29,* 148–161.

Benoit, W. L. (1987). Argumentation and credibility appeals in persuasion. *Southern Speech Communication Journal, 52,* 181–197.

Bochner, S., & Insko, C. (1966). Communication discrepancy, source credibility, and opinion change. *Journal of Personality and Social Psychology, 4,* 614–621.

Bock, D., & Saine, T. (1975). The impact of source credibility, attitude valence, and task sensitivity on trait errors in speech evaluation. *Speech Monographs, 37,* 229–236.

Bowers, J. W. (1965). The influence of delivery on attitudes toward concepts and speakers. *Speech Monographs, 32,* 154–158.

Bowers, J. W., & Osborn, M. M. (1966). Attitudinal effects of selected types of concluding metaphors in persuasive speeches. *Speech Monographs, 33,* 148–155.

Bradac, J. J., Courtright, J. A., Schmidt, G., & Davies, R. A. (1976). The effects of perceived status and linguistic diversity upon Judgments of speaker attributes and message and effectiveness. *Journal of Psychology, 93,* 213–220.

Bradac, J. J., Courtright, J. A., Schmidt, G., & Davies, R. A. (1976). The effects of perceived status and linguistic diversity upon judgments of speaker attributes and message and effectiveness. *Journal of Psychology, 93,* 213–220.

Bradac, J. J., Desmond, R. J., & Murdock, J. I. (1977). Diversity and density: Lexically determined evaluative and informational consequences of linguistic complexity. *Communication Monographs, 44,* 273–283.

Brehm, J. W., & Cohen, A. R. (1962). *Explorations in cognitive dissonance.* New York: Wiley.

Brewer, M., & Crano, W. (1968). Attitude change as a function of discrepancy and source of influence. *Journal of Social Psychology, 76,* 13–18.

Brock, T. C. (1967). Communication discrepancy and intent to persuade as determinants of counterargument production. *Journal of Experimental Social Psychology, 3,* 296–309.

Buller, D. B. (1986). Distraction during persuasive communication: A meta-analytic review. *Communication Monographs, 53,* 91–114.

Cacioppo, J. T., Harkins, S. G., & Petty, R. E. (1981). The nature of attitudes and cognitive response and their relationships to behavior. In R. E. Petty, T. M. Ostrom, & T. C. Brock (Eds.), *Cognitive responses in persuasion* (pp. 31–54). Hillsdale, NJ: Erlbaum.

Cacioppo, J. T., & Petty, R. E. (1979a). Attitudes and cognitive responses: An electrophysiological approach. *Journal of Personality and Social Psychology, 37,* 2181–2199.

Cacioppo, J. T., & Petty, R. E. (1979b). Effects of message repetition and position on cognitive responses, recall, and persuasion. *Journal of Personality and Social Psychology, 37,* 97–109.

Cacioppo, J. T., & Petty, R. E. (1981). Social psychological procedures for cognitive response assessment: The thought-listing technique. In T. V. Merluzzi, C. R. Glass, & M. Genest (Eds.), *Cognitive assessment* (pp. 309–342). New York: Guilford Press.

Calder, B. J., Insko, C. A., & Yandell, B. (1974). The relation of cognitive and memorial processes to persuasion in a simulated jury trial. *Journal of Applied Social Psychology, 4,* 62–93.

Chaiken, S. (1980). Heuristic versus systematic information-processing and the use of source versus message cues in persuasion. *Journal of Personality and Social Psychology, 39,* 752–766.

Choo, T. (1964). Communicator credibility and communication discrepancy as determinants of attitude change. *Journal of Social Psychology, 64,* 65–76.

Cook, T. D. (1969). Competence, counterarguing, and attitude change. *Journal of Personality, 37,* 342–58.

Craig, R. T. (1979). Information systems theory and research: An overview of individual information processing. In D. Nimmo (Ed.), *Communication yearbook 3* (pp. 99–121). New Brunswick, NJ: Transaction.

Dean, R., Austin, J., & Watts, W. (1971). Forewarning effects in persuasion: Field and classroom experiments. *Journal of Personality and Social Psychology, 18,* 210–221.

Feather, N. T. A. (1967). A structural balance approach to the analysis of communication effects. In L. Berkowitz (Ed.), *Advances in experimental social psychology* (Vol. 3, pp. 100–166). New York: Academic Press.

Feldman, S. (Ed.). (1966). *Cognitive consistency.* New York: Academic Press.

Festinger, L. (1957). *A theory of cognitive dissonance.* Palo Alto, CA: Stanford University Press.

Festinger, L. (1964). *Conflict, decision, and dissonance.* Palo Alto, CA: Stanford University Press.

Greene, J. O. (1984). Evaluating cognitive explanations of communication phenomena. *Quarterly Journal of Speech, 70,* 241–254.

Greenberg, B. S., & Miller, G. R. (1966). The effects of low-credible sources on message acceptance. *Speech Monographs, 33,* 127–136.

Greenberg, B. S., & Tannenbaum, P. H. (1961). The effects of bylines on attitude change. *Journalism Quarterly, 38,* 535–37.

Greenwald, A. G. (1968a). Cognitive learning, cognitive response to persuasion, and attitude change. In A. G. Greenwald, T. C. Brock, & T. M. Ostrom (Eds.), *Psychological foundations of attitudes* (pp. 147–170). New York: Academic Press.

Greenwald, A. G. (1968b). On defining attitude and attitude theory. In A. G. Greenwald, T. C. Brock, & T. M. Ostrom *Psychological foundations of attitudes* (pp. 361–388). New York: Academic Press.

Greenwald, A. G., Brock, T. C., & Ostrom, T. M. (1968). *Psychological foundations of attitudes.* New York: Academic Press.

Gillig, P. M., & Greenwald, A. G. (1974). Is it time to lay the sleeper effect to rest? *Journal of Personality and Social Psychology, 29*, 132–139.

Haiman, F. (1949). An experimental study of the effects of ethos in public speaking. *Speech Monographs, 16*, 190–202.

Hample, D. (1980). A cognitive view of argument. *Journal of the American Forensic Association, 16*, 151–58.

Hass, R. G. (1972). Resisting persuasion and examining message content: The effects of source credibility and recipient commitment on counterargument production (Doctoral dissertation, Duke University). *Dissertation abstracts international, 33*, 1305–B.

Hass, R. G. (1981). Effects of source characteristics on cognitive responses and persuasion. In R. E. Petty, T. M. Ostrom, & T. C. Brock (Eds.), *Cognitive responses in persuasion* (pp. 44–72). Hillsdale, NJ: Erlbaum.

Heider, F. (1946). Attitudes and cognitive organization. *Journal of Psychology, 21*, 107–112.

Horai, J., Naccari, N., & Fatoullah, E. (1974). The effects of expertise and physical attractiveness upon opinion agreement and liking. *Sociometry, 37*, 601–606.

Hovland, C. I., & Weiss, W. (1951). The influence of source credibility on communication effectiveness. *Public Opinion Quarterly, 15*, 635–650.

Husek, T. R. (1965). Persuasive impacts of early, late, or no mention of the negative source. *Journal of Personality and Social Psychology, 2*, 125–128.

Insko, C. A. (1967). *Theories of attitude change*. New York: Appleton-Century-Crofts.

Insko, C. A., Turnbull, W., & Yandell, B. (1974). Facilitating and inhibiting effects of distraction on attitude change. *Sociometry, 37*, 508–28.

Johnson, H. H., & Scileppi, J. A. (1969). Effects of ego-involvement conditions on attitude change to high and low communicators. *Journal of Personality and Social Psychology, 13*, 31–36.

Kelman, H. C. (1958). Compliance, identification, and internalization: Three processes of attitude change. *Journal of Conflict Resolution, 2*, 51–60.

Kelman, H. C. (1961). Processes of opinion change. *Public Opinion Quarterly, 25*, 57–78.

Koslin, B., Stoops, J., & Loh, W. (1967). Source characteristics and communication discrepancy as determinants of attitude change and conformity. *Journal of Experimental Social Psychology, 3*, 230–42.

Littlejohn, S. (1971). A bibliography of studies related to variables of source credibility. In N. A. Shearer (Ed.), *Bibliographic Annual in Speech Communication, 1971, 2*, 1–40.

Lorge, I., & Curtis, C. (1936). Prestige, suggestion, and attitudes. *Journal of Social Psychology, 7*, 386–402.

Love, R. E., & Greenwald, A. G. (1978). Cognitive responses to persuasion as mediators of opinion change. *Journal of Social Psychology, 104*, 231–241.

Maddux, J. E., & Rogers, R. W. (1980). Effects of source expertness, physical attractiveness, and supporting arguments on persuasion: A case of brains over beauty. *Journal of Personality and Social Psychology, 39*, 235–244.

Markus, H, & Zajonc, R. B. (1985). The cognitive perspective in social psychology. In G. Lindsey & E. Aronson (Eds.), *Handbook of social psychology* (3rd ed., Vol. 1, pp. 137–230). New York: Random House.

McCroskey, J. C. (1967). The effects of evidence in persuasive communication. *Western Speech, 31*, 189–99.

McCroskey, J. C. (1970). The effects of evidence as an inhibitor of counterpersuasion. *Speech Monographs, 37*, 188–194.

McCroskey, J. C., & Mehrley, R. S. (1969). The effects of disorganization and nonfluency on attitude change and source credibility. *Speech Monographs, 36*, 13–31.

McGinnies, E., & Ward, C. D. (1980). Better liked than right—Trustworthiness and expertise as factors in credibility. *Personality and Social Psychology Bulletin, 6*, 467–472.

Miller, N., & Baron, R. S. (1973). On measuring counterarguing. *Journal for the Theory of Social Behavior, 3,* 101–118.

Miller, G. R., & Basehart, J. (1969). Source trustworthiness, opinionated statements, and responses to persuasive communication. *Speech Monographs, 36,* 1–7.

Miller, G. R., & Hewgill, M. A. (1964). The effect of variations in nonfluency on audience ratings of source credibility. *Quarterly Journal of Speech, 50,* 36–44.

Miller, N., Maruyama, G., Bealer, R. J., & Valone, K. (1976). Speed of speech and persuasion. *Journal of Experimental Social Psychology, 34,* 615–624.

Mills, J., & Harvey, J. (1972). Opinion change as a function of when information about the communicator is received and whether he is attractive or expert. *Journal of Personality and Social Psychology, 21,* 52–55.

Nofsinger, R. (1986). Special section on "Consciousness and communication." *Western Journal of Speech Communication, 50.*

O'Keefe, D. J. (1987). The persuasive effects of delaying identification of high- and low-credibility communicators: A meta-analytic review. *Central States Speech Journal, 38,* 63–72.

Osgood, C. E., & Tannenbaum, P. H. (1955). The principle of congruity in the prediction of attitude change. *Psychological Review, 62,* 42–55.

Osterhouse, R. A, & Brock, T. C. (1970). Distraction increases yielding to propaganda by inhibiting counterarguing. *Journal of Personality and Social Psychology, 15,* 344–58.

Pearce, W. B., & Brommel, B. J. (1972). Vocalic communication persuasion. *Quarterly Journal of Speech, 58,* 298–306.

Perloff, R. M., & Brock, T. C. (1980). . . . 'And thinking makes it so': Cognitive responses to persuasion. In M. E. Roloff & G. R. Miller (Eds.), *Persuasion: New directions in theory and research* (pp. 67–100). Beverly Hills, CA: Sage.

Petty, R. E., & Brock, T. C. (1981). Thought disruption and persuasion: Assessing the validity of attitude change experiments. In R. E. Petty, T. M. Ostrom, & T. C. Brock (Eds.), *Cognitive responses in persuasion* (pp. 55–79). Hillsdale, NJ: Erlbaum.

Petty, R. E., & Cacioppo, J. T. (1977). Forewarning, cognitive responding, and resistance to persuasion. *Journal of Personality and Social Psychology, 35,* 645–655.

Petty, R. E., & Cacioppo, J. T. (1979a). Effects of forewarning of persuasive intent and involvement on cognitive responses and persuasion. *Personality and Social Psychology Bulletin, 55,* 173–176.

Petty, R. E., & Cacioppo, J. T. (1979b). Issue involvement can increase or decrease persuasion by enhancing message-relevant cognitive processes. *Journal of Personality and Social Psychology, 37,* 1915–1926.

Petty, R. E., & Cacioppo, J. T. (1986a). *Communication and persuasion: Central and peripheral routes to attitude change.* New York: Springer-Verlag.

Petty, R. E., & Cacioppo, J. T. (1986b). The elaboration likelihood model of persuasion. In L. Berkowitz (Ed.), *Advances in experimental social psychology.* New York: Academic Press.

Petty, R. E., Cacioppo, J. T., & Goldman, R. (1981). Personal involvement as a determinant of argument-based persuasion. *Journal of Personality and Social Psychology, 41,* 847–855.

Petty, R. E., Cacioppo, J. T., Kasmer, J. A., & Haugtvedt, C. P. (1987). A reply to Stiff and Boster. *Communication Monographs, 54,* 257–63.

Petty, R. E., Kasmer, J. A., Haugtvedt, C. P., & Cacioppo, J. T. (1987). Source and message factors in persuasion: A reply to Stiff's critique of the Elaboration Likelihood Model. *Communication Monographs, 54,* 233–249.

Petty, R. E., Ostrom, T. M., & Brock, T. C. (Eds.). (1981a). *Cognitive responses in persuasion.* Hillsdale, NJ: Erlbaum.

Petty, R. E., Ostrom, T. M., & Brock, T. C. (1981b). Historical foundations of the cognitive responses approach to attitudes and persuasion. In R. E. Petty, T. M. Ostrom, & T. C. Brock (Eds.), *Cognitive responses in persuasion* (pp. 5–29). Hillsdale, NJ: Erlbaum.

Petty, R. E., Wells, G. L., & Brock, T. C. (1976). Distraction can enhance or reduce yielding to propaganda: Thought disruption versus effort justification. *Journal of Personality and Social Psychology, 34,* 874–884.

Planalp, S., & Hewes, D. (1982). A cognitive approach to communication theory: *Cogito ergo dico?* In M. Burgoon (Ed.), *Communication yearbook 5* (pp. 49–77). New Brunswick, NJ: Transaction.

Rhine, R. J., & Severance, L. J. (1970). Ego-involvement, discrepancy, source credibility, and attitude change. *Journal of Personality and Social Psychology, 16,* 175–190.

Roberts, D. F., & Maccoby, N. (1973). Information processing and persuasion: Counterarguing behavior. In P. Clarke (Ed.), *New models for mass communication research* (pp. 269–307). Beverly Hills, CA: Sage.

Sereno, K. K., & Hawkins, G. J. (1967). The effects of variations in speaker's nonfluency upon audience ratings of attitude toward the speech topic and speaker's credibility. *Speech Monographs, 34,* 58–64.

Sherif, M., & Hovland, C. I. (1961). *Social judgment: Assimilation and contrast effects in communication and attitude change.* New Haven, CT: Yale University Press.

Sherif, C. W., & Sherif, M. (Eds.). (1967). *Attitude, ego-involvement, and change.* New York: John Wiley.

Sherif, C. W., Sherif, M., & Nebergall, R. E. (1965). *Attitude and attitude change: The social judgment-involvement approach.* Philadelphia, PA: W. B. Saunders.

Sternthal, B., Dholakia, R., & Leavitt, C. (1978). The persuasive effect of source credibility: Tests of cognitive response. *Journal of Consumer Research, 4,* 252–260.

Sternthal, B., Phillips, L. W., & Dholakia, R. (1978). The persuasive effect of source credibility: A situational analysis. *Public Opinion Quarterly, 42,* 285–314.

Stiff, J. B. (1986). Cognitive processing of persuasive message cues: A meta-analytic review of the effects of supporting information on attitudes. *Communication Monographs, 53,* 75–89.

Stiff, J. B., & Boster, F. J. (1987). Cognitive processing: Additional thoughts and a reply to Petty, Kasmer, Haugtvedt, and Cacioppo. *Communication Monographs, 54,* 250–256.

Tannenbaum, P. H. (1967). The congruity theory revisited: Studies in the reduction, induction, and generalization of persuasion. In L. Berkowitz (Ed.), *Advances in experimental social psychology* (Vol. 3, pp. 271–320). New York: Academic Press.

Thompson, W. (1949). A study of the attitude of college students toward Thomas E. Dewey before and after hearing him speak. *Speech Monographs, 16,* 125–134.

Ward, C. D., & McGinnies, E. (1974). Persuasive effect of early and late mention of credible and non-credible sources. *Journal of Psychology, 86,* 17–23.

Wicklund, R. A., & Brehm, J. W. (1976). *Perspectives on cognitive dissonance.* Hillsdale, NJ: Erlbaum.

Zimbardo, P. G., Weisenberg, M., Firestone, I., & Levy, B. (1965). Communicator effectiveness in producing public conformity and private attitude change. *Journal of Personality, 33,* 233–255.

2 Uncertainty and Communication

Charles R. Berger
Department of Communication Studies
Northwestern University

William B. Gudykunst
Department of Speech Communication
California State University, Fullerton

Since the beginning of the study of communication science, researchers have argued that related theoretical constructs such as entropy (Shannon & Weaver, 1949), uncertainty (Garner, 1962), and novelty (Berlyne, 1960) are crucial to our understanding of how communication works (Berlo, 1960; Broadhurst & Darnell, 1965; Schramm, 1954). Considering the importance attached to the uncertainty construct by these writers, it is surprising that relatively few communication researchers have employed it explicitly in their theoretical thinking about, and research on, communication processes. Consistent with the thinking of these early researchers, it is our contention that the uncertainty construct can provide considerable explanatory power in understanding a variety of communication phenomena. In this chapter, we will demonstrate the plausibility of this assertion.

As the communication discipline has developed, inevitable pressures toward specialization have manifested themselves. We cannot provide a detailed account of the reasons for these trends (see Delia, 1987); however, at the present time there are persons who are comfortable identifying themselves as instructional, intercultural, interpersonal, health, mass, organizational, and political communication researchers. While some view this growing pluralism as a positive development, others have pointed out that delineating the communication discipline with a *context* template may be an egregious error (Berger & Chaffee, 1987). Such divisions of the field suggest that different theories are needed to explain communication phenomena within each subdomain. This view countervails against the development of general theories that transcend this contextual parochialism.

We believe that the processes associated with the creation and reduction of uncertainty are sufficiently abstract to qualify as candidates for general theory status. In the first section of this chapter, we explicate the construct of uncertainty. We then examine relevant research done in the domains of interpersonal and intercultural communication to demonstrate the utility of our formulation. Our division of the paper into interpersonal and intercultural domains is designed to illustrate how theory can transcend contexts. It is *not* meant to imply that the two domains should be considered separately in developing theories. We also note research reported in other subdomains of communication science that has employed uncertainty as a central construct. Finally, we suggest some future directions for research. A fully developed theory is not presented here; however, we articulate the potential boundaries of such a theory.

I. UNCERTAINTY AND UNCERTAINTY REDUCTION

A. Defining Uncertainty

The construct of *uncertainty* enjoys wide usage across a number of different domains of concern to the public. The term has been used extensively in such areas as economic forecasting, stock market analysis, corporate decision making, insurance underwriting, and political and government planning. Within these spheres of concern, uncertainty is viewed as something with which one must cope and something that one would be better off without. This use of the term comes quite close to the sense in which uncertainty was used by information theorists (Shannon & Weaver, 1949). For these theorists, uncertainty is the product of the number of alternative things that might happen in a given situation and the relative likelihoods of their occurrence. Increasing the number of alternatives produces greater uncertainty and as the probabilities of occurrence of the alternatives approaches equality, uncertainty also increases. In short, as the ability of persons to predict which alternative or alternatives are likely to occur next decreases, uncertainty increases.

This information theory-based conception of uncertainty was augmented by Berger and Calabrese (1975) and Berger, Gardner, Parks, Schulman, and Miller (1976) to include an explanatory component. These researchers argued that one might be able to predict with a high level of confidence the next action or actions of a given person, but when asked to explain these actions, be unable to do so. The addition of the explanatory dimension of uncertainty was prompted by the work of those theorists who view persons as intuitive scientists (Heider, 1958; Jones & Davis, 1965; Kelly, 1955; Kelley, 1967, 1971). These theorists emphasize the needs that persons have to develop explanations for others' behaviors. In addition, Bem (1972) extended these notions to explanations involving the behavior of the self. Berger et al. (1976) argued that, because deriving predictions for others' actions might be easier than developing explanations for them, most persons would not have extensive amounts of explanatory knowledge about particular others. Knowledge at this level would be limited to relatively few persons in individuals' social networks.

The relationship between prediction and explanation is somewhat problematic in the social sciences in general. Some philosophers of science take the view that they are symmetrical; that is, successful prediction implies explanation, and successful explanations give rise to accurate predictions. Others argue that predictions can be derived from explanations, but explanations cannot necessarily be extrapolated from successful predictions (Hempel, 1965). We believe that the asymmetrical view is more appropriate to naive explanations of others' conduct. Clearly, one might be able to predict, with a high degree of accuracy, the circumstances in which a target other will become angry. At the same time, our highly successful predictor may be unable to explain why the target person becomes angry in these situations and not others, or what events in the socialization of the target person are responsible for the appearance of anger responses in the particular circumstances.

Most probably, persons' abilities to generate explanations for others' attitudes and actions stem from at least two sources. First, persons have implicit general theories of behavior that are similar to implicit personality theories. These general theories contain such propositions as "aggressive adults were raised in homes with aggressive parents" or "shy people had domineering parents." In addition to these general theories are specific ones that are developed for individuals. These specific theories are based upon information acquired over time about particular individuals. Specific theories might contain such propositions as "Joe is always angry because his father was" or "Mary is withdrawn because she was dominated by her mother." Specific propositions may or may not agree with those contained in general theories. Since most persons do not have the time to acquire detailed information about a large number of other persons, most individuals have only a few well-developed, specific theories about other persons. In any case, it is the knowledge contained in both general and specific theories that is used to explain the conduct of others.

The question of what constitutes, in social terms, an adequate explanation for other person's actions cannot be dealt with in detail here. We raise the issue, however, because it is one that has not been dealt with to any great extent by attribution theorists but is, nevertheless, an important question. In their everyday interactions with others, persons frequently proffer explanations for their own and others' actions. When do persons challenge their own and others' explanations and theories? What are the characteristics of acceptable and unacceptable explanations? To what extent are such explanations accurate? These issues are deserving of research attention.

B. Types of Uncertainty

Berger (1979) argued that *cognitive uncertainty* could be distinguished from *behavioral uncertainty*. One might have little knowledge about a particular person and thus have a high level of cognitive uncertainty, but be able to behave in a predictable manner in an interaction with the other person, thus demonstrating a low level of behavioral uncertainty. This situation is illustrated best in initial interactions between strangers. Persons who have little knowledge of each other can carry out initial interactions because they possess knowledge about general interaction procedures. Persons know what to do even though they do not know each other well. If their relationship is to progress beyond this initial interaction phase, however, they must acquire information that *individuates* the other person. The acquisition of this information reduces cognitive uncertainty by limiting the large set of possible beliefs that one person can have about another person to relatively few. Moreover, information acquisition also limits the large set of potential alternative behaviors that could be engaged in once the actional constraints of initial interaction situations themselves are reduced. Reduction of cognitive uncertainty may or may not lead to reduction of behavioral uncertainty. If an individual believes that another has certain preferences, the individual may not be certain exactly what actions should be deployed to comport with those preferences. Reduced cognitive uncertainty should, nevertheless, lead to increased behavioral certainty in many situations.

In addition to the distinction between cognitive and behavioral uncertainty, Baxter and Wilmot (1984) and Duck and Miell (1986) proposed that persons may have varying levels of uncertainty concerning their *relationships* with others; that is, rather than conceiving of uncertainty as a phenomenon solely focused upon individuals, including the self, these theorists argue that persons can have uncertainties about their interpersonal relationships as well. It is, of course, possible for persons to have uncertainties regarding even larger social aggregates like groups or institutions.

Lester (1987) suggested that a particularly important source of uncertainty for new employees in formal organizations is others' *evaluations* of their performance. Individuals strive to predict whether they will succeed or fail in their new organizational culture. In order do this, they must determine what actions are likely to be rewarded and punished in their new environments. Although this type of uncertainty resembles those discussed previously, it is unique in that it is focused on the evaluative dimension rather than only on the procedural dimension; that is, it is one thing to know what things need to be done to do a particular job, but is it quite another to know what things count for job success. Furthermore, even if one knows what must be done to obtain organizational rewards, one may be uncertain about the evaluations of one's performance by superiors.

Several of the previously cited works are the basis for what has become to be known as *uncertainty reduction theory,* or URT (Berger, 1979; Berger & Bradac, 1982; Berger & Calabrese, 1975). URT is an axiomatic theory originally developed to explain communicative action occurring in the context of initial interactions between strangers (Berger & Calabrese, 1975; see Table 1 for a summary of the original axioms and theorems).

Recently the theory has been extended beyond initial interaction situations to more developed relationships (Gudykunst, Yang, & Nishida, 1985; Parks & Adelman, 1983; Planalp & Honeycutt, 1985; Planalp, Rutherford, & Honeycutt, 1988). Parks and Adelman, for example, elaborated the theory adding shared communication network as a major variable (see Table 2 for the axiom and theorems derived from their work).

Researchers in such areas as organizational communication (Lester, 1987; Schlueter, Barge, & Case, 1987; Wilson, 1986), intercultural communication (Gudykunst, 1985a) and health communication (Albrecht & Adelman, 1984; Ray, 1987) have found URT to be a potentially useful explanatory system beyond the bounds of informal social interactions. The broadening of the theory's scope suggests the potential usefulness of reconceptualizing and extending the original formulation. We now begin that task.

Table 1.   Axioms and Theorems from Berger and Calabrese's (1975) Theory

Axioms

1. Given the high level of uncertainty present at the onset of the entry phase, as the amount of verbal communication between strangers increases, the level of uncertainty for each interactant in the relationship will decrease. As uncertainty is further reduced, the amount of verbal communication will increase.
2. As nonverbal affiliative expressiveness increases, uncertainty levels will decrease in an initial interaction situation. In addition, decreases in uncertainty level will cause increases in nonverbal affiliative expressiveness.
3. High levels of uncertainty cause increases in information seeking behavior. As uncertainty levels decline, information seeking behavior decreases.
4. High levels of uncertainty in a relationship cause decreases in the intimacy level of communication content. Low levels of uncertainty produce high levels of intimacy.
5. High levels of uncertainty produce high rates of reciprocity. Low levels of uncertainty produce low reciprocity rates.
6. Similarities between persons reduce uncertainty, while dissimilarities produce increases in uncertainty.
7. Increases in uncertainty level produce decreases in liking; decreases in uncertainty produce increases in liking.

Theorems

1. Amount of verbal comunication and nonverbal affiliative expressiveness are positively related.
2. Amount of communication and intimacy level of communication are positively related.
3. Amount of communication and information seeking behavior are inversely related.
4. Amount of communication and reciprocity rate are inversely related.
5. Amount of communication and liking are positively related.
6. Amount of communication and similarity are positively related.
7. Nonverbal affiliative expressiveness and intimacy level of communication content are positively related.
8. Nonverbal affiliative expressiveness and information seeking are inversely related.
9. Nonverbal affiliative expressiveness and reciprocity rate are inversely related.
10. Nonverbal affiliative expressiveness and liking are positively related.
11. Nonverbal affiliative expressiveness and similarity are positively related.
12. Intimacy level of communication content and information seeking are inversely related.
13. Intimacy level of communication content and reciprocity rate are inversely related.
14. Intimacy level of communication content and liking are positively related.
15. Intimacy level of communication content and similarity are positively related.
16. Information seeking and reciprocity rate are positively related.
17. Information seeking and liking are negatively related.
18. Information seeking and similarity are negatively related.
19. Reciprocity rate and liking are negatively related.
20. Reciprocity rate and similarity are negatively related.
21. Similarity and liking are positively related.

Table 2.   Axiom and Theorems Emerging from Parks and Adelman's (1983) Study

Axiom

  8. Shared communication networks reduce uncertainty, while lack of shared networks increases uncertainty.

Theorems*

22. Shared communication networks and the amount of verbal communication are related positively.
23. Shared communication networks and nonverbal affiliative expressiveness are related positively.
24. Shared communication networks and information seeking are related inversely.
25. Shared communication networks and intimacy level of communication are related positively.
26. Shared communication network and reciprocity rates are related inversely.
27. Shared communication networks and similarities are related positively.
28. Shared communication networks and liking are related positively.

  * The theorems were generated by the same procedure used by Berger and Calabrese (1975).

C. Uncertainty and Action Generation

Recently, Berger (1988a) argued for the utility of viewing communicative behavior as an instrument for reaching goals. Obviously, not all communicative activity is instrumental; however, persons frequently use their communicative capabilities to reach various social goals. Although the goals for which persons strive are understudied (McCann & Higgins, 1988), research suggests that inferences concerning goals and plans for reaching them are critical to the understanding of narrative text and generic experience (Abbott & Black, 1986; Bruce, 1980; Hobbs & Evans, 1980; Miller, Galanter, & Pribram, 1960; Sacerdoti, 1977; Schank & Abelson, 1977; Schmidt, 1976; Wilensky, 1983). Thus, in order for individuals to understand the actions of others, they must develop inferences concerning the goals being pursued by others and the plans others are using to attain their goals. In the case of action generation, once individuals decide to pursue goals, they must find plans that enable them to reach their goals. If plans are not available in memory, they must be fabricated or the goal abandoned.

Berger (1988a) pointed out that persons do not necessarily have conscious access to planning knowledge; however, their levels of consciousness concerning planning are raised when goal failure occurs. Moreover, while persons may have a focal goal in mind, it is assumed that, in most situations, persons pursue multiple goals simultaneously. A given individual's goal, for example, might be to persuade another, but, for the sake of maintaining a friendship, the individual might not employ certain influence strategies and tactics. Thus, the goal of maintaining the friendship might play as much of a role in the selection of persuasion strategies and the deployment of persuasion tactics as the primary goal of influencing the friend. This type of multiple goal situation can be distinguished from one in which a person pursues a series of subgoals in order to reach a main goal, e.g., acquiring bachelor's degree in order to become a candidate for advanced degrees.

Like goals, plans can be thought of in terms of their complexity. In order to reach a specific goal, an individual might develop a plan that includes a number of alternative paths for reaching the goal, while another individual seeking the same goal might develop a plan that consists of only one path. Some planners can anticipate goal failures and develop contingency plans to circumvent goal blockages. Others may not anticipate such failures and blockages. Finally, optimal planners are likely to know when to cease striving for goals in the face of failure; whereas suboptimal planners are more likely to iterate the same planning strategies in case of failure and to continue to do so even when it is obvious that the plan will not work. Berger (1988a) and Berger and Bell (1988) found that complex planners performed better in their interactions with others. Also, planning ability appears to be specific to particular domains rather than a general trait (Berger & Bell, 1988).

While the analysis just presented suggests that optimal planners are more likely to reach their social goals, there are a number of factors that complicate the picture. First, when persons interact, their goals may also interact. Persons may be uncertain about the goals of their interaction partners and as a result be uncertain about their own goals in the interaction. When persons ask, "What are your intentions?" they are seeking information that will reduce their uncertainties about their co-interactants' goals. It is also possible, of course, for persons to be unsure of what their own goals are and they may develop goals in an opportunistic manner (Hayes-Roth & Hayes-Roth, 1979); that is, goals may be formulated on the basis of what is perceived to be achievable in the situation. Secondly, although persons may be certain of their own goals and those of their partner, they may be unsure of how best to go about achieving the goal. There are at least two reasons for this. The person may be at a complete loss to think of a plan for achieving the goal, or the person may have a number of alternative planning paths for reaching the goal and may be unable to determine which of these paths might be the optimal ones for attaining the goal. Uncertainties associated with the planning process may also be the product of interacting plans (Bruce & Newman, 1978). Persons may be forced to alter their plans based upon their assessments of their interaction partners' plans.

In addition to uncertainties that arise with respect to goals and plans, there are those regarding the tactical deployments of actions. Tactics are the low-level behavioral routines that are used to realize plans or strategies. Once one has settled on a particular plan of action, decisions must be made about how the strategy or plan will be represented actionally. One might decide, for example, that to achieve a persuasion goal it is necessary to use a threat strategy; however, since there are a very large number of combinations of verbal and nonverbal behaviors that might be perceived as instances of threat, the individual must select from these alternatives those action sequences deemed to be optimal in the situation. These tactical decisions are not likely to be taken consciously (Norman, 1981); nevertheless, given the large number of alternatives involved, considerable uncertainty can occur at the tactical level.

Distinguishing among goal, plan, and tactical uncertainty has distinct theoretical advantages. Although any one of these kinds of uncertainty is likely to prove to be debilitating to communicative performance, understanding the precise source of the uncertainty enables one to sharpen predictions about the relationships between cognition and human action. Uncertainty with reference to goals, for example, does not imply that an individual lacks optimal plans for reaching particular goals once the decision is made to pursue them. Poorly articulated plans may or may not be associated with uncertainties at the tactical level. Furthermore, uncertainties of various kinds may have differential influences on how action sequences are enacted. Uncertainty with respect to goals, for example, may manifest itself early in an action sequence. Once the goal is decided upon, and assuming that there are optimal plans and tactics available, the action sequence should proceed smoothly. Persons with well-articulated goals, in contrast, but uncertainty about plans or tactics should experience difficulties in pursuing a course of action over the entire action sequence. Whether these different kinds of uncertainty manifest themselves in different ways is a question for future research. In addition to these theoretical issues, attempts to improve the communicative performances of individuals must take into account the possibility that observed communicative deficits may be caused by deficiencies in one or more of these domains; that is, the source of uncertainty must be taken into account before any move can be made to ameliorate the performance problem.

This discussion of goal, plan, and tactical uncertainty generally has assumed an informal, face-to-face communication situation. It is not difficult, however, to generalize these concepts to interactions occurring in organizational, instructional, political, or health communication contexts. Moreover, we assume, along with those who view the mass media as potentially providing gratifications for persons' needs (Atkin, 1985; Blumler & Katz, 1974; Rosengren, Wenner, & Palmgreen, 1985), that persons may seek and consume media information in order to reach certain goals. In addition, we also assume that media consumers generally pursue multiple goals *simultaneously*. This position differs somewhat from work done in the uses and gratifications tradition. This research has recognized the multitude of reasons that persons consume various media, but generally has not been sensitive to the fact that persons may seek to achieve multiple goals at the same time during media exposure. Much of this research asks persons to rank or rate reasons for consuming media, e.g., passing time, learning, entertainment, and so forth. This methodological approach itself encourages respondents to think of these goals as occurring one at a time rather than in parallel, as they most likely do. More recent thinking in this area evidences some recognition of this problem (Wenner, 1985).

Regardless of the communication context within which goal, plan, and tactical uncertainties are researched, it is critical to recognize that these three components of strategic communicative action change frequently during many communication episodes. Thus, it would be a mistake to believe that persons frequently formulate goals and plans consciously before they enter into conversations with others, as one might do when preparing for a public speech. An equally infrequent scenario is one in which mass media consumers approach their TV sets and newspapers with well formulated goals concerning the types of information that they want from the particular medium at that point in time; however, persons may do such things as seek morning weather and traffic reports before leaving for work in order to facilitate getting to their jobs. We suggest that such purposive media consumption is relatively rare, and that much mass media consumption is done out of *habit*. Particular goals may be activated opportunistically by the content of the medium while it is being consumed rather than by needs that occur *before* exposure to the medium. Certainly, a priori activation of goals sometimes does direct persons to seek specific media content, as we have pointed out; however, we believe that such activation is the exception rather than the rule.

The dynamic nature of strategic communicative conduct not only implies that goals may change rapidly in any given communication episode, but that plans and tactics must change to match these reformulated goals. If one accepts this conception, then it is difficult to justify research that only takes a snapshot approach to measurement. Analyses of action through time are crucial. Moreover, the theoretical machinery necessary to explain strategic communicative conduct must be capable of accounting for changes in these components. In order to explain why some goals take precedence over others, it is necessary to develop goal hierarchies that can account for choices to pursue various goals. At a certain point, for example, the physiological necessity for excretion takes precedence over all media consumption goals, no matter how important these goals are. Although such physiological necessities seem far removed from the study of strategic communicative action, because they impinge upon such action, they cannot be ignored. Furthermore, communicative action itself becomes instrumental in reaching these noncommunicative goals; e.g., "Where's the bathroom?" The potential for high rates of goal, plan, and tactical change in many communication situations suggests that uncertainty levels can fluctuate considerably within them.

Since goals, plans, and tactics can change frequently during the course of particular communication episodes, persons in the pursuit of various goals must be motivated to reduce uncertainty in order to achieve their goals. Of course, if one lacks the desire to achieve a particular goal, then the necessity for reducing uncertainties concerning subgoals, plans, and tactics is obviated. Given the motivation to achieve a goal, however, motivation for uncertainty reduction almost has to increase. Before attempting to reach persuasion goals, for example, even persons who know their targets well may attempt to gather information about their targets' current emotional states in order to optimize their chances for success. Furthermore, assuming that the target appears to be "in the right mood" to be persuaded, and that the persuader initiates the persuasion episode, the persuader must continue to update his or her estimates of the target's mood state in order to avoid pushing the target too much and inducing a boomerang effect. We believe that the acquisition of social information is a crucial prerequisite for the achievement of most social goals; thus, by implication, uncertainty reduction is central to the achievement of social goals.

D. Measuring Uncertainty

Two distinct approaches have been used to measure uncertainty. First, various aspects of communication behavior itself have been indexed to estimate uncertainty levels. Pause rate and verbal productivity (Lalljee & Cook, 1973), mean word length and type/token ratio (Sherblom & Van Rheenen, 1984), and question-asking rate (Berger & Kellermann, 1983; Calabrese, 1975; Douglas, 1987) have all been used as empirical indicators of uncertainty. Second, several studies have assessed subjective estimates of uncertainty, using Clatterbuck's (1979) CLUES scale or some variant of that scale, e.g., Gudykunst & Nishida's (1986a) measure designed to assess attributional confidence in low- and high-context cultures. CLUES items ask respondents to indicate, on a 0%–100% continuum, the extent to which they feel certain that they know a variety of things about a particular target person, for example, the target's attitudes, values, behavior in situations, etc. Clatterbuck (1979) argues that the CLUES scale taps attributional confidence.

Earlier it was pointed out that uncertainty is the product of the number of alternatives in a domain and the relative likelihood of their occurrence. We would expect that, as the number of alternatives increase, for example, the number of actional alternatives available to individuals, persons would experience increased difficulty in choosing any one alternative to enact. This would also be the case if one were faced with trying to predict a person who could act in a very large number of alternative ways. In both cases, the increased availability of alternatives would make decision making about one's actions more difficult, including, perhaps, decisions about what they should say.

As the number of alternative possibilities increase with reference to another person's beliefs and behavior, a person's felt ability to predict confidently particular beliefs and actions should decline. When we say that we are unsure whether a person believes X or whether a person will do Y, we are implicitly saying that there are so many possible alternatives that we cannot imagine which one might be chosen or that the alternatives are so close to being equiprobable that we cannot pick one that is most likely to be the case. When there is only one alternative or one very highly probable alternative among many, in contrast, persons should feel very confident of their abilities to predict. Presumably, the CLUES scale taps these feelings of confidence (see Clatterbuck, 1979, for a discussion of this instrument's reliability and validity).

We are aware of only one investigation that has examined the relationship between a subjective measure of uncertainty and a speech behavior that might be indicative of uncertainty (Sherblom & La Riviere, 1987). This study found subjective feelings of uncertainty, as measured by a modified version of CLUES (Parks & Adelman, 1983), to be a significant covariate of utterance rate accommodation. While this finding is encouraging, in the same study subjective feelings of uncertainty were not related significantly to either speech rate accommodation or vocal jitter accommodation. There are several possible reasons for slippage between subjective measures and speech behavior measures of uncertainty. Individuals may, for example, manifest uncertainty in their behavior but not feel it subjectively. Or persons might have considerable felt uncertainty, but be able to mask the behavioral manifestations of uncertainty using various impression management techniques. Persons may be unsure of the preferences of another, but, instead of allowing this uncertainty to disrupt their verbal output, they might concentrate on being as fluent as possible during the interaction. Use of this strategy might cause the person to say something with which the other disagrees, but the persons' overall performance would be fluent. Despite the complications suggested here, studies reviewed in the next section of this chapter show that behavioral measures and subjective measures of uncertainty generally produce similar findings.

II. UNCERTAINTY AND INTERPERSONAL COMMUNICATION

We assume that uncertainty reduction is critical to the conduct of interpersonal encounters. In order to coordinate their interactions with others and to develop relationships with them, persons must acquire information that individuates particular others from all other members of the culture and social groups within the culture. Failure to obtain requisite information means that relationships cannot develop beyond the most superficial levels. This view of interpersonal communication is similar to one advocated by Miller and Steinberg (1975), who argue that relationships become interpersonal when persons exchange information at the psychological level. Exchanging psychological level information dealing with personal preferences, attitudes, opinions, and values serves to differentiate individuals from various social categories of which they are members. This view of interpersonal communication is more useful than one that defines interpersonal communication as communication between two persons; since communication between two persons can take place at several different levels. Cappella (1987), however, suggested that it might be more useful to define interpersonal communication and interpersonal relationships using criteria associated with behavioral influence rather than employing type of information exchanged as the only defining attribute. Nevertheless, we take it as a given that reducing uncertainty through information exchange is vital for both coordinating social interaction and developing long-term relationships.

In the remainder of this section, we review evidence from studies that have examined relationships between uncertainty and various interaction process and outcome measures. We relate these findings to the original version of URT (Berger & Calabrese, 1975) and to the modifications suggested in the previous section. Unfortunately, most of the research conducted to date has not examined the distinctions among goal, plan, and tactical uncertainty outlined in the preceding section; however, we try to draw some connections between these constructs and extant findings.

A. Uncertainty Reduction Over Time

Berger and Calabrese (1975) argued that uncertainty is reduced by increased verbal and nonverbal interaction over time. There is considerable evidence to support this contention. Clatterbuck (1979) reviewed evidence for eight studies finding support for the hypothesis that, the longer persons know each other and the more they have contact with each other, the less uncertainty they have about each other. Frequent interaction generally produces perceptions of increased ability to predict the attitudes, opinions, and actions of another. Clatterbuck also pointed out, however, that the correlations observed in this study were in the moderate range. Several of the studies reported in his review employed cross-sectional designs, making interpretation of observed changes in uncertainty over time subject to the usual limitations of such designs. A longitudinal study by Berger, Douglas, and Rodgers (1980) found that uncertainty about new acquaintances, as measured by CLUES, decreased significantly over a month and a half interval. This study also revealed consistent correlations between the amount of communication with new acquaintances and the amount of uncertainty about these acquaintances, the greater the reported communication the less the uncertainty. Cross-lagged panel correlations of these two variables, however, failed to establish any particular causal priority. A more recent longitudinal study (Van-Lear & Trujillo, 1986) reported that uncertainty levels, again measured by CLUES, showed significant decreases from Week 1 to Week 2. After this time period, there were no further decreases in uncertainty. This exponential decrease in uncertainty may explain why Clatterbuck's (1979) linear correlations were only in the moderate range. Douglas (1987) observed significant reductions in CLUES after stranger dyads conversed for six minutes.

The studies just considered all indexed subjective feelings of uncertainty.

Studies examining behavioral indicators of uncertainty have also suggested that uncertainty decreases over time. Persons interacting in interview situations, for example, showed decreased pausing and increased verbal productivity as their interactions progressed (Lalljee & Cook, 1973). Pause rate and verbal productivity are considered to be indicators of uncertainty of linguistic decision making. Analyses of interviews conducted on a radio talk show produced similar results (Sherblom & Van Rheenen, 1984). These investigators found that mean word length and type/token ratios increased over time during interviews; however, measures of linguistic immediacy did not yield unequivocal evidence of reduced uncertainty during the interview period. Three additional studies have shown that question asking between strangers during initial interactions decreases exponentially with passage of time, suggesting that uncertainty tends to be reduced over time (Berger & Kellermann, 1983; Calabrese, 1975; Douglas, 1987). The findings of these studies converge nicely with those that have indexed subjective feelings of uncertainty to support the proposition that uncertainty in face-to-face interactions tends to be reduced over time. The exact shape of the function describing this decrease is still in doubt, but it would not be surprising to find some kind of power curve to be most descriptive of this relationship.

Although the research reviewed supports the contention that uncertainty in interpersonal relationships is reduced over time, Berger and Bradac (1982) recognized that persons might intentionally create uncertainty for strategic purposes in their interactions with others. Persons who wish to remain unknown to others may accomplish this goal by providing information about themselves that is ambiguous or potentially misleading (Berger & Kellermann, 1989). Strategic use of uncertainty in relationship disengagement has been observed by Eckel (1988). Her study revealed that persons who were in the process of terminating relationships reported engaging in behaviors designed to increase their partners' levels of uncertainty about them. Persons trying to maintain their relationships, in contrast, indicated that they engaged in fewer uncertainty increasing behaviors. In addition to these strategic possibilities, persons might receive information about another that simply contradicts an already established fact about that person. Such information might not be divulged for any strategic purpose, but it might create uncertainty just the same. Planalp and Honeycutt (1985) investigated this latter possibility by asking persons to indicate events that increased their uncertainties about relationship partners and the effects these events had upon their relationships. Competing relationships, unexplained loss of contact, aspects of sexual behavior, deception, change in personality/values, and betraying confidences were categories of uncertainty increasing events delineated in this investigation. Not surprisingly, persons experienced negative emotional responses during these events and respondents reported that these events significantly changed their relationships or resulted in their termination.

Although the Planalp and Honeycutt (1985) study demonstrated that, even in "established relationships," uncertainty can be increased by specific events, it would be erroneous to conclude that uncertainty-provoking events in long-term relationships always have negative consequences. The question used to elicit uncertainty-provoking events in this study was worded in such a way that it encouraged respondents to think of negative events. It is quite possible for persons to be surprised by positive events; for example, a husband who rarely does so brings his wife candy and flowers. This problem in the original Planalp and Honeycutt (1985) study was corrected in a subsequent investigation (Planalp et al., 1988). In this study, the item used to elicit uncertainty increasing events included both positive and negative examples. Although this modification of the instructions increased the number of positive uncertainty increasing events elicited, the predominant uncertainty increasing events recalled by respondents were still negative. While there were some other variations between the results of the two studies, the findings of the second study generally replicated those of the first study. In a related study, Bullis and Baxter (1986) reported that relationship turning points that increased ambivalence or uncertainty generally were assigned negative valences by respondents, while turning points that decreased uncertainty generally were judged to be more positive.

There is compelling evidence to support the proposition that uncertainty is reduced as specific interaction episodes and long-term relationships progress, although there are circumstances that can subvert this overall trend, as evidenced by Eckel's (1988), Planalp and Honeycutt's (1985) and Planalp et al.'s (1988) findings. Throughout this section we have emphasized the importance of reducing uncertainty for the smooth conduct of particular interaction episodes and the development of relationships. While this position comports well with a rational view of decision making and communication, one could ask whether highly predictable persons and relationships might not become tedious. After all, variety is allegedly "the spice of life." The world view captured in this aphorism suggests that some uncertainty might have favorable effects on relationships. We now consider this possibility as part of a more general discussion of the relationships between uncertainty and affect.

B. Uncertainty and Affect

In the original version of URT, Berger and Calabrese (1975) proposed that reductions of uncertainty were likely to be associated with increases in attraction between persons. The rationale underlying this proposition was that unpredictability in interactions with others makes the conduct of these interactions difficult, thus rendering unpredictable others to be less attractive than those who are more predictable. This axiom of URT was met with skepticism from some quarters. Scheidel (1977), for example, argued that, in the process of reducing uncertainty, persons might find out undesirable things about their partners and become less attracted to them. The act of reducing uncertainty itself might not lead to increased attraction to the other. In short, to know another might *not* be to love another. In a review of several studies examining the relationship between subjective feelings of uncertainty toward a target person as measured by CLUES and degree of attraction to the person, Clatterbuck (1979) reported an average correlation between the two variables of -.36, with values ranging from near zero to -.70; high levels of uncertainty were found to be associated with low levels of attraction. Subsequent studies have reported similar relationships between the two variables (Gudykunst et al., 1985; Van Lear & Trujillo, 1986). During the second week of the Van Lear and Trujillo (1986) study, however, VanLeer and Trujillo found the relationship between uncertainty and attraction reversed; that is, high levels of uncertainty were associated with high levels of attraction ($r = .52$). During the other four weeks of this five week study, the uncertainty-attraction correlations were negative ($r = -.37$ to $r = -.63$).

Although the bulk of correlational evidence supports the inverse relationship between uncertainty and attraction originally predicted by URT (Berger & Calabrese, 1975), the Van Leer and Trujillo (1986) study, as well as recent theoretical thinking, suggest that the relationship between uncertainty and affect is not as simple as predicted originally by URT. Berger (1987, 1988b) pointed out that the uncertainty–attraction correlations can be interpreted as suggesting that it is when persons become attracted to others that they expend the effort necessary to reduce their uncertainty about them. Uncertainty levels do not cause attraction; rather, it is the other way around. It may be next to impossible to disentangle the causal direction in this relationship. There is a good possibility that the two variables are related reciprocally.

In addition to the obvious problems involved in inferring a causal link between uncertainty and attraction from correlational evidence, recent interest in the relationships between affect and cognition (see Isen, 1984) suggests a more complex relationship between uncertainty and affect. Several researchers have argued that the high levels of positive affect experienced in the early stages of romantic relationships are the product of uncertainty (Berscheid, 1983; Livingston, 1980; Sternberg, 1986). Berscheid (1983), drawing upon the work of Mandler (1975), argues that unpredictable events produce arousal in the autonomic nervous system (ANS). This ANS arousal is experienced as affect. Since the early stages of romantic relationships are likely to produce more unpredictable events, both ANS arousal and the resulting experience of affect are frequent. As relationships develop over time, unpredictability decreases and the frequency of ANS arousal declines. With the decline in the frequency of ANS arousal, romantic feelings to diminish.

Although the reasoning presented has been applied to the development of romantic relationships, there is no reason why it could not be used to explain communicative activity in a variety of other contexts. Generalizing this model suggests that unpredictable events occurring in both face-to-face and mass communication situations are likely to produce affective consequences. These unpredictable events may produce either positive or negative affect, depending upon the type of event. Furthermore, reducing uncertainties about such events may also have positive or negative affective consequences. This line of reasoning leads to the proposition that, contrary to the original version of URT, high levels of uncertainty may produce either positive or negative affect, and that in the process of acquiring information to reduce these uncertainties, persons may have either positive or negative affective responses.

Zajonc (1980, 1984) argued for the primacy of affect over cognition. He contends, for example, that, in making decisions, persons have initial affective responses to decision alternatives that strongly influences the ultimate choice. The cognitive analyses that persons often do when they make decisions are simply an effort to justify the initial affective choice. Thus, lists of pros and cons for choosing between or among decision alternatives are actually post hoc attempts to support choices already made on an affective basis. This position is not without its detractors (e.g., Lazarus, 1982, 1984); however, if it is plausible, it raises some interesting questions concerning the relationship between affect and uncertainty, including the possibility that affect induces uncertainty rather than the other way around. If affect is preeminent over uncertainty, the position advocated by Berscheid (1983), Livingston (1980), Mandler (1975), and Sternberg (1986) would be undermined.

The induction of uncertainty seems to be the prelude to the onset of affect. For the sake of parsimony, it would be tempting to argue that any change in uncertainty paves the way for affect to arise. While it seems plausible that elevated uncertainty is associated with increased affect, it is not clear whether uncertainty reduction per se necessarily is associated with heightened affect. It is, nevertheless, obvious that, in the process of reducing uncertainty about ourselves and others, we may acquire specific pieces of information that influence our affective reactions, but it is not at all obvious that the process of uncertainty reduction is associated with elevated affect. In any case, the possibilities that have been outlined in this presentation are considerably more complex than the simple relationship between uncertainty and attraction posited in the original version of URT (Berger & Calabrese, 1975).

C. Reducing Uncertainty

1. Conditions Motivating Uncertainty Reduction.   Persons are not always preoccupied with reducing uncertainty and many activities aimed at uncertainty reduction are not carried out consciously. Berger (1979) argued that persons would be more motivated to reduce their uncertainties about others when: (a) they anticipate interaction with them, (b) others mediate rewards and punishments for them, and (c) others behave in deviant and unexpected ways. These factors could operate independently or in combinations. There are several studies that support these relationships. When persons anticipate interacting with a stranger for the first time and are given the opportunity to gather information about that person before the interaction, they spend more time acquiring information about that person and they remember more about that person than they do about persons with whom they do not anticipate interaction (Berscheid, Graziano, Monson, & Dermer, 1976; Douglas, 1985; Harvey, Yarkin, Lightner, & Towne, 1980). Berger and Douglas (1981) found that persons who anticipated interaction with a target stranger chose to observe the target in informal rather than in formal situations. This finding was taken as support for the general proposition that persons anticipating interactions try to maximize the amount of information they pick up about the other person. In this case observing a target in an informal situation with fewer actional constraints would provide more information about the target than observing the same person in a more formal context.

Two additional studies have examined anticipated interaction effects in a somewhat different situation. These studies have had individuals actually interact with a target person while believing that they would be interacting with the target in the future. Using this experimental paradigm, Calabrese (1975) found that persons who expected to interact with their partners on a second occasion gathered more biographic and demographic information about them than did persons who expected no future interaction with their partners. Kellermann (1986) discovered that persons anticipating a second interaction with their partners did not experience any more subjective uncertainty than those not expecting future interaction; however, this latter study ignored the fact that Berger's (1979) prediction regarding the effects of anticipated interaction involves levels of motivation to reduce uncertainty, not the levels of uncertainty themselves. Motivation to reduce uncertainty is conceptually distinct from levels of uncertainty; that is, persons might have high levels of uncertainty, but not really be interested in reducing them for a variety of reasons. Furthermore, this study employed only paper-and-pencil, subjective ratings of uncertainty. As we noted above, persons may not be able to report consciously about their desires to reduce uncertainty. Also, the numerous studies showing anticipated interaction effects employed either information storage measures (recall) or measures based upon behavior. None of them employed subjective assessments of information-gathering activities to demonstrate that such activities occurred. Finally, all participants in this study may have reduced their uncertainty levels in their interactions to the point that any potential effects of anticipated interaction were obviated.

The previously cited Berscheid et al. (1976) study lends support to the second condition triggering uncertainty reduction, that is, the rewards and punishments that others mediate for the observer. This study demonstrated that persons pay more attention to those upon whom their outcomes dependent than to those upon whom their outcomes are not dependent. Furthermore, there is considerable evidence to support the proposition that persons with higher levels of power receive more attention from lower power persons than to low power persons from higher power persons. These differential attention rates are assumed to reflect the fact that persons with greater power can mediate more rewards for their low power counterparts than the lows can mediate for the highs (see Berger, 1985, for a review). Clearly, then, observers are motivated to reduce their uncertainties about targets who mediate rewards or punishments for them.

Finally, work reported by Newtson (1976) and Newtson, Engquist, and Bois (1977) demonstrates that, when persons' expectations regarding a sequence of events are violated, they attend more closely to actions that follow the unexpected event than when their expectations are not violated, thus providing support for the third condition motivating uncertainty reduction specified above. Newtson (1973) argued that the increased monitoring of action sequences after observing deviant actions represents attempts by observes to reduce their uncertainties about the meaning of the events in the sequence. Of course, we have noted previously that, even when uncertainty itself is high, persons may not necessarily be motivated to reduce it. Newtson's subjects may have been motivated to attend more closely to his videotaped action sequences after observing deviant events in order to receive their extra credit points or money. Thus, uncertainty provoking events *may* promote attempts to reduce uncertainty, but no deterministic relationship is implied.

2. Uncertainty Reduction Strategies.   Since the original formulation of URT, considerable research energy has been expended to investigate various strategies persons employ to acquire information about others in order to reduce their uncertainties about them (Berger, 1979; Berger & Bradac, 1982; Berger & Douglas, 1981; Berger, Gardner, Parks, Schulman, & Miller, 1976; Berger & Kellermann, 1983, 1986, 1989; Berger & Perkins, 1978; Berger & Perkins, 1979; Kellermann & Berger, 1984). This research program has investigated the passive, active and interactive strategies that persons use to acquire social information about others (Berger, 1979; Berger & Bradac, 1982). Passive strategies are those employed by unobtrusive observers to collect information about targets. Active strategies involve acquisition of information about targets from third parties or the active manipulation of environments by observers to maximize information gain about targets. Interactive strategies are used when observers interact on a face-to-face basis with targets.

The research done in this area has been summarized by Berger and Kellermann (in press). It, therefore, is not reviewed here in detail, but some of the major findings of this line of research can be summarized briefly. Passive strategies research has revealed that observers show differential preferences for observational contexts in terms of how informative they are likely to be about a target person. Observers judge social situations in which the target person is actively involved with others to be potentially more informative about the target as an individual than nonsocial situations or situations in which the target is not actively involved with the others present (Berger & Douglas, 1981; Berger & Perkins, 1978; Berger & Perkins, 1979). While little work has been done to assess how persons structure environments to maximize their information gain about targets, considerable research has been directed toward the question of how persons evaluate information about targets from third party sources (Doelger, Hewes, & Graham, 1986; Hewes, Graham, Doelger, & Pavitt, 1985; Hewes & Planalp, 1982). Hewes et al. (1985) reported that persons frequently rely upon third-party sources to provide them with information about target persons and that persons are aware that the information provided by these sources may be biased. Moreover, participants in the Hewes et al. study felt that they could compensate for the biases in the information provided by the third parties.

Interactive strategies research has isolated three main approaches persons use to acquire information about others in face-to-face encounters (Berger & Kellermann, 1983). Interrogation, disclosure, and relaxing the target person may be used alone or in combination to acquire information from a target. Berger and Kellermann (1983) and Kellermann and Berger (1984) suggested that strategies are deployed in terms of their potential efficiency and their social appropriateness. At times, these two dimensions may be consistent with each other; however, at other times they may be in tension; that is, the most efficient way to acquire information may be the least socially appropriate. A series of studies has investigated the specific verbal and nonverbal behaviors used to realize interactive strategies at the tactical level (Berger & Kellermann, 1983, 1986, 1989; Kellermann & Berger, 1984). We will not describe the details of these studies here. The reader is referred to the original studies and to the Berger and Kellermann (in press) review.

Although the goal of this discussion has been to illuminate the conditions that motivate uncertainty reduction attempts and the strategies that are used to reduce uncertainty, in line with previous discussion we should emphasize that, under certain conditions, persons may try to *increase* uncertainty in their face-to-face encounters with others. We are not aware of a large body of systematic work dealing with this issue; however, Goffman's (1969) discussion of strategic interaction suggests ways in which members of opposing intelligence organizations try to mislead their competitors. Moreover, Berger and Kellermann (1989) have explored some of the tactics that persons use to remain opaque to others during their interactions with them (see also Eisenberg's, 1984, analysis of strategic ambiguity). Some of these tactics involve the deployment of vague and ambiguous messages about the self. Although attempts to ambiguate interactions may be associated with lying, they may serve functions like discouraging future interaction (Eckel, 1988). It would be a mistake to assume that uncertainty-increasing interaction strategies are only associated with deceptive intent.

III. CULTURAL VARIABILITY IN UNCERTAINTY

Like any other communication theory, URT has been developed and researched primarily in one culture. An implicit scope/boundary condition of the theory, therefore, is that it is applicable only in the culture in which it was constructed; i.e., the United States. For this scope/boundary condition to be removed and for the theory to be generalized across cultures, either the theory must be demonstrated to explain communication in other cultures or a theory of culture must be integrated with URT in order to explain cultural variability in uncertainty reduction processes. Research on URT has been conducted using both options. Before examining this research, however, it is necessary to discuss how a theory of culture can be integrated with URT.

Differences between particular cultures are not of theoretical interest; rather, specific cultures are of theoretical interest only when they are used to operationalize dimensions of cultural variability. Foschi and Hales (1979) succinctly outline the issues involved in treating culture as a theoretical variable: "a culture X and a culture Y serve to operationally define a characteristic *a*, which the two cultures exhibit to different degrees" (p. 246). There are at least two theories of cultural variability (Hall, 1976; Hofstede, 1980) that can be integrated with URT (for applications of these theories to a wide variety of interpersonal phenomena, see Gudykunst & Ting-Toomey, 1988).

Hall (1976) differentiates cultures on the basis of the communication that predominates in the culture. "A high-context (HC) communication or message is one in which more of the information is either in the physical context or internalized in the person, while very little is in the coded, explicit part of the message. A low-context communication is just the opposite; i.e., the mass of information is vested in the explicit code" (Hall, 1976, p. 79). While no culture exists at either end of the low–high-context continuum, the culture of the United States is toward the low end, sightly above the German, Swiss, and Scandanavian cultures. Most Asian cultures (e.g., Japanese, Chinese, Korean), on the other hand, fall at the high-context end of the continuum. The level of context influences all other aspects of communication. Hall (1976) points out that:

> High-context cultures make greater distinctions between insiders and outsiders than low-context cultures do. People raised in high-context systems expect more of others than do the participants in low-context systems. When talking about something that they have on their minds, a high-context individual will expect his [or her] interlocutor to know what's bothering him [or her], so that he [or she] doesn't have to be specific. The result is that he [or she] doesn't have to be specific. The result is that he [or she] will talk around and around the point, in effect putting all the pieces in place except the crucial one. Placing it properly—this keystone—is the role of his [or her] interlocutor. (p. 98)

Okabe (1983) extended this analysis, arguing that verbal skills are more necessary and prized more highly in low-context cultures than in high-context cultures. In high-context cultures, verbal skills are considered suspect and confidence is placed in nonverbal aspect of communication.

An alternative multidimensional theory was developed by Hofstede (1980,

1983). Hofstede isolated four dimensions of culture: uncertainty avoidance, individualism, masculinity, and power distance. *Uncertainty avoidance* is "the extent to which people feel threatened by ambiguous situations and have created beliefs and institutions that try to avoid these" (Hofstede & Bond, 1984, p. 419). This dimension is related to how people deal with conflict and aggression, how they release energy and use formal rules, and the tolerance they have for ambiguity. Members of high uncertainty avoidance cultures try to avoid uncertainty, while members of low uncertainty avoidance cultures have greater tolerance for uncertainty. Hofstede's conceptualization of uncertainty avoidance is related closely to Levine's (1985) discussion of the use of ambiguity across cultures.

Hofstede's (1980) second dimension involves a bipolar continuum between individualism and collectivism. In *individualistic* cultures, "people are supposed to look after themselves and their immediate family only," while, in *collectivistic* cultures, "people belong to in-groups or collectivities which are supposed to look after them in exchange for loyalty" (Hofstede & Bond, 1984, p. 419). Triandis (1986) sees the key distinction between individualistic and collectivistic cultures as the focus on the ingroup in collectivistic cultures. Collectivistic cultures emphasize goals, needs, and views of the ingroup over those of the individual, the social norms of the ingroup rather than individual pleasure, shared ingroup beliefs rather than unique individual beliefs, and a value on cooperation with ingroup members rather than maximizing individual outcomes.

Hofstede's (1980) third dimension is a bipolar continuum, *masculinity–femininity*. Masculinity predominates in countries where dominant values "are success, money, and things," while femininity predominates where "caring for others and quality of life" are predominate values (Hofstede & Bond, 1984, pp. 419–210). Cultures high in masculinity differentiate sex roles clearly, while cultures low in masculinity (high in femininity) tend to have fluid sex roles.

Power distance, Hofstede's (1980) final dimension, involves the degree to which members of a culture accept the unequal distribution of power in the society. People in high power distance cultures assume that inequality should exist, that most people should be dependent on others, and that hierarchy is due to existential inequality. Members of lower power distance cultures, in contrast, assume that inequality should be minimized, that people should be interdependent, and that hierarchy is due to role inequality and roles are established for convenience.

A. Conditions Motivating Uncertainty Reduction

Cross-cultural difference in the conditions motivating uncertainty reduction appear to be related to Hall's (1976) low/high-context distinction and Hofstede's (1980) individualism–collectivism dimension. The conceptual link is clearest to low/high-context, but this dimension appears to be isomorphic with individualism–collectivism. Specifically, low-context communication predominates in individualistic cultures, while high-context communication is prevalent in collectivistic cultures. While there are no empirical data to support this claim, Hall's description of high-context cultures is consistent with Triandis' (1986) description of collectivistic cultures and virtually all low-context cultures Hall discusses are individualistic and all high-context cultures are collectivistic (see Gudykunst & Ting-Toomey, 1988, for further support of this claim).

Because of the emphasis on nonverbal communication, members of high-context cultures need to know whether others understand them when they do not verbally express their ideas and feelings. It is also necessary for members of high-context cultures to know whether others will make allowances for them when they communicate. The concept *sassi* in Japan illustrates this claim. Nishida (1977) defines *sassi* as meaning conjecture, surmise, guess, judgment, understanding what a person means, and what a sign means. In its verb form (*sassuru*) its meaning is expanded to include imagine, suppose or empathize with, feel for, or make allowances for. This concept is so important in Japan that Ishii (1984) used it as the basis for his model of Japanese interpersonal communication. While these forms of uncertainty are not absent in low-context cultures, they are emphasized less.

In low-context cultures, verbal (or written) messages require less knowledge of the context in order to be interpreted correctly. Members of low-context cultures, therefore, can gather information about others' attitudes, values, emotions, and past behavior and use it to predict their future behavior (i.e., reduce uncertainty). The type of information gathered is individual specific. Members of high-context cultures, in contrast, seek out social information (e.g., where others went to school, their company). To illustrate, Alexander, Cronen, Kang, Tsou, and Banks (1986) found that Chinese college students infer more about others' intellectual and academic potential based on knowing their high school background than do college students in the United States. Nakane (1974) similarly argued that Japanese ignore individuals whose backgrounds are unknown, because their behavior is unpredictable and it is unknown whether they will follow the norms/conventions appropriate in the context. In order to be able to predict others' behavior, their background and relative status must be known. Background information not only tells members of high-context cultures whether strangers' behavior is predictable, but it also tells them how to talk with strangers (i.e., it tells them how to address strangers and which form of the language to use). Without this knowledge, it is impossible to communicate with strangers with any degree of comfort.

Exploratory research by Gudykunst (1983b) with international students in the United States partially supported these theoretical claims. Gudykunst's study revealed that members of high-context cultures are more cautious in initial interactions with strangers and make more assumptions about strangers based upon their background. As would be predicted from Hall's (1976) theory, Gudykunst and Nishida (1984) found that Japanese display a higher level of attributional confidence about strangers' behavior than people in the United States. Moreover, higher levels of interrogation and self-disclosure were reported in the United States sample than in the Japanese sample. These results are consistent with Nakane (1974), Johnson and Johnson (1975), and Okabe (1983) who point out people in the United States engage in more verbal communication, including interrogation and self-disclosure than do Japanese. Japanese also reported displaying more nonverbal affiliative expressiveness than the respondents from the United States. Gudykunst and Nishida's findings are consistent with predictions that would be made using Hofstede's (1980) uncertainty avoidance dimension; members of high uncertainty avoidance cultures (e.g., Japan) should express emotions more in interpersonal relationships than members of low uncertainty avoidance cultures (e.g., United States).

Gudykunst and Nishida (1986a) found that two types of attributional confidence can be isolated across cultures. These correspond to low- and high-context patterns of communication. Significant differences in low- and high-context attributional confidence scores emerged by culture and stage of relationship. As would be expected from research on interpersonal relationship development (Altman & Taylor, 1973), both low- and high-context attributional confidence increased as relationships increased in intimacy. The interaction effect between culture and stage of relationship that emerged suggests there may be differences in the perceived intimacy of relationships across cultures. At least one of the findings is consistent with previous research. Members of high-context cultures, for example, establish relationships with classmates early in their school careers. These relationships are part of the ingroup and last for life (Nakane, 1974). It, therefore, would be expected that members of high-context cultures would have more low- and high-context attributional confidence regarding classmates than acquaintances. Members of low-context cultures, however, do not establish the same type of relationships with classmates. Rather, acquaintance relationships tend to be perceived as more intimate and members of low-context cultures are more confident in predicting acquaintances' than classmates' behavior.

Gudykunst, Nishida, and Schmidt (1988) examined the influence of cultural variability in individualism–collectivism on communication in ingroup and outgroup relationships and cultural variability in masculinity–femininity influences communication in same- and opposite-sex relationships. They also examined the effects of self-monitoring (Snyder, 1974) and predicted outcome value (Sunnafrank, 1986) of the relationships on uncertainty reduction processes in these relationships. Gudykunst, Nishida, and Schmidt collected data from respondents in Japan (a collectivistic and masculine culture) and the United States (an individualistic and feminine culture).

When controlling for culture, Gudykunst, Nishida, and Schmidt (1988) found several differences in the effect of predicted outcome value on the dependent variables. Predicted outcome value had a significant positive effect on all dependent variables in the United States sample and on all dependent measure in the

Japanese sample. The effect for predicted outcome value, however, was stronger in the Japanese sample than in the United States sample for self-disclosure, attraction, shared networks, low-context attributional confidence, and high-context attributional confidence. Only similarity had a larger effect in the United States sample than in the Japanese sample. These findings are consistent with previous research. Predictability of others' behavior is important in collectivistic, high-context cultures (Hall, 1976). This is one reason members of collectivistic cultures are comfortable with members of their ingroups. If people's behavior is not predictable, they are ignored (e.g., Nakane, 1974).

Self-monitoring had a significant effect on three dependent variables (interrogation, nonverbal, and low-context attributional confidence) in the United States sample and one variable (nonverbal) in the Japanese sample when Gudykunst, Nishida, and Schmidt (1988) controlled for culture. These findings appear to be consistent with the cultural differences in self-monitoring observed in Gudykunst, Yang, and Nishida's (1987) study. Specifically, since Snyder's (1974, 1979) conceptualization (and measurement) of self-monitoring does not incorporate status or ingroup–outgroup relationships, it has less of an influence on communication in collectivistic cultures than it does in individualistic cultures.

Gudykunst, Nishida, and Schmidt (1988) observed a significant multivariate effect for ingroup vs. outgroup in the Japanese sample, but found no significant effect in the United States sample. The specific patterns that emerged in the mean scores for the dependent measures were relatively consistent. As expected, there were significantly more shared networks with members of ingroups than with members of outgroups in the Japanese sample. There also was a tendency for more interrogation and display of nonverbal affiliative expressiveness with members of ingroups than with members of outgroups. No apparent differences between ingroup and outgroup communication occurred with respect to attraction, similarity, low-context or high-context attributional confidence. The one unexpected result was for self-disclosure; that is, there was more self-disclosure with members of outgroups than with members of ingroups in the Japanese sample. The multivariate findings for culture and dyadic composition generally supported Gudykunst, Nishida, and Schmidt's predictions from Hofstede's (1980) theory of cultural differentiation. Specifically, there was a main effect for dyadic composition in the Japanese sample, but not in the United States sample. The pattern in the mean scores that emerged was consistent with Gudykunst and Nishida's (1986b) study of social penetration in Japan and the United States.

Gudykunst, Gao, Schmidt, Nishida, Bond, Leung, Wang, and Barraclough (1988) extended Gudykunst, Nishida, and Schmidt's (1988) study of the effect of individualism–collectivism, adding data from Australia, Taiwan, and Hong Kong. The data from the study indicated that there are differences in communication with members of ingroups and outgroups in collectivistic cultures (Japan, Hong Kong, and Taiwan), but not in individualistic cultures (Australia and United States).

B. Cross-Cultural Generalizability

In the previous section, we discussed cultural differences in the composition of uncertainty, the conditions motivating uncertainty reduction, and illustrated how Hall's (1976) and Hofstede's (1980) theories of culture can be integrated with URT. While differences exist, there also appears to be cross-cultural support for the generalizability of URT. There are no clear criteria, however, for determining whether scope/boundary conditions are necessary in a theory. Lack of support for an axiom or theorem in one or two studies does not necessarily suggest that scope/boundary conditions are necessary. For purpose of the present analysis, an argument for scope/boundary conditions is made when there is *consistent* lack of support for an axiom or theorem across studies (only axioms/theorems consistently not supported, therefore, are identified specifically below).

Gudykunst and Nishida (1984) found support for three of four axioms from Berger and Calabrese's (1975) theory tested in their cross-cultural study, and Gudykunst, Nishida, Koike, and Shiino's (1986) data revealed support for four of seven axioms tested. Gudykunst and Hammer (1987) found that two of four axioms tested are supported in initial black–black communication. The one axiom consistently is not supported outside white–white interaction in the United States is Axiom 3 (information seeking and uncertainty reduction). The reason for the lack of support, however, is not clear at the present time.

Gudykunst, Yang, and Nishida (1985) examined a structural model of URT in acquaintance, friend, and dating relationships in Japan, Korea, and the United States. Their study revealed that a model of URT derived from Berger and Calabrese (1975) provides an acceptable fit to the data in all three relationships in all three cultures. Gudykunst, Yang, and Nishida (1985) also examined the parameter estimates in their model which correspond to axioms and/or theorems in Berger and Calabrese's (1975) original version of the theory. While there were a few differences in the support for specific axioms/theorems across cultures, there was much more consistency. The majority of the parameter estimates for acquaintances yielded consistent results across cultures. Similar patterns emerged for friend and dating relationships. The results for this study and those cited above suggest that, even though there are cultural differences in mean scores for variables associated with URT, there is a high level of consistency in the relationships among the variables across the cultures and ethnic groups studied to date. It, therefore, appears that culture is *not* a scope/boundary condition for URT. The majority of research to date, however, has been conducted in Japan and Korea. While Japan and Korea differ on most dimensions of cultural variability and provide a rigorous test of the cross-cultural generalizability of URT, additional research is needed in cultures in other parts of the world (e.g., Latin America, Africa, other Asian cultures) before a claim of cross-cultural generalizability can be made.

IV. UNCERTAINTY AND INTERCULTURAL COMMUNICATION

We now consider the role played by uncertainty in communication between members of different cultures. Intercultural interactions provide a unique forum within which to study the relationships between uncertainty and communication, because levels of uncertainty are likely to be considerably higher in these encounters than in intracultural encounters. Intercultural encounters differ from intracultural encounters in that cultural dissimilarities are present. Given that Axiom 6 of URT focuses on the general similarity construct (not attitude similarity specifically), cultural similarity/dissimilarity easily can be integrated into the theory.

When cultural dissimilarities exist, communication is, in part, a function of group membership. "Whenever individuals belonging to one group interact collectively or individually, with another group or its members *in terms of their group identifications,* we have an instance of intergroup behavior" (Sherif, 1966, p. 12). Tajfel (1978) argued that behavior can be viewed as varying along a continuum from purely interpersonal to purely intergroup. Recent conceptualizations, however, suggest that a single continuum may over-simplify the analysis. Stephenson (1981) and Gudykunst and Lim (1986), for example, contend that both interpersonal and intergroup factors are salient in every encounter between two individuals and that intergroup salience affects interpersonal processes (and vice versa).

Cultural dissimilarities appear to have a differential impact on relationships at different levels of intimacy. Altman and Taylor (1973) argue that, in the affective exchange stage (i.e., close friendships), "the dyad has moved to the point where interaction is relatively free in both peripheral and in more central areas of personality. Cultural stereotype is broken down in these more intimate areas and there is willingness to move freely in and out of such exchanges" (Altman & Taylor, 1973, pp. 139–140). If cultural stereotype is broken down, the culture from which a person comes should not be a major factor influencing interaction. This line of reasoning is consistent with Bell's (1981) conceptualization of friendship: "The development of friendship is based on private negotiations and is not imposed through cultural values or norms" (p. 10).

The position outlined here also is compatible with Miller and Steinberg's (1975) "developmental" theory of interpersonal relationships. Specifically, when communicators move from using cultural and sociological data in making predictions about their partners to the use of psychological data, the culture from which individuals come is no longer a major relevant variable in making predictions about their communication behavior. When individuals base their predictions about their partner on psychological data, intracultural and intercultural relationships should not differ as a function of culture.

A. Cultural Similarity

Simard's (1981) research with Francophones and Anglophones in Canada revealed that both groups "perceive it as more difficult to know how to initiate a conversation, to know what to talk about during the interaction, to be interested in the other person, and to guess in which language they should talk" (p. 179) when communicating with someone culturally different than when communicating with someone culturally similar. Her research also indicated the subjects who formed an acquaintance relationship with a culturally different person perceived this person to be as similar to them as did subjects who formed an acquaintance with a person who was culturally similar.

Other research is consistent with Simard's (1981) findings. Gudykunst (1983a), for example, found that people make more assumptions about strangers, prefer to talk less, ask more questions about strangers' backgrounds, and have less attributional confidence about predicting strangers' behavior in initial intercultural encounters than in initial intracultural encounters. Similarly, in a study of Japanese and North Americans, Gudykunst and Nishida (1984) discovered that cultural similarity/dissimilarity has an effect on intent to self-disclose and interrogate, as well as the intent to display nonverbal affiliative expressiveness. Specifically, they found that both interactive uncertainty reduction strategies (self-disclosure and interrogation) and nonverbal affiliative expressiveness are used more under the conditions of cultural dissimilarity than cultural similarity. These findings are consistent with URT.

Gudykunst (1985b) found a significant interaction effect between cultural similarity and stage of relationship (e.g., acquaintance vs. friend). The univariate analyses revealed significant independent effects on two variables: attributional confidence and shared communication networks, while interrogation and self-disclosure approached significance. With respect to self-disclosure and attributional confidence, the mean scores were higher for dissimilar acquaintances than similar ones, but higher for culturally similar friends than dissimilar ones. The level of attributional confidence in culturally dissimilar friendships was significantly higher than culturally dissimilar and culturally similar acquaintances. Results for shared communication networks indicated that the mean scores were approximately the same for culturally similar and dissimilar acquaintances, but culturally similar friends shared twice as many networks as culturally dissimilar friends. Culturally dissimilar friends, however, shared significantly more communication networks than culturally similar acquaintances. This difference can be explained by Blau and Schwartz's (1984) theory of intergroup relations. Drawing upon Simmel's (1950) analysis of "cross-cutting social circles," they point out that close relations between people who do not share similar ethnic or cultural backgrounds "tend to be the result of their having other social relations in common" (Blau & Schwartz, 1984, p. 88).

Gudykunst, Chua, and Gray's (1987) research revealed significant interaction effects between dissimilarities on all of Hofstede's (1980) dimensions of cultural variability and stage of relationship development. Specifically, they found that power distance interacted with stage and relationship to influence self-disclosure, attraction, similarity, shared networks, low- and high-context attributional confidence; uncertainty avoidance interacted with stage of relationship to influence self-disclosure, similarity, low- and high-context attributional confidence; individualism interacted with stage of relationship to influence self-disclosure, interrogation, shared networks, low- and high-context attributional confidence; and masculinity interacted with stage of relationship to influence self-disclosure, similarity, shared networks, low- and high-context attributional confidence. The data suggest that, as relationships become more intimate, cultural dissimilarities have less effect on uncertainty reduction processes.

B. Social/Ethnolinguistic Identity

Gudykunst, Sodetani, and Sonoda's (1987) research supports extensions of ethnolinguistic identity theory (Beebe & Giles, 1984) to interethnic uncertainty reduction processes. Overall, their data indicated that ethnolinguistic identity influences the set of uncertainty reduction processes examined. Specifically, the data revealed that the more positive the interethnic comparisons (e.g., comparison between ingroup and outgroups), the weaker other group identification, and that the less the perceived vitality, the greater the perceived similarity. Gudykunst, Sodetani, and Sonoda's (1987) study also suggested that the greater the perceived vitality, the less the self-disclosure, interrogation, and low-context attributional confidence. Similarly, they found that the stronger the interethnic comparisons, the less the high-context attributional confidence. Finally, their study indicated that the more positive the interethnic comparisons, the more interethnic networks overlap.

Recent work by Gudykunst and Hammer (1988a) demonstrated that social identity is related to uncertainty reduction processes in general and that it is related positively to interethnic attributional confidence. While inconsistent with the initial version of Giles's (e.g., Giles & Byrne, 1982) intergroup theory of second language acquisition, this finding is consistent with a recent revision (Giles, Garrett, & Coupland, 1987). Gudykunst and Hammer's finding also is compatible with Hall and Gudykunst's (1986) results, which indicated that the stronger the ingroup identification, the greater the perceived competence in the outgroup language. Moreover, Gudykunst and Hammer's results are consistent with Lambert, Mermigis, and Taylor's (1986) study, which suggests that the more secure and positive members of a group feel about their identity, the more tolerant they are of members of other groups. Similar observations emerge from other studies (e.g., Bond & King, 1985; Pak, Dion, & Dion, 1985).

Gudykunst and Hammer's (1988a) research further revealed that social identity only influences uncertainty reduction when members of the outgroup are perceived as typical of their group. When members of the outgroup are perceived as atypical, social identity does not affect uncertainty reduction in interethnic relationships. Gudykunst and Hammer also found that social identity only influences uncertainty reduction when ethnic status is activated. There findings are consistent with Gerard's (1963) research, which indicated that uncertainty produces a desire in individuals to compare themselves with others. It also appears that ethnic identity influences the anxiety strangers experience in new cultures; the stronger the identification with the native culture, the more anxiety (Dyal & Dyal, 1981; Padilla, 1980).

Ethnolinguistic identity also appears to influence Berger and Bradac's (1982) four alternative models regarding the relationship between language and uncertainty reduction (Gudykunst & Hall, 1987). Model 1 specifies that people develop hypotheses about others' group affiliations based on the language they use, and that, on the basis of these hypotheses, judgments of similarity are made. The greater the similarity, the more uncertainty is reduced. Model 2 is similar except that a "judgment of psychological trait or state" replaces the judgment of group membership as the mediator for judging similarity. Model 3 posits that language leads to a judgment of group membership, which in turn leads to a judgment of psychological trait or state, which then forms the basis of a judgment of similarity. Similarity then leads to uncertainty reduction. Model 4 posits that only a judgment of similarity intervenes between language and uncertainty reduction.

Each of the four models "is probably valid in particular circumstances" (Berger & Bradac, 1982, p. 55); however, Berger and Bradac do not specify the circumstances under which each model might be valid. Gudykunst and Lim's (1986) argument that the interpersonal–intergroup salience of encounters are orthogonal dimensions provides a way to define the circumstances under which each of Berger and Bradac's models should be valid. Four quadrants can be isolated: (I) high interpersonal and high intergroup salience, (II) high interpersonal and low intergroup salience, (III) low interpersonal and high intergroup salience, and (IV) low interpersonal and low intergroup salience. The major generative mechanism for intergroup behavior is social/ethnolinguistic identity, while the major generative mechanism for interpersonal behavior is personal identity.

Gudykunst and Hall (1987) suggest that, when intergroup salience is high and interpersonal low (Quadrant III), and ethnolinguistic identity is a major generative mechanism for behavior, individuals use language to make judgments of group affiliation on which judgments of similarity are made and uncertainty is reduced (Model 1). When the intergroup salience is high and interpersonal also is high (Quadrant I), and both ethnolinguistic and personal identity are generative mechanisms for behavior, it is plausible that judgments of group membership are used to make judgments of psychological traits which form the basis for the judgment of similarity which reduces uncertainty (Model 3). When intergroup salience is low and interpersonal salience is high (Quadrant II), and person, *not* ethnolinguistic identity, is the major generative mechanism for behavior, language should lead directly to judgments of psychological traits which form basis of judgments of similarity that are used to reduce uncertainty (Model 2). Finally, when both interpersonal and intergroup salience are low (Quadrant IV), language may only cue similarity judgment (Model 4), because the interaction is of relatively low importance.

C. Type of Relationship

Gudykunst, Sodetani, and Sonoda's (1987) research revealed that type of relationship influences uncertainty reduction processes. Not only was there a significant multivariate effect by stage of relationship, there was a significant univariate effect for all dependent variables (e.g., self-disclosure, interrogation, attributional confidence, attraction). The findings were consistent with Altman and Taylor's (1973) social penetration theory. Uncertainty reduction processes, therefore, appear to vary systematically as stage of relationships changes, intraculturally, interculturally, and interethnically.

Using dyadic data, Gudykunst, Nishida, and Chua (1986) discovered that high intimacy dyads involved significantly greater self-disclosure, interrogation, shared networks, amount of communication, and low-context attributional confidence than low intimacy dyads. Their analysis also revealed that high intimacy dyads are more consistent in the amount they self-disclose and the degree of high-context attributional confidence the partners have about each other.

Several noteworthy patterns also emerged in Gudykunst, Nishida, and Chua's (1986) post hoc correlational analysis. Their data indicated that self-disclosure, interrogation, amount of communication, length of relationship, and shared networks are correlated with low-context, but not high-context attributional confidence. The associations for amount of communication and self-disclosure supported two of the axioms of Berger and Calabrese's (1975) original theory, but the data revealed the axioms cannot be extended to high-context attributional confidence in intercultural dyads. Gudykunst, Sodetani, and Sonoda's (1987) findings suggest this may be due to differences between the North American and Japanese partners. In their study, amount of communication and high-context confidence were correlated for Caucasians, but not Japanese-Americans. Similarly, Gudykunst and Nishida's (1986a) research revealed that amount and length of relationship are correlated with both low-context and high-context confidence for North Americans, but only related to low-context confidence for Japanese.

Perceived second language competence was correlated with self-disclosure, interrogation, low-context attributional confidence, and length of relationship in Gudykunst, Nishida, and Chua's (1986) study. Closely related to second language competence, clear patterns emerged for perceived intercultural effectiveness. Specifically, perceived intercultural effectiveness was related to self-disclosure, interrogation, attraction, and similarity, as well as both low- and high-context attributional confidence. These results are consistent with Hammer, Gudykunst, and Wiseman's (1978) conceptualization of intercultural effectiveness. Finally, communication satisfaction was correlated with self-disclosure, interrogation, attraction, similarity, effectiveness, and low- and high-context attributional confidence. These findings compare with Hecht's (1978) conceptualization of communication satisfaction.

As indicated earlier, Planalp and Honeycutt's (1985) intracultural research indicated that surprising events resulted in an increase in uncertainty and this increase has negative consequences for interpersonal relationships. Sodetani and Gudykunst's (1987) intercultural study, in contrast, revealed both positive and negative outcomes for interpersonal relationships between members of different cultures following an increase in uncertainty. While there are potential methodological explanations for the different results of the two studies (e.g., Planalp and Honeycutt gave only negative examples of uncertainty increase, while Sodetani and Gudykunst did not provide examples), another plausible explanation involves differences in intracultural and intercultural relationships. It may be that some surprising events may reveal information that, while surprising, also provides information about the partner and, therefore, reduces uncertainty in intercultural relationships. Partial support emerges for the methodological explanation in Planalp et al.'s (1988) study. They found both positive and negative consequences emerging from events that increased uncertainty. Future research comparing intra- and intercultural relationships, however, is necessary to differentiate between the two explanations.

D. Uncertainty and Anxiety

Rose (1981) argued that intergroup (including intercultural) contact is a novel form of interaction for most people. Herman and Schield (1961) pointed out that "the immediate psychological result of being in a new situation is lack of security. Ignorance of the potentialities inherent in the situation, of the means to reach a goal, and of the probable outcomes of an intended action causes insecurity" (p. 165). Attempts to adapt to the ambiguity of new situations involves a cyclical pattern of tension reducing and information seeking behaviors (Ball-Rokeach, 1973). Information seeking is directed towards individuals increasing their ability to predict or explain their own and others' behavior in the environment, that is, reducing cognitive uncertainty. Tension reduction, on the other hand, is directed toward reducing the anxiety individuals experience.

Stephan and Stephan (1985) point out that intergroup "anxiety stems from the anticipation of negative consequences. People appear to fear four types of negative consequences: psychological or behavior consequences for the self, and negative evaluations by members of the outgroup and the ingroup" (p. 159). Stephan and Stephan (1984) argued that lack of knowledge of the other group is one of the major causes of intergroup anxiety. Stephan and Stephan's (1985) study revealed that negative stereotypes and intergroup attitudes, previous "unfavorable" contact (e.g., contact that was *not* intimate, rewarding, etc.), and an increase in dissimilarities between the ingroup and outgroup are associated with higher levels of anxiety in intergroup situations. Other research (e.g., Dyal & Dyal, 1981; Padilla, 1980) suggests that the stronger individual's ethnolinguistic identities, the greater the anxiety they experience in interacting with members of other groups.

Gudykunst (1988) suggests that uncertainty and anxiety have independent influences on intergroup and intercultural communication. As our earlier discussion of communication and affect suggests, however, there is likely to be some connection between uncertainty and anxiety in intercultural encounters. Specification of this relationship awaits further research.

E. Intercultural Generalizability

The axioms and theorems by URT were designed to explain intracultural communication. To the degree that Berger and Calabrese's (1975) axioms and theorems are supported in intercultural communication, the generalizability of URT is increased. The same criteria are utilized in the present analysis as were used in the examination of cross-cultural generalizability; namely, only axioms or theorems consistently not supported across studies is viewed as needing a scope/boundary condition (accordingly, only these axioms or theorems are identified specifically in the discussion below).

Gudykunst's (1985a) structural model of uncertainty reduction in intercultural encounters indicated that the axioms and theorems of URT can be extended to intercultural encounters. Gudykunst's (1985b) intercultural research also found support for four of the five axioms tested and six of the 10 theorems examined. Gudykunst, Nishida, Koike, and Shiino (1986) found that four of the seven axioms and 13 of the 21 theorems are supported for Japanese speaking English with North Americans. Gudykunst, Chua, and Gray (1987) found that five of the six axioms and six of 13 theorems tested are supported for international students' communication with people in the United States. They also found that Parks and Adelman's (1983) axiom (shared networks lead to uncertainty reduction) and five of six theorems related to this axiom also are supported. Gudykunst, Sodetani, and Sonoda (1987) examined five of the original, as well as Parks and Adelman's axioms, finding support for five axioms and 11 of 15 theorems for Caucasian and four axioms and 7 of 15 theorems for Japanese-Americans vis-á-vis interethnic communication in Hawaii. Finally, Gudykunst (1986) found that there is more self-disclosure, perceived similarity, and attributional confidence in intra- than interethnic (black–white) relationships in the United States. This study also reveals that the greater the percent of communication networks shared with the ingroup, the greater the difference between intra- and interethnic attributional confidence. Gudykunst's analysis and difference scores between intra- and interethnic relationships supports the applicable axioms and theorem of Berger and Calabrese's (1975) original theory.

The research cited clearly indicates that the axioms and theorems of URT generalize to intercultural encounters. The studies, however, also suggest there may be a scope/boundary condition for at least one axiom. Consistent with the cross-cultural studies, Gudykunst, Nishida, Koike, and Shiino's (1986) study, for example, suggests that Axiom 3 (information seeking and uncertainty) may not be applicable in Japanese-North American communication. This axiom also has not been supported in other intercultural studies (e.g., Gudykunst et al., 1987) as well as cross-cultural studies (e.g., Gudykunst & Hammer, 1987; Gudykunst & Nishida, 1984), and it, therefore, may be limited to white–white interactions in the United States. No other axiom has failed to be supported consistently across studies.

While the vast majority of the axioms and theorems of URT appear to generalize to intercultural encounters, an URT of intercultural/ intergroup communication must include additional concepts that are not included in the original theory. Gudykunst (1985a) argues that these minimally include cultural/ethnolinguistic identity, cultural/group similarity, second language ability, intercultural/intergroup attitudes and stereotypes (attitudes and stereotypes are incorporated under expectancies in Gudykunst's, 1988, theory). Recent work (Gudykunst & Hammer 1988b; Gudykunst, 1988) also includes intercultural/intergroup anxiety as a critical variable in extending URT to explain intercultural/intergroup communication. An initial extension of the theory has been proffered (Gudykunst, 1988), but it has not been tested empirically to date (see Table 3 for a summary of the assumptions and axioms in the theory). This theory incorporates aspects of ethnolinguistic identity theory (Giles & Johnson, 1987) and expectation states theory (Berger & Zelditch, 1985). It is designed to be applicable to interpersonal and intergroup/intercultural encounters. Gudykunst's theory explicates the factors which account for the reduction of uncertainty and anxiety. Some variables in the original theory are subsumed under higher level concepts (e.g.,nonverbal affiliative expressiveness and intimacy of communication content are subsumed under interpersonal salience) and additioanl concepts (e.g., expectancies) are incorporated. Gudykunst points out that interpersonal salience and expectancies also may be able to be combined and thereby integrate Sunnafrank's (1986) notion of predicted outcome value. The theory also inks uncertainty and anxiety to effectiveness and adaptation.

V. FUTURE DIRECTIONS

In this chapter we have spent considerable time reviewing prior research that has either directly or indirectly tested URT. We now turn our attention to theoretical and empirical issues in need of resolution.

Table 3. Axioms from Gudykunst's (1988) Theory of Interpersonal and Intergroup Communication

Assumptions

1. At least one participant in an intergroup encounter is a stranger vis-a-vis the ingroup being approached.
2. Strangers' initial experiences with a new ingroup are experienced as a series of crises; that is, strangers are not cognitively sure of how to behave (i.e., cognitive uncertainty) and they experience the feeling of a lack of security (i.e., anxiety).
3. Uncertainty and anxiety are independent dimensions of intergroup communication.
4. Strangers' behavior takes place at high levels of awareness.
5. Both intergroup and interpersonal factors influence intergroup communication.
6. Strangers overestimate the influence of group membership in explaining members of other group's behavior.

Axioms

1. An increase in the strength of strangers' ethnolinguistic identities will produce an increase in their attributional confidence regarding members of other group's behavior and an increase in the anxiety they experience when interacting with members of other groups. This axiom *only* holds when members of the outgroup are perceived as "typical" and when ethnic status is activated.
2. An increase in strangers' positive expectations will produce an increase in their attributional confidence regarding members of other groups' behavior and a decrease in the anxiety they experience when interacting with members of other groups.
3. An increase in the similarity between strangers' ingroups and other groups will produce an increase in their attributional confidence regarding members of other groups' behavior and a decrease in the anxiety strangers experience when interacting with members of other groups.
4. An increase in the networks strangers share with members of other groups will produce an increase in their attributional confidence regarding members of other group's behavior and a decrease in the anxiety strangers experience when interacting with members of other groups.
5. An increase in the interpersonal salience of the relationship strangers form with members of other groups moderates the effect of group dissimilarities and will produce an increase in their attributional confidence regarding members of other group's behavior, as well as a decrease in the anxiety strangers experience when interacting with members of other groups.
6. An increase in strangers' second language competence will produce an increase in their attributional confidence regarding members of other group's behavior and a decrease in the anxiety experienced when interacting with members of other groups.
7. An increase in strangers' self-monitoring will produce an increase in their attributional confidence regarding members of other group's behavior and a decrease in the anxiety experienced when interacting with members of other groups.
8. An increase in strangers' cognitive complexity will produce an increase in their attributional confidence regarding members of other groups' behavior and a decrease in the anxiety experienced when interacting with members of other groups.
9. An increase in strangers' tolerance for ambiguity will produce an increase in their attributional confidence regarding members of other groups' behavior and a decrease in the anxiety experienced when interacting with members of other groups.
10. An increase in strangers' attributional confidence regarding members of other groups' behavior will produce an increase in their intergroup adaptation and effectiveness.
11. A decrease in the anxiety strangers experience when interacting with members of other groups will produce an increase in their intergroup adaptation and effectiveness.
12. An increase in collectivism will produce an increase in the differences in attributional confidence between ingroup and outgroup communication.
13. An increase in uncertainty avoidance will produce an increase in the anxiety strangers experience when interacting with members of other groups.

A. Theoretical Directions

At several junctures, we have pointed to some problems with the original formulation of URT. Since the development of URT over a decade ago, research has
suggested that some of the axioms of URT may be in error. Moreover, Sunnafrank (1986) proposed that, by adding new constructs to the theory, its
scope/boundary conditions can be expanded to explain relationship development
beyond the initial phases of relationships. He argues that attempts to reduce
uncertainty are determined by the kinds of outcomes that persons predict in their
relationships with others. When favorable outcomes are predicted, attempts to
reduce uncertainty increase; however, negative expectations regarding relational
outcomes are likely to dampen uncertainty reduction efforts. In response to these
suggested modifications, Berger (1986) pointed out that predicted outcome values themselves are arrived at by uncertainty reduction processes; that is, one
cannot generate such values without reducing uncertainty. Given the importance
of uncertainty reduction to the determination of predicted outcome values,
Berger (1986) contended that Sunnafrank's (1986) insistence on the primacy of
predicted outcome values in determining the magnitude of uncertainty reduction
efforts is misplaced.

At least one study suggests that Sunnafrank's (1986) predicted outcome value
theory is supported less than Berger and Calabrese's (1975) uncertainty reduction
theory. Jones (1988) compared predictions from the two theories using self-
reports of communication in acquaintance relationships. Her findings revealed
that all axioms except number 3 of uncertainty reduction theory were supported.
Further, all of the propositions of Sunnafrank's theory were supported in the
positive predicted outcome condition, but none of the propositions in the negative predicted outcome condition were supported. Jones argues that positive
predicted outcome may be a form of the perceived rewards available from the
partner and, therefore, the results for positive predicted outcome are compatible
with Berger's (1979) discussion of the assumptions of uncertainty reduction
theory. Minimally, Jones' study indicates that Sunnafrank's theory cannot be
extended outside the initial interaction context.

It is not clear whether research findings themselves can resolve this debate.
What may be needed is a reformulation of the theory that would not only
incorporate predicted outcome values but also the modes used to reduce uncertainty. This latter concern is prompted by the extensive research, reviewed earlier, concerning the passive, active, and interactive strategies persons employ to
reduce uncertainty. Much of the research reported in that domain has been
descriptive; that is, the objective of the research has been to enumerate the
strategies persons use to reduce uncertainty. Now that the outlines of those
strategies have been clarified, it is necessary to explain the conditions under
which they are or are not deployed. What is the nature of the mechanism that
determines strategy use? To answer this question, the original version of URT

will have to be expanded. Some steps have already been taken in this direction by suggesting that the metagoals of *efficiency* and *social appropriateness* partially determine strategy deployment (Berger & Kellermann, 1983; Kellermann & Berger, 1984). These two dimensions do not constitute the whole story, however, and more theoretical development must be done in this direction.

Another issue that must be dealt with in future theoretical efforts concerns the possibility that persons may reduce their uncertainties about themselves and others by predicting that they and others are likely to be unpredictable. Expecting the unexpected when the subject of one's expectations is likely to do the unexpected in an adaptive strategy. While such a prediction does not enable one to respond in a specific way to one's self or another on the basis of one's expectations, it does alert one to the potential necessity of being ready to respond in a wide variety of ways when interacting with a given person. How frequently interactants are forced to employ this strategy as a way of coping with uncertainty is a potentially important issue.

As we noted at the beginning of this chapter, the term *uncertainty* usually takes on a negative connotation when it is used in the public domain. This theme has pervaded this chapter, with the exception of the discussion of the relationship between uncertainty and feelings of romantic love (Berscheid, 1983; Livingston, 1980; Sternberg, 1986). In addition to its potential role as a precursor of feelings of romantic love, uncertainty in relationships may be functional. After all, complete predictability in relationships is likely to lead to boredom, which in turn is likely to prompt dissolution of relationships. While Berger and Calabrese (1975) suggested this possibility, it was not formalized in their theory. Uncertainty, nevertheless, may not be quite as villanous as it is portrayed in the public domain. *Optimal uncertainty* may be a construct worth consideration in future theoretical efforts.

Gudykunst (1988) also has pointed out that the way uncertainty operates in relationships may follow a dialectical process. That is, there are continual shifts from an increase to a decrease in uncertainty and back to increase in uncertainty and so on occurring throughout a relationship. Such a view might suggest an unpatterned relationship between uncertainty and intimacy of relationships. This, however, is not necessarily the case. Work on *chaos* in the physical and social sciences suggests that while disorder or chaos may appear to lurk under the facade of order, ordered patterns undergrid the chaos (see Gleick, 1987, for an introduction to the study of chaos). The study of chaos, therefore, may provide a powerful heuristic for future theorizing regarding uncertainty and communication.

B. Research Directions

Along with the theoretical issues just discussed are empirical concerns that need to be addressed by research. A large proportion of studies done to assess the predictions of URT have employed some variant of Clatterbuck's (1979) CLUES scale. This scale indexes attributional confidence. Although CLUES has a high degree of internal consistency, it only taps subjective feelings of confidence. Earlier we cited the few studies that have used behavioral indicators to measure uncertainty in ongoing interactions. While we recognize that interaction studies of uncertainty are considerably more time consuming to execute than studies employing self-report measures like CLUES, they have the potential for providing more detailed answers to research questions concerned with such issues as modes of uncertainty reduction. We hope that the future brings with it an increase in the number of the studies employing interactive measures of uncertainty reduction processes.

As we noted in the previous section, considerable research effort has already been expended to delineate the strategies and tactics persons employ to gather social information about others. We also pointed to the need for developing theoretical explanations for strategy choice. Thus, future research on information acquisition strategies needs to be directed away from description and toward explanation. One way this move can be accomplished is by varying relevant metagoals like efficiency and social appropriateness to see how strategy deployment is affected. Of course, efficiency and social appropriateness may not be the only metagoals governing strategy choice, so this line of experimentation needs to be guided by a more fully elaborated theory. Levine's (1985) theorizing about ambiguity in general, Eisenberg's (1984) work on strategic ambiguity, and Doelger, Hewes, and Graham's (1986) research on "second guessing" may be useful in guiding work on information acquisition strategies.

Finally, further work needs to be done to assess the cross-cultural and intercultural generality of URT. Several studies reviewed in this chapter have made such comparisons. Most cross-cultural studies to date, however, have examined uncertainty reduction processes in only two or three cultures. While using a small number of cultures allows for the generalizability of the relationships among the variables in the theory to be tested, it does not allow theoretical predictions of the influence of culture on uncertainty reduction processes to be tested adequately. In order to accomplish this, studies with multiple (e.g., four or more) cultures need to be conducted. The influence of individualism–collectivism on uncertainty reduction processes in ingroup–outgroup communication, for example, should be examined with at least two individualistic and two collectivistic cultures (this was done in the Gudykunst et al., 1988, study cited above, and the conclusions were firmer than in a similar study with only two cultures, i.e., Gudykunst, Nishida, & Schmidt, 1988). Two additional issues need to be addressed in future intercultural research. First, more research needs to be conducted on the effect of cultural similarity/dissimilarity on uncertainty reduction processes. Of particular interest is whether or not cultural similarity/dissimilarity has a differential influence across cultures. Second, the role of social/ethnolinguistic identity in intercultural/intergroup uncertainty reduction processes needs to be investigated in more detail, including research on its affect across cultures.

C. Conclusion

Although we have not presented a reformulation of URT in this chapter, we believe we have demonstrated the potential explanatory power of a theory that focuses upon the relationships between uncertainty and communication. We believe that the approach to studying human communication advocated in this chapter serves to unify theoretical thinking in several subareas of communication science. While we have confined most of our review to intercultural and interpersonal communication contexts, there are signs that uncertainty reduction is becoming an attractive starting point for mass, organizational, and health communication research. Certainly, URT is not the only perspective capable of explaining communicative action across these diverse communication contexts. Nevertheless, we feel that theories focusing on uncertainty, like URT, are attractive because both communication and the reduction of uncertainty are vital for human adaptation and social coordination. What could be a more basic foundation upon which to build a general theory of human communication?

REFERENCES

Abbott, V., & Black, J. B. (1986). Goal-related inferences in comprehension. In J. A. Galambos, R. P. Abelson, & J. B. Black (Eds.), *Knowledge structures.* Hillsdale, NJ: Erlbaum.

Albrecht, T. L., & Adelman, M. B. (1984). Social support and life stress: New directions for communication research. *Human Communication Research, 11,* 3–32.

Alexander, A., Cronen, V., Kang, K., Tsou, B., & Banks, J. (1986). Patterns of topic sequencing and information gain: A comparative study of relationship development in Chinese and American cultures. *Communication Quarterly, 34,* 66–78.

Altman, I., & Taylor, D. (1973). *Social penetration: The development of interpersonal relationships.* New York: Holt, Rinehart, and Winston.

Atkin, C. K. (1985). Informational utility and selective exposure to entertainment media. In D. Zillmann & J. Bryant (Eds.), *Selective exposure to communication.* Hillsdale, NJ: Erlbaum.

Ball-Rokeach, S. J. (1973). From pervasive ambiguity to a definition of the situation. *Sociometry, 36,* 378–389.

Baxter, L. A., & Wilmot, W. W. (1984). "Secret tests": Social strategies for acquiring information about the state of the relationship. *Human Communication Research, 11,* 171–201.

Beebe, L. M., & Giles, H. (1984). Speech accommodation theories: A discussion in terms of second-language acquisition. *International Journal of the Sociology of Language, 46,* 5–32.

Bell, R. (1981). *World of friendship.* Beverly Hills, CA: Sage.

Bem, D. J. (1972). Self-perception theory. In L. Berkowitz (Ed.), *Advances in experimental social psychology* (Vol. 6). New York: Academic Press.

Berger, C. R. (1979). Beyond initial interactions. In H. Giles & R. St. Clair (Eds.), *Language and social psychology.* Oxford, England: Basil Blackwell.

Berger, C. R. (1985). Social power and interpersonal communication. In M. L. Knapp & G. R. Miller (Eds.), *Handbook of interpersonal communication*. Beverly Hills, CA: Sage.

Berger, C. R. (1986). Uncertain outcome values in predicted relationships: Uncertainty reduction theory then and now. *Human Communication Research, 13,* 34–38.

Berger, C. R. (1987). Communicating under uncertainty. In M. E. Roloff & G. R. Miller (Eds.), *Interpersonal processes: New directions in communication research*. Newbury Park, CA: Sage.

Berger, C. R. (1988a). Planning, affect and social action generation. In L. Donohew, H. Sypher, & E. T. Higgins (Eds.), *Communication, social cognition and affect*. Hillsdale, NJ: Erlbaum.

Berger, C. R. (1988b). Uncertainty and information exchange in developing relationships. In S. Duck (Ed.), *Handbook of personal relationships*. Chichester, England: John Wiley.

Berger, C. R., & Bell, R. A. (1988). Plans and the initiation of social relationships. *Human Communication Research, 15,* 217–235.

Berger, C. R., & Bradac, J. J. (1982). *Language and social knowledge: Uncertainty in interpersonal relations*. London: Edward Arnold.

Berger, C. R., & Calabrese, R. (1975). Some explorations in initial interactions and beyond: Toward a developmental theory of interpersonal communication. *Human Communication Research, 1,* 99–112.

Berger, C. R., & Chaffee, S. H. (1987). The study of communication as a science. In C. R. Berger & S. H. Chaffee (Eds.), *Handbook of communication science*. Newbury Park, CA: Sage.

Berger, C. R., & Douglas, W. (1981). Studies in interpersonal epistemology III: Anticipated interaction, self-monitoring, and observational context selection. *Communication Monographs, 48,* 183–196.

Berger, C. R., Douglas, W., & Rodgers, M. J. (1980, May). *Communication and uncertainty in long and short term relationships*. Paper presented at the annual convention of the International Communication Association, Acapulco, Mexico.

Berger, C. R., Gardner, R. R., Parks, M. R., Schulman, L., & Miller, G. R. (1976). Interpersonal epistemology and interpersonal communication. In G. R. Miller (Ed.), *Explorations in interpersonal communication*. Beverly Hills, CA: Sage.

Berger, C. R., & Kellermann, K. A. (1983). To ask or not to ask: Is that a question? In R. Bostrom (Ed.), *Communication yearbook 7*. Beverly Hills, CA: Sage.

Berger, C. R., & Kellermann, K. A. (1986, May). *Goal incompatibility and social action: The best laid plans of mice and men often go astray*. Paper presented at the annual convention of the International Communication Association, Chicago, IL.

Berger, C. R., & Kellermann, K. A. (1989). Personal opacity and social information gathering: Explorations in strategic communication. *Communication Research, 16,* 314–351.

Berger, C. R., & Kellermann, K. A. (in press). Acquiring social information. In J. A. Daly & J. M. Wiemann (Eds.), *Communicating strategically: Strategies in interpersonal communication*. Hillsdale, NJ: Erlbaum.

Berger, C. R., & Perkins, J. (1978). Studies in interpersonal epistemology I: Situational attributes in observational context selection. In B. Ruben (Ed.), *Communication yearbook 2*. New Brunswick, NJ: Transaction.

Berger, C. R., & Perkins, J. W. (1979, November). *Studies in interpersonal epistemology II: Self-monitoring, involvement, facial affect, similarity and observational context selection*. Paper presented at the annual convention of the Speech Communication Association, San Antonio, TX.

Berger, J., & Zelditch, M. (Eds). (1985). *Status, rewards and influence*. San Francisco, CA: Jossey-Bass.

Berlo, D. K. (1960). *The process of communication*. New York: Holt, Rinehart, & Winston.

Berlyne, D. (1960). *Conflict, arousal, and curiosity*. New York: McGraw-Hill.

Berscheid, E. (1983). Emotion. In H. H. Kelley, E. Berscheid, A. Christensen, J. H. Harvey, T. L. Huston, G. Levinger, E. McClintock, L. Peplau, & D. R. Peterson (Eds.), *Close relationships*. New York: Freeman.

Berscheid, E., Graziano, W., Monson, T., & Dermer, M. (1976). Outcome dependency: Attention, attribution, and attraction. *Journal of Personality and Social Psychology, 34*, 978–989.

Blau, P., & Schwartz, J. (1984). *Cross-cutting social circles: Testing a macro theory of intergroup relations*. New York: Academic Press.

Blumler, J. G., & Katz, E. (Eds.). (1974). *The uses of mass communications: Current perspectives on gratifications research*. Beverly Hills, CA: Sage.

Bond, M. H., & King, A. Y. C. (1985). Coping with the threat of westernization in Hong Kong. *International Journal of Intercultural Relations, 9*, 351–364.

Broadhurst, A. R., & Darnell, D. K. (1965). Introduction to cybernetics and information theory. *Quarterly Journal of Speech, 51*, 442–453.

Bruce, B. C. (1980). Plans and social actions. In R. J. Sprio, B. C. Bruce, & W. F. Brewer (Eds.), *Theoretical issues in reading comprehension*. Hillsdale, NJ: Erlbaum.

Bruce, B., & Newman, D. (1978). Interacting plans. *Cognitive Science, 2*, 195–233.

Bullis, C., & Baxter, L. (1986, February). *A functional typology of turning point events in the development of romantic relationships*. Paper presented at the annual convention of the Western Speech Communication Association.

Calabrese, R. J. (1975). *The effects of privacy and probability of future interaction on initial interaction patterns*. Unpublished doctoral dissertation, Department of Communication Studies, Northwestern University.

Cappella, J. N. (1987). Interpersonal communication: Definitions and fundamental questions. In C. R. Berger & S. H. Chaffee (Eds.), *Handbook of communication science*. Newbury Park, CA: Sage.

Clatterbuck, G. W. (1979). Attributional confidence and uncertainty in initial interactions. *Human Communication Research, 5*, 147–157.

Delia, J. G. (1987). Communication research: A history. In C. R. Berger & S. H. Chaffee (Eds.), *Handbook of communication science*. Newbury Park, CA: Sage.

Doelger, J. A., Hewes, D. E., & Graham, M. L. (1986). Knowing when to "second guess": The mindful analysis of messages. *Human Communication Research, 12*, 301–338.

Douglas, W. (1985). Anticipated interaction and information seeking. *Human Communication Research, 12*, 243–258.

Douglas, W. (1987). *Uncertainty, information seeking, and liking for a partner: Toward a test of uncertainty reduction theory*. Unpublished paper, School of Communication, University of Houston, Houston, TX.

Duck, S. W., & Miell, D. E. (1986). Charting the development of personal relationships. In R. Gilmour & S. W. Duck (Eds.), *The emerging field of relationships*. Hillsdale, NJ: Erlbaum.

Dyal, J. A., & Dyal, R. Y. (1981). Acculturation, stress, and coping. *International Journal of Intercultural Relations, 5*, 301–328.

Eckel, L. E. (1988, February). *Relationship disengagement: An extension of uncertainty reduction theory*. Paper presented at the annual convention of the Western Speech Communication Association, San Diego, CA.

Eisenberg, E. (1984). Ambiguity as a strategy in organizational communication. *Communication Monographs, 51*, 227–242.

Foschi, M., & Hales, W. H. (1979). The theoretical role of cross-cultural comparisons in experimental social psychology. In L. H. Eckensberger, W. J. Lonner, & Y. H. Poortinga (Eds.), *Cross-cultural contributions to psychology*. Lisse, Netherlands: Swets & Zeitlinger.

Garner, W. (1962). *Uncertainty and structure as psychological concepts*. New York: John Wiley.

Gerard, H. G. (1963). Emotional uncertainty and social comparison. *Journal of Abnormal and Social Psychology, 66,* 568–573.

Giles, H., & Byrne, J. L. (1982). An intergroup approach to second language acquisition. *Journal of Multilingual and Multicultural Development, 3,* 17–40.

Giles, H., Garrett, P., & Coupland, N. (1987, September). *Language acquisition in the Basque country: Invoking and extending the intergroup model.* Paper presented at the Second World Basque Congress: Basque Language Conference, San Sabastian, Basque Country, Spain.

Giles, H., & Johnson, P. (1987). Ethnolinguistic identity theory: A social psychological approach to language maintenance. *International Journal of the Sociology Language, 68,* 69–99.

Gleick, J. (1987). *Chaos: Making a new science.* New York: Viking.

Goffman, E. (1969). *Strategic interaction.* Philadelphia, PA: University of Pennsylvania Press.

Gudykunst, W. B. (1983a). Similarities and difference in perceptions of initial intracultural and intercultural encounters. *The Southern Speech Communication Journal, XLIX,* 49–65.

Gudykunst, W. B. (1983b). Uncertainty reduction and predictability of behavior in low- and high-context cultures. *Communication Quarterly, 31,* 49–55.

Gudykunst, W. B. (1985a). A model of uncertainty reduction in intercultural encounters. *Journal of Language and Social Psychology, 4,* 79–98.

Gudykunst, W. B. (1985b). The influence of cultural similarity, type of relationship, and self-monitoring on uncertainty reduction process. *Communication Monographs, 52,* 203–217.

Gudykunst, W. B. (1986). Ethnicity, type of relationship, and intraethnic and interethnic uncertainty reduction. In Y. Kim (Ed.), *Interethnic communication.* Beverly Hills, CA: Sage.

Gudykunst, W. B. (1988). Uncertainty and anxiety. In Y. Y. Kim & W. B. Gudykunst (Eds.), *Theory in intercultural communication.* Newbury Park, CA: Sage.

Gudykunst, W. B., Chua, E., & Gray, A. (1987). Cultural dissimilarities and uncertainty reduction process. In M. McLaughlin (Ed.), *Communication yearbook 10.* Beverly Hills, CA: Sage.

Gudykunst, W. B., Gao, G., Schmidt, K. L., Nishida, T., Bond, M., Leung, K., Wang, G., & Barraclough, R. (1989, May). *The influence of individualism–collectivism, self-monitoring, and predicted outcome value on communication in ingroup and outgroup relationships.* Paper presented at the Annual Convention of the International Communication Association, San Francisco, CA.

Gudykunst, W. B., & Hall, B. J. (1987, July). *Ethnolinguistic identity and uncertainty reduction in intergroup and interpersonal encounters.* Paper presented at the Third International Conference on Language and Social Psychology, Bristol, England.

Gudykunst, W. B., & Hammer, M. R. (1987). The effects of ethnicity, gender, and dyadic composition on uncertainty reduction in initial interactions. *Journal of Black Studies, 18,* 191–214.

Gudykunst, W. B., & Hammer, M. R. (1988a). The influence of social identity and intimacy of interethnic relationships on uncertainty reduction processes. *Human Communication Research, 14,* 569–601.

Gudykunst, W. B., & Hammer, M. R. (1988b). Strangers and hosts: An uncertainty reduction based theory of intercultural adaptation. In Y. Y. Kim & W. B. Gudykunst (Eds.), *Cross-cultural adaptation: Current history and research.* Newbury Park, CA: Sage.

Gudykunst, W. B., & Lim, T. S. (1986). A perspective for the study of intergroup communication. In W. B. Gudykunst (Ed.), *Intergroup communication.* London: Edward Arnold.

Gudykunst, W. B., & Nishida, T. (1984). Individual and cultural influences on uncertainty reduction. *Communication Monographs, 51,* 23–36.

Gudykunst, W. B., & Nishida, T. (1986a). Attributional confidence in low- and high-context cultures. *Human Communication Research, 12,* 525–549.

Gudykunst, W. B., & Nishida, T. (1986b). The influence of cultural variability on perceptions of communication behavior associated with relationship terms. *Human Communication Research, 13,* 147–166.

Gudykunst, W. B., Nishida, T., & Chua, E. (1986). Uncertainty reduction in Japanese-North American dyads. *Communication Research Reports, 3,* 39–46.

Gudykunst, W. B., Nishida, T., Koike, H., & Shiino, N. (1986). The influence of language on uncertainty reduction: An exploratory study of Japanese-Japanese and Japanese-North American interactions. In M. McLaughlin (Ed.), *Communication yearbook 9.* Beverly Hills, CA: Sage.

Gudykunst, W. B., Nishida, T., & Schmidt, K. L. (1988, May). *Cultural, personality, and relational influences on uncertainty reduction in ingroup vs. outgroup and same- vs. opposite-sex relationships: Japan and the United States.* Paper presented at the International Communication Association Convention, New Orleans.

Gudykunst, W. B., Sodetani, L. L., & Sonoda, K. (1987). Uncertainty reduction in Japanese-American-Caucasian relationships in Hawaii. *Western Journal of Speech Communication, 51,* 256–278.

Gudykunst, W. B., & Ting-Toomey, S. (in press). *Culture and interpersonal communication.* Newbury Park, CA: Sage.

Gudykunst, W. B., Yang, S. M., & Nishida, T. (1985). A cross-cultural test of uncertainty reduction theory: Comparisons of acquaintance, friend, and dating relationships in Japan, Korea, and the United States. *Human Communication Research, 11,* 407–454.

Gudykunst, W. B., Yang, S. M., & Nishida, T. (1987). Cultural differences in self-consciousness and self-monitoring. *Communication Research, 14,* 7–36.

Gudykunst, W. B., Yoon, Y. C., & Nishida, T. (1987). The influence of individualism-collectivism on perceptions of communication in ingroup and outgroup relationships. *Communication Monographs, 54,* 295–306.

Hall, B. J., & Gudykunst, W. B. (1986). The intergroup theory of second language ability. *Journal of Language and Social Psychology, 5,* 291–302.

Hall, E. T. (1976). *Beyond culture.* New York: Doubleday.

Hammer, M., Gudykunst, W., & Wiseman, R. (1978). Dimensions of intercultural effectiveness. *International Journal of Intercultural Relations, 2,* 382–393.

Harvey, J. H., Yarkin, K. L., Lightner, J. M., & Towne, J. P. (1980). Unsolicited interpretation and recall of interpersonal events. *Journal of Personality and Social Psychology, 38,* 551–568.

Hayes-Roth, B., & Hayes-Roth, F. (1979). A cognitive model of planning. *Cognitive Science, 3,* 275–310.

Hecht, M. (1978). The conceptualization and measurement of communication satisfaction. *Human Communication Research, 4,* 253–264.

Heider, F. (1958). *The psychology of interpersonal relations.* New York: John Wiley.

Hempel, C. G. (1965). *Aspects of scientific explanation.* New York: Free Press.

Herman, S., & Schield, E. (1961). The stranger group in a cross-cultural situation. *Sociometry, 24,* 165–176.

Hewes, D. E., Graham, M. K., Doelger, J. A., & Pavitt, C. (1985). "Second guessing": Message interpretations in social networks. *Human Communication Research, 11,* 299–334.

Hewes, D. E., & Planalp, S. (1982). There is nothing as useful as a good theory . . . The influence of social knowledge of interpersonal communication. In M. E. Roloff & C. R. Berger (Eds.), *Social cognition and communication.* Beverly Hills, CA: Sage.

Hobbs, J. R., & Evans, D. A. (1980). Conversation as planned behavior. *Cognitive Science, 4,* 349–377.

Hofstede, G. (1980). *Cultures consequences.* Beverly Hills, CA: Sage.

Hofstede, G. (1983). Dimensions of national cultures in fifty countries and three regions. In J. Deregowski, S. Dziurawiec, & R. Annis (Eds.), *Explications in cross-cultural psychology.* Lisse, Netherlands: Swets & Zeitlinger.

Hofstede, G., & Bond, M. (1984). Hofstede's culture dimensions: An independent validation using Rokeache's value survey. *Journal of Cross-Cultural Psychology, 15,* 417–433.

Isen, A. M. (1984). Toward understanding the role of affect in cognition. In R. S. Wyer & T. K. Srull (Eds.), *Handbook of social cognition.* Hillsdale, NJ: Erlbaum.

Ishii, S. (1984). Enryo-sasshi communication: A key to understanding Japanese interpersonal relations. *Cross-Currents, XI,* 49–58.

Johnson, C., & Johnson, F. (1975). Interaction rules and ethnicity. *Social Forces, 54,* 452–466.

Jones, E. E., & Davis, K. E. (1965). From acts to dispositions: The attribution process in person perception. In L. Berkowitz (Ed.), *Advances in experimental social psychology* (Vol. 2). New York: Academic Press.

Jones, E. K. (1988). *Uncertainty reduction versus predicted outcome value: A test of two competing theories.* Unpublished master's thesis, Arizona State University.

Kellermann, K. A. (1986). Anticipation of future interaction and information exchange in initial interaction. *Human Communication Research, 13,* 41–75.

Kellermann, K. A., & Berger, C. R. (1984). Affect and the acquisition of social information: Sit back, relax, and tell me about yourself. In R. Bostrom (Ed.), *Communication yearbook 8.* Beverly Hills, CA: Sage.

Kelley, H. H. (1967). Attribution theory in social psychology. In D. Levine (Ed.), *Nebraska symposium on motivation.* Lincoln, NE: University of Nebraska Press.

Kelley, H. H. (1971). *Attribution in social interaction.* Morristown, NJ: General Learning Press.

Kelly, G. A. (1955). *The theory of personal constructs.* New York: Norton.

Lalljee, M., & Cook, M. (1973). Uncertainty in first encounters. *Journal of Personality and Social Psychology, 26,* 137–141.

Lambert, W. E., Mermigis, L., & Taylor, D. M. (1986). Greek Canadian's attitudes toward own group and other Canadian ethnic groups: A test of the multiculturalism hypothesis. *Canadian Journal of Behavioural Sciences, 18,* 35–51.

Lazarus, R. S. (1982). Thoughts on the relations between emotion and cognition. *American Psychologist, 37,* 1019–1024.

Lazarus, R. S. (1984). On the primacy of cognition. *American Psychologist, 39,* 124–129.

Lester, R. E. (1987). Organizational culture, uncertainty reduction, and the socialization of new organizational members. In S. Thomas (Ed.), *Communication—methodology, behavior, artifacts and institutions.* Norwood, NJ: Ablex Publishing Corp.

Levine, D. N. (1985). *The flight from ambiguity.* Chicago, IL: University of Chicago Press.

Livingston, K. R. (1980). Love as a process of uncertainty reduction—cognitive theory. In K. S. Pope (Ed.), *On love and loving.* San Francisco, CA: Jossey-Bass.

Mandler, G. (1975). *Mind and emotion.* New York: John Wiley.

McCann, C. D., & Higgins, E. T. (1988). Goals and orientations in interpersonal relations: How intrapersonal discrepancies produce negative affect. In L. Donohew, H. Sypher, & E. T. Higgins (Eds.), *Communication, social cognition and affect.* Hillsdale, NJ: Erlbaum.

Miller, G. A., Galanter, E., & Pribram, K. H. (1960). *Plans and the structure of behavior.* New York: Holt, Rinehart, & Winston.

Miller, G. R., & Steinberg, M. (1975). *Between people.* Chicago, IL: Science Research Associates.

Nakane, C. (1974). The social system reflected in interpersonal communication. In J. Condon & M. Saito (Eds.), *Intercultural encounters with Japan.* Tokyo, Japan: Simul Press.

Newtson, D. (1973). Attribution and the unit of perception of ongoing behavior. *Journal of Personality and Social Psychology, 38,* 28–38.

Newtson, D. (1976). Foundations of attribution: The perception of ongoing behavior. In J. Harvey, W. Ickes, & R. Kidd (Eds.), *New directions in attribution research* (Vol. 1). Hillsdale, NJ: Erlbaum.

Newtson, D., Engquist, G., & Bois, J. (1977). The objective basis of behavior units. *Journal of Personality and Social Psychology, 35,* 847–862.

Nishida, T. (1977). An analysis of a cultural concept affecting Japanese interpersonal communication. *Communication, 6,* 69–80.

Norman, D. A. (1981). Categorization of action slips. *Psychological Review, 88,* 1–15.

Okabe, R. (1983). Cultural assumptions of east and west: Japan and the United States. In W. Gudykunst (Ed.), *Intercultural communication theory: Current perspectives.* Beverly Hills, CA: Sage.

Padilla, A. M. (1980). The role of cultural awareness and ethnic loyalty in acculturation. In A. Padilla (Ed.), *Acculturation: Theory, models, and some new findings.* Boulder, CO: Westview Press.

Pak, A., Dion, K. L., & Dion, K. K. (1985). Correlates of self-confidence with English among Chinese students in Toronto. *Canadian Journal of Behavioural Sciences, 17,* 369–378.

Parks, M. R., & Adelman, M. B. (1983). Communication networks and the development of romantic relationships: An expansion of uncertainty reduction theory. *Human Communication Research, 10,* 55–80.

Planalp, S., & Honeycutt, J. (1985). Events that increase uncertainty in interpersonal relationships. *Human Communication Research, 11,* 593–604.

Planalp, S., Rutherford, D. K., & Honeycutt, J. M. (1988). Events that increase uncertainty in relationships II. *Human Communication Research, 14,* 516–547.

Ray, E. B. (1987, May). *Support, uncertainty and occupational stress in the workplace.* Paper presented at the annual convention of the International Communication Association, Montreal, Quebec.

Rose, T. L. (1981). Cognitive and dyadic processes in intergroup contact. In D. Hamilton (Ed.), *Cognitive processes in stereotyping and intergroup behavior.* Hillsdale, NJ: Erlbaum.

Rosengren, K. E., Wenner, L. A., & Palmgreen, P. (Eds.). (1985). *Media gratifications research: Current perspectives.* Beverly Hills, CA: Sage.

Sacerdoti, E. D. (1977). *A structure for plans and behavior.* New York: Elsevier.

Schank, R. C., & Abelson, R. P. (1977). *Scripts, plans, goals and understanding: An inquiry into human knowledge structures.* Hillsdale, NJ: Erlbaum.

Scheidel, T. M. (1977). Evidence varies with phases of inquiry. *Western Journal of Speech Communication, 41,* 20–31.

Schlueter, D. W., Barge, J. K., & Case, K. D. (1987, May). *Uncertainty reduction in the employee selection process: Model development and preliminary investigation.* Paper presented at the annual convention of the International Communication Association, Montreal, Quebec.

Schmidt, C. F. (1976). Understanding human action: Recognizing the plans and motives of other persons. In J. S. Carroll & J. W. Payne (Eds.), *Cognition and social behavior.* Hillsdale, NJ: Erlbaum.

Schramm, W. (1954). How communication works. In W. Schramm (Ed.), *The process and effects of mass communication.* Urbana, IL: University of Illinois Press.

Shannon, C., & Weaver, W. (1949). *The mathematical theory of communication.* Urbana, IL: University of Illinois Press.

Sherblom, J., & La Riviere, C. (1987, November). *Speech accommodation and the effects of cognitive uncertainty and physiological arousal upon it.* Paper presented at the annual convention of the Speech Communication Association, Boston, MA.

Sherblom, J., & Van Rheenen, D. E. (1984). Spoken language indices of uncertainty. *Human Communication Research, 11,* 221–230.

Sherif, M. (1966). *In common predicament: Social psychology of intergroup conflict and cooperation.* New York: Houghton Mifflin.

Simard, L. (1981). Cross-cultural interaction. *Journal of Social Psychology, 113,* 117–192.

Simmell, G. (1950). The stranger. In K. Wolff (Ed. & Trans.), *The sociology of Georg Simmel.* New York: Free Press.

Snyder, M. (1974). Self-monitoring of expressive behavior. *Journal of Personality and Social Psychology, 30*, 526–537.

Snyder, M. (1979). Self-monitoring processes. In L. Berkowitz (Ed.), *Advances in experimental social psychology* (Vol. 12). New York: Academic Press.

Sodetani, L. L., & Gudykunst, W. B. (1987). The effects of surprising events on intercultural relationships. *Communication Research Reports, 4*(2), 1–6.

Stephan, W. G., & Stephan, C. W. (1984). The role of ignorance in intergroup relations. In N. Miller & M. Brewer (Eds.), *Groups in contact.* New York: Academic Press.

Stephan, W. G., & Stephan, C. W. (1985). Intergroup anxiety. *Journal of Social Issues, 41*, 157–166.

Stephenson, G. (1981). Intergroup bargaining and negotiation. In J. Turner & H. Giles (Eds.), *Intergroup behavior.* Chicago, IL: University of Chicago Press.

Sternberg, R. J. (1986). A triangular theory of love. *Psychological Review, 93*, 119–135.

Sunnafrank, M. (1986). Predicted outcome value during initial interactions: A reformulation of uncertainty reduction theory. *Human Communication Research, 13*, 3–33.

Tajfel, H. (1978). Social categorization, social identity, and social comparison. In H. Tajfel (Ed.), *Differentiation between social groups.* London: Academic Press.

Triandis, H. C. (1986). Collectivism vs. individualism: A reconceptualization of a basic concept in cross-cultural psychology. In C. Bagley & G. Verma (Eds.) *Personality, cognition, and values: Cross-cultural perspectives of childhood and adolescence.* London: MacMillan.

VanLear, C. A., & Trujillo, N. (1986). On becoming acquainted: A longitudinal study of social judgment processes. *Journal of Personal and Social Relationships, 3*, 375–392.

Wenner, L. A. (1985). Transaction and media gratifications research. In K. E. Rosengren, L. A. Wenner, & P. Palmgreen (Eds.), *Media gratifications research: Current perspectives.* Beverly Hills, CA: Sage.

Wilensky, R. (1983). *Planning and understanding: A computational approach to human reasoning.* Reading, MA: Addison-Wesley.

Wilson, C. E. (1986, November). *Organizational socialization, uncertainty reduction and communication networks.* Paper presented at the annual convention of the Speech Communication Association, Chicago, IL.

Zajonc, R. B. (1980). Feeling and thinking: Preferences need no inferences. *American Psychologist, 35*, 151–175.

Zajonc, R. B. (1984). On the primacy of affect. *American Psychologist, 39*, 117–123.

3

A Microsocietal Approach to Marital Communication

Mary Anne Fitzpatrick
Professor and Director, Center for Communication Research
University of Wisconsin
Madison, WI

* This manuscript was completed while the author was Visiting Professor of Psychiatry, Center for Family Research, George Washington University Medical Center, Washington, D.C. The author would like to thank the director of the Center, Dr. Peter Steinglass, Dr. David Reiss, Director of the Division of Research in the Department of Psychiatry, and the members of the Center for their support of this endeavor.

I. INTRODUCTION

The majority of adults in contemporary Western society marry and establish a family. During this century, many of the classic functions of the family have gradually been delegated to other social agencies (e.g., its economic function, care for the aged, education of the children and so forth). The only major function currently served by the family is the nurturance of its members (Lasch, 1977). Two new marital roles—the therapeutic role and the leisure role—illustrate this concern for nurturance (Nye, 1976). In addition to being a good house-keeper, breadwinner, and sexual partner, the good spouse listens to the worries and anxieties of a partner and is a leisure-time companion and friend. Both of these new marital roles place greater demands on each spouse's ability to communicate.

In both public opinion and in the theoretical literature, a surprisingly consistent viewpoint about communication and marriage has crystallized. Almost everyone agrees that communication difficulties are the major cause of marital unhappiness and hence marital failure. Thus, the quality of a marriage or the subjective evaluation of a marriage as good, happy, or satisfying (Lewis & Spanier, 1979) depends upon good communication between husbands and wives. The meaning of *good* marital communication, however, varies by couple. What constitutes functional marital communication (i.e., that which leads to satisfaction in the relationship) differs according to the underlying beliefs husbands and wives hold about the nature of marriage (Fitzpatrick, 1984). For some couples, *communication* means close, supportive, and flexible speech. Their marriage and the communication between them is analyzed, taken apart, and put back together in an improved form, for this is how these couples "work" on their relationships (Katriel & Philipsen, 1981). For other couples, good marital communication is the clear specification and discussion of mutual rights and obligations (Sillars, Weisberg, Burgraff, & Wilson, 1987).

Not only can married couples be found to hold differing views on the relationship between communication and marriage, but theorists also have a number of different points of view on the issue. Theories range on a continuum anchored at one end by those who see communication and relationships as isomorphic processes (e.g., Millar & Rogers, 1976); to those in the midrange who see communication as one major manifestation of relational development (e.g., Baxter, 1985; Miller, 1976); to those at the other end of the continuum who view the exchange of messages as less important than an underlying cognitive (e.g., Planalp, 1984) or emotional/physiological (e.g., Levenson & Gottman, 1983) process. The type of connection, and the intensity of the link, between communication and the state of a relationship vary in these viewpoints depending on where the theories rest on this continuum. The basic question for all theorists in this area is: How do husbands and wives actively perceive, interpret, create and negotiate their relationship? My position is the following:

1. The ideological values that spouses hold concerning marriage and the family, and the state of the relationship between the partners, are displayed in their communication with one another.
2. To explain marital communication, both individual and interactional levels of analysis are needed. Conversation is individual in that it involves cognitive activity by the spouses. Conversation is also social in that it involves the transmission of messages between spouses.

To support my position, I survey the major microsocietal theories related to marital communication: the biological, psychological and primary group processes that affect communication in marriage. Two levels of analysis are implicated in these microsocietal theories. The first is the *individual level,* which uses the person as the unit of analysis and attempts to interpret and explain marital behavior (e.g., attitudes, values, motives, and experiences) in those terms. Of concern at this level of analysis are the processes that occur within the individual spouse in reference to communicative activities. The second is the *interactional level,* which uses the marital system as the unit of analysis and attempts to interpret and explain how the mutual influence each spouse exerts on the other, relative to their typical or baseline patterns (Cappella, 1987), affects the emergence of, and the stability or change in, the marital dyad.

The levels of analysis framework implied in this review is a necessary analytical device to be read with caution. Not only can individuals and dyads be affected by a large number of causal conditions, emerging from inside and outside the marriage, but causation can also occur on a number of levels simultaneously. Great difficulty obtains in assessing the relative contributions of any given effect. Both levels of analysis are included in this review, because the blind spots of one level are often the strengths of the other. And, as I demonstrate herein, these levels of analysis are neither contradictory nor mutually exclusive and could benefit from theoretical integration (see Hewes & Planalp, 1987).

What we know about communication in marriage is largely determined by how we know what we know. Therefore, after tracing the theoretical lines represented in the microanalytic tradition, I discuss the methodological techniques, problems, and advances made in the study of communication in marriage.

II. THE INDIVIDUAL AND THE MARRIAGE

This section considers the biological and psychological models that have been related to marriage. Considering biological processes in a chapter on marriage follows from the argument that gender differences are not merely a creation of socialization, patriarchy, or capitalism (Rossi, 1985). These differences are grounded in a sex-dimorphism that serves the fundamental purpose of reproducing the species. The psychological processes section reminds us that husbands and wives are cognitive creatures. This section overviews personality processes, social competence models, and cognitive theories related to marital communication.

A. Biological Processes

Differences between men and women, and the variations in the extent to which such differences are found throughout the life course, are a function, not only of social and historical processes (Shorter, 1982), but also the underlying biological processes of sexual differentiation and maturation (Rossi, 1985). Marriage may be a social institution, yet it is based on a biological fact of sexual dimorphism. Concepts like class, roles, groups, networks, and so forth tend to divert us from the effects of this dimorphism on many aspects of marital interaction.

Even the relative numbers of males and females available for marriage appears to exert influence on the nature and type of personal relationships in a society (Guttentag & Secord, 1983). When there are fewer women than men, the division of labor between the sexes is strong, and women are more likely to find themselves in the traditional roles of wife and mother. When there are more women than men, society places less value on marriage and the family and more on sexual libertarianism and feminism.

How does the analyst estimate whether biological variability produces differences in social behavior? Any two of the following patterns suggest that biological factors are involved in social behavior (Parsons, 1982; Rossi, 1985). Pattern (a) involves consistent correlations between social behavior and a physiological sex attribute (sex chromosome type, neural organization in the brain, hormonal type, and so forth); (b) is found in infants and young children before major socialization influences take hold or emerges with the onset of puberty, when body morphology and hormonal secretion change rapidly; (c) is stable across cultures; (d) is found across species, particularly the higher primates most genetically like humans. Demonstrating these patterns is enormously difficult. In the search for human universals (c), for example, even establishing that something as simple as the human smile is inborn rather than learned, and signifies happiness or pleasure in all societies, is a complex undertaking (see Knapp, 1978). How much and how strong the proof a reader demands before accepting a conclusion about biological influences on social behavior is a matter of individual judgment, embedded within the fabric of one's belief system. Radical feminists rush to replace biologically reductive theories of male–female relationships with socially reductive views. Sociobiologists who adopt simple, unidirectional models of biological control of human behavior misconstrue the facts of biology (Fausto-Sterling, 1985). Although an analytical consideration of how biological processes affect marital communication must not necessarily discuss sex differences, these differences are usually the concern, particularly within the family context.

I cannot cover all the potential genetic, neurological, and hormonal differences between males and females that may influence their communicative behaviors in marriage, or the differences between male and female neonates. Strong and consistent sex differences with potential biological contributions can be claimed in four areas that impact on marital communication (But, see the counterarguments by Fausto-Sterling, 1985). These four areas are: sensory sensitivity (e.g., Haviland & Malatesta, 1981); general activity level and aggression (e.g., Gove, 1985); cognitive skills such as spatial visualization and, to a lesser extent, verbal skills (e.g., Hyde, 1981); and parenting behavior (Peterson, 1980; Rossi, 1985).

A physiological theory of marital interaction (Gottman & Levenson, 1988) posits fundamental biological differences between males and females which directly affect their reactions to marital conflict. Wives are significantly more negative during marital conflict, yet their husbands react more strongly physiologically to their wives' negative speeches than the wives do in response to their husbands (Notarius & Johnson, 1982). Wives may appear to be more upset, but husbands are more aroused during marital conflict and are slower to return to baseline or calm down after a negative interaction (Levenson & Gottman, 1983). During conflict, distressed couples, compared to satisfied couples, show greater physiological interrelatedness or *linkage*. Sixty percent of the variance in marital satisfaction can be accounted for using measures of physiological linkage alone (Levenson & Gottman, 1983). Note that questionnaire measures usually account for about 10% of the variance in marital satisfaction (Burgess, Locke, & Thomas, 1971): observational studies have fared somewhat better by accounting for 25% of the variance (Gottman, 1979). And such linkages predict subsequent declines in marital satisfaction 3 years later. Moreover, greater declines in marital satisfaction are strongly correlated with poorer health ratings at follow-up (Levenson & Gottman, 1985). These effects are stronger for unhappily married husbands (Gottman & Levenson, 1988). Extreme physiological arousal may be very punishing to the distressed husband and causes him to withdraw, emotionally, from the marital relationship. Furthermore, frequent, extreme physiological arousal is associated with a number of life-threatening, stress-related diseases (Gottman & Levenson, 1988).

Such negative physiological effects may not be limited to males. Studying females, Kiecolt-Glaser and her colleagues suggest that autonomic arousal is one pathway through which chronically abrasive relationships might mediate immune function (Kiecolt-Glaser, Fisher, Ogrocki, Stout, Speicher, & Glaser, 1987). Along with increased physiological arousal, concurrent persistant alterations in endocrine function occur and mediate immunologic changes. The actual health impact of these changes in immune function is not yet known. Kiecolt et al. (1987), however, show that, among a sample of married women, poorer marital quality is associated with greater depression and a poorer response on three measures of immune function. Women who had been separated 1 year or less demonstrated significantly poorer qualitative and quantitative immune function than their matched married counterparts. Among separated and divorced women, shorter separation periods and greater attachment to the (ex) husband were associated with poorer immune function and greater depression. These data were consistent with epidemologic evidence linking marital disruption with increased morbidity and mortality (See Fitzpatrick, 1987b, pp. 597–598).

Marriage is stable across cultures and may be said to fit pattern (c). All societies contain provisions for some relationship between adults of the opposite sexes which may be designated by the term *marriage* (Reiss, 1976). Marriage clearly does not fit pattern (d) because it is pivotal in the evolution of our species. In many theories dealing with evolution, the ability of an adult male and female to bond, share, and work together in the raising of their offspring *differentiates* us from other higher order primates. The division of labor between the sexes, paternal investment patterns, and prolonged periods of juvenile dependency on parents are viewed as the crucial characteristics of human societies (Lancaster, 1985). The division of labor between male hunting and female gathering fosters a unique human pattern of parental partnership—the feeding of juveniles. Once mother monkeys or apes wean infants, these juveniles are responsible for feeding themselves. Only in human groups is there a collective familial responsibility for gathering and sharing food between adults and offspring.

Ignoring the fact that the essential basis for marriage is that of a joining of a male and a female leads to a number of conceptual blind spots. The work of Levenson and Gottman (1983) represents one of the few theories in this area that seeks an integration of physiological, affective, and behavioral marital phenomena. As more knowledge becomes available concerning the neurological, hormonal, and physiological differences between males and females, theories of marriage and the family will suffer if they fail to include these factors. This is not to argue for a simple-minded theory of biological determinism but a call for the incorporation of biological factors in theories of marital and family development when warranted.

At the beginning of the century women's brains were "proven" to be smaller than those of men. Such scientific work both reinforced and grew out of the climate of Social Darwinism rampant at the time (Gould, 1981). Theoretical moves toward studying the biological bases of human behavior probably are tied to the conservative trends now on the rise in Western culture: Science is, after all, a socially embedded activity. Each step in the scientific method is profoundly affected by the values, opinions, biases, beliefs, and even political interests of the scientists (Bleier, 1977). Many feminists categorically object to any theory arguing for a biological component in human behavior. Fears about the policy implications of scientific evidence should not, however, constrain the construction and testing of scientific theories of human behavior.

B. Psychological Processes

In this section, I overview three psychological orientations to the study of marriage.[1] The first is an individual difference approach often called the *trait model*. Trait approaches to communication in marriage place the locus of action in the predispositions of husbands and wives to initiate or react to communication from their spouses. The second is the *competence model*, which examines the quality of a spouse's communication performance overall in the marriage. The third is the *cognitive model*, which emphasizes a spouse's complex cognitive abilities to produce and interpret marital messages. Husbands and wives represent external reality internally, often in a language-like form. Spouses can manipulate this internal representation in a variety of ways.

1. Trait Models. The individual perspective on marriage has persisted throughout this century. Initially, sociodemographic factors (e.g., social class, religion, and so forth) were correlated to marital happiness. This enterprise was supplanted by the investigation of the psychological traits, characteristics, and abilities of individual spouses that makes a marriage stable and mutually satisfying or unstable and full of discontent. The areas pursued today include: (a) psychological variables in mate selection (e.g., Buss & Barnes, 1986) (b) the relationship between such variables and marital satisfaction (e.g., Baucom & Aiken, 1984), and (c) the relationship between the accuracy of interspousal perceptions of personality or role behavior and marital satisfaction (Sillars, Pike, Jones, & Murphy, 1984). Major longitudinal investigations linked low neuroticism in both partners, and high impulse control on the part of the husband, to the long-term maintenance of a marriage (see Kelly & Conley, 1987). Among Americans seeking spouses, preferences in mate choices have changed: Good heredity or housekeeping no longer ranked first. In rank order, the highly valued traits for a mate were: Kind, exciting, intelligent, physically attractive, and healthy. Buss and Barnes (1986) posited these traits served as clues to marital survival and satisfaction (e.g., the kind person is understanding and easy to get along with) or signalled that the mate was a good reproductive investment (e.g., the physically attractive person is usually young and healthy).

Psychological differences between males and females in general may also influence the interaction in a marriage. The level of marital satisfaction experienced by husbands and wives often interacts with the gender of the commu-

---

[1] Many theories of communication in marriage are *logocentric* (Bradac, 1983). Marriage may be viewed as a private culture, and culture is both displayed and transmitted by the language patterns of group members. Conversations between couples have been examined, for example, for topic shifts in marital dialogues (Crow, 1983), decision-making in the dual-career couple (Lenk-Krueger, 1982), and metaphoric descriptions of marriage (Stephens, 1986). In this review, I have not included such perspectives on language and marriage, because these views do not explicitly tie particular linguistic patterns to marital inputs or outcomes. As these views represent a different order of explanation, they need to be covered elsewhere.

nicator (e.g., Noller, 1984). Men are likely to prefer their spouses to be physically attractive, whereas women are likely to prefer mates who are college-educated with good earning potential. Such consensually valued characteristics probably enter into the equity and exchange processes in the marital marketplace. In addition to these gender differences in assortative mating, males and females may place different relative values on satisfying and close relationships. Morality for females may be more intricately tied to human relationships than it is for males. Across the life cycle, women emphasize intimacy, attachments, and caring, whereas men value justice and equality more than connection and nurturance between people (Gilligan, 1982). The position that males and females may differ fundamentally in their emphasis on justice versus connection is not without controversy (Kerber, Greeno, Maccoby, Luria, Stack, & Gilligan, 1986).

The concern for maintaining connections may explain why females appear to monitor relationships more closely and are aware of interpersonal problems sooner than males (Rubin, Peplau, & Hill, 1981). The work of maintaining relationships and the consequent decreases in self-esteem when relationships fail may be the women's burden (Fitzpatrick & Indvik, 1982). During high conflict in distressed marriages, Gottman (1979) found that wives reacted to their husbands' changes of emotional expressions significantly more than the husbands reacted to their wives'. A number of interesting husband-and-wife differences are documented in Noller and Fitzpatrick (1988): Particular interaction patterns appear to be initiated more by wives than by husbands (Christensen, 1988; Schaap, Buunk, & Kerkstra, 1988); communication channels used effectively by husbands and wives differ (Noller & Gallois, 1988); and the physiological responses of husbands and wives differ to marital messages (Gottman & Levenson, 1988). Burgraff and Sillars (1986), however, compared sex differences in marital communication during conflict and found that the ideological values, and levels of companionship in the marriage, were significantly more predictive of the conflict tactics used in conversation than was the sex of the speaker.

Recently, the personality variables relevant to the explanation of individual behavior have been reconstructed in terms of flexible mental structures and processes, rather than the stable and consistent behavioral dispositions envisaged by conventional psychometric approaches. Aspects of Bem's (1984) work on gender schemata and Markus's (1977) work on self-schemata could be profitably applied to understanding individual differences in marital communication. Although extremely promising, very little of this new look in personality has been applied to marital interaction.

2. Social Competence Models. On reading the work completed on marital communication, the proverbial visitor from Mars would be convinced that competent marital communication in our milieu was accomplished solely through self-disclosure or the revealing of private thoughts and feelings about the self to the spouse (Fitzpatrick, 1987c). On the empirical side, self-report studies show a positive correlation between the self-disclosures of husbands and wives (Burke, Weir, & Harrison, 1976; Hendrick, 1981). Discrepancies in affective self-disclosure between married partners may be related to dissatisfaction with marriage (Davidson, Balswick, & Halverson, 1983). A high correlation is often found between the disclosure of positive, but not negative, feelings and marital satisfaction (Chelune, Waring, Vosk, Sultan, & Ogden, 1984; Levinger & Senn, 1967). The outcomes for disclosing negative emotions depend less on the unpleasantness of the emotion expressed than on the degree to which the expressed emotion honors or threatens the receiver. Disclosing hostilities in conversations with the spouse toward persons other than the spouse appears to prompt spouses to respond with more positive messages and to comply with the requests of the speaker (Shimanoff, 1986).

Although the early research viewed self-disclosure as a personality trait, more recent research treats self-disclosure as the process of social exchange. According to Altman and Taylor's (1973) theory of social penetration, the gradual exchange of personal information increases in both breadth and depth of topic as relationships develop. This assumption that relationships progress in a linear and unidirectional fashion with increasing openness between partners, however, is debatable (Altman, Vinsel, & Brown, 1981). Marital communication functions dialectically and not linearly in at least two senses. First, relationships are dialectical in that they continually cycle through superficial and deeper contact with repeated ebbs and flows of self disclosure. Second, marital communication performs at least five functions around which spouses must continually balance opposite ends of a continuum. The need to open and disclose to one's spouse, for example, must be balanced against the need to protect the spouse from the consequences of such openness (Bochner, 1983).

Is competent marital discourse strategic? That is, under what conditions do husbands and wives plan their exchanges to achieve certain goals? And, when do couples interact mindlessly? (Berger & Roloff, 1982). I hypothesize that the relationship between monitoring what one is about to say, and the predicted stress in a conversation, is linear during the planning phase. During the planning phase, the more difficulty a husband and wife expect to experience, the more aware they are of their message behavior. During an ongoing interaction, however, the relationships is curvilinear. In other words, during low stress interactions, husbands and wives are relatively unaware of their message behaviors, become more aware at moderately stressful levels, and less aware again during high stress conversations. Compliance gaining (Witteman & Fitzpatrick, 1986), generating liking for one's self with an interaction partner (Bell, 1986), and strategies for maintaining one's marriage (Dindia & Baxter, 1986) are examples of strategic message choice studies. In all these situations one may expect difficulty with a spouse; hence, messages choices are probably made with extreme awareness.

These types of studies represent good ways to examine strategic messages behavior. The researcher may expect that spouses can report on what they do, particularly if the questions are phrased to understand specific instances of interaction.

Nonverbal communication is central to the social competence model. Harmonious marital relationships are marked by closer physical distances, direct body orientation, and more immediate and relaxed posture than are less harmonious ones (Beier & Sternberg, 1977). Newlywed couples are better able to read the nonverbal messages of their spouse than are dating couples. The wife's skill seems to be particularly important here (Sabatelli, Buck, & Dreyer, 1982). Wives who are good encoders (easy for judges to read) have husbands with few marital complaints and are relatively satisfied themselves. Wives who are especially skilled at decoding their husband's poorly sent nonverbal messages are also in happier marriages. Contrary to this finding is that of Gottman and Porterfield (1981), who suggest that the husband's ability to read his wife's nonverbal communication is more predictive of the degree of marital happiness than the wife's ability to read the husband's.

Noller (1984), who has extensively studied this issue, argues that husbands in distressed marriages seem to suffer a "communication-skills deficit." Husbands in unhappy marriages appear unable to receive the messages of their spouses correctly and have problems in sending clear messages, especially positive ones. In comparing spouses and strangers, however, what appears to be a "communication-skills deficit" is actually a "performance deficit." Husbands and wives in distressed marriages do less well in reading the marital communication of their spouses than they do in reading the communication of strangers. Individuals in unhappy marriages appear capable of reading nonverbal communication but they fail to do so when interacting with one another.

Are the happily married more socially or communicatively competent than the unhappily married? As we have seen, a good deal of research emphasizes the cataloging of self-report and behavioral communication differences between the happily and the unhappily married (see Fitzpatrick & Badzinski, 1985). *Because* individuals are happily married, their communication practices must be the competent ones. The working assumption of this research is that the set of communication practices adopted by the happily married cause that marital happiness. Equally valid is its opposite: A happy marriage causes the use of certain interactional practices. There are two problems with the catalogue studies. First is the aforementioned 'correlation does not imply causality' problem. Second, cataloguing yet other communication differences between the happily and the unhappily passes for an *explanation* for communication in marriage, deflecting deeper and more serious considerations of the issues. Basically, social competence cannot be identified with any absolute standard of behavior but rather needs to be viewed as the spouse's ability to adapt to a given situation.

Before pursuing any study of social competence in marriage, the researcher must have a clear theory explicating the relationships among what he or she expects to observe. For example, a symbolic interactionist framework on marital competence hypothesizes that the greater the ability to function effectively in a long-term and fairly complex relationship such as marriage, the greater the marital satisfaction. Effective functioning includes role-taking ability, role skills, the capacity for negotiation and the degree of differentiation. The question for communication researchers within this theoretical framework is, how do couples communicatively demonstrate their role-taking ability, their role skills, and so forth?

Many therapeutic and intervention programs operate on the assumption that individuals need to be taught communication skills to improve their marriages. The finding that husbands and wives may have the skills to communicate accurately and effectively, yet choose not to use their skills with the spouse, suggests very different intervention techniques. Dealing with either the cognitive or motivational processes underlying these decisions may be necessary for successful intervention.

3. Cognitive Models. Under the discussion of cognitive models, I include: implicit theories of communication in relationships, attribution theories, and social cognitive models of marital interaction. Individuals have implicit theories of relationships that guide their information processing: They can hold dysfunctional beliefs about relationships (Eidelson & Epstein, 1982). I consider the strong correlations between marital satisfaction and self-reports of communication behavior as evidence for strongly held beliefs in our culture about the role of communication in marriage (Fitzpatrick & Badzinski, 1985). The happily married believe that they have remarkably good marital communication. "Good" communication includes openness (Chelune, 1979), self-disclosure of thoughts and feelings (Levinger & Senn, 1967), perceived accuracy of nonverbal communication (Navran, 1967), and frequent successful communicative exchanges (Bienvenu, 1970).

Attribution theories consider how couples arrive at estimates of the causes of their own as well as their spouses' behavior (e.g., Bernal & Golann, 1980; Doherty, 1981; Newman, 1981). Sillars and his colleagues (1987) have developed a coding scheme to study content themes in marital interaction which has a strong attributional flavor (see Holtzworth-Munroe & Jacobson, 1985). Dissatisfied spouses often dwell on the attributed personality deficits of the partner, at the same time overlooking situational and interactional causes of behavior (Orvis, Kelley, & Butler, 1976). Distressed spouses tend to form rigid attributions about the partner's motives and personality (Fincham, 1985). Attribution theory cannot, however, be directly imported from laboratory tests with strangers into the study of marital interaction. Traditional attribution theories tend to describe quasiscientific judgments about causal influence as formulated by a reasonably disinterested observer. Statements about the cause of one's own marital behavior or that of the spouse tend to have strong evaluative implications (Fincham, Beach, & Nelson, 1987).

Husbands and wives may act less like scientists with one another and more like lawyers (Fincham & Jaspars, 1980). In other words, models of responsibility attribution that focus on the spouses' concerns with establishing accountability may be more important in understanding marital dynamics (Fincham, 1985). Accountability or responsibility attributions are concerned with the acceptability of the outcome (behavior) according to a set of standards. A spouse may cause an outcome but not be blamed for it because his or her actions met expected standards. In support of this contention, empirical attempts to focus on happily and unhappily married couples' distinctions between internal and external causes for spouse behavior have produced mixed results (Jacobson, McDonald, Follette, & Berley, 1985; in contrast, Fincham & O'Leary, 1983). More consistent results have obtained when other properties of causes have been examined (e.g., global versus specific: Fincham, 1985; Holzworth-Munroe & Jacobson, 1985; positive versus negative attribution biases for self versus spouse: Fincham, Beach, & Baucom, 1987). Responsibility attributions predict both affective impact and one's intended response to the behavior of the spouse (Fincham, et al., 1987). In sum, relative to nondistressed spouses, distressed spouses view the causes of their partners' negative behavior as reflecting enduring, global characteristics of their partners and consider the behavior more negative in intent, selfishly motivated, and blameworthy, whereas they tend to view their partners' positive behavior as reflecting temporary, situation-specific causes. The inverse pattern holds for the nondistressed.

Two areas within the attribution framework could benefit from a communication perspective. First, how and when do attributions occur in conversation? Both Holtzworth-Munroe and Jacobson (1985) and Bradbury and Fincham (1988) offer methodological and conceptual considerations in assessing spontaneous attributions in marital conversations. Second, a variety of other attributions that couples can make (e.g., self-presentational, interpersonal, descriptive, and so forth) could profitably be examined.

Despite their merits, attribution theories present static models of cognition. Such perspectives argue that individuals assign causes to the behaviors of themselves and of others but ignore how such processes operate. Furthermore, most experimental tests of attribution theory focus exclusively on how perceivers make sense of the situations that are already defined, not how they incorporate information in attempting to define social situations. A more comprehensive explanation for cognitive processes underlying marital communication is needed.

A theoretical explanation for the regularities in marital interaction observed in different types of couples has been proposed by the current author (Fitzpatrick, 1987a,b). My explanation is a social cognitive one. Specifically, individuals are hypothesized to have *marital schemata*. Marital schemata are knowledge structures that represent the external world of marriage and provide guidelines about how to interpret incoming data. Marital schemata operate to specify the nature and organization of information relevant to the partner and the marriage and to plan and direct activity relevant to the schemata (Neisser, 1967). The proposition that individuals possess marital schemata emerges from a program of research on marriage conducted over the past 10 years (for a summary, see Fitzpatrick, 1983, 1984).

When individuals are asked to respond to the Relational Dimensions Instrument (Fitzpatrick, 1977), a series of questions on major dimensions of marriage, three definitions emerge: Traditional, independent, or separate. *Traditionals* hold conventional values about marriage and the family, are very interdependent with their spouses, and willingly argue over serious issues. *Independent* are more liberal in their orientation toward marriage and family values, are moderately interdependent in their marriages, and are habituated to conflict. *Separates* are ambivalent about their family values, not very interdependent in their marriages, and tend to avoid marital conflict.

Although the Relational Dimensions Instrument does not contain all of the major dimensions of marital interaction, nor does it isolate the content of an individual's schema, the instrument can tap subgroups of individuals who hold similar marital schema. Thus, traditionals, independents, and separates differentially encode, retrieve, and process information about the spouse and the marriage.

My colleagues and I have completed three studies to demonstrate that the relational types are marital schema. The first was a reaction time study which demonstrated that couples in the various marital types could be clearly differentiated in their reaction times to viewing schematic and aschematic marriages (Fitzpatrick, 1987d). The second study demonstrated that couples in the various types used significantly different codes in marital interaction. These differential codes reflected dissimilar cognitive organizations among the couple types (Fitzpatrick, Bauman, & Lindaas, 1987). The third study differentiated couples on their accuracy in the recognition of emotion (Noller & Fitzpatrick, 1987).

Having established that the typology is a marital schemata, we intend to test and refine this social cognitive theory of marital interaction. Of particular concern to me in the future will be the addition of affect to this model. Bradbury and Fincham (1987) have developed one integrative model of affect and cognition in close relationships. Their model explains the empirical conclusion that distressed couples are less positive, more negative and more likely to reciprocate negative behaviors, more predictable, and interact less often. These differences are most pronounced when couples are in situations where they need to settle conflicts or resolve differences (see Fitzpatrick & Badzinski, 1985; Noller, 1984, for reviews). Theories concerned with the cognitive bases of affect suggest that some combination of cognitive interpretation and arousal causes emotion (e.g., Mandler, 1984). A violation of expectation of schema-inconsistent information may cause arousal, which is subsequently considered as a positive or negative affect. I have recently linked the typology to Berscheid's (1983) model of emotion to explain couple differences in self-disclosure (Fitzpatrick, 1988). I am currently pursuing research on this topic.

C. Summary

In this section, I have reviewed the major individual level approaches to the study of marriage. Three trends are apparent in this literature. The first is the renewed interest in gender and sex differences in marital communication. The second is the concern for more dynamic models of cognitive processes that can account for how spouses perceive and interpret one another's messages. The third trend is the integration of affect and cognition into one model by linking the cognitive processes that underlie affect and the affective processes that may underlie cognition. In the next section, I argue that husbands and wives are social as well as cognitive creatures. Born into established and continuing social contacts, generally dependent on others, spouses are seldom, if ever, completely alone.

III. MODELS OF MARITAL INTERACTION

The assessment of marital interaction, which by definition reflects an interpersonal focus, entails conceptual and methodological considerations distinct from the consideration of the individual. Given space limitations, this section focuses exclusively on the marital unit, ignoring the developmental work on the transition to parenthood (e.g., Belsky, Ward, & Rovine, 1986) and other family-oriented themes (Reiss, 1981). I focus here on how the intricate system connecting two intimate partners can be described, analyzed and explained. In this section, I examine three major approaches to marital interaction: symbolic interactionist models, typological models of marital interaction, and transactional models.

A. Symbolic Interactionist Models

Symbolic interactionist assumptions and principles show up in two current approaches to explaining marital communication: the social construction of reality model, and the coorientational model. Both of these approaches take from symbolic interactionism a concern for how communication between couples builds consensus and agreement on basic issues.

Berger and Kellner (1975) argued that the central task of early marriage was for two individuals to redefine the realities they brought with them into the relationships and construct a new, jointly shared reality. This jointly shared reality is a perceptual consensus that defines for the couple both the nature of the world in which they live and their identity within that world. This jointly shared reality is constructed through talk. The work of Wamboldt and his associates (Wamboldt & Reiss, 1989; Wamboldt & Wolin, 1988) has begun to expand and test this reality construction process with engaged couples. These researchers are demonstrating the central role of the family of origin in shaping this reality construction process. Married couples also demonstrate that a couple identity is kept in a state of repair and ongoingly refurbished through their conversational topics and themes. The ideological values that couples hold concerning marriage, and the state of the relationship between the couples, is differentially displayed in their mutual conversational focus on communal, individual, or impersonal themes (Sillars et al., 1987).

Coorientational models (Laing, Phillipson, & Lee, 1966; McLeod & Chaffee, 1972) of marital interaction distinguish between individual-level (cognitive) comparisons, which can be experienced by (and only by) a given spouse, and social-level (communicative) comparisons, which can not be directly observed by the husbands and wives. The best measure of "perfect communication" is accuracy or the degree to which each spouse's impressions of the other spouse's cognitions match the other person's actual cognitions.

These models are concerned with the psychological reality of the husband and wife. The psychological reality for one member of the dyad may differ considerably from that of the spouse, and both can, of course, differ from the reality constructed by a group of observers. Coorientational models measure whether spouses agree, whether they are accurate about this agreement, and whether they know (understand) that they are accurate (or inaccurate). Agreement is measured from the outsider's perspective; a husband and wife are asked their opinions about various issues, but it is the researcher (the outsider) who compares their answers to see if the couple agree. There are two types of accuracy, which might also be called *awareness of agreement. Coorientational accuracy* is concerned with the ability of one spouse to predict the opinions of the other spouse. Communication accuracy involves the ability of a spouse to interpret the other's messages as they were intended. *Communication accuracy* may be the reason that coorientational accuracy exists. Noller and Gallois (1988), studying communication accuracy, link these constructs back to the specific behaviors of husbands and wives as they communicate.

These models are considered estimates of dyadic processes because they measure responses across individuals. Sillars and Scott (1983) review research on accuracy of interpersonal perception in close relationships and suggest a number of conditions under which accuracy in perception may falter. Knudson, Sommers, and Golding (1980) measured the interpersonal perceptions of couples as they watched a videotape of one of their own conflicts. Couples who resolved the issue by engaging the conflict at hand were contrasted to those who avoided discussing the issue. Engaging the issue at hand was related to increases in spouse's access to one another's interpersonal perceptions, whereas avoidance was associated with decreases in shared perceptions.

Gage and Cronbach (1955) posed the question: Is understanding or accuracy, as measured, merely a collection of perceptual biases? Accuracy scores are factorially complex and may be misleading as an index of understanding. Coorientational accuracy scores may be partitioned into three "error" components and differential accuracy. In other words, the accuracy score of one spouse in reference to the partner may be biased due to projection (high assumed similarity), or stereotypy (all spouses respond this way), or response sets (may respond positively or negatively toward others in general). One implication of these components is that those couples who agree may appear to have more "understanding" of one another than those who disagree. Couples who have high levels of agreement may guess one another's position via projection or the imputation of a similar response to the partner. The researcher must sort out accuracy due to stereotypic responses, differential accuracy, and so forth. But biases such as projective and stereotypic accuracy may be important to study in their own right (Fitzpatrick & Indvik, 1979). Many communication situations occur, even between intimates, when stereotypic information is all that is needed. Couples do not necessarily have to use all the information at their disposal about one another in all their exchanges. And couples may rely on nonverbal communication or even self-disclosure to understand one another.

B. Typological Models

Typological models are attempts to categorize some aspect of marital functioning (see Christensen & Arrington, 1987, pp. 272–277). Within any sample of couples, there are a limited number of marital patterns which can be isolated. Couples within different types are assumed to communicate similarly to couples in the same type and differently than couples in other types. In my work over the past decade (Fitzpatrick, 1977, 1984, 1988), I have developed an empirical, polythetic classification scheme of marriage which categorizes couples according to three basic dimensions of married life: *ideology, interdependence,* and *expressivity.* These dimensions combine systematically to isolate, in any population of married couples, three basic definitions of marriage—traditional, independent, and separate. The unit of analysis in my typology is the couple; thus, husbands and wives are compared on the three basic definitions and categorized in a pure type if they agree and a mixed type if they disagree. My system would be elegant but relatively useless were it not for the fact that the reliable assignment of a couple to a marital type predicts a number of self-report assessments of the marriage, and a variety of communication rates, frequencies, and patterns (for a summary, see Fitzpatrick, 1988).

In contrast to my approach, others assume that the best way to categorize couples or families is through their interaction patterns. Some researchers observe couples and families and name particular marital types. Steinmetz (1979), for example, in her work on family violence distinguished two interactional styles. "Saturday night brawlers" are typified by reciprocally escalating, violent interaction, with either spouse likely to be the victim in a given fight, whereas the "chronic battered syndrome" is charactericized by the wife's sense of powerlessness and extreme fear, and repeated, intense beating by the perpetuator.

Some begin with a theoretical perspective and a clear idea of what they wish to observe. A major typological approach is based on particular patterns of control in conversations with the spouse (Ericson & Rogers, 1973). In addition to its manifest content, each turn in an interaction offers a definition of how the speaker sees his or her relationship to the other interactant. The conversational partner may accept, reject, or ignore this relational bid. Linking messages together to examine message sequences uncovers predominant patterns in marital communication. Based on observations of couples as they communicate with one another, two types of couples can be discriminated: symmetrical and complementary.

Symmetrical couples (i.e., those whose predominant pattern of communication involves the exchange of similar control moves) have higher levels of role discrepancy. When these couples are defined by a high number of competitive attempts to be in control, however, they have lower levels of marital satisfaction (Rogers, 1972). In other terminology, these symmetrical couples may be considered equalitarian. Complementary couples (i.e., those whose predominant pattern of communication with the spouse is opposite in control maneuvering) differ in marital satisfaction and role discrepancy, depending on which spouse is in the controlling position. Husband-dominant couples report higher levels of satisfaction and less role-discrepancy than do wife-dominant couples (Millar & Rogers, 1976; Courtwright, Millar, & Rogers-Millar, 1979). These findings on complementary couples are consonant with the general research in the area of power and marital satisfaction. The self-reports of decision making and marital satisfaction indicate that wife-dominated marriages are less happy than equalitarian or husband-dominant ones. Furthermore, interaction studies support this notion (see Gray-Little & Burks, 1983). One explanation for these findings is the *husband-incapacity role hypothesis:* when the husband retreats from the marriage and refuses to fulfill his marital role, a vacuum is created which the wife must fill. She does so, but with deleterious consequences for the marriage.

The development, validation, and refinement of marital and family typologies will remain a valued (and valuable) enterprise (Olson, 1981). The variations in marital types are clear to both researchers and clinicians, and the search for the correct measurement approach and discriminating dimensions will continue. Normative data is needed. Typological work, based either on dimensions or on interactional styles, needs to use broad-based samples, including a range of ethnic and socioeconomic status groups. Most typological work has been cross-sectional and many developmental issues await exploration. A consideration of the effects of normative and nonnormative transitions on the couple's marital type moves the typological approach in an important conceptual direction.

C. Transactional Models

The study of transaction processes, defined as the sequential analysis of verbal and nonverbal messages involving chains of interpersonal exchanges, represents a revolution in thinking and research about interpersonal relationships (Gottman, 1982; Penman, 1980). Over 25 years ago, Haley (1962) argued that such a perspective required a new language to include dyadic constructs. More recently, new research technologies have been called for (Gottman, 1982; Lamp, Suomi, & Stephenson, 1979). This approach advocates the observation of patterns of communication, directly assessed and systematically coded. Theoretical arguments in the interactional framework (Watzlawick, Beavin, & Jackson, 1967) and in the family literature (Kantor & Lehr, 1975) are replete with statements about the primacy of transactional sequences. Therapeutic programs are built on such concepts as "quid pro quo" (Lederer & Jackson, 1968). Five major theories or models have been proposed as explanations of interaction in marriage. These models are summarized as follows:

1. Behavior Exchange Model of Marital Interaction. The quality of the exchanges, such as the ratio of positive to negative exchanges, determines the degree of marital distress. Further, the reactivity hypothesis argues that recent events are particularly salient to distressed spouses, whereas for nondistressed spouses subjective satisfaction is relatively independent of such events (Jacobson, Follette, & McDonald, 1982). Recently, the cognitions that couples hold about the relationship, the spouse, and the nature of the rewards and costs are seen as important (Jacobson, 1984).

2. Behavioral Competency Model. This model isolates the coping skills and external stresses, relevant for all couples, as they progress through normal developmental changes (Markman, 1982). The basic thesis of this model is that interactional deficits precede the development of marital distress. Excellent support in longitudinal investigations exists for this model (Kelly, Huston, & Cate, 1985).

3. Social Learning Model. This model emphasizes social reinforcement through the *quid pro quo*. Behaviors displayed by partners are lawfully related; that is, each spouse's behavior is controlled by discriminative and reinforcing stimuli provided by the other partner. The role of nonverbal communication in contextualizing and modifying conversations between intimates is stressed (Weiss, 1981).

4. Structural Model of Marital Interaction (SMMI).   Marital interaction is patterned: Structure is constraint determined by the reduction in uncertainty in temporal patterns of communication between partners (Gottman, 1979). This model offers four hypotheses that are well supported by the research conducted by Gottman (1979). Schaap et al. (1988) have extended the structural model and developed a modification based on their research.

5. Interdependence Model.   Couples develop organized behavioral sequences which necessitate the spouse as a partner in the action in order to achieve successful completion (Berscheid, 1983). When these organized behavioral sequences are interrupted, alternate routes to complete the sequence are blocked; emotion occurs. Negative affect occurs under most conditions that are interrupting. Positive affect occurs if the interruption is seen as benign or controllable, and leads to the accomplishment of a goal sooner than expected, or removes something previously disruptive (Mandler, 1984). No marital research has, as yet, been conducted using this model.

Despite the elegance of these interactional models and their concern for sequences and pattern, many investigators do not go beyond examining separate frequency measures of behaviors that husbands and wives emit in one another's presence. Many excellent studies stop short of analyzing the patterning in the communication between spouses over time. The exclusive use of rate or frequency data may promote inferential errors. Interactional researchers refer to one major error as the *pseudounilaterality problem* (Duncan, Kanki, Mokros, & Fiske, 1984). For example, suppose the researcher finds that dissatisfied husbands make more justifications for their behavior than do wives. The conclusion might be that justifications are related to male marital dissatisfaction (an individual-level explanation). Because the coded behaviors (in this case, justifications) emerged during marital interaction, an equally plausible interpretation of these rates is that the wives of the dissatisfied husbands act in some way that makes their spouses feel compelled to justify their behavior. The link between marital discord could then be made at the interactional rather than the individual level. The use of frequency or rate measures obscures the level of analysis at which the theorist is working. There are a growing number of important and notable research programs that emphasize the interactional level (Fitzpatrick, 1984; Gottman, 1979; Hahlweg & Jacobson, 1984; Margolin & Wampold, 1981; Raush, Barry, Hertel, & Swain, 1974; Schaap, 1982; Sillars, Pike, Jones, & Redmon, 1983; Ting-Toomey, 1983).

D. Summary

I have discussed the three major conceptual approaches to examining the interaction between husbands and wives. Each approach tries to examine how the messages exchanged between spouses affect the overall quality of the marriage.

Symbolic interactionist approaches emphasize agreement, accuracy and understanding. These models isolate the inputs and outputs of communicative exchanges yet can often be accused of ignoring the exchanges themselves. Typological approaches emphasize different recurring organizational patterns in order to classify marriages. These approaches focus on the complexity of human relationships but give less attention to communication processes and outcomes. Transaction models emphasize the structure and patterning in marital dialogues. These models often capture the complexity of human communication but ignore the complexity of relationships. My work on marriage has viewed these three approaches as panels of a triptych: although these approaches can stand alone, taken together, they form a more complete picture of marital interaction. In my research, I have carefully described types of marital relationships, examined the sequence and patterning of the couple types during casual and conflict interaction, and related both to agreement, accuracy, marital satisfaction and so forth (see Fitzpatrick, 1988).

IV. METHODOLOGY IN STUDIES OF MARITAL INTERACTION

In the accepted wisdom of the social sciences, theory is expected to guide observations about a phenomenon and to impose patterns on an otherwise complex world. In this view, it is theory that determines method. What we can know, however, is determined by the methods available for knowing (Gottman, 1982). The types of constructs and propositions in our theories, as well as the degree of certainty we attach to them, are dependent on our methodological repertoire. Rather than argue that theory determines method, I agree with Poole and McPhee (1985) who see theory and method as dialectically related. A clear example of this dialectical relationship is the development of the social relations model (Kenny & La Voie, 1984). This model allows the analyst to test both individual and interactional levels of explanation in the same study. With this model, we can examine how much of the variance in communication behavior is dependent on the individual and how much is dependent on the emergent properties of the interaction between people. Indeed this model represents one way to merge individual and interactional levels of analysis in studies of marital communication.

In the next sections, I discuss a variety of measurement and data gathering issues peculiar to an examination of marital communication.

A. Measurement Issues

The techniques for studying marital interaction have involved both insider and outsider perspectives (Olson, 1977). The insider perspective includes what the spouses say about the marriage. The outsider perspective includes anyone outside the relationship: the researcher, a couple's children, their friends, and so forth. Both perspectives can involve subjective and objective types of data. In recent years, there has been considerable turmoil about which mode of inquiry is "best" for the study of marital communication. Taken together, these critiques and countercritiques demonstrate that a good case can be made for the employment of all types of perspectives on the topic of marital interaction. And these critiques also show that there are disadvantages or problems with the employment of any mode.

1. Tests and Questionnaires. A substantial proportion of the research on marital interaction depends on the use of questionnaires, interviews, and similar techniques for eliciting spouse's descriptions of marital interaction. Such data represents the major access to personal experience and behavior. Traditionally, interviews and self-reports aimed at general impressions and evaluations of the marriage have been the hallmark of the research. With the advent of behaviorism and systems theory, some more objective-insider measures were developed. Spouse and self-monitoring procedures like the Spouse Observation Checklist (Weiss & Perry, 1979) and the Interaction Record (Peterson, 1979) were introduced. Unfortunately, techniques designed to measure the same construct do not relate to one another in a systematic manner.

Using 27 couples, Margolin (1978) examined the intercorrelations of two self-report measures of marital satisfaction (insider-subjective), two observer-rated measures (outsider-objective), and two measures requiring spouses to monitor each other's behavior (insider-objective). Only three significant correlations obtained among the possible 15, and these were between the two self-report measures, the two observational measures, and one self-report and one spouse-monitoring measure which were both from the same person. Multitrait, multimethod studies (Campbell & Fiske, 1959) are needed to untangle these confusing relationships among measurement techniques. Such studies are appearing in the literature (e.g., Boals, Peterson, Farmer, Mann, & Robinson, 1982). Conceptual work is also needed, however, to explain why divergence and convergence in ratings of marital satisfaction occur not only between husbands and wives but between insiders' and outsiders' perspectives with various types of data. Indeed, it may be unreasonable to assume that different types of data taken from different perspectives necessarily lead to the same conclusions.

Subjective data from the insider's perspective has several well-known problems: tenuous relationships to behavior and interaction, social desirability concerns, memory distortions, differential use of scale boundaries, and so forth. Objective data from the insider's perspective may have some of these problems along with reactivity to observing one's own behavior. Objective data from the outsider's perspective also suffers from the reactivity problem (Christensen & Nies, 1980). In addition, research from this perspective is very expensive and has been limited to small, select samples of couples. A recent development in studies of marital interaction is to take the marital patterns and sequences observed in laboratory settings and turn them into questionnaires (Christensen, 1988; Eggeman, Moxley, & Schumm, 1985). These questionnaires are more complex than most. The practical advantages of isolating interaction patterns through questionnaires are obvious: It takes about 28 hours to code the verbal and nonverbal behaviors in one hour of interaction. Some research evidence, however, indicates that the unhappily married are especially unreliable as observers of events in their own relationship (Elwood & Jacobson, 1982; Jacobson & Moore, 1981).

The major dependent variable, marital quality, is primarily measured with subjective-insider methods, in particular either the Locke-Wallace (1959) or the Spanier (1976) scale. A major problem in this literature is the negative skewness of the distributions when individuals are asked for overall evaluations of their marriage. This skewness has been obtained for almost 50 years. About 95% of the respondents in Terman's (1938) study reported their marriages as significantly happier than average. Very few people in national surveys report themselves or their marriages as unhappy overall, although individuals appear willing and able to report specific stresses and strains in the marriage.

A second problem with the marital quality measures is the reliance on descriptive questions. Here, the focus is on the frequency of activities such as fighting, kissing, or having an interesting exchange of ideas. With descriptive questions, the researcher makes a number of assumptions about what makes a marriage happy. For example, Spanier (1976) assumes that quarreling, leaving the house after an argument, and being too tired for sex are all detrimental to marital satisfaction. On the other hand, he sees having a stimulating exchange of ideas, working together on a project, and confiding in one another as being good for marital satisfaction. As I have shown in my research (Fitzpatrick, 1984), these factors do not work in the same way for all couples. Some couples, for example (i.e., independents) find conflict less threatening than do other couples.

The third problem involves summing across evaluations of a marriage in different domains (e.g. attitudinal agreement and sexual expression); thus, the measures obscure what they should clarify (Norton, 1983). For example, by including communication measures in an overall marital quality index, the relative contribution of communication to marital quality is obscured. The dyadic adjustment scale (DAS) is a multidimensional marital assessment scale (Spanier & Thompson, 1982), and hence the subscales should not be summed but each subscale should be used independently. And, a new overall marital quality assessment should be added to the battery.

A fourth problem concerns the appropriate unit of analysis. To make the leap from the level of the individual respondent to that of the couple or dyad requires a procedure for combining individual data into dyadic (structural) measures. Although devising structural measures is a problem in many areas of marriage and family study, the problem is particularly acute in the study of marital quality. A lack of consensus on marital quality between husbands and wives can represent inaccuracy of perception, different criteria for evaluating the quality of the marriage, differential sensitivity to response sets, and so forth. Although it is possible that disagreement stems from the difference between one valid and one invalid report, it is more likely that both reports, although they disagree, represent important statements about the nature and quality of the marriage (White & Brinkerhoff, 1978).

The typical way that *individual* assessments of a marriage are aggregated to assign *couples* to a happy or unhappy category unnecessarily loses a good deal of information in the interest of maximizing the variance between groups and minimizing the variance within groups. Paradigmatic research in this area proceeds by having each husband and wife independently complete scales of some aspect of marital quality. The husbands and wives who score above a certain average are assigned to the happily married groups, while those husbands and wives who score below a certain score are assigned to the unhappily married group. These methods may be confounding *agreement* between a husband and wife on their level of marital quality with the actual level of marital quality. Couples in the happily married group are those who evaluate their marriage as qualitatively high on the dimensions of interest and who agree on those evaluations. These couples are contrasted with those who score lower and who may either agree or disagree with the spouse on these dimensions. Rather than obscuring agreement and marital quality, agreement on the level of marital quality may be the important variable to study. Unwittingly, we are focusing on couples who agree that they are happily or unhappily married.

Agreement between husbands and wives on marital quality is rarely high. On the Snyder Marital Satisfaction Inventory, for example, the average correlation for marital satisfaction for husbands and wives is .37 (Snyder, Wills, & Kesler, 1981). The research I have conducted over the past 10 years finds a similar level of disagreement on dimensions of marriage of .40 for husbands and wives. Locke (1951) explicitly took earlier researchers (Burgess & Cottrell, 1939) to task because they found a correlation of .88 between the marital satisfaction scores of husbands and wives. Such a high correlation occurs because of collusion between spouses. Locke (1951) found a correlation of .36 between husband and wife happiness. Across the literature this finding is so robust that there are two marriages in any given relationship: his marriage and her marriage (Bernard, 1972).

In general, the frequently used measures of marital satisfaction overemphasize agreement and consensus and underemphasize expressions of affection and cohesion. Less emphasis should be placed on the number of conflicts experienced by a couple and more on how they are resolved and handled. Greater attention needs to be paid to the issues of marital companionship between husbands and wives.

Although the debate continues on the definition of this construct, the fact remains that the intercorrelations among the self-report instruments used to measure these various concepts are very high. The use of dependent variables that are both methodologically and conceptually related to one another suggests that a meta-analysis (Glass, McGaw, & Smith, 1981) of the relationship between communication and satisfaction would resolve some of the theoretical and methodological confusion.

2. Data Analysis. The major statistical problem endemic to the study of marital communication is that the observations are not independent of one another. Such nonindependence may be thought of as links between pairs of observations and may be positive or negative. The self-reports of husbands and wives are linked to one another as is their communication behavior. These nonindependent observations exert a severe biasing effect on the mean square estimates (Kenny & Judd, 1986). The combined effects of the bias in each of the mean squares can lead to either too large or too small F ratios. Researchers sometimes handle this problem by separately analyzing the data for husbands and wives. Not only does this lose power by cutting the degrees of freedom in half, but this solution also does not directly test husbands and wives on the dependent variables of interest. A better solution is a repeated-measure design which loses degrees of freedom yet allows a direct test of husbands and wives.

The social relations model (Kenny & LaVoie, 1984), which is a model for the analysis of social interaction data, explicitly examines the nonindependence in social interaction data as a way of studying reciprocity and compensation in social interaction. This model turns a statistical problem into a substantive one. Fitzpatrick and Dindia (1986) have extended the social relations model to the spouse–stranger interaction question. My colleague and I estimated the effects on communication of pairing all possible combinations of interactants (males with females, husbands with wives, males with males, females with females). This design estimates effects on each person's behavior due to his or her own general tendencies, the general tendencies of the other with whom he or she is interacting, the specific relationship of the two, and occasion-specific error variance. This design also allows us to examine the similarities and differences between marriage and other social relationships.

Recent advances in social interaction analysis techniques measure communication behavior while preserving the timing and sequence of events (Morley, 1987). These techniques center on the analysis of dependencies in the sequential, categorical data of two interactants: How does one spouse's communication behavior at time one influence the communication behavior of the partner at time two? The conditional probability of this event is a function not only of the joint dependency in the partner's behavior but also of the serial dependency or autocorrelation in the first partner's behavior. Methods to control for this autocorrelation in lag sequential analysis are being developed (Kenny & Judd, 1986).

Aside from the autocorrelation problem, lag sequential analysis may also capitalize on chance. The use of the Markov tests (e.g., Williamson & Fitzpatrick, 1985) before the lag sequential tests establishes whether the interaction data has demonstrable structure. A researcher may also consider the values in the

Markov transition matrix as dependent variables in a causal model and specify the factors that determine the transition probabilities. This approach moves the Markov techniques from merely describing interaction data to testing theoretical models (see Cappella, 1979).

Alternative analyses of categorical data can be accomplished with log-linear analysis. This is a statistical technique specifically designed for the analysis of contingency tables involving multiple categorical variables (e.g., Witteman & Fitzpatrick, 1986) Or multivariate repeated measures designs in which the dependent variables, now proportions, are arcsin transformed to stabilize the variances, can be used.

3. Observational Techniques.   There are two major forms of observational techniques used in the marital research: stimulated recall and observational analysis. Stimulated recall introduces the spouses into the observational technique, because spouses are asked to view a tape of their interaction and comment on it. Some researchers structure the form of the comments that they wish their participants to make (Guthrie & Noller, 1988), whereas others have couples provide a continuous report of their feelings during the interaction (Gottman & Levenson, 1985). Stimulated recall has a number of important benefits. It allowed Noller and her associates to hone in on the major affective moments in marital conversations and do more intensive analyses of these points in the conversation. Gottman and Levenson (1985) found that their stimulated recall ratings were significantly related to coders' judgment of the marital interaction and to online physiological measurements taken during the communication episode.

Interaction analysis includes any systematic method of classifying verbal and nonverbal behavior. Interaction studies have typically been used to compare the communication behaviors that discriminate distressed and nondistressed couples (Schaap et al., 1988), spouses and strangers (Fitzpatrick & Dindia, 1986), and couples who have been in treatment from those who have not been in treatment (Hahlweg & Jacobson, 1984). The type of data generated from coding studies includes a variety of coorientational measures (Noller, 1984): intent-impact measures, which relate to accuracy but are more subjective (Markman, 1982); outsider or insider ratings of behavior, including ratings of different channels and combinations of ratings (Noller & Gallois, 1988); and the coding of actual verbal (Dillard & Fitzpatrick, 1985) behaviors.

Bakeman and Gottman (1986) provide a primer on sequential interaction analysis that starts with the development of communication coding schemes and then introduces ways to handle sequence and pattern in communication. Coding schemes can be abstract (e.g., Witteman & Fitzpatrick, 1986) or concrete (e.g., Fitzpatrick & Dindia, 1986). Markman and Notarius (1987) make a persuasive case that most marital interaction coding uses six dimensions: dominance, affect, communication clarity, information exchanges, conflict (overt tension), and support/validation.

In addition to the verbal and nonverbal content of an interaction, the characteristics of verbal and nonverbal codes such as the quality, intensity (activity, tension, tempo), and diversity can be examined. Overall interactional quality has received very little attention from observational researchers of marriage. Courtwright, Millar, and Rogers (1980) have examined intensity by weighting the control messages in their scheme. Williamson and Fitzpatrick (1985) have studied the intensity of the control moves of husbands and wives defined into one of the Fitzpatrick (1984) marital typology clusters. Diversity has not been the object of much sequential analysis unless it is defined as the different communication strategies spouses use in discussing different topics (Fitzpatrick, 1984). In one study, Gottman (1979) examined flexibility (similar to diversity) by looking at the size of the Z scores in the lag sequential analysis. This approach was criticized, however, by Allison and Liker (1982). The issue of diversity in interaction needs further considerations, because diversity in interactional style may be the key ingredient in effective communication between spouses. In summary, communication coding schemes privilege each communication behavior or message equally. Some attention to measures of quality, intensity, and diversity is needed. These characteristics of communication may be better able to approximate what various messages mean to the husbands and wives in the conversations.

Coding has typically been plagued by reliability and validity difficulties. Coding reliability can be separated into two components: *unitizing,* which refers on the coder's ability to agree on how the conversation should be parsed into units; and *classificatory reliability,* which refers to the level of agreement on how the units should be classified. At times, researchers have needed to combine codes in order to achieve appropriate levels of reliability (Birchler, Weiss, & Vincent, 1975; Raush et al., 1974).

Both construct and representational validity problems occur in marital interaction studies. Concerning construct validity, a comparative analysis of some of the major schemes to examine conflict and power demonstrated that these coding schemes use the same behaviors to signify different constructs (Bavelas, Rogers, & Millar, 1985). Further, functional approaches to nonverbal behavior (Patterson, 1983) posit that coding nonverbal cues without systematically examining the interrelationships among the cues is erroneous. A given nonverbal cue taken out of the context of the other cues may lead to misinterpretation. Talk time, for example, can be taken as a measure of involvement, of affection, or of power, depending on the conversational partner(s), the context of the interaction, and the presence or absence of other nonverbal behaviors. Studying human communication in an ongoing relationship like marriage also poses representational validity problems. Marriage may be seen as a private culture with its own rules and idiosyncratic communication codes. Cracking these codes may not be easy. To demonstrate the representational validity of a marital communication coding scheme demands matching of the researcher, couple, and community perspectives on the meaning of verbal and nonverbal codes. Representational validity

(Folger, Hewes, & Poole, 1984) may be needed to understand how individual husbands and wives assign meaning to messages.

B. Summary

In this section, I have discussed some of the methodological decisions and trade-offs that researchers have made in an attempt to understand marital communication. To ask couples about their level of marital happiness, when that construct is defined as the subjectively experienced contentment with the relationship, is a reasonable and appropriate operational strategy. Asking couples to report on their communication patterns and sequences is somewhat more problematic and needs to be approached with great care. This section has also shown that the movement to study the interactional level of analysis requires some fairly sophisticated data analysis. Demonstrating pattern and sequences, independent of the individual's level of behavior, is a complex yet clearly manageable research agenda. Finally, the development of new statistical methods, like the social relations model, allows us to test both levels of analysis, thus, more clearly articulating the relationship between the individual and the interaction.

V. CONCLUSION

This chapter has attempted to review some of the major theoretical and methodological issues in the study of marital interaction. I begin with a discussion of the centrality of communication in modern marriage and organize the chapter around the individual in marriage, the interactional system of marriage, and the methods and practices generally followed in marital communication research. At each level of analysis, we have seen that the ideological values that couples have about marriage and husband and wife roles, as well as about the current state of their relationship, affect their communication behavior. We have also seen the necessity of including both levels of analysis for understanding marital communication. The anomalies at one level of analysis become less problematic at another level. The common disparities in individual reports of marital satisfaction may be explained by difficulty in negotiating transactional sequences: Such difficulties may be apparent to one interactional partner, yet not to the other.

One other rationale for including both individual and interactional models of marital communication in the same review is that such a course might lead to new models including both individual and interactional concepts. The physiological linkage concept (Gottman & Levenson, 1988), clearly an interactional one, fits with the longitudinal investigations that suggest low neuroticism and high impulse control affect marital satisfaction. Both of these individual difference variables are related to an individual's ability (or lack thereof) to control their physiological arousal (cf. Kelly & Conley, 1987). What seem at first glance remarkably different explanations for marital satisfaction are explaining different, related pieces of the puzzle.

In addition to constructing models linking individual and interactional levels of analysis, the almost exclusive focus on marital satisfaction needs to be reconsidered. Across a number of theoretical perspectives the marital system is considered to have a central role in regulating all the other relationships within the family. Thus, linking individual and marital interaction processes to outcomes other than marital satisfaction would tell us a great deal about family life in general. Of basic theoretical and clinical interest would be the documentation of the effects of marital communication on a variety of functional and dysfunctional outcomes for the children.

REFERENCES

Allison, P. D., & Liker, J. K. (1982). Analyzing sequential categorical data on dyadic interaction: A comment on Gottman. *Psychological Bulletin, 91,* 393–403.

Altman, I., & Taylor, D. A. (1973). *Social penetration: The development of interpersonal relationships.* New York: Holt, Rinehart and Winston.

Altman, I., Vinsel, A., & Brown, B. B. (1981). Dialectical conceptions in social psychology. In L. Berkowitz (Ed.), *Advances in experimental social psychology* (pp. 107–160). New York: Academic.

Bakeman, R., & Gottman, J. M. (1986). *Observing interaction.* Cambridge, England: Cambridge University Press.

Baucom, D. H., & Aiken, P. A. (1984). Sex role identity, marital satisfaction, and response to behavioral marital therapy. *Journal of Consulting and Clinical Psychology, 52,* 438–444.

Bavelas, J. B., Rogers, L. E., & Millar, F. E. (1985). Interpersonal conflict. In T. A. Van Dijk (Ed.), *Handbook of discourse analysis: Vol. 4* (pp. 9–26). London: Academic.

Baxter, L. (1985). Accomplishing relationships disengagement. In S. Duck & D. Perlman (Eds.), *Personal relationships* (pp. 243–265). Beverly Hills, CA: Sage.

Beier, E. G., & Sternberg, D. P. (1977). Subtle cues between newlyweds. *Journal of Communication, 27,* 92–103.

Bell, R. (1986, November). *Affinity seeking among married couples.* Paper presented at the Speech Communication Association, Denver, CO.

Belsky, J., Ward, M. J., & Rovine, M. (1986). Prenatal expectations, postnatal experiences and the transition to parenthood. In R. Ashmore & D. Brodzinsky (Eds.), *Thinking about the family: Views of parents and children* (pp. 119–145). Hillsdale, NJ: Erlbaum.

Bem, S., (1984). Androgeny and gender schema theory: A conceptual and methodological integration. In T. B. Sonderegger (Ed.), *Psychology and gender: Nebraska symposium on motivation* (pp. 179–226). Lincoln, NE: University of Nebraska Press.

Berger, C. R., & Roloff, M. (1982). Thinking about friends and lovers. In M. Roloff & C. R. Berger (Eds.), *Social cognition and communication* (pp. 151–192). Beverly Hills, CA: Sage.

Berger, P., & Kellner, H. (1975). Marriage and the construction of reality. In D. Brisset & C. Edgeley (Eds.), *Life as theatre* (pp. 225–239). Chicago, IL: Aldine.

Bernal, G., & Golann, S. (1980). Couple interaction: A study of the punctuation process. *International Journal of Family Process, 2,* 47–56.

Bernard, J. (1972). *The future of marriage*. New York: World Publications.

Berscheid, E. (1983). Emotion in close relationships. In H. Kelley, E. Berscheid, A. Christensen, J. J. Harvey, T. L. Huston, G. Levinger, E. McClintock, L. A. Peplau, & D. R. Peterson (Eds.), *Close relationships* (pp. 110–168). New York: W. H. Freeman.

Bienvenu, M. J. (1970). Measurement of marital communication. *Family Coordinator, 19,* 26–31.

Birchler, G. R., Weiss, R. L., & Vincent, J. P. (1975). Multi-method analysis of social reinforcement exchange between maritally distressed and non-distressed spouse and stranger dyads. *Journal of Personality and Social Psychology, 31,* 349–360.

Bleier, R. (1977). *Science and gender*. Elmsford, NY: Pergamon.

Boals, G. F., Peterson, D. R., Farmer, L., Mann, D. F., & Robinson, D. l. (1982). The reliability, validity and utility of three data modes in assessing marital relationships. *Journal of Personality Assessment, 46,* 85–95.

Bochner, A. P. (1983). The functions of human communication in interpersonal bonding. In C. C. Arnold & J. W. Bowers (Eds.), *Handbook of rhetorical and communication theory* (pp. 544–621). Boston, MA: Allyn & Bacon.

Bradac, J. (1983). The language of lovers, flovers, and friends: Communicating in social and personal relationships. *Journal of Language and Social Psychology, 2,* 141–162.

Bradbury, T. N., & Fincham, F. D. (1987). Affect and cognition in close relationships: Towards an integrative model. *Cognition and Emotion, 1,* 59–87.

Bradbury, T. N., & Fincham, F. D. (1988). Assessing spontaneous attributions in marriage. *Journal of Social and Clinical Psychology, 7,* 122–130.

Burgess, E. W., & Cottrell, L. S. (1939). *Predicting success or failure in marriage*. New York: Prentice-Hall.

Burgess, E. W., Locke, H. J., & Thomes, M. M. (1971). *The family*. New York: Van Nostrand Reinhold.

Burgraff, C., & Sillars, A. (1986, November). *A critical examination of sex differences in marital communication*. Paper presented at the Speech Communication Association, Chicago.

Burke, R. J., Weir, T., & Harrison, D. (1976). Disclosure of problems and tensions experienced by marital partners. *Psychological Reports, 38,* 531–542.

Buss, D. M., & Barnes, M. (1986). Preferences in human mate selection. *Journal of Personality and Social Psychology, 50,* 559–570.

Campbell, D. T., & Fiske, D. W. (1959). Convergent and discriminant validation by the multitrait, multimethod matrix. *Psychological Bulletin, 56,* 81–105.

Cappella, J. N. (1979). Talk-silence sequences in informal conversations I. *Human Communication Research, 6,* 3–17.

Cappella, J. N. (1987). Interpersonal communication. In C. R. Berger & S. H. Chaffee (Eds.), *Handbook of interpersonal communication* (pp. 184–238). Newbury Park, CA: Sage.

Chelune, G. J. (1979). Measuring openness in interpersonal communication. In G. J. Chelune (Ed.), *Self disclosure* (pp. 1–27). San Francisco, CA: Jossey Bass.

Chelune, G. J., Waring, E. M., Vosk, B. N., Sultan, F. E., & Ogden, J. K. (1984). Self-disclosure and its relationship to marital intimacy. *Journal of Clinical Psychology, 40,* 216–219.

Christensen, A. (1988). Dysfunctional interaction patterns in couples. In P. Noller & M. A. Fitzpatrick (Eds.), *Perspectives on marital interaction* (pp. 31–52). Philadelphia, PA & Clevedon, England: Multilingual Matters.

Christensen, A., & Arrington, A. (1987). Research issues and strategies. In T. Jacob (Ed.), *Family interaction and psychopathology* (pp. 259–296). New York: Plenum.

Christensen, A., & Nies, D. C. (1980). The spouse observation checklist: Empirical analysis and critique. *American Journal of Family Therapy, 8,* 69–79.

Courtwright, J., Millar, F., & Rogers-Millar, E. (1979). Domineeringness and dominance. *Communication Monographs, 46,* 179–192.

Courtwright, J., Millar, F., & Rogers, E. (1980). Message control intensity as a predictor of transactional redundancy. In D. Nimmo (Ed.), *Communication yearbook 4* (pp. 199–216). New Brunswick, NJ: Transaction Press.

Crow, B. (1983). Topic shifts in couple's conversations. in R. T. Craig & K. Tracy (Eds.), *Conversational coherence* (pp. 136–156). Beverly Hills, CA: Sage.

Davidson, B., Balswick, J., & Halverson, C. (1983). Affective self-disclosure and marital satisfaction. *Journal of Marriage and the Family, 45,* 93–102.

Dillard, J., & Fitzpatrick, M. A. (1985). Compliance-gaining in marital interaction. *Personality and Social Psychology Bulletin, 11,* 419–433.

Dindia, K., & Baxter, L. (1986, May). *Strategies used by marital partners to maintain their relationships.* Paper presented at the International Communication Association, Chicago.

Doherty, W. J. (1981). Cognitive processes in intimate conflict. *American Journal of Family Therapy, 9,* 1–13.

Duncan, S., Kanki, B. G., Mokros, H., & Fiske, D. W. (1984). Pseudounilaterality, simple-rate variables, and other ills to which interaction research is heir. *Journal of Personality and Social Psychology, 46,* 1335–1348.

Eggeman, K., Moxley, V., & Schumm, W. (1985). Assessing spouses' perceptions of Gottman's temporal form in marital conflict. *Psychological Reports, 57,* 171–181.

Eidelson, R. J., & Epstein, N. (1982). Cognition and relationship maladjustment. *Journal of Consulting and Clinical Psychology, 50,* 715–720.

Elwood, R. W., & Jacobson, N. S. (1982). Spouses' agreement in reporting their behavioral interactions: A clinical replication. *Journal of Consulting and Clinical Psychology, 50,* 783–784.

Ericson, P. M., & Rogers, E. L. (1973). New procedures for analyzing relational communication. *Family Process, 12,* 245–267.

Fausto-Sterling, A. (1985). *Myths of gender.* New York: Basic.

Fincham, F. (1985). Attributions in close relationships. In J. H. Harvey & G. Weary (Eds.), *Attribution: Basic issues and applications* (pp. 203–234). New York: Academic.

Fincham, F., Beach, S., & Baucom, D. H. (1987). Attribution processes in distressed and non-distressed couples: 4. Self-partner attribution differences. *Journal of Personality and Social Psychology, 52,* 739–758.

Fincham, F., Beach, S., & Nelson, G. (1987). Attribution processes in distressed and nondistressed couples: 3. Causal and responsibility attributions for spouse behavior. *Cognitive Therapy and Research, 11,* 71–86.

Fincham, F., & Jaspars, J. M. F. (1980). From man the scientist to man as lawyer. In L. Berkowitz (Ed.), *Advances in experimental social psychology* (Vol. 13, pp. 43–85). New York: Academic.

Fincham, F., & O'Leary, K. D. (1983). Causal inferences for spouse behavior in maritally distressed and nondistressed couples. *Journal of Social and Clinical Psychology, 1,* 42–57.

Fitzpatrick, M. A. (1977). A typological approach to communication in relationships. In B. Rubin (Ed.), *Communication yearbook 1* (pp. 263–275). New Brunswick, NJ: Transaction Press.

Fitzpatrick, M. A. (1983). Predicting couples' communication from couples' self-reports. In R. N. Bostrom & B. H. Westley (Eds.), *Communication yearbook 7* (pp. 49–82). Beverly Hills, CA: Sage Publishers.

Fitzpatrick, M. A. (1984). A typological approach to marital interaction: Recent theory and research. In L. Berkowitz (Ed.), *Advances in experimental social psychology, 18* (pp. 1–47). Orlando, FL: Academic Press.

Fitzpatrick, M. A. (1987a, May). *The effect of marital schemata on marital communication.* Paper presented at International Communication Association, Montreal, Canada.

Fitzpatrick, M. A. (1987b). Marital interaction. In C. R. Berger & S. H. Chaffee (Eds.), *Handbook of communication science* (pp. 564–618). Newbury Park, CA: Sage.

Fitzpatrick, M. A. (1987c). Marriage and verbal intimacy. In V. J. Derlega & J. Berg (Eds.), *Self-disclosure: Theory, research, and therapy*. New York: Plenum.

Fitzpatrick, M. A. (1987d). *Final report on the effect of marital schemata on marital communication*. Submitted to NIMH (RO1-MH-40813-01).

Fitzpatrick, M. A. (1988). *Between husbands and wives: Communication in marriage*. Newbury Park, CA: Sage.

Fitzpatrick, M. A., & Badzinski, D. (1985). All in the family: Communication in kin relationships. In M. L. Knapp & G. R. Miller (Eds.), *Handbook of interpersonal communication* (pp. 687–736). Beverly Hills, CA: Sage.

Fitzpatrick, M. A., Bauman, I., & Lindaas, M. (1987, May). *A schematic approach to marital interaction*. Paper presented at the International Communication Association, Montreal, Canada.

Fitzpatrick, M. A., & Dindia, K. (1986). Couples and other strangers: Talk-time in spouse-stranger interaction. *Communication Research, 13*, 625–652.

Fitzpatrick, M. A., & Indvik, J. (1979, November). *What you see may not be what you have: Communicative accuracy in marital types*. Paper presented at the Speech Communication Association Convention, San Antonio, TX.

Fitzpatrick, M. A., & Indvik, J. (1982). The instrumental and expressive domains of marital communication. *Human Communication Research, 8*, 195–213.

Folger, J., Hewes, D., & Poole, M. S. (1984). Coding social interaction. In B. Dervin & M. Voight (Eds.), *Progress in communication sciences* (Vol. 5, pp. 115–161). Norwood, NJ: Ablex Publishing Corp.

Gage, N. L., & Cronback, L. J. (1955). Conceptual and methodological problems in interpersonal perception. *Psychological Review, 62*, 411–422.

Gilligan, C. (1982). *In a different voice*. Cambridge, MA: Harvard University Press.

Glass, G. V., McGaw, B., & Smith, M. L. (1981). *Meta-analysis in social research*. Beverly Hills, CA: Sage.

Gottman, J. M. (1979). *Marital interaction: Experimental investigations*. New York: Academic Press.

Gottman, J. M. (1982). Temporal form. *Journal of Marriage and the Family, 44*, 943–962.

Gottman, J. M., & Levenson, R. W. (1988). The social psychophysiology of marriage. In P. Noller & M. A. Fitzpatrick (Eds.), *Perspectives on marital interaction* (pp. 182–200). Clevedon, England & Philadelphia, PA: Multilingual Matters.

Gottman, J. M., & Porterfield, A. L. (1981). Communicative competence in the nonverbal behavior of married couples. *Journal of Marriage and the Family, 43*, 817–824.

Gould, S. J. (1981). *The mismeasure of man*. New York: Norton.

Gove, W. R. (1985). The effect of age and gender on deviant behavior. In A. S. Rossi (Ed.), *Gender and the life course* (pp. 115–144). Hawthorne, MA: Aldine.

Gray-Little, B., & Burks, N. (1983). Power and satisfaction in marriage: A review and critique. *Psychological Bulletin, 93*, 513–538.

Guthrie, D. M., & Noller, P. (1988). Spouses' perceptions of one another in emontional situations. In P. Noller & M. A. Fitzpatrick (Eds.), *Perspectives in marital interaction* (pp. 153–181). Clevedon, England: Multilingual Matters.

Guttentag, M., & Secord, P. (1983). *Too many women?: The sex ratio question*. Beverly Hills, CA: Sage.

Hahlweg, K., & Jacobson, N. S. (1984). *Marital interaction: Analysis and modification*. New York: The Guilford Press.

Haley, J. (1962). Family experiments. *Family Process, 1*, 265–293.

Haviland, J., & Malatesta. C. (1981). The development of sex differences in nonverbal signals. In C. Mayo & N. Henley (Eds.), *Gender and nonverbal behavior* (pp. 182–208). New York: Springer-Verlag.

Hendrick, S. S. (1981). Self disclosure and marital satisfaction. *Journal of Personality and Social Psychology, 40,* 1150–1159.

Hewes, D., & Planalp, S. (1987). The individual's place in communication science. In C. R. Berger & S. H. Chaffee (Eds.), *Handbook of communication science* (pp. 146–183). Newbury Park, CA: Sage.

Holtzworth-Munroe, A., & Jacobson, N. S. (1985). Causal attributions of married couples. When do they search for causes? What do they conclude when they do? *Journal of Personality and Social Psychology, 48,* 1398–1412.

Hyde, J. (1981). How large are cognitive differences? *American Psychologist, 36,* 892–901.

Jacobson, N. S. (1984). A component analysis of behavioral marital therapy: The relative effectiveness of behavior exchange and communication/problem-solving training. *Journal of Consulting and Clinical Psychology, 52,* 295–305.

Jacobson, N. S., Follette, W. L., & McDonald, D. W. (1982). Reactivity to positive and negative behavior in distressed and nondistressed married couples. *Journal of Consulting and Clinical Psychology, 50,* 706–714.

Jacobson, N. S., McDonald, D. W., Follette, W. C., & Berley, R. A. (1985). Attribution processes in distressed and nondistressed married couples. *Cognitive Therapy and Research, 9,* 35–50.

Jacobson, N. S., & Moore, D. (1981). Spouses as observers of events in their relationships. *Journal of Consulting and Clinical Psychology, 49,* 269–277.

Kantor, D., & Lehr, W. (1975). *Inside the family.* New York: Harper & Row.

Katriel, T., & Philipsen, G. (1981). "What we need is communication": "Communication" as a cultural category in some American speech. *Communication Monographs, 48,* 301–318.

Kelly, E. L., & Conley, J. J. (1987). Personality and compatibility: A prospective analysis of marital stability and marital satisfaction. *Journal of Personality and Social Psychology, 52,* 27–40.

Kelly, C., Huston, T., & Cate, R. (1985). Premarital relationship correlates of the erosion of satisfaction in marriage. *Journal of Social and Personal Relationships, 2,* 137–178.

Kenny, D. A., & Judd, N. (1986). Handling correlated data. *Psychological Bulletin, 94,* 101–132.

Kenny, D. A., & LaVoie, L. (1984). The social relations model. In L. Berkowitz (Eds.), *Advances in experimental social psychology* (Vol. 18, pp. 48–101). New York: Academic Press.

Kerber, L. K., Greeno, C. G., Maccoby, E. E., Luria, Z., Stack, C. B., & Gilligan, C. (1986). "In a different voice": An interdisciplinary forum. *Signs, 11,* 304–333.

Kiecolt-Glaser, J. K., Fisher, L. D., Ogrocki, P., Stout, J. C., Speicher, C., E., & Glaser, R. (1987). Marital quality, marital disruption, and immune function. *Psychomatic Medicine, 49,* 13–330.

Knapp, M. L. (1978). *Nonverbal communication.* Boston, MA: Allyn & Bacon.

Knudson, R. M., Sommers, A. A., & Golding, S. L. (1980). Interpersonal perception and mode of resolution in marital conflict. *Journal of Personality and Social Psychology, 38,* 751–763.

Laing, R. D., Phillipson, H., & Lee, A. R. (1966). *Interpersonal perception.* New York: Springer.

Lamb, M., Suomi, S., & Stephenson, G. (1979). *Social interaction analysis.* Madison, WI: University of Wisconsin Press.

Lancaster, J. (1985). Evolutionary perspectives on sex differences in the higher primates. In A. Rossi (Ed.), *Gender and the life course* (pp. 3–27). Hawthorne, MA: Aldine.

Lasch, C. (1977). *Haven in a heartless world.* New York: Basic.

Lederer, W. J., & Jackson, D. D. (1968). *The mirages of marriage.* New York: W. W. Norton.

Lenk-Krueger, D. (1982). Marital decision-making. *Quarterly Journal of Speech, 68,* 273–287.

Levenson, R. W., & Gottman, J. M. (1983). Marital interaction: Physiological linkage and affective exchange. *Journal of Personality and Social Psychology, 45,* 587–597.

Levenson, R. W., & Gottman, J. W. (1985). Physiological and affective predictors of changes in marital satisfaction. *Journal of Personality and Social Psychology, 49,* 85–94.

Levinger, G., & Senn, D. J. (1967). Disclosure of feelings in marriage. *Merrill-Palmer Quarterly, 13,* 237–249.

Lewis, R. A., & Spanier, G. (1979). Theorizing about the quality and the stability of marriage. In W. R. Burr, R. Hill, F. I. Nye, & I. L. Reiss (Eds.), *Contemporary theories about the family* (Vol. 1, pp. 268–294). New York: Free Press.

Locke, H. J. (1951). *Predicting adjustment in marriage: A comparison of a divorced and happily married group.* New York: Henry Holt.

Locke, H. J., & Wallace, K. M. (1959). Short marital-adjustment tests: Their reliability and validity. *Marriage and Family Living, 21,* 251–255.

Mandler, G. (1984). *Mind and body: The psychology of emotion and stress.* New York: W. W. Norton.

Margolin, G. (1978). A multilevel approach to the assessment of communicative positiveness in distressed married couples. *International Journal of Family Counseling, 6,* 81–89.

Margolin, G., & Wampold, B. E. (1981). Sequential analysis of conflict and accord in distressed and nondistressed marital partners. *Journal of Consulting and Clinical Psychology, 49,* 554–567.

Markman, H. J. (1982, November). *Couples' observation of their own communication.* Paper presented at the meeting of the association for the Advancement of Behavioral Therapy, Los Angeles.

Markman, H. J., & Notarius, C. (1987). Coding marital and family interaction. In T. Jacob (Ed.), *Family interaction and psychopathology* (pp. 329–390). New York: Plenum.

Markus, H. (1977). Self schemata and processing information about the self. *Journal of Personality and Social Psychology, 35,* 63–78.

McLeod, J. M., & Chaffee, S. H. (1972). The construction of social reality. In J. T. Tedeschi (Ed.), *The social influence processes* (pp. 50–99). Chicago, IL: Aldine-Atherton.

Millar, F. E., & Rogers, L. E. (1976). A relational approach to interpersonal communication. In G. R. Miller (Ed.), *Explorations in interpersonal communication* (pp. 87–104). Beverly Hills, CA: Sage.

Miller, G. R. (1976). Foreword. In G. R. Miller (Ed.), *Explorations in interpersonal communication* (pp. 9–16). Beverly Hills, CA: Sage.

Morley, D. D. (1987). Revised lag sequential analysis. In M. L. Mc Laughlin (Ed.), *Communication Yearbook 10* (pp. 172–182). Newbury Park, CA: Sage.

Navran, L. (1967). Communication and adjustment in marriage. *Family Process, 6,* 173–184.

Neisser, U. (1967). *Cognitive psychology.* New York: Appleton Press.

Newman, H. (1981). Communication within ongoing intimate relationships: An attributional perspective. *Personality and Social Psychology Bulletin, 7,* 59–70.

Noller, P. (1980). Misunderstandings in marital communication. *Journal of Personality and Social Psychology, 39,* 1135–1148.

Noller, P. (1984). *Nonverbal communication and marital interaction.* New York: Pergamon Press.

Noller, P., & Fitzpatrick, M. A. (1987, July). *Nonverbal communication accuracy in couple types.* Paper presented at the Third International Conference on Social Psychology and Language, Bristol, England.

Noller, P., & Fitzpatrick, M. A. (1988). *Perspectives on marital interaction.* Clevedon, England & Philadelphia, PA: Multilingual Matters.

Noller, P., & Gallois, C. (1988). Nonverbal communication and accuracy in marital communications. In P. Noller & M. A. Fitzpatrick (Eds.), *Perspectives on marital interaction* (pp. 53–77). Clevedon, England & Philadelphia, PA: Multilingual Matters.

Norton, R. (1983). Measuring marital quality: A critical look at the dependent variable. *Journal of Marriage and the Family, 45,* 141–151.

Notarius, C., & Johnson, H. (1982). Physiological responses during marital interaction. *Journal of Marriage and the Family, 44,* 418–432.

Nye, F. I. (1976). *Role structure and an analysis of the family.* Beverly Hills, CA: Sage.

Olson, D. H. (1977). Insiders' and outsiders' views of relationships: Research strategies. In G.

Levinger & H. L. Raush (Eds.), *Close Relationships: Perspectives in the meaning of intimacy* (pp. 115–136). Amherst, MA: University of Massachusetts Press.

Olson, D. H. (1981). Family typologies: Bridging family research and family therapy. In E. E. Filsinger & R. A. Lewis (Eds.), *Assessing marriage: New behavioral approaches* (pp. 74–89). Beverly Hills, CA: Sage.

Orvis, B. B., Kelley, H. H., & Butler, D. (1976). Attributional conflict in young couples. In J. H. Harvey, W. J. Ickes, & R. E. Kidd (Eds.), *New directions in attribution research* (Vol. 1, pp. 353–386). Hillsdale, NJ: Erlbaum.

Parsons, J. E. (1982). Biology, experience, and sex dimorphic behaviors. In W. R. Gove and G. R. Carpenter (Eds.), *The fundamental connection between nature and nurture* (pp. 137–170). Lexington, MA: Lexington Books.

Patterson, M. (1983). *Nonverbal behavior: A functional perspective.* New York: Springer-Verlag.

Peterson, A. C. (1980). Biopsychosocial processes in the development of sex-related differences. In J. E. Parsons (Ed.), *The psychology of sex differences and sex roles* (pp. 31–56). Washington, DC: Hemisphere.

Peterson, D. R. (1979). Assessing interpersonal relationships by means of interaction records. *Behavioral assessment, 1,* 221–236.

Penman, R. (1980). *Communication processes and relationships.* New York: Academic.

Planalp, S. (1984). *Relational schemata: An interpretive approach to relationships.* Unpublished doctoral dissertation, University of Wisconsin-Madison.

Poole, M. S., & McPhee, R. (1985). Methodology in interpersonal communication research. In M. Knapp & G. R. Miller (Eds.), *Handbook of interpersonal communication* (pp. 28–62). Beverly Hills, CA: Sage.

Raush, H. L., Barry, W. A., Hertel, R. K., & Swain, M. A. (1974). *Communication, conflict, and marriage.* San Francisco, CA: Jossey-Bass.

Reiss, D. (1981). *The family's construction of reality.* Cambridge, MA: Harvard University Press.

Reiss, I. (1976). *Family systems in America* (2nd ed.). New York: Holt.

Rogers, L. A. (1972). *Dyadic systems and transactional communication in a family context.* Unpublished doctoral dissertation, Michigan State University, East Lansing, MI.

Rossi, A. (1985). Gender and parenthood. In A. S. Rossi (Ed.), *Gender and the life course* (pp. 161–192). New York: Aldine.

Rubin, Z., Peplau, L. A., & Hill, C. T. (1981). Loving and leaving: Sex differences in romantic attachments. *Sex Roles, 7,* 821–835.

Sabetelli, R. M., Buck, R., & Dreyer, A. (1982). Nonverbal communication accuracy in married couples: Relationship to marital complaints. *Journal of Personality and Social Psychology, 43,* 1088–1097.

Schaap, C. (1982). *Communication and adjustment.* Lisse, The Netherlands: Swets & Zeitlinger, B. V.

Schaap, C., Buunk, B., & Kerkstra, A. (1988). Marital conflict resolution. In P. Noller & M. A. Fitzpatrick (Eds.), *Perspectives on marital interaction* (pp. 203–244) Philadelphia, PA & Clevedon, England: Multilingual Matters.

Shimanoff, S. (1986, May). *Types of emotional disclosures and request compliance between spouses.* Paper presented at the International Communication Association Convention, Chicago.

Shorter, E. (1982). *A history of women's bodies.* New York: Basic.

Sillars, A., Pike, G. R., Jones, T. S., & Murphy, M. A. (1984). Communication and understanding in marriage. *Human Communication Research, 10,* 317–350.

Sillars, A., Pike, G. R., Jones, T. S., & Redmon, K. (1983). Communication and conflict in marriage: One style is not satisfying to all. In R. Bostrom (Ed.), *Communication yearbook 7* (pp. 414–431). Beverly Hills, CA: Sage.

Sillars, A. L., & Scott, M. D. (1983). Interpersonal perception between intimates: An integrative review. *Human Communication Research, 10,* 153–176.

Sillars, A. L., Weisberg, J., Burgraff, C. S., & Wilson, E. A. (1987). Content themes in marital conversations. *Human Communication Research, 13,* 495–528.

Snyder, D. K., Wills, R. M., & Kesler, T. W. (1981). Empirical validation of the Marital Satisfaction Inventory. *Journal of Consulting and Clinical Psychology, 49,* 262–268.

Spanier, G. B. (1976). Measuring dyadic adjustment: New scales for assessing the quality of marriage and similar dyads. *Journal of Marriage and the Family, 38,* 15–28.

Spanier, G. B., & Thompson, L. (1982). A confirmatory factor analysis of the dyadic adjustment scale. *Journal of Marriage and the Family, 44,* 731–738.

Steinmetz, S. (1979). Wife beating: A critique and reformulation of existing theory. *Bulletin of the American Academy of Psychiatry and the Law, 6,* 322–334.

Stephens, T. (1986). Communication and interdependence in geographically separated relationships. *Human Communication Research, 13,* 191–210.

Terman, L. M. (1938). *Psychological factors in marital happiness.* New York: McGraw-Hill.

Ting-Toomey, S. (1983). An analysis of verbal communication patterns in high and low marital adjustment groups. *Human Communication Research, 9,* 306–319.

Wamboldt, F., & Reiss, D. (1989). Defining a family heritage. *Family Process, 28,* 317–335.

Wamboldt, F., & Wolin, S. (in press). Reality and myth in family life. *Journal of Psychotherapy and the Family, 4,* 141–165.

Watzlawick, P., Beavin, J. H., & Jackson, D. D. (1967). *Pragmatics of human communication.* New York: W. W. Norton.

Weiss, R. L. (1981). The new kid on the block: Behavioral systems approach. In E. E. Filsinger & R. A. Lewis (Eds.), *Assessing marriage: New behavioral approaches* (pp. 22–37). Beverly Hills, CA: Sage.

Weiss, R. L., & Perry, B. A. (1979). *Assessment and treatment of marital dysfunction.* Eugene, OR: University of Oregon.

White, L. K., & Brinkerhoff, D. B. (1978). Measuring dyadic properties. *International Journal of the Sociology of the Family, 8,* 219–229.

Williamson, R. N., & Fitzpatrick, M. A. (1985). Two approaches to marital interaction: Relational control patterns in marital types. *Communication Monographs, 52,* 236–252.

Witteman, H., & Fitzpatrick, M. A. (1986). Compliance-gaining in marital interaction: Power bases, power processes, and outcomes. *Communication Monographs, 53,* 130–143.

4

New Communications Media and the Family: Practices, Functions, and Effects

Thomas R. Lindlof
Associate Professor
Department of Telecommunications
University of Kentucky

I. INTRODUCTION

During the past decade, an accelerated diffusion of several electronic media intended for home use has occurred in the United States, suggesting a fragmentation of the audience's normal ways of selecting and using media. The family is the social setting in which most mediated communication is situated and in which acculturation to the practices of media usage normally takes place. The newest technologies, most notably the microcomputer and the videocassette recorder (VCR), seem to alter the premises underlying much of our earlier thinking about family interactions with mass media. These media also have implications for social action outside the household, since they often integrate with friendship networks, schools, the workplace, and other settings. In the wake of this technological expansion, speculation about its effects on family functioning and child socialization is steadily being replaced by an empirical base of research.

This chapter will present a synoptic view on what is known and what has been hypothesized about the role of new communications media in the functional processes of family life. A high proportion of the research literature on social impacts of new communications media in the home has focused on the microcomputer and the VCR, and this review will reflect that emphasis.[1] The review is organized primarily by topical demarcations of the existing research literature: (a) changes in household time allocations, (b) content or software use practices, (c) relational communication, and (d) child socialization processes and outcomes. The media adoption phase will not receive extensive attention here for two reasons: the subject has been explicated very adequately elsewhere (e.g., Dutton, Rogers, & Jun, 1987; Klopfenstein & Swanson, 1987; Lindlof & Shatzer, in press), and this review is primarily interested in processes and activities that are contingent on relatively stable, postadoption usage regimens.

It should be noted that research of family uses of new media has been mostly intermittent, unprogrammatic, or reported only as individual variables included in projects conducted for other purposes. Moreover, many of the studies have sought to explore the relationships that are forming between new media acquisition and family functioning by means of ethnographic case studies and descriptive surveys. This research has directed detailed attention to the manner in which family members define, refer to, account for, and act in relation to these media. Much of the initial thrust in studying the use phenomena associated with new home media, then, has been qualitative, descriptive, and localistic. Inclusion of the small-sample studies enables insight into actual enactments of mediated communication, but typically without assurance of controls for sampling bias or observational error.

This chapter will couple a critical assessment of the conduct and conceptualizations of audience research with an agenda of research directions to im-

---

[1] Much social research of other new media, such as electronic text services and advanced-feature telephones, has been conducted under proprietary auspices and is unavailable for public inspection.

prove on our present levels of understanding. Towards that end, a discussion of three research perspectives that assert ways in which new media innovations influence audience formations and activity will be presented. Other comments regarding needed research initiatives will be found throughout this review, accompanying the discussions of domains of home microcomputing and VCR operation. The chapter will conclude with a set of issues for further exploration of this field.

II. THE FAMILY, MASS MEDIA, AND THE NEW MEDIA: AN OVERVIEW OF ISSUES

For as long as there has been an interest in the social-contextual determinants of audience behavior, the family has been a major focus of inquiry. Much of this research effort has been directed at understanding children's relationships with mass media, particularly television, and has been predicated on some characteristics of those media that have changed little during this century. This emphasis has been recently augmented by work that explicates television's contribution to the maintenance of interpersonal roles and rules, and to the construction of social realities in the family. This section briefly surveys the prominent research themes emerging from the interest in mass media and the family, and then considers the promise of discontinuity as well as continuity that the new communications media may hold for family adaptation.

Young people's unabated consumption of movies, comic books, radio, and television has been arguably a response to some characteristics held in common by all of those media: their near-universal accessibility, low unit cost, ease of use, and content that is unabashedly "popular" and often targeted to the interests and desires of youth cultures. These media have also been viewed as subversive to the interests of the family, since they present children with portrayals of morally complex adult behavior (Meyrowitz, 1985). The family's ability to regulate the socialization experiences of children is seen to be degraded by the economic and technological imperatives of mass communication. Thus, a similar moral panic seems to accompany successive developments in mass media (Davis, 1976). Much of the social research exploring family mediation of communications media and content has been conducted with these concerns as either explicit or implicit pretexts. As a consequence, the study of the influences on children's content reception becomes framed in terms of political accountability for alleged effects (Meyer & Hexamer, 1982). In terms of research design, however, these concerns have largely *not* been expressed as measures of monolithic impact that occur at the level of the individual. Indeed, the history of research on children and the media is marked by the study of *conditional* influences on exposure, usage, and effects, including the local conditions of home and peers (Meadowcroft & McDonald, 1986; Wartella & Reeves, 1985).

More recently, the family has been studied as a mediating influence in such communications-related aspects of development as comprehension ability (Reid, 1979; Desmond, Singer, Singer, Calam, & Colimore, 1985), conceptions of realism and morality (Messaris, 1987), aggressive and prosocial behavior learning (Collins, Sobol, & Westby, 1981; Eron, 1982; Singer & Singer, 1981), and consumer socialization (Robertson, 1979; Wackman, Wartella, & Ward, 1977). As early as infancy, children's physical and emotional orientations to television are contextualized in specific parent–child patterns of question–response–evaluation (Lemish, 1987). Children's cognitive skills for processing social information from television are likely to be influenced by the interactional patterns and specific tasks structured in the family (Messaris & Sarett, 1981; Wackman et al., 1977). Social mediation, as it might occur in the family context, has also been shown to moderate the probability that children will imitate or model (perhaps through a disinhibition process) televised displays of aggression and other behaviors (Bandura, 1977; Brown & Linne, 1976). In the preadolescent years and later, selection of media sources is more likely to involve considerations of self-identity and peer group acceptance than family norms (Christenson, DeBenedittis, & Lindlof, 1985; Faber, Brown, & McLeod, 1979). Whereas mechanisms of biological maturation constrain the attentional and memorial capacities of the individual's engagement with media, the institutions of the social world (including the family) seem to shape the actual content of media-related performances and their cultural meanings.

Communication scholars have also sought to examine the manner in which family member relationships, role performances, and affective functioning are contingent on patterns of mass media reception. Attention has been directed to the ways that television use affects the functioning of family subsystems, such as spousal dyads (Fallis, Fitzpatrick, & Friestad, 1985; McDonald, 1985; Wolf, Meyer, & White, 1982) and sibling interaction (Alexander, Ryan, & Munoz, 1984; Zahn & Baran, 1984). For example, it has been found that married couples classified as "separates" (or spouses whose relational dissatisfaction is reflected in little talk about emotional concerns) are more likely to discuss topics derived from televiewing, including marital issues, than couples that rate themselves as more interdependent emotionally and communicatively (Fallis et al., 1985). Television is also vital in regulating the family's spatial-temporal organization (Bryce, 1987; Leichter, Ahmed, Barrios, Bryce, Larsen, & Moe, 1985; Rosenblatt & Cunningham, 1976). With regard to the regulation of time, Bryce (1987) concluded that television plays a key role in the "clocking" processes of family interaction. Families that function in a *monochronic* mode engage viewing as a singular activity, emphasizing advance scheduling and purposive attention behavior, while *polychronic* families treat television as a casual, unplanned affair embedded among other concurrent activities. Thus, television is an exceptionally malleable component in the timing, tempo, and duration of events in the family microculture. The application of qualitative field methods has expanded the range of phenomena studied in this area (Lindlof & Traudt, 1983; Lindlof & Meyer, 1987).

One index of the progress in this field can be seen in the increasing specificity of family variables employed as intervening or antecedent conditions. For example, adult mediation measures—applied through such treatments as adult comments indicating approval or disapproval of televised content as the child subject views—are no longer readily accepted as a surrogate for the family. Such verbal queries, reinforcements, or commentaries on manifest content have been demonstrated to enhance children's learning (Corder-Bolz & O'Bryant, 1978; Reiser, Tessmer, & Phelps, 1984) or to provide them with defenses against advertising messages (Prasad, Rao, & Sheikh, 1978). However, there is now greater interest in how normative aspects of the child's intact family affect those and other outcomes. Forms of family mediation are now conceptualized as media use rules or norms (Lull, 1982), family communication patterns (Chaffee, McLeod, & Atkin, 1971), and disciplinary styles (Abelman, 1986). Despite concerns about the validity and reliability of operationalizations of these mediation concepts, most notably the Family Communication Pattern measures (McLeod, Fitzpatrick, Glynn, & Fallis, 1982; Tims & Masland, 1985), the interest in forms of mediation has introduced the notion that differences in family communicative environments can affect the ecologies of information found in the home.

As more complex, processual explanations of how mass media regulate or inform social action in family life have been produced, several new communication products were introduced to augment, or even supersede, the traditional media of mass communication. The term *new communications media* covers those technologies that are distinguished by one attribute: their recency. (Even here, there are equivocations: Cable television has existed almost since the beginning of network television transmission, yet the large channel capacity cable system with addressable converters and satellite interconnection with which most of us are now familiar appears to be a "new" medium.) The recency attribute, however, is not only nonspecific, it simply does not reference the features of such media which seem to be important in assessing family functioning.

Microcomputers are different from television and other mass media in a number of decisive respects which portend differences in their role in family life. First, the microcomputer's technological nature diverges quite significantly from those of the mass media by virtue of the former's programmable microprocessing features, including the ability to manipulate binary data representing almost any symbolic array and to exchange those data with other computers. While it is possible for the television viewer to program the set by also becoming a producer with the acquisition and use of additional gear, the multipurpose microcomputer is expressly designed as an instrument for the creation of virtual products by the user, some of which may be stored and worked on later. The interactivity attributed to the computer and other microprocessor-based media—evinced in its most elemental form by the prompt-and-command couplet—demands a continual focus by the user. Television, on the other hand, makes no such demands and can actually be adapted in almost ideal fashion to any level of inattention operative in the household. The characteristically solitary condition of home computing for most applications is in part a function of this focused interactivity.

Second, as Chen (1984, p. 276) has pointed out with regard to the economic impetus of each, "the demand for television has been largely a demand for entertainment, [while] usage of microcomputers is based upon more instrumental pursuits." Relations between socialization institutions (mostly schools and the church) and television have been palpably tense, if not openly combative, since the medium's introduction. In contrast, the computer has been enthusiastically welcomed by educational institutions for the instrumental tasks it performs so well, despite the effort often required of practitioners to understand its operation and how it integrates with traditional classroom objectives.

Finally, the literature on children's uses of and responses to television has not been referenced very much in the first studies of microcomputers and children. The negative effects tenor of the television studies has simply not been viewed as relevant to the concerns of computing, which have to do with such matters as motivation, learning, problem-solving skills, writing skills, peer teaching, and attitudinal orientation to computing (Chen, 1984). However, the studies that consider family mediation of computing have in fact been interested in many of the same topics as the early television-family research. Such topics as time allocation shifts, parent–child communication, and gender socialization to the medium recur in the first examples of household computing research (Dutton, Kovaric, & Steinfield, 1985).

The videocassette recorder represents a much less radical departure from the mass media model, if only because the VCR is essentially an accessory to the television set. The VCR extends to the consumer the capabilities of magnetic tape recording and playback that have long been the preserve of professional broadcast facilities. In further contrast to the computer, the VCR can operate only as a *stand-alone* unit, rather than as *networked* units, deriving from the telephone model, which retrieve, store, process, and/or send information over publicly accessible circuits or frequency bands (Baer, 1985). Networked technologies, such as interactive cable television, teletext, videotex, and microcomputers with modems, permit the household user to link with networks providing online data bases and other services, and, in some instances, linking also with modular technologies inside the home.

The stand-alone status of the VCR, however, belies certain social nuances of networking which have closely followed the product's diffusion and the concomitant development of a vast prerecorded video market. The VCR has, in effect, forced the viewer out of the household in search of the unique video product (one that cannot be obtained through time-shifting alone): the film just out of theatrical release; the obscure film that is no longer, or never was, in broadcast distribution; the collection of sports highlights that a friend has custom edited; the office party captured live on camcorder. In other words, the privatistic appeal of the VCR is more than complemented by the active strategies employed by VCR owners for servicing their desires for specific viewing occasions.

It is well substantiated that VCR ownership correlates with households rich in both traditional and advanced consumer electronics media (Gunter & Svennevig, 1987). It may be that the most salient motive that impels these households in their media adoption behavior is that of control—of product choice, of exposure opportunity, of social context. The ongoing shift away from broadcast-only television may be subtle, as Gunter and Svennevig (1987, pp. 79–80) suggest, but its significance may lie in the development of a long-term orientation to what one expects from household media:

> The new media do not seem to be completely replacing the old. The evidence suggests that displacement can occur and does so when a new medium provides the same gratifications as an old one, but in a more attractive package. . . . Children in media rich environments (usually those living with both parents) may be learning which media can satisfy certain interests and produce certain benefits best of all, and they select from among those available according to their needs at the time.

Despite the recent slowing growth rates of the VCR (Mahler, 1987) and home computer (Dutton et al., 1987), both technologies have achieved significant household penetration levels. The early microcomputer adopter profile of high levels of formal education, income, and occupational status (Dickerson & Gentry, 1983; Dutton et al., 1987; Rogers, 1985) may have broadened somewhat, but not to the same extent as the present VCR-owning population, which exceeded 65% penetration in the U.S. in 1989. Carey and Moss (1985, p. 145) argue that, in order to achieve appreciable market acceptance, a new telecommunications service "must be cost-competitive with other ways of doing things . . . must be compatible with users' skills as well as their work or home environment; and it must provide a specific service which the user values." As will be apparent later in this review, such criteria are more easily met by the VCR than the microcomputer.

The initially high adoption rate for the microcomputer was probably abetted by the transient excitement over videogames as well as the product's image as the nonpareil in-home educational technology. The attractiveness of the former use was not sufficient to sustain high purchase levels of sophisticated, multipurpose computers. The initial inadequacy of educational software may have contributed to a certain disillusionment that home microcomputing can make a demonstrable difference in children's formal learning skills. However, some recent research indicates that potential adopters' expectations of noneconomic benefit from microcomputers (in terms of savings in time and effort) may be somewhat unassociated with the perceived complexity of the technology (Hamilton & Young, 1986). Indeed, it was reported by Link Resources Corp., an information industries research firm (cited in Phillips, 1986), that the high end of the home computer product line was increasingly being used for such productivity tools as word processing, spreadsheets, and filing/storing programs, as well as for telecommunicating via modem.

It is difficult to forecast the ultimate extent to which American households will embrace communication technologies, particularly the more advanced networked types. Some observers believe that the future in household information services involves a convergence of broadcasting, print, and telephony (Pool, 1983) as well as the invention of new media forms that emphasize highly "personalizing" modes of engagement (Brand, 1987). One recent projection (Vitalari & Venkatesh, 1987) envisions a 40%–60% share of U.S. households with networked data access, retrieval, and processing capabilities by 2008. The scenario is based on the development of a responsive infrastructure consisting of such elements as adequate levels of computer literacy, standardization of software and hardware interfaces at many levels, security safeguards, easily obtained maintenance and support, and the emplacement of electronic networks.

Such projections are reminiscent of the "wired city" proposed nearly two decades ago (Sloan Commission, 1971) in its vision of a holistic information utility operated through coaxial cable communications. Incarnated as interactive cable systems in the early 1980s, the two-way facility and accompanying program services were not sufficiently compelling to be widely incorporated into the customs and needs of subscribing families. Long-range forecasting is only as valuable as the validity of its assumptions, which are necessarily based on the uncertain empirical reality of today's events. Yet, such trends as the development of storage media, like CD-ROM (Consumer Electronic, 1987), that may underpin the digital convergence of many consumer electronic products, and the formation of an aggregate public opinion favorable to the introduction of powerful communications technologies (Reese, Shoemaker, & Danielson, 1987) would seem to suggest that fundamental changes in the way consumers think about and transact information may yet be underway. It is difficult to discern high fidelity patterns from the confusion of the present, even for those whose business is to plan and evaluate marketing innovations. Clearly, though, the vitality of product demand for both home microcomputers and VCRs favors those technologies' continued development.

III. THREE RESEARCH PERSPECTIVES ON AUDIENCES OF NEW MEDIA

Before encountering the empirical work on the family and new communications media, three prominent perspectives on the role of new media in constituting audience formations and activities will be explicated. The discussion is intended to inform the reader of the kinds of conceptual categories that are applied in such studies. An underlying dimension of all three perspectives concerns the extent to which *autonomy of choice* devolves from the acquisition and use of new media. In other words, all three differ in where they situate the locus of control for information-seeking and use behavior. It should also be pointed out that all three positions draw on different scientific or critical traditions of argument, and that the data each position utilizes for support is probably not commensurable with the other positions. In that sense, each perspective functions as an ideology for its adherents, providing grounds for the exclusion of competing ideologies' evidence and conceptualizations.

A. Critical Perspective

The first perspective to be considered admits that a modest increase of individual choice may result from the diffusion of media innovations. Without concomitant changes in the political control of resources for the production and distribution of media, however, no real realignment of social relations can occur. Therefore, the human emancipatory purposes which information technology might be expected to serve are actually subverted or coopted by the control over technical standards, distribution, interconnection, and marketing exerted by the technology's corporate sponsors (Golding & Murdock, 1986; Mosco, 1982).

The critical perspective assumes that the individual audience member turns to media under the false presumption that there is freedom in the choice of sources and content. Moreover, any social actions deriving from those acts of media exposure, such as choices formulated in response to advertising appeals, are thought to be motivated by the agency of self determination. The media are thus seen as implements in the enjoyment of free domestic leisure time. Such an illusion, actively promoted by commercial media interests, makes it possible for the individual audience member to work for them without recognizing it (Jhally & Livant, 1986; Mosco, 1982; Smythe, 1977). What is produced by audience attendance is ratings data that are sold to media time buyers and advertisers. By operating under the illusion of free choice and autonomy, the individual audience member becomes effectively dispossessed of the means to understand the modes by which the media "reproduce" society's social control mechanisms. The introduction of home information technologies does not change the terms of the proposition. If anything, the proponents of this perspective view the process of getting family members to work for the sponsors of information and entertainment services as vastly more efficient through the deployment of highly interactive, involving communications products.

In somewhat different terms, Carey (1980) views the introduction of electronic information technologies in the context of an ongoing erosion of community-based public discourse. In effect, the public, originally founded in oral culture customs of dialectical persuasion, became privatized through the technical development of "public opinion" and marketing segmentation. Rather than an organic relationship of the citizen to democratic institutions, the concept of the public came to mean an aggregate of responses to political or retail options. The large-circulation, advertiser-supported newspaper, and later radio and television, atomized the functioning public through the identification of specific strata of interests. The appearance of new forms of electronic communication, Carey argues, is neither revolutionary nor particularly decisive in altering social relations. Instead, the social change potential of the technologies that he reviews—satellite transmission, cable television, text services, home satellite reception, and home video recording—is seen as determined by the corporate groups that will eventually dominate the field. Increasing channel capacity simply becomes a more effective way of differentiating and evaluating audience segments. Carey (1980, p. 43) concludes that "the new wave of innovation in communications is more of a rebellion than a revolution, more a reallocation of power than a fundamental alteration of its location, more of an intensification of long-standing patterns of audience distributions than an abrupt change in the nature of the audience."

In summary, audience forms and consciousness cannot change unilaterally through the arrival and market-positioning of a media innovation. The innovation is not value-neutral, but rather brings with it an ideological bias that represses the possibility of fundamental change. This perspective of the impact of new communications media—of the audience continuing essentially unchanged in its relationship to content producers and distributors—has been submitted as a brief in policy and institutional studies, and as a component of critical argument regarding the meanings of cultural texts. Although the perspective has prompted few user studies, the available research does suggest some points of agreement with what is empirically known about both VCR and microcomputer adoption rates and use patterns, particularly with regard to gender role alignments in families and the existence of societal access inequities. However, the tenets of this perspective regarding actual determinants of content choice and use (as well as the intentions of corporate sponsors) remain largely untested.

B. Rationalist Perspective

A second perspective on the audience proposes that new media—including those, like cable and satellite delivery systems, which are distinguished by their broadband signal carriage capacity—offer a genuine diversity of message choices, which in turn facilitates an increase in selectivity in audience exposure behavior. With the decline in effective limits on signal carriage, pluralistic program materials are more likely to emerge that will appeal to audience segments. The new environment of television, involving broadband as well as storage/replay capabilities, alters the old rules by which program strategy was oriented for large, undifferentiated audiences. The audience that selects a specialized channel from a pluralistic array is motivated by either a transitory need or interest (e.g., attendance to a weather channel) or a need that is consistently salient (e.g., replay of a video of a classic movie). In effect, the individual audience member seeks a path of least resistance: efficient search-and-use strategies are employed in order to minimize physical and cognitive expenditures in the face of increased gratification opportunities. The primary constraints on selective exposure are no longer structural, but rather those constraints inhering in the information processing limits of the individual.

New research models are being designed and tested for tracking perceived changes in user activity. Rice (1984) advocates making use of computer-monitored data generated during the course of interactions in computer-mediated communications systems as an unobtrusive method for recording real-time user behavior. Webster (1986), observing trends in the commercial utilization of new television technologies, sees the profit-making interests of program producers and distributors as driving the specialization of individual channels. (In Webster's scheme, the term *channels* references home video plays as well as program services.) In effect, programming becomes correlated with channels, much like format radio. In addition, the channels themselves are differentially available to the audience by virtue of varying cable system configurations and tiering strategies. One consequence of these developments is that audiences become polarized into extremes of use and nonuse for those channels that are highly correlated with a certain type of content. His reanalysis of ratings data confirmed that specialized content channels do appear to pull audience subsets that are not shared with the more mainstream channels.

Heeter and associates (Heeter, 1985; Heeter & Greenberg, 1985) posit that the expansion of channel availability structure on cable systems has demonstrable effects on viewer selection strategy. Following a model of cognitive information processing, channel changing behavior is assessed in terms of the exhaustiveness, elaboration, and automaticity of searches. Cable viewers are found to display particular styles, depending on how *active* or *passive* they are in the frequency of channel reevaluations, and the length of time spent with individual channels. Younger adult viewers are identified as possessing the most sophisticated information processing skills, since they "are the most aware of programming options and presumably should exhibit the best fit between preferences and needs and program exposure" (Heeter & Greenberg, 1985, p. 214).

Uses and gratifications theory has also been proposed as well suited for explaining the selectivity of new media audience behavior (Urban, 1984; Williams, Phillips, & Lum, 1985). Since uses and gratifications assumes conscious, rational analysis by the individual of mediated and interpersonal communication choices (Rubin & Rubin, 1985), it could effectively explain how viewers make choices in a pluralistic televiewing environment. The videocassette rental market, for example, would seem to be a highly appropriate arena for examining differences between media consumption and gratifications actually obtained from consumption (Palmgreen, 1984).

The rationalist perspective has been applied in studies of information selection behavior, and in studies of household activity and functions in relation to new communications media, including microcomputers. The assumption of rationalistic adaptation by the individual user to expanded and specialized viewing choices, albeit constrained by limitations of group viewing and channel selector technology (Heeter & Greenberg, 1985), would appear to be viable for investigating generic settings of selective exposure. It should be noted, however, that data collected at the level of the individual cannot be used to make inferences about the social action dynamics of the group. There also needs to be greater clarification of the thresholds and operations of conscious activity attributed to patterns of content selection (cf. Biocca, 1988).

C. Accommodation Perspective

The third perspective incorporates some conceptual aspects of the first two. Here, the media user is constituted at neither the aggregate level nor as an ideal-type individual. Instead, the user is conceptualized and studied in terms of the natural language and behavioral forms of life of which the media are observed to be constituent parts (Leichter et al., 1985; Lindlof & Meyer, 1987). The question, what is the audience, becomes relevant as an ontological concern. It can be answered only by understanding the modes of interaction and interpretation through which social actors define the relevance of media in their lives. The part of this conceptualization borrowed from the critical perspective is the interest in explaining the roots of the different levels of consciousness characteristic of audience members or users of technology. The part appropriated from the rationalist perspective consists of the interest in activeness in selectivity and content interpretation. Audience members are viewed as involved in mediated communication in order to construct a sensible world. But, essentially, the hegemonic assumption of the critical perspective is rejected, as is the assumption of individualistic rational analysis as the basis of usage decisions.

In examining media use from the accommodation perspective, a particular set of considerations about the operation of media is encountered. A first consideration is to conceive of audiences as existing in cultures, with their own rules for initiation, socialization, competence, and valuation. A second consideration is to understand the media as sets of symbols and narrative forms that function as their own culture, apart from but also partaking in the other cultures that constitute human society. When media become implicated in the arena of a culture (such as the family), interpretations of the mediated content become inflected (or systematically accented) by the norms and valuations that operate among the relations of its members. The culture accommodates the technical features, stylistic modes, and content output of a communications medium to its own purposes (Kling & Scacchi, 1980; Michaels, 1985).

The individuals constituting a family are members of an intact group with a shared social history who organize their communicative conventions partly on the basis of certain stable values (Lull, 1980; Tims, 1986). In reciprocal fashion, the medium's technical design and the modes of use that its full exploitation implies will affect, though not with uniform impact, the definitions that the family members create of its purposes and being. The social uses of those instances of mediated communication are used to define self and others in interaction (Roe & Salomonsson, 1983; Turkle, 1984). The individual cannot act as an isolable individual, but rather as a member of a social collectivity in which certain standardized media uses and meanings will be recognized.

The accommodation perspective has been operationalized in research of diverse categories of media users (but principally children; e.g., Eastman, 1986; Eastman & Agostino, 1986; Wolf, 1987) and diverse cultures (but principally families; e.g., Morley, 1986), in studying their characteristic ways of accommodating communications media. Qualitative methods have been used in recent years to elucidate the accommodation process of mass media, but with uncertain success due to some lack of agreement about protocol, reporting, and the nature of its scientific claims (Anderson, 1987). It may be that a useful conceptual innovation directly attributable to the application of qualitative methods will have to be produced before the accommodation perspective is more widely adopted.

D. Summary

The second perspective, the rationalist, has dominated in the empirical study of the family and new communications media. Therefore, most of the studies to be reviewed in the rest of this essay examine data at the level of the individual user and assume that the individual is the locus of control in the information environment. Although a discussion of the origins of this emphasis is beyond the scope of this review, the notion that media with high user-control capabilities empower the individual may be partly responsible. It is also possible that this perspective is preferred because of its perceived high scientific standards. Later in this chapter, we will return to issues involved in the limitations of these perspectives, and the possibilities of exploiting them to better effect.

IV. MICROCOMPUTING IN THE FAMILY

Part of the impetus for much of the research on home microcomputing derived from debate about its impacts on normal family interactions and household functions. These alleged impacts range from predictions that in-home learning, information retrieval, and household tasks may be radically transformed (Baer, 1985; Vail, 1980; Vitalari & Venkatesh, 1987; Wakefield, 1986) to hypotheses that such variables as sociability, achievement expectations, and new forms of affiliation based in the computing subculture will subtly change (Morrisroe, 1984; Turkle, 1984).

Another source of interest has centered on the child's contact with a computer in the home. That contact has been variously thought to engender such outcomes as high self-esteem; low self-esteem (apparently for girls only); asocial tendencies; creativity; skill-building in such areas as programming, writing, and graphic design; and academic inequities due to socioeconomic advantage or sex-role bias. It has even been speculated that children's use of computers and other technologies loosens their dependence on their parents as sources of rules and norms (Roberts, 1986). In recent years, several areas of investigation relating to household usage of computer technology have yielded an informative body of evidence. In assessing the studies, one should remember that sometimes the household is the analytic focus rather than the family, and that this distinction affects the inferences that can be validly drawn about social processes of the family. If our interest is in how microcomputing affects the communicative processes, goals, and outcomes of familial *relationships* (e.g., father–son, mother–daughter, sibling–sibling), then data analyzed at the level of household may well obscure the nature of those relational concerns.

A. Time Allocations

The extent to which acceptance of a microcomputer into the home reorganizes how time is distributed to existing activities is a salient indicator of the product's effect on family life. As Dutton et al. (1987) note, even the lowest average figure of the 6 to 17 weekly computing hours per family reported in the surveys they assessed is a nontrivial amount of time to be extracted from a week. This is particularly true when it is realized that computing is generally a solitary event and cannot be "time-shared" with other tasks. Computer-induced changes in time allocated to household activities, however, have been typically measured by retrospective self reports and may be subject to unknown reporting distortions. (A 4-year longitudinal study now underway by Venkatesh and Vitalari of the University of California-Irvine could resolve this methodological issue.) It must be stressed that the number of studies focusing on time allocation shifts are still very few, and are often based on convenience samples that cannot be considered representative of the full range of adopters.

In the most thorough study yet of postadoption changes in time allocations (Vitalari, Venkatesh, & Gronhaug, 1985), a sample of 282 computer club members reported overall decreases in television viewing, outdoor recreation, hobbies, sports, sleeping, and time spent with family following adoption of computers. (Rogers, 1985, also cites widespread television viewing decreases among Silicon Valley respondents following adoption.) Activities in which there were significant increases were time spent alone and studying/homework. In partitioning for number of children in the family, a nonlinear pattern emerged: families without children showed the least change; families with one child, however, showed the greatest disruption across most activities, compared with families with two or more children. Length of ownership also affected time allocation, with respondents who had no computing experience before adoption reporting significantly larger decreases in televiewing, leisure time with family, leisure time with friends, reading, outdoor recreation, and sleeping, and a significant increase in studying/homework.

Vitalari et al. (1985) proposed a homeostatic model in which short-term perturbations in time spent on important activities, especially within the home, do occur but soon modulate due to increasing adaptation. Cognate activities (e.g., television, hobbies, and reading) would be affected the most since they would be partially displaced by computing. It was speculated that long-term, cumulative changes in time allocations could be significant.

The few data available indicate that microcomputer use does not seem to increase over time, but neither is complete discontinuance typical. The most probable pattern is a slight decline in time spent using the computer, perhaps because the product's novelty fades (Dutton et al., 1987; Mitchell, 1985). Trend data reported by Link Resources Corp. offer indirect support for this pattern, with declines of daily computer use in consecutive samples over 1984 to 1986 (cited in Phillips, 1986). Unfortunately, there are no data demonstrating the methods by which family members manage their computer use over the course of a discrete period of time—e.g., by devising either ad hoc or informally codified rules for turn taking among family members. Such time series data might account for the sources of use decreases over the tenure of computer ownership. It may be that increasing sophistication in using applications programs, as well as greater competency in managing computing in the midst of other household responsibilities, might reduce the time devoted to computing without really reducing dependency on computing itself. Such factors as the availability of workplace microcomputers, the addition of peripherals with faster access and greater storage, and changes in family composition should also be investigated in that regard. The imprecision of the "novelty fade" explanation demands a more ecological and multivariate approach to the problem.

B. Software Usage Practices

As the quintessential multifunctional information technology, the types and rankings of microcomputer uses found in any given family depend on a variety of key factors, including: capabilities of the system, previous knowledge and training in computing, number and ages of children with computing interests, membership in computer clubs, other personal and mediated information sources, and compatibility of the system with work-related tasks.

Perhaps not surprisingly, use patterns are critically dependent on which members of the family report on their home computing. Watkins and Brimm (1985) studied the "media environments" of a suburban Michigan community, with some specific questions for the computer-owning respondents who comprised

7% of the 607 completed interviews. Computer-owning children under 12 years of age ranked their computer uses as education and games; children over 12 preferred education, programming, and games, in that order. On the other hand, the computer-owning adult subsample ranked their uses in order as games, work, finances, education, and programming (with no gender differences). These differences are substantially similar for other reported studies. Word processing (or text editing), however, does constitute a major portion of use for other adult samples (Caron, Giroux, & Douzou, 1985; Phillips, 1986; Rogers, 1985; Vitalari et al., 1985). There are indications that word processing has been growing in recent years as a household computer activity, although all forms of entertainment/game use continue to rank high. Children's uses of multipurpose microcomputers, as opposed to the less complex systems, tend to coalesce around school-related tasks (e.g., word processing, drill-and-practice programs, BASIC programming), graphics, and entertainment, with telecommunicating via modem used intensively by a small number of older children at home (Carey & Gall, 1986; Haefner, Hunter, & Wartella, 1986).

It is interesting that such utilitarian software as home budgeting/management, personal finance, and other home-related functions rank relatively low (Dutton et al., 1987). Any time savings that those applications produce, itself a questionable proposition, would not necessarily reduce the overall time devoted to household-related tasks. This speculation derives from historical analyses indicating that technological advances in automating household tasks do not result in less time devoted to housework (Arnold, 1985; Cowan, 1976). In fact, any time saved through mechanization is apparently moved to other tasks to be executed by "the only unspecialized worker left in America" (Cowan, 1976, p. 23), the female head of household. In other words, "housework is not so much a clearly defined set of tasks as the sum of the jobs *not* done by husbands and children" (Arnold, 1985). This implication is relevant to the relational outcomes of home computing. The automation of certain clerical functions, which most microcomputers are quite capable of accomplishing, is unlikely to cause any shift of gender-assigned work or re-allocations of time for work or leisure. Particularly for female users, computing is unlikely to result in the liberation of time for the self.

The survey studies under review did not attempt to categorize users in terms of predominant computing style or orientation. In their theoretical analysis of receptivity conditions for households' interfaces with technology, however, Venkatesh and Vitalari (1984) propose three dimensions by which a technology's attributes can be assessed for adoption: instrumental/expressive, passive/active, and task-oriented/pleasure-oriented. Using the matrix, it is presumably possible to conceptualize a family's likely compatibility with specific kinds of computer hardware and software applications. In her analysis of ethnographic data for 16 families, Tinnell (1985) categorizes users as either Addict (one who "gets lost" in computing), Dabbler (whose use is light and selective, but "devoted"), or Applicationist (whose orientation is narrowly instrumentalist). These categories were inductively developed from unstructured verbal self-descriptions, and should not be considered personality assessments in any theoretical or clinical sense. But, as Tinnell observed, the behavioral correlates of these user types were consistent with traditional gender roles: the husbands in the Addict and Dabbler groups, and the wives in the Applicationist group, expressed guilt about their involvement with computing. Beyond this effort, no attempt has been made at defining typologies of user profiles that are related to family roles. By contrast, Turkle's (1984) descriptions of identity expression in microcomputer manipulation, based on depth interviews and analysis of computing-related artifacts, are convincing, richly textured case studies. Turkle also provides ample evidence of the specific products of her participants' computing arts, including descriptions of the programs' stylistic features, how they connect with formal academic or conceptual domains, and their etiology in the computing subcultures. All of this suggests that computer use in the family extends beyond the category of generic activity (e.g., word processing). Perhaps there should be more explicit attention to the way that family members compute, and the manner in which outcomes (printout, banner, screen display, game result, etc.) become implicated in normal family processes. In other words, family-related manifestations or outcomes of computing could define the categories of usage, instead of the labels of program type.

C. Relational Communication

Other than measures of isolation/sociability, most quantitative studies of microcomputer owners have not assessed the effects of the technology and its use patterns on such areas as family communication, behavioral interaction patterns, or marital satisfaction. In line with findings cited above, owners tend to report somewhat more time spent alone and less time with friends and family members (Dutton et al., 1987). To understand the difficulty of drawing meaningful inferences from such data, one needs to go no further than Venkatesh and Vitalari's (1984, p. 198) statement that, "because 95 percent of the users [in the Orange County study] are predominantly male and in families with children, it appears that the computer is creating opportunities for the father to interact with his children." It is quite possible, however, that males' interest in, and uses of, home computing may have the effect of reducing the incidence of shared family activity. Despite the authors' otherwise excellent analyses, the warrant for their claim is not supported by relevant data.

For insights into the relational effects of home computing, qualitative research projects and open-ended survey responses provide the only useful guidance at this point. With the husband often leading in making the purchase decision and dominating in subsequent use, misunderstandings, conflicts, and overt frustrations between spouses are a frequent theme of the reports (Ferrari, Klingzing, Paris, Morris, & Eyman, 1985; Rogers, 1985; Tinnell, 1985). The major source of these effects seems to be the wife's dissatisfaction with the time the husband spends alone in computing. There is an almost total lack of systematic data on such conflicted situations and messages regarding computer use. This is particularly unfortunate, since gender role socialization regarding computer competence may partly originate in family orientations to the technology (see next section); young females' observations of spousal stress induced by a computer use regimen may affect their own disposition toward computing.

On the other hand, there is evidence that in computer-owning families parents actively support their older children's efforts at understanding computers (Krendl, Gantz, & Fitzmaurice, 1986). Actual computer-centered family conviviality is reported mainly in instances of arcade-style game use (Mitchell, 1985; Haefner et al., 1986). Although these gaming episodes are mostly characterized by male participation in games with masculine-oriented themes or objectives, Mitchell's longitudinal study of 23 families does document instances of heightened father–daughter interaction and enjoyment. The following capsule descriptions provide brief glimpses of video games' centripetal effects in two families:

> The records from [one] family show the mother and father playing together late in the evening, competing against each other with scores going higher and higher as the weeks progressed.
>
> A non-employed mother of three teenage girls viewed the videogames as a revolution in family life. The game set, attached to the television in the family living room, provided a focal point for family interaction. While this mother did not play often herself, all family members confirmed that they were talking with each other more, competing in a friendly way, appreciating the tactics and skill shown by other family members, and generally having more fun together as a family than they had ever known. (Mitchell, 1985, p. 126)

Evidence that children (again, mostly boys) engage their peers and siblings in gaming and more instrumental pursuits, especially when the machine is privately accessible (Creasey & Myers, 1986; Mitchell, 1985), calls into question the popular idea that engagement with computers fosters isolation, or dysfunctional communication syndromes like reticence. However, even parents who purchase microcomputers sometimes fear that their children will become "hooked on" computers, displacing more obviously sociable activities (Giacquinta, Ely, & Smith-Burke, 1984). Mitchell's study did find that only children spent a greater amount of time alone in video-game playing than did children with siblings. Since only children are indistinguishable from or surpass nononly children in nearly all developmental outcomes (Falbo & Polit, 1986), corroboration of a finding of greater "isolation" of only children with home computers should not be taken as a sign of deprivation. Interestingly, Mitchell found that boys in all-boy families spent about half their video-game time playing alone, while girls in all-girl families played alone only about 8% of the time; the author concluded that "boys tend to find time to practice on their skills when they were not playing in family competition. Girls tended not to find or take time to practice alone" (p. 132). Chen (1987) also found that high school boys encouraged other boys' computer use to a much greater extent than high school girls, while the girls reported a higher percentage of computer-knowledgeable mothers than did boys. Chen concluded that this same-sex orientation to social affiliation involving computers seems to replicate a more general socializing role of gender-separate cultures (Maccoby, 1986). These findings may therefore indicate differential "natural" skill levels such that, for boys, the most important goal in computer games is winning, while for girls, competitive computer interaction with friends need not lead to individualistic winning to be considered fulfilling.

As Ferrari et al. (1985, p. 43) observe, "it seems . . . plausible that part of the computer's influence on family communication may be to clarify and/or magnify one subsystem within the family (e.g., father–son, marital subsystem, siblings) while isolating others." There is a need for more substantial research of these important computer-related interactional processes. A less impressionistic approach to qualitative studies would contribute more to an understanding of the gender-based and situational determinants of computing in family subsystems.

D. Child Socialization

The socialization issue that has received the most attention, indicated in a modest but growing empirical literature, is that of a gender differential in home computer access and use. In part, this awareness is due to the increasingly widespread utilization of microcomputer technology by elementary and secondary schools as both a method and subject of instruction. The day that the learning of at least some computing skills becomes a common experience for nearly all American children is fast approaching.

This circumstance has ramifications for the role of home computing. A first consideration concerns the extent to which early computing experience "prepares" a child for competency in particular school subjects. More precisely, there is an interest in identifying the home environmental components with regard to computer access that contribute to academic competencies. Second, there is ample evidence that children's interactions with microcomputers in school and camp settings often entail cooperative problem solving and creative exploration with groups of peers (Daiute, 1985; Diem, 1985; Eastman & Agostino, 1986; Ferrari et al., 1985; Lieberman, 1985). These positive contacts with computing may have an effect, perhaps a stimulative one, on children's propensity for computer use at home. The social milieu of computing that young girls encounter in the home may be decisive for the nature of their expectations for occupational selection and advancement, but also more proximally, for achievements in such academic areas as programming, science, mathematics, and computer-aided writing and graphics. Two questions arise from this discussion. First, *is* there a gender differential in girls' attitudes, uses, and performance levels in school computing? If such a differential exists, what part can be attributed to home computing environments and experiences?

A brief summary addressing the first question will have to suffice. Young children in general show little anxiety in their first computing encounters, but gender differences regarding microcomputers do appear by the onset of adolescence in both home and school settings (Lockheed, 1985). However, the degree of difference seems to depend on the kind of computer application. Girls generally express more anxiety (Chen, 1986), less enthusiasm (Krendl et al., 1986; however, see Chen, 1986), more negative sex-typing (Wilder, Mackie, & Cooper, 1985) and more difficulty in using computers (Hawkins, 1985; Krendl et al., 1986; Williams, Coulombe, & Lievrouw, 1983). Girls are greatly outnumbered by boys in computer-camp enrollments, with the enrollment ratios widening with advancing grade level, curriculum difficulty, and tuition cost (Hess & Miura, 1985). Eastman and Krendl (1987) do report that structured computing experiences can reduce both boys' and girls' preexisting sex-typed attitudes about computers and gender role to a relatively low level, and with nonsignificant difference for sex. Similarly, after applying controls for amount of formal and informal computer experience, Chen (1986) found no differences between male and female high school students' reported interest in and attraction towards computers.

Girls typically report less access than boys to computer technology at home (Chen, 1986; Fetler, 1985), less weekly use of home computers (Chen, 1986), as well as less attendance than boys at community video arcades (Fetler, 1985; Lin & Lepper, 1987), where initial contacts with electronic interactivity may be experienced and mutually reinforced with peers (Wigand, Borstelmann, & Boster, 1986). Indeed, as alluded to in the previous section, the greater propensity of boys to involve computing activity in their friendship networks probably carries over to computing opportunities in the home and at school (Chen, 1986, 1987). Boys seem to be more positively disposed than girls to home computers, in relation to other household media (Haefner et al., 1986). However, Krendl et al. (1986) found that parents' computer attitudes and activities do not seem to contribute significantly to their adolescent children's orientations as differentiated by gender, even with the fathers reporting more experience and more comfort with computers than the mothers. Even in families for whom educational microcomputing is important, ambivalence over the degree of "partnership" to encourage may be manifested in several kinds of parental response (Giacquinta et al., 1984, p. 10): "Those who 'stand over' their children and give direction; those who 'stand by' their children in case they need help or direction; those [who] 'stand by wringing their hands' hoping things will work out; and those [who] simply 'stand aside,' allowing their children maximum leeway to do what they want."

Despite inconclusive evidence about the family origins of attitudinal formation about computing, the case for family practices positively affecting other early schooling outcomes is convincing. Several family variables have been identified as predicting achievement in reading performance, including value placed on literacy, parents' press for achievement in reading, availability of reading and writing material, parents' reading with children, and children's opportunities for verbal interaction with parents (Hess & Holloway, 1984). *Computing* could be transposed in those statements to obtain a short inventory of social practices in the home that might enhance girls' interests and self esteem regarding computers.

As a first approximation to the specific nature of parental involvement, one can consider the accounts of parents and children in households in which educational computing is emphasized. For example, it is clear from a qualitative study (Giacquinta et al., 1984) that, in cases where the computer has been delegated a role in supplementing the child's education, parents and children often share a common ideology regarding the value of such activities as programming skills and telecommunicating. The following fieldnote from that study illustrates the level of involvement demanded by such parents, and its effect on the child's orientation to schoolwork:

> "Mother [explained] that Daughter practices her reading and mathematics lessons [on the computer] . . . and that the lessons on the disk are similar to the material that she is doing in school. I asked, 'How do you know what work Daughter is doing in school?' Mother replied, I know exactly what each of them (meaning Daughter and Son) are doing in school because I make it my business to know! She continued on and explained that prior to purchasing the software, she met with each of their teachers and obtained the information relative to their curriculum in mathematics, reading and spelling . . ."
>
> In a later field visit, the researcher asked the daughter about her feelings toward the things her mother had her doing on the micro at home:
>
> "She described that the program that her mother had obtained on math and reading was good and it seemed to help her in her classwork. I asked her to detail exactly how the software material helped her . . . She said, 'Well, for one thing, I am always ready in class because I practice at home.' She also indicated that she likes to be at the top of her class because some kids come to depend upon her for help." (p. 14)

Mutual support in the issue of computer competence—manifested in markedly high self concept of the child—may itself be a significant form of family cohesion. Parent–child or peer interactions with the computer as a co-orienting focus may also have unintended consequences for how children communicate, as indicated in observations of their utilization of "precise" language for instructing peers (Ferrari et al., 1985, p. 54).

Chen (1986) has pointed out that the low rate of computer activity noted for girls, particularly in such exploratory and quasiscientific uses as programming, seems to indicate "willingness to engage such experiences" as a potential mitigating factor. One could profitably study the intrafamily practices and ideologies that correlate with different levels of self-concept and competency among high and low computer-using females. It is conceivable that computer-using parents constitute compelling models for daughters, and that reverse-modeling (i.e., parents adopting computer-using patterns from their children) may occur more often with male children, given their typically greater involvement in social networks where computers and videogames are implicated. It is also conceivable that the decision to purchase a microcomputer in the first place may be based in large part on the gender, and thus the attributed interests, of the family's children. The distribution of use and decision making regarding home computer access may therefore be associated with modes of family communication, similar to family television use (Chaffee & Tims, 1976). But with computing so closely connected with the content domains and expectations of schools and peer networks, the contribution of the family group to gender differentials of attitudes toward and competency with computers is a difficult question that requires much additional study, preferably longitudinal.

V. THE VCR IN THE FAMILY

In discussions of how to regard the VCR, ambivalence is sometimes expressed about how *revolutionary* the phenomenon actually is. Levy (1987) believes that the VCR is indeed an "important" change in the television landscape, though concedes that only further research can reveal *how* important it is. Putting aside the issue that researchers themselves are in a position to place a topic high on the importance scale (which Levy recognizes), the ambivalence hinges to some degree on whether the changes in family television use that the VCR has wrought are primarily quantitative or qualitative. Does the VCR result in simply more hours of viewing and more control of choice, or does the VCR evoke different patterns of usage, family communication, and socialization?

A. Time Allocations

Recent data indicate that the addition of VCR's in households results in increased overall viewing: a daily average of 7 hours and 4 minutes in non-VCR households, compared to a daily average of 7 hours and 25 minutes in VCR households, according to the Television Bureau of Advertising (cited in "More TV," 1987). The typical VCR household appears to be a relatively media-rich environment, being significantly more likely to also have a computer, cable access, premium channels, and several television receivers (Greenberg & Heeter, 1987). (For example, in 1985, the ELRA Group estimated VCR penetration to be 41% in cable homes and 31% in nonsubscribing homes passed by cable; cited in "Audience Outlook," 1986.) Since VCR households are more likely to be cable subscribers, and cable households also view more on average than noncable households, the independent effect of the VCR is difficult to discern. There is no reason to believe, however, that VCR adoption would not also increase viewing in cable-subscribing families.

Harvey and Rothe's (1985/1986) study of 745 VCR owners found that, in addition to increasing overall viewing time, the adoption of a VCR seems to increase time allocated to entertaining at home and time spent with family. They noted a large decrease for moviegoing and slighter decreases for frequency of eating out, time spent reading, and time spent on hobbies. Since the study did not measure the magnitude of the increases or decreases, or utilize significance tests, it is difficult to assess the meanings of the reported changes. A study of adolescents (Greenberg & Heeter, 1987) found that VCR ownership was associated with higher levels of movie viewing of all types (including in theaters), group viewing, print media reading, school activity participation, and dating behavior (although these comparisons with non-VCR adolescents cannot be attributed to the effect of VCR adoption). In a study of 485 video club members, Donohue and Henke (1985) found moviegoing to suffer a dramatic decline following VCR adoption. Viewing choices that declined after adoption included news and regularly scheduled network programs and movies; choices that increased were premium cable channels, sports events, network specials, mini series, and adult or X-rated movies.

In general, it may be concluded that the VCR does negatively affect some out-of-home activity associated with entertainment (especially such cognate activities as moviegoing). However, the social function that moviegoing serves for adolescents apparently persists despite the VCR. The reported increases in time spent with family and group televiewing call for more precise specification of group composition, activity type, and level of interaction. It is likely that, over time, families develop rule-like occasions for renting or viewing time-shifted material in the presence of certain family members. It would also be desirable to use time-logging techniques. Using such an approach, for example, Timmer, Eccles, and O'Brien (1985) found differences in the viewing time of children of employed mothers versus children of full-time homemaker mothers, as well as differences in children's viewing time as a function of the gender of the parent. Examining the effects of the VCR on time allocation in a similar analytic scheme could yield interesting conclusions regarding the issue of whether the VCR augmentation induces qualitative changes in person-and-family interactional variables.

B. Content Usage Patterns

Previous research of VCR behavior has focused on the displacement effects of VCR introduction on content preferences and the distributions of such practices as time-shifting and library building (Agostino & Zenaty, 1980; Beville, 1986;

Donohue & Henke, 1985; Harvey & Rothe, 1985/1986; Levy, 1980, 1983; Levy & Fink, 1984). The general conclusion of most of this research is that the use of the VCR for rather immediate demands, such as time-shifting because of absence from the household or conflicting real-time program choices, outweighs other more long-term uses. Donohue and Henke (1985, p. 12) state that "taping is a somewhat self-indulgent activity whose purposes are immediate gratification and not archival in nature as people place low priorities on building libraries, taping for others or chronicling news events."

The multifunctionality of the VCR is apparent in the range of both content uses and technical features that are available. Assembling findings from several sources (Donohue & Henke, 1985; Greenberg & Heeter, 1987; Harvey & Rothe, 1985/1986), the ranges of the various content uses can be grouped in terms of their importance for family purposes. The *most important* uses include: (a) recording one program while watching another; (b) recording a program while away from home or while engaged in another activity; and (c) viewing pre-recorded rental tapes. VCR uses that can be categorized as *somewhat important* are (a) recording programs for children; (b) recording and viewing events with own camera; and (c) archiving major sports events for later viewing. The *less important* uses include: (a) archiving major news events; (b) recording programs or movies for friends; (c) purchasing prerecorded tapes; and (d) archiving favorite regular programs.

The uses in the "very important" category tend to be somewhat universalistic among VCR owning families. The uses in the "somewhat important" category are much more dependent on the specific interests and composition of individual families; to a lesser extent, this is also true of the uses grouped as "less important." In order to examine the demographic correlates of prominent VCR uses, Rubin and Bantz (1987) performed canonical correlations between a set of demographic and media experience variables and a set of VCR-use motives. Three canonical roots were obtained, indicating the following relationships: (a) younger females, who frequently use VCRs to store and play back music videos, view exercise tapes, and use videos for socializing, time shifting, and critical viewing; (b) younger males, who use VCRs to socialize, watch music videos, and critically view prerecorded programs; and (c) older males with lower incomes, using VCRs frequently to time-shift and to view more critically, but not to socialize. These findings indicate a high degree of intentionality, selectivity, and utility on the part of VCR users. One can conclude from this study that the significance of the VCR's role is partly dependent on lifestyle and life span position.

Among the program types that are time-shifted the most are daytime soap operas (Donohue & Henke, 1985; Greenberg & Heeter, 1987). The soap opera often airs when individuals are out of the household or are unable to devote complete attention to the program at its scheduled airing time. It has been observed in qualitative studies that women are not only the primary tapers and ultimate audience of this material, but will often view the recorded program at a later time under solitary circumstances (Lindlof, Shatzer, & Wilkinson, 1988; Morley, 1986). The dominance of VCR and program choice control by males in many families during the evening period appears to confine female viewing of taped programs, especially soap operas and related female-targeted programming, to those times of day when no VCR-viewing conflicts are likely. This pattern of attendance is consistent with other gender-related orientations to the operations and uses of television.

Among the technical features available on nearly all VCR models that afford great control over the presentation of taped content are the pause function (which allows *zapping,* or commercial break deletion during taping), and the visual-scan fast-forward function (which allows the viewer to *zip* quickly and quietly through a commercial break in previously recorded material). Both of these features, particularly the latter, are executed much more easily with a remote control device. Donohue and Henke (1985) found that 37% of the overall survey sample engaged in occasional zapping, while 68% of all those who tape programs off-air engage in zipping. Although the frequency of those acts was not ascertained, the authors' determination that younger viewers, even children, were the more active zipping viewers in families has implications for control of the VCR-augmented set in such families. (As noted in Heeter and Greenberg's, 1985, review, remote control users are more likely to engage in frequent reevaluations of programming and more extensive orienting searches of channels; certainly, the remote control should facilitate active channel-changing and channel-sampling *between* zapping opportunities while recording.) These data also imply that the altering of recorded content, and the tactical use of the remote control/visual scan capability to circumvent advertising exposure, may become an accepted viewing practice in some American households. Although there is some indication that male family members are more prone than females to use the remote control (Morley, 1986), more study on the hierarchy of competence and implementation among family members of the VCR's technical features, as it influences use, needs to be done.

C. Relational Communication

The VCR is thought to have consequences for the place of the individual in social formations (Levy, 1987). One area in which some evidence converges is the manner in which the VCR may amplify patterns of gender-related power relations in the family. In the Donohue and Henke (1985) survey, the male head of household was reported as the dominant household decision maker in playing back tapes, although the female head of household ranked a relatively close second in taping decisions. Harvey and Rothe (1985/1986) found that the male head of household maintained the most important role in all phases of VCR purchasing.

Morley (1986) conducted depth interviews with members of 18 British families to investigate the domestic origins of television content decoding patterns.

The interview accounts yielded a consistent portrayal of male viewing preferences, male television-related talk, and male leisure time taking precedence in
nearly all the families. The female respondents, particularly the households'
wives, spoke of viewing their favorite programs—typically soap opera and other
dramatic programs—in the absence of company. Each of the 18 families had a
VCR, and most also had remote control capability, giving Morley the opportunity to examine the social dynamics of video use in those family situations. He
found that the VCR and remote control were operated in terms of the gender
differentiation identified in other areas of television decision making and attendance. The women exhibited little interest for operating the VCR, and this
aversion was interpreted by many of the men as a lack of understanding of
technological matters. A participant observation study of six families possessing
VCRs conducted by Lindlof et al. (1988) largely confirms Morley's conclusions.
In general, each family observed a "satisficing" approach to the use of the VCR
in that the learning of the machine's technical features advanced only to the point
that the original purchasing motives were satisfied. Most of the women's uses
were minimal, and several mentioned difficulty in overcoming a reluctance to
learn such aspects as programming channel recording.

Interest in the effects of the VCR on relational communication has also centered on the possible encouragement of "privatistic behavior" (Levy, 1987, p.
467). In other words, the VCR's capability to mediate program choice conflicts
by time-shifting may lead to an individualistic mode of reception. The findings
on this issue are mixed. Gunter and Levy (1987) discovered that British VCR
households reported higher percentages of viewing alone when playing back
tapes as opposed to watching off-air television programming. On the other hand,
adolescents with VCR access report more viewing with friends (Greenberg &
Heeter, 1987). Although the Lindlof et al. study (1988) did not include aggregate
measures of group and self VCR viewing, both observer and respondent reports
indicate a great range of viewing participation, even within individual families;
in particular, family members would view with friends and relatives on prear-
ranged occasions for such video materials as taped family events, major sporting
events, and soap operas. It is apparent that the VCR is a powerful technology, not
just in terms of objective technical capabilities, but also for altering and recon-
stituting joint acts for family members. Control is more accurately defined in
family-action terms: It is what family members do with the VCR in accomplishing any number of goals. The inventory of uses and goals observed in, or
reported by, these families was impressively varied. Many of the family members, when queried about their reasons for purchasing the VCR or their reasons
for using it, mentioned applications that related directly to control over content
selection, content exposure, or their social environment.

This "control" motif emerged through references to individualistic need or
interest while many of the observed uses of the VCR showed evidence of *accommodative structures* operating in family subsystems. Because the VCR-augmented set was often located in an open access area of the family homes,

intended for whole family use, the kinds of maximal control that the machine could potentially offer an individual—e.g., playing back recorded programs, rewinding and viewing for close analysis, zipping through unwanted program parts—typically occurred only by invoking some interpersonal methods, usually tacit, for making use decisions.

As an example of accommodative structures at work, in two families an R-rated movie (either a rented tape or a program time-shifted from a premium channel) would often be scheduled later in the evening, mostly when the wife was free from household activities to devote her complete attention to it and when she and her husband could relax together without distraction. In one of the families, the older children would be upstairs at that time (where their own television was in use). The movie would not start until they were securely there for the duration of the evening. In both families, the youngest children, aged 3 and 5, respectively, could and did wander through the viewing area of the family room while the parents viewed those movies. The inference was that whatever morally problematic acts might appear would not be understood by them.

For more than one family, the VCR caused revisions in the manner by which the older children negotiated viewing access. Specifically, the capability of the VCR to record a program away from the children's physical presence, either by programming or by a parent monitoring a taping session, meant that the children could make a request for any program. The parents would typically design a structure (i.e., decision rules plus account, or moral warrant) that would allow such an extension of the children's viewing control without disrupting either the parents' viewing perquisites or the overall family ideology. In one family, the mother mentioned that it was her perception that television viewing during the Christmas holiday period became more polarized; with the shopping and other activities, there was less viewing, but the special programs scheduled during that period made the television they did watch more important. She referred to a tape-now-watch-later rule stipulating that, if a program aired after the children's bedtime, it would be taped and watched later. For another family, the mother taped a variety of programs for the children on a "standing order" basis, both because their bedtimes did not permit the children viewing them at the scheduled hour and because she performed nearly all the family's recording.

It should be noted that the accommodation of the VCR was not always successfully accomplished, in that the communicative efforts of family members were not sufficient to resolve conflicting purposes. In one family, the husband's desire to view the cable news channel (on what he considered to be his television) was continually thwarted by the interests of other family members to use the set's VCR for playing back material. In another family, the viewing styles of the husband and wife sharply conflicted over the use of the VCR; she enjoyed playing back her favorite programs more than once (she compared this style to "playing albums"), while her husband expressed distaste for seeing the same program more than once.

The dialectic of control and accommodation is differently manifested according to how the family's dominant constructions of reality specify access rights to media. Bochner and Eisenberg's (1987, p. 547) description of the constructivist view of family process is relevant here:

> Ordinarily, an individual's sense of belonging to a particular family is tied to the reality-organizing structures shared by family members. These structures constitute a "family ideology," a set of belief-oriented constructs that are recursively tied to the family's interaction patterns. *The interaction patterns evolve from the family's ideology and reinforce it.* (emphasis in original)

Although these findings represent only a part of the evidential coherence for VCR incorporation in family life represented in the ethnographic arguments (Lindlof et al., 1988; Lindlof & Shatzer, in press), it is apparent that, regardless of its technical control capabilities, the VCR is in a sense captured by prevailing modes of family interaction. At the same time, though, the extensions of television use afforded by the VCR do in fact exert changes in such matters as the timing, duration, and quality of interactions.

D. Child Socialization

In terms of overt parental mediation of child viewing, there seem to be only slight differences attributable to the presence of a VCR. Kim, Baran, and Massey (1988) interviewed 110 parents and 110 children in their homes in order to assess differences in responses to questions about control of the viewing situation, VCR control, and family perceptions of viewing. Both parents and children answered that they decided together about which movies to rent approximately half the time; according to parents' responses, children had the smallest degree of individual influence on rental decisions. Both children and parents substantially agree that the communicative environment of viewing had not changed with VCR adoption, although the children reported much less viewing with parents than did the latter when tapes rented expressly for the children were played. Differences between the VCR and broadcast television as resources for parental disciplinary intervention were minimal. Parental prescreening of children's movies was rated as low, although parents reported somewhat greater levels of prescreening of their own tapes before letting children view them; the number of children was positively correlated with the frequency of prescreening of videos rented for children. In Greenberg and Heeter's (1987) study of adolescent VCR usage, no increased parental efforts at mediating or controlling VCR exposure was evident.

The manner in which children become acculturated to the content codes and the social placement of television viewing qua family activity may be fundamentally altered by the experience of growing up with the VCR. At one level, there is the matter of having unprecedented, albeit perhaps inadvertent, access to depictions of complex moral behavior. As is evident from the summary of the ethnography presented above, as well as from other interpretive research (e.g., Traudt & Lont, 1987, p. 152), parents interested in viewing taped material that would be restricted from broadcast channels typically develop accounts that justify such usage in the presence of young children. Adolescents in VCR households are apparently exposed to more R-rated films and a marginally higher number of televised sexual acts and references (Greenberg & Heeter, 1987). An interest in renting, purchasing, and/or exchanging videos featuring scandalous violent or sexual themes, including those produced for musical performances, may form part of the basis for subcultural group ties (Roe & Salomonsson, 1983; Roe, 1987). At present, almost nothing is known about patterns of purchase and rental of video materials by young people, much less their actual exposure patterns. There is clearly a need for such data as well as for information about situated uses of video in peer groups.

Finally, the effects of specific practices of VCR usage on cognitive skills of children merits further empirical study. In the study of six VCR-owning families (Lindlof et al., 1988), the research team observed a phenomenon across all of the families with very young children (ages ranging from 3 to 6) in which multiple playbacks of individual taped programs would be requested and granted by the parents. The attention levels observed during such playback occasions, and also as reported by parents, were very high, even when the program had been viewed as many as 10 times by the child. The children would often predict and speak lines of dialogue as they were emitted by program characters, sing songs simultaneously with the program's soundtrack, and even rewind or fast-forward to parts of the program that they preferred. The implications for children's operational and interpretive competencies resulting from a pragmatic grasp of VCR functions are potentially significant for their cognitive development. It is conceivable that their schematic representation of story events, and their integration of complete stories, could be enhanced by being able to experience and control multiple viewings of individual programs. The events of VCR-induced response by children described here, however, do not occur de novo. Family-level definitions of the VCR phenomenon, expressed as practices that observe rule-like enactments (Lull, 1982), probably offer "zone of proximal development" requirements (Vygotsky, 1978)[2] for a child's recall and performance achievements. In other words, VCR use situations must be structured with the proper interactional inducements, all of which are conveyed in ways that are understandable

---

[2] Len Vygotsky's "zone of proximal development" concept refers to the gap that may exist for a child at a given time between his or her level of performance on some task and his or her potential for performing at a higher level of ability when assisted by someone's instruction. This and related concepts of Vygotsky's form a social constructionist alternative to Piaget's essentially biological explanation of cognitive development. The Vygotskian approach allows an expanded role for the child's communicative competence, and has been applied in such projects as narrative recognition and comparison in child psychotherapy (Russell & van den Broek, in press).

and salient to the child. Examination of how those situations come to be structured by parents and other family members, and whether they do in fact instigate certain competencies in children, is a research priority.

VI. CONCLUSION

This section contains some prescriptive statements for addressing lacunae in our present state of knowledge regarding new communications media as part of the family setting. It should be evident by now, however, that much of the agenda has already been articulated in this review. Most of the areas covered in the sections on the VCR and the microcomputer were leavened with critiques and calls for future investigation. That leaves this conclusion section, then, for remarks that may or may not possess immediate potential for operationalization, but that may be useful for long-term thinking about technology and families.

A. Getting Out of the Family in Order to Know the Family Better

While the household unit is the logical research site for investigating the family processes involving new media (hardware and software), there are characteristics of these media that call that approach into question. One notices that both the microcomputer and the VCR are household nodes for inflows and outflows of information and goods in a much more explicit way than the stand-alone broadcast media. This is overtly true in the economic sense. Not only the media treated here, but other new media in development such as videotex and teletext, *demand* the household user to state preferences and make transactions in order to conduct ordinary business through the system (Borgman, 1982; Henke & Donohue, 1986; Urbany & Talarzyk, 1983). But this proposition is also true in the sense that specific ways of organizing social action and ideas about the uses of those media overlap the bounds of the household. The microcomputer has spawned computer clubs, software copying and pirating, software inventions and improvisations, bulletin boards, special interest groups, and other forms of networking. Some similar VCR phenomena include tape trading, tape copying and pirating, customized editing and archiving, and special group viewing occasions. Several observers, noting these developments, have called for intensive study of the subcultural elements of media use (Brown, 1985; Morley, 1983), or "interpretive communities" (Jensen, 1987; Lindlof, 1988) in which media user activity is seen as constituted by formations of meanings and social actions. The study of networks of social relationships could be facilitated by examining the meanings they propagate and negotiate (Fine & Kleinman, 1983).

In other words, these new media may involve people in many other ways than just their family roles. However, paradoxically, in order to fully understand their family rules, it may be necessary to inquire about how household media are used by people to connect with constituencies outside the family itself.

B. Returning "Communication" to the Study of New Media and Families

Earlier in this review, it was claimed that the study of the family's interaction with mass media had recently attained a methodological and conceptual sophistication. The family's ways of managing television qua symbolic and commodity-like resource—via such constructs as rules, norms, disciplinary styles, and even ethnomethods—are now seen as a central part of its self-expression. Moreover, those family expressions of "doing television" possess both stability and developmental change over time. It is therefore important that television viewing is conceived within a framework of family communication.

Why has this framework not been widely applied to the case of new media? In some studies, the unit of analysis has been the household; in others, family differences in new media variables have been attributable to measures of family composition, or measures of time spent with media or other activities. With few exceptions, the communicative action of the family and its subsystems—whether studied by self report, diagnostic testing, controlled observation, or naturalistic observation—has not been a critical focus. Yet it is apparent from this review that a great deal of the explanatory potential for answering important questions about new media effects lies with understanding communicative acts of affiliation, persuasion, and valuation.

In general, it seems propitious to move towards identifying useful metaphors of communicative action from which specific lines of research may be developed. A modest beginning is presented in the form of the following two metaphors. A *systems metaphor,* which emphasizes the relationships of functional interpersonal communication patterns, could address such questions as what family-related variables affect child socialization to microcomputers and VCRs. In the rationalistic vein, for example, such factors as parental involvement, birth spacing, and degree of peer network connectedness could mediate the child's dependency on microcomputing. The technology's functional contribution to the stability of family life variables could be estimated in terms of a theoretic statement of reciprocal effects. On the other hand, a *cultural metaphor* would focus on reality construction and negotiation as constituting the principal "work" of the family. Here, an accommodation-oriented hypothesis regarding the patriarchal bias of the VCR would, for example, call for intensive analysis of the discourses, within the home as well as in other social formations, that indicate gendered inflections of the medium's usage.

C. Now That We Know the New Media are Qualitatively Different, How Do We Recognize It Conceptually and Operationally?

Inherent in the subordinate clause above is a premise that is still controversial in the current literature. In effect, the premise operates axiomatically, as a statement that must be accepted for now in order to get the work done. The main clause, of course, points to the work ahead; to wit:

1. Much of the family's involvement with new media involves explicit problem solving. Yet the family's problem solving is of a different order than that of the solution-oriented small group (Weick, 1971). According to Weick, family members have unequal access to primary data, there is frequent "masking of expertness," and the problem solving itself is "embedded" (i.e., takes place in an ongoing stream of other unfinished business). Any productive research model of family decision making vis-á-vis the new media must take account of the peculiarities of the family group.

2. Much of the family discourse concerning new media involves moral talk regarding access rights, content property rights, and obligations to various communities. Aggregate public opinion offers a broad but superficial view of the nature of these cognitions. Precisely because morality formation occurs in specific situations and through the medium of oral discourse, the rationalist perspective of new media research is unable to contribute to this issue. Some variant of the accommodation perspective will need to be adapted to examining the family's moral warrants for utilizing new media.

3. Gender socialization and gender relations in regard to new media use equity and other areas of family life are important subjects that will require reassessments of measurement and sampling techniques (cf. Atkinson, 1987). Here, a macroperspective such as afforded by critical communications theories can provide analytic direction in studying the maintenance mechanisms for sex-role inequities. Time use and ecological activity studies (Bloch, 1987; Timmer, Eccles, & O'Brien, 1985) could yield baseline information on normative behavior of males and females, both in the household and in the community. The notion that standards for certain kinds of "appropriate" gender conduct, including computer use, may actually originate in schools and other formal socialization arenas—and then work their way into behavior at home—should also be investigated.

4. The study of communications media other than the two reviewed in this chapter will be required. Of course, the devotion of resources to this task awaits judgments about the significance of the new medium in the family context in terms of adoption rate, technical features, "content," and other factors. For example, the significance of the family-process implications of the audio compact disc, its enormous consumer acceptance notwithstanding, is dubious. Of somewhat more interest for family communication research might be the advent of a variety of innovations in household telephony, including answering machines, cordless units, call forward and phone list storage capabilities, and so on. Judgments of research significance cannot be systematized, and so will continue to be made on the basis of highly informal and subjective assessments.

5. Finally, our notions of researchable family configurations and life span positions need to be substantially expanded to accommodate demographic reality. Elderly households and linguistic minority families are steadily increasing their representation in the U.S. population as well as acquiring new occupational

and social identities. The one-parent family, the two-wage earner family, the empty nest family, and the reconstituted family are all much more frequent types today than even as recently as 10 years ago. The new media could actually be serving ameliorative roles for those families which have special needs for social support. Some research problems of new media in the near future will undoubtably call for obtaining and analyzing data from samples of conceptually significant family types.

REFERENCES

Abelman, R. (1986). Children's awareness of television's prosocial fare: Parental discipline as an antecedent. *Journal of Family Issues, 7*(1), 51–66.

Agostino, D., & Zenaty, J. (1980). *Home VCR owners' use of television and public television: Viewing, recording, and playback.* Washington, DC: Office of Communication Research, Corporation for Public Broadcasting.

Alexander, A., Ryan, M. S., & Munoz, P. (1984). Creating a learning context: Investigations on the interaction of siblings during television viewing. *Critical Studies in Mass Communication, 1,* 345–364.

Anderson, J. A. (1987). *Communication research: Issues and methods.* New York: McGraw Hill.

Arnold, E. (1985, April 18). The appliance of science: Technology and housework. *New Scientist,* pp. 12–15.

Atkinson, J. (1987). Gender roles in marriage and the family. *Journal of Family Issues, 8,* 5–41.

Audience outlook. (1986, July). *Broadcast Marketing & Technology News, 3*(6), 4–5.

Baer, W. S. (1985). Information technology comes home. *Telecommunications Policy, 9*(1), 3–22.

Bandura, A. (1977). *Social learning theory.* Englewood Cliffs, NJ: Prentice-Hall.

Beville, M. (1986, February 17). VCR usage patterns begin to emerge. *Electronic Media, 5,* 26.

Biocca, F. (1988). Opposing conceptions of the audience: The active and passive hemispheres of mass communication theory. In J. A. Anderson (Ed.), *Communication yearbook 11* (pp. 51–80). Newbury Park, CA: Sage.

Bloch, M. N. (1987). The development of sex differences in young children's activities at home: The effect of the social context. *Sex Roles, 16*(5/6), 279–301.

Bochner, A. P., & Eisenberg, E. M. (1987). Family process: Systems perspectives. In C. R. Berger & S. H. Chaffee (Eds.), *Handbook of communication science* (pp. 540–563). Newbury Park, CA: Sage.

Borgman, C. L. (1982). The videotex user interface: Design considerations and a feature analysis. *Videodisc/Videotex, 2*(2), 115–131.

Brand, S. (1987). *The media lab: Inventing the future at MIT.* New York: Viking.

Brown, J. R., & Linne, O. (1976). The family as a mediator of television's effects. In R. Brown (Ed.), *Children and television* (pp. 184–198). Beverly Hills, CA: Sage.

Brown, J. S. (1985). Process versus product. In M. Chen & W. Paisley (Eds.), *Children and microcomputers* (pp. 248–266). Beverly Hills, CA: Sage.

Bryce, J. W. (1987). Family time and television use. In T. R. Lindlof (Ed.), *Natural audiences* (pp. 121–138). Norwood, NJ: Ablex Publishing Corp.

Carey, J. (1980). Changing communications technology and the nature of the audience. *Journal of Advertising, 9*(2), 3–9, 43.

Carey, J., & Moss, M. L. (1985). The diffusion of new telecommunications technologies. *Telecommunications Policy, 9*(2), 145–158.

Carey, R., & Gall, M. (1986). Patterns of microcomputer use at home and at school by secondary school students. *Educational Technology, 26*(10), 29–31.

Caron, A. H., Giroux, L., & Douzou, S. (1985, May). *The presence of microcomputers in the home: Uses and impacts.* Paper presented at the meeting of the International Communication Association, Honolulu, HI.

Chaffee, S. H., & Tims, A. R. (1976). Interpersonal factors in adolescent TV use. *Journal of Social Issues, 32,* 98–115.

Chaffee, S. H., McLeod, J., & Atkin, C. K. (1971). Parental influences on adolescent media use. *American Behavioral Scientist, 14,* 323–340.

Chen, M. (1984). Computers in the lives of our children: Looking back on a generation of television research. In R. E. Rice (Ed.), *The new media* (pp. 269–286). Beverly Hills, CA: Sage.

Chen, M. (1986). Gender and computers: The beneficial effects of experience on attitudes. *Journal of Educational Computing, 2*(3), 265–282.

Chen, M. (1987). Gender differences in adolescents' uses of and attitudes toward computers. In M. McLaughlin (Ed.), *Communication yearbook 10* (pp. 200–216). Beverly Hills, CA: Sage.

Christenson, P., DeBenedittis, P., & Lindlof, T. R. (1985). Children's use of audio media. *Communication Research, 12,* 327–343.

Collins, W. A., Sobol, B. L., & Westby, S. D. (1981). Effects of adult commentary on children's comprehension and inferences about a televised aggressive portrayal. *Child Development, 52,* 158–163.

Consumer electronic product adoption. (1987, March). *CD-1 News,* pp. 11, 15.

Corder-Bolz, & O'Bryant, S. (1978). Teacher vs. program. *Journal of Communication, 28*(1), 97–103.

Cowan, R. S. (1976). The 'Industrial Revolution' in the home: Household technology and social change in the 20th. century. *Technology and Culture, 17*(1), 1–23.

Creasey, G. L., & Myers, B. J. (1986). Video games and children: Effects on leisure activities, schoolwork, and peer involvement. *Merrill-Palmer Quarterly, 32*(3), 251–262.

Daiute, C. (1985). Issues in using computers to socialize the writing process. *Educational Communication and Technology Journal, 33,* 41–50.

Davis, R. E. (1976). *Response to innovation: A study of popular argument about new mass media.* New York: Arno Press.

Desmond, R. J., Singer, J. L., Singer, D. G., Calam, R., & Colimore, K. (1985). Family mediation patterns and television viewing: Young children's use and grasp of the medium. *Human Communication Research, 11*(4), 461–480.

Dickerson, M. D., & Gentry, J. W. (1983). Characteristics of adopters and non-adopters of home computers. *Journal of Consumer Research, 10,* 225–235.

Diem, R. A. (1985). A study of children's attitudes and reactions to the new technology. *Social Education, 49*(4), 318–320.

Donohue, T. R., & Henke, L. L. (1985). *The impact of video cassette recorders on traditional television and cable viewing habits and preferences.* Washington, DC: National Association of Broadcasters.

Dutton, W. H., Kovaric, P., & Steinfield, C. (1985). Computing in the home: A research paradigm. *Computers and the Social Sciences, 1,* 5–18.

Dutton, W. H., Rogers, E. M., & Jun, S.-H. (1987). Diffusion and social impacts of personal computers. *Communication Research, 14,* 219–250.

Eastman, S. T. (1986). A qualitative study of computers and printouts in the classroom. *Educational Communication & Technology Journal, 34*(4), 207–222.

Eastman, S. T., & Agostino, D. (1986). Commanding the computer: Functions and concepts of videotex technology for eighth-grade students. *Journal of Research and Development in Education, 19*(2), 49–57.

Eastman, S. T., & Krendl, K. (1987). Computers and gender: Differential effects of electronic search on students' achievement and attitudes. *Journal of Research and Development in Education,* *20.*

Eron, L. D. (1982). Parent–child interaction, television violence, and aggression of children. *American Psychologist, 37,* 197–211.

Faber, R. J., Brown, J. D., & McLeod, J. M. (1979). Coming of age in the global village: Television and adolescence. In E. Wartella (Ed.), *Children communicating* (pp. 215–250). Beverly Hills, CA.: Sage.

Falbo, T., & Polit, D. R. (1986). Quantitative review of the only child literature: Research evidence and theory development. *Psychological Bulletin, 100*(2), 176–189.

Fallis, S. F., Fitzpatrick, M. A., & Friestad, M. S. (1985). Spouses' discussion of television portrayals of close relationships. *Communication Research, 12,* 59–81.

Ferrari, M., Klingzing, D. G., Paris, C. L., Morris, S. K., & Eyman, A. P. (1985). Home computers: Implications for children and families. *Marriage & Family Review, 8,* 41–58.

Fetler, M. (1985). Sex differences on the California statewide assessment of computer literacy. *Sex Roles, 13*(3/4), 181–191.

Fine, G. A., & Kleinman, S. (1983). Network and meaning: An interactionist approach to structure. *Symbolic Interaction, 6*(1), 97–110.

Giacquinta, J. B., Ely, M., & Smith-Burke, T. (1984). *Educational microcomputing at home: A comparative analysis of twenty families.* Unpublished manuscript. School of Education, Health, Nursing, and Arts Professions, New York University.

Golding, P., & Murdock, G. (1986). Unequal information: Access and exclusion in the new communications marketplace. In M. Ferguson (Ed.), *Communication technologies and the public interest* (pp. 71–83). London: Sage.

Greenberg, B. S., & Heeter, C. (1987). VCRs and young people. *American Behavioral Scientist, 30,* 509–521.

Gunter, B., & Levy, M. R. (1987). Social contexts of video use. *American Behavioral Scientist, 30,* 486–494.

Gunter, B., & Svennevig, M. (1987). *Behind and in front of the screen: Television's involvement in family life.* London: John Libbey & Co.

Hawkins, J. (1985). Computers and girls: Rethinking the issues. *Sex Roles, 13*(3/4), 165–179.

Haefner, M. J., Hunter, L. S., & Wartella, E. (1986, May). *Parents, children, and new media: Expectations, attitudes, and use.* Paper presented at the meeting of the International Communication Association, Chicago.

Hamilton, M. A., & Young, K. A. (1986, May). *The home computer as innovative medium: Predicting adoption.* Paper presented at the meeting of the International Communication Association, Chicago.

Harvey, M. G., & Rothe, J. T. (1985/1986). Video cassette recorders: Their impact on viewers and advertisers. *Journal of Advertising Research, 25*(6), 19–27.

Heeter, C. (1985). Program selection with abundance of choice: A process model. *Human Communication Research, 12,* 126–152.

Heeter, C., & Greenberg, B. (1985). Cable and program choice. In D. Zillman & J. Bryant (Eds.), *Selective exposure to communication* (pp. 203–224). Hillsdale, NJ: Lawrence Erlbaum Associates.

Henke, L. L., & Donohue, T. R. (1986). Teletext viewing habits and preferences. *Journalism Quarterly, 63,* 542–545, 553.

Hess, R. D., & Holloway, S. D. (1984). Family and school as educational institutions. In R. D. Parke (Ed.), *Review of child development research 7. The family* (pp. 179–222). Chicago, IL: The University of Chicago Press.

Hess, R. D., & Miura, I. T. (1985). Gender differences in enrollment in computer camps and classes. *Sex Roles, 13*(3/4), 193–203.

Jensen, K. B. (1987). Qualitative audience research: Toward an integrative approach to reception. *Critical Studies in Mass Communication, 4*(1), 21–36.

Jhally, S., & Livant, B. (1986). Watching as work: The valorization of audience consciousness. *Journal of Communication, 36*(3), 124–143.

Kim, W. Y., Baran, S. J., & Massey, K. K. (1988). Impact of the VCR on control of television viewing. *Journal of Broadcasting & Electronic Media, 32*(3), 351–357.

Kling, R., & Scacchi, W. (1980). Computing as social action: The social dynamics of computing in complex organizations. In M. C. Yovits (Ed.), *Advances in computers* (Vol. 19, pp. 249–327). New York: Academic Press.

Klopfenstein, B. C., & Swanson, D. A. (1987, May). *An analysis of VCR adopter characteristics and behavior.* Paper presented at the International Communication Association, Montreal.

Krendl, K., Gantz, W., & Fitzmaurice, M. (1986, May). *Equity issues in computer use: A view from the parents' perspective.* Paper presented at the International Communication Association, Chicago.

Leichter, H. J., Ahmed, D., Barrios, L., Bryce, J., Larsen, E., & Moe, L. (1985). Family contexts of television. *Educational Communication and Technology Journal, 33,* 26–40.

Lemish, D. (1987). Viewers in diapers: The early development of television viewing. In T. R. Lindlof (Ed.), *Natural audiences: Qualitative research of media uses and effects* (pp. 33–57). Norwood, NJ: Ablex Publishing Corp.

Levy, M. R. (1987). Some problems of VCR research. *American Behavioral Scientist, 30,* 461–470.

Levy, M. R. (1983). Time-shifting use of home video recorders. *Journal of Broadcasting, 27*(3), 263–266.

Levy, M. R. (1980). Home video recorders: A user survey. *Journal of Communication, 30*(4), 23–27.

Levy, M. R., & Fink, E. L. (1984). Home video recorders and the transience of television broadcasts. *Journal of Communication, 34*(2), 56–71.

Lieberman, D. (1985). Research on children and microcomputers: A review of utilization and effects studies. In M. Chen & W. Paisley (Eds.), *Children and microcomputers* (pp. 59–83). Beverly Hills, CA: Sage.

Lin, S., & Lepper, M. (1987). Correlates of children's usage of videogames and computers. *Journal of Applied Social Psychology, 17*(1), 72–93.

Lindlof, T. R. (1988). Media audiences as interpretive communities. In J. A. Anderson (Ed.), *Communication yearbook 11* (pp. 81–107). Newbury Park, CA: Sage.

Lindlof, T. R., & Meyer, T. P. (1987). Mediated communication as ways of seeing, acting, and constructing culture: The tools and foundations of qualitative research. In T. R. Lindlof (Ed.), *Natural audiences: Qualitative research of media uses and effects* (pp. 1–30). Norwood, NJ: Ablex Publishing Corp.

Lindlof, T. R., & Traudt, P. J. (1983). Mediated communication in families: New theoretical approaches. In M. S. Mander (Ed.), *Communications in transition* (pp. 260–278). New York: Praeger.

Lindlof, T. R., & Shatzer, M. J. (in press). VCR usage in the American family. In J. Bryant (Ed.), *Television and the American family.* Hillsdale, NJ: Erlbaum.

Lindlof, T. R., Shatzer, M. J., & Wilkinson, D. (1988). Accommodation of video and television in the American family. In J. Lull (Ed.), *World families watch television* (pp. 158–192). Newbury Park, CA: Sage.

Lockheed, M. E. (1985). Women, girls, and computers: A first look at the evidence. *Sex Roles, 13*(3/4), 115–122.

Lull, J. (1982). A rules approach to the study of television and society. *Human Communication Research, 8,* 3–16.

Lull, J. (1980). The social uses of television. *Human Communication Research, 6,* 197–209.

Maccoby, E. E. (1986). Social groupings in childhood: Their relationships to prosocial and antisocial behavior in boys and girls. In D. Olweus, J. Block, & M. R. Yarrow (Eds.), *Development of antisocial and prosocial behavior: Research, theories, and issues.* Orlando, FL: Academic Press.

Mahler, R. (1987, June 1). VCR boom leveling off. *Electronic Media,* p. 25.

McDonald, D. G. (1985). Spousal influences on television viewing. *Communication Research, 12,* 530–545.

McLeod, J. M., Fitzpatrick, M. A., Glynn, C. J., & Fallis, S. F. (1982). Television and social relations: Family influences and consequences for interpersonal behavior. In National Institute of Mental Health, *Television and behavior: Ten years of scientific progress and implications for the eighties* (DHHS Publication No. ADM 82-1196) (pp. 272–286). Washington, DC: U.S. Government Printing Office.

Meadowcroft, J. M., & McDonald, D. G. (1986). Meta-analysis of research on children and the media: Atypical development? *Journalism Quarterly, 63,* 474–480.

Messaris, P. (1987). Mothers' comments to their children about the relationship between television and reality. In T. R. Lindlof (Ed.), *Natural audiences* (pp. 95–108). Norwood, NJ: Ablex Publishing Corp.

Messaris, P., & Sarett, C. (1981). On the consequences of television-related parent-child interaction. *Human Communication Research, 7,* 226–244.

Meyer, T. P., & Hexamer, A. (1982). The use and abuse of media effects research in the development of telecommunications social policy. In J. R. Schement (Ed.), *Telecommunications policy handbook* (pp. 222–235). New York: Praeger.

Meyrowitz, J. (1985). *No sense of place: The impact of electronic media on social behavior.* New York: Oxford University Press.

Michaels, E. (1985). Constraints on knowledge in an economy of oral information. *Current Anthropology, 26*(4), 505–510.

Mitchell, E. (1985). The dynamics of family interaction around home video games. *Marriage & Family Review, 8*(1/2), 121–135.

More TV in homes than ever before. (1987, August 3). *NAB Today,* p. 3.

Morley, D. (1986). *Family television: Cultural power and domestic leisure.* London: Comedia Publishing Group.

Morley, D. (1983). Cultural transformations: The politics of resistance. In H. Davis & P. Walton (Eds.), *Language, image, media* (pp. 104–117). Oxford, England: Basil Blackwell.

Morrisroe, P. (1984, January 9). Living with the computer. *New York,* pp. 22–31.

Mosco, V. (1982). *Pushbutton fantasies.* Norwood, NJ: Ablex Publishing Corp.

Palmgreen, P. (1984). Uses and gratifications: A theoretical perspective. In R. N. Bostrom (Ed.), *Communication yearbook 8* (pp. 20–55). Beverly Hills, CA: Sage.

Phillips, C. (1986, June 16). Who needs it? *The Wall Street Journal,* p. 30D.

Pool, I. de Sola (1983). *Technologies of freedom: On free speech in an electronic age.* Cambridge, MA: Harvard University Press.

Prasad, V. K., Rao, T. R., & Sheikh, A. A. (1978). Can people affect television? Mother versus commercial. *Journal of Communication, 28*(1), 91–96.

Reid, L. (1979). The impact of family group interaction on children's understanding of television advertising. *Journal of Advertising, 8*(3), 13–19.

Reiser, R. A., Tessmer, M. A., & Phelps, P. C. (1984). Adult-child interaction in children's learning from "Sesame Street." *Educational Communication and Technology Journal, 32,* 217–223.

Reese, S. D., Shoemaker, P. J., & Danielson, W. A. (1987). Social correlates of public attitudes toward new communication technologies. *Journalism Quarterly, 64*(4), 675–682, 692.

Rice, R. E. (1984). Evaluating new media systems. In J. Johnston (Ed.), *Evaluating the new information technologies* (pp. 53–71). San Francisco, CA: Jossey-Bass.

Roberts, D. F. (1986). Comments on the communication revolution in the United States. *Communicare, 5*(1), 4–11.

Robertson, T. (1979). Parental mediation of television advertising effects. *Journal of Communication, 29*(1), 12–26.

Roe, K. (1987, May). *Adolescents' VCR use: How and why.* Paper presented at the meeting of the International Communication Association, Montreal.

Roe, K., & Salomonsson (1983). *The uses and effects of video viewing among Swedish adolescents* (Report No. 31). Sweden: Media Panel, University of Lund.

Rogers, E. M. (1985). The diffusion of home computers among households in Silicon Valley. *Marriage & Family Review, 8*(1/2), 89–102.

Rosenblatt, P. C., & Cunningham, M. R. (1976). Television watching and family tensions. *Journal of Marriage and the Family, 38*(1), 105–111.

Rubin, A. M., & Bantz, C. R. (1987). Utility of videocassette recorders. *American Behavioral Scientist, 30,* 471–485.

Rubin, A. M., & Rubin, R. B. (1985). Interface of personal and mediated communication: A research agenda. *Critical Studies in Mass Communication, 2,* 36–53.

Russell, R. L., & van den Broek, P. (in press). A cognitive/developmental account of storytelling in child psychotherapy. In S. R. Shirk (Ed.), *Cognitive development and child psychotherapy.* New York: Plenum Press.

Singer, J. L., & Singer, D. G. (1981). *Television, imagination, and aggression: A study of preschoolers.* Hillsdale, NJ: Erlbaum.

Sloan Commission on Cable Communications. (1971). *On the cable: The television of abundance.* New York: McGraw-Hill.

Smythe, D. (1977). Communications: Blindspot of Western Marxism. *Canadian Journal of Political and Social Theory, 1*(3), 1–27.

Television's shifting balance of power. (1987, October 12). *Broadcasting,* pp. 40–44.

Timmer, S. G., Eccles, J., & O'Brien, K. (1985). How children use time. In F. T. Juster & F. P. Stafford (Eds.), *Time, goods, and well-being.* Ann Arbor, MI: Institute for Social Research.

Tims, A. R. (1986). Family political communication and social values. *Communication Research, 13*(1), 5–17.

Tims, A. R., & Masland, J. L. (1985). Measurement of family communication patterns. *Communication Research, 12*(1), 35–57.

Tinnell, C. S. (1985). An ethnographic look at personal computers in the family setting. *Marriage & Family Review, 8*(1/2), 59–69.

Traudt, P. J., & Lont, C. M. (1987). Media logic-in-use: The family as locus of study. In T. R. Lindlof (Ed.), *Natural audiences* (pp. 139–160). Norwood, NJ: Ablex Publishing Corp.

Turkle, S. (1984). *The second self: Computers and the human spirit.* New York: Simon & Schuster.

Urban, C. (1984). Factors influencing media consumption: A survey of the literature. In B. M. Compaigne (Ed.), *Understanding new media* (pp. 213–282). Cambridge, MA: Ballinger.

Urbany, J. E., & Talarzyk (1983). Videotex: Implications for retailing. *Journal of Retailing, 59*(3), 76–92.

Vail, H. (1980). The home computer terminal: Transforming the household of tomorrow. *The Futurist, 14* (6), 52–58.

Venkatesh, A., & Vitalari, N. (1984). Households and technology: The case of home computers—some conceptual and theoretical issues. In M. L. Roberts & L. H. Wortzel (Eds.), *Marketing to the changing household* (pp. 187–204). Cambridge, MA: Ballinger.

Vitalari, N. P., & Venkatesh, A. (1987). In-home computing and information services. *Telecommunications Policy, 11,* 65–81.

Vitalari, N. P., Venkatesh, A., & Gronhaug, K. (1985). Computing in the home: Shifts in the time allocation patterns of households. *Communications of the ACM, 28*(5), 512–522.

Vygotsky, L. (1978). *Mind in society.* Cambridge, MA: Harvard University Press.

Wackman, D. B., Wartella, E., & Ward, S. (1977). Learning to be consumers: The role of the family. *Journal of Communication, 27,* 138–151.

Wakefield, R. A. (1986). Home computers & families: The empowerment revolution. *The Futurist, 20*(5), 18–22.

Wartella, E., & Reeves, B. (1985). Historical trends in research on children and the media, 1900–1960. *Journal of Communication, 35*(2), 118–133.

Watkins, B., & Brimm, D. (1985). The adoption and use of microcomputers in homes and elementary schools. In M. Chen & W. Paisley (Eds.), *Children and microcomputers* (pp. 129–150). Beverly Hills, CA: Sage.

Webster, J. (1986). Audience behavior in the new media environment. *Journal of Communication, 36*(3), 77–91.

Weick, K. E. (1971). Group processes, family processes, and problem solving. In J. Aldous, T. Condon, R. Hill, M. Straus, & I. Tallman (Eds.), *Family problem solving* (pp. 3–32). Hinsdale, IL: Dryden Press.

Wigand, R. T., Borstelmann, S. E., & Boster, F. J. (1986). Electronic leisure: Video game usage and the communication climate of video arcades. In M. McLaughlin (Ed.), *Communication yearbook 9* (pp. 275–293). Beverly Hills, CA: Sage.

Wilder, G., Mackie, D., & Cooper, J. (1985). Gender and computers: Two surveys of computer-related attitudes. *Sex Roles, 13*(3/4), 215–228.

Williams, F., Coulombe, J., & Lievrouw, L. (1983). Children's attitudes toward small computers: A preliminary study. *Educational Communication & Technology Journal, 31*(1), 3–7.

Williams, F., Phillips, A. F., & Lum, P. (1985). Gratifications associated with new communications technologies. In K. E. Rosengren, L. A. Wenner, & P. Palmgreen (Eds.), *Media gratifications research: Current perspectives* (pp. 241–252). Beverly Hills, CA: Sage.

Wolf, M. A. (1987). How children negotiate television. In T. R. Lindlof (Ed.), *Natural audiences* (pp. 58–94). Norwood, NJ: Ablex Publishing Corp.

Wolf, M. A., Meyer, T. P., & White, C. (1982). A rules-based study of television's role in the construction of social reality. *Journal of Broadcasting, 26,* 813–829.

Zahn, S. B., & Baran, S. J. (1984). It's all in the family: Siblings and program choice conflict. *Journalism Quarterly, 61,* 848–852.

5

Bearing Bad News in Clinical Settings*

Douglas W. Maynard
Department of Sociology
University of Wisconsin
Madison, WI

* Different parts of this chapter have been presented at the annual meetings of the International Communication Association, Honolulu, May 1985, and Chicago, May 1986; at the Developmental Biology and Psychology Colloquium series, Waisman Center on Mental Retardation and Human Development, University of Wisconsin, Madison, May, 1986; and at the Developmental Disabilities Conference, sponsored by the Institute for Continuing Medical Education, Hurley Medical Center, and Mott Children's Health Center, Flint, Michigan, May, 1986. I would like to thank participants at these meetings and others, including Norman Jensen, Pam Laikko, Courtney Marlaire, Albert J. Meehan, and David Steele, who were helpful in the development of the paper. Richard Frankel, Christian Heath, and an anonymous reviewer provided extremely useful written comments.

One of the most difficult of clinical tasks is that of conveying bad news, especially of a severe diagnosis or death. The question of how the professional can perform such communication efficaciously is a natural one for social and communication scientists concerned with "naturally occurring" interaction and conversation. However, the concept of communication can be a very clouded one. The aim of this chapter is to discuss some common misconceptions of communication, as exhibited in the literature on bearing bad news, and to then suggest investigative strategies that deal with the complexities of the news delivery process.

Thus, there are two parts to this chapter. First is a review of literature regarding the disclosure of information in clinical settings. Writers suggest that better communication is needed and make extensive recommendations regarding the presentation of diagnoses; "Deliver bad news tactfully" is the title of one article (Michaels, 1983). But few, if any, of the recommendations are based on systematic study. Moreover, investigators target the discourse practices of clinicians; although concerned about patients' emotional and other reactions, very little is said about how these parties also employ interactional devices that are constitutive features of the communicative process. The second part of the chapter explores how communication must be understood in nontraditional ways to handle the complexities of the delivery and receipt of diagnostic news. In terms of conceptual development, I use my own research to illustrate these complexities and to point the direction for further study. Three particular issues are addressed: (a) how one decides what communication effectiveness is, (b) the difficulty of designing strategies for intervention, and (c) the nature of debates about the disclosure of information.

Two matters are preliminary to the literature review and conceptual development. For one, a terminological problem surrounds the fact that the bearing of bad new occurs in a variety of clinical and nonclinical settings. As for the clinical settings, medical researchers and practitioners have expressed profound concerns for properly managing the delivery of diagnostic news. Usually, the medical practitioners who deliver news are doctors, and those who receive it are patients. In addition, the field of developmental disabilities demonstrates a similar interest in the *informing interview,* which is the name given to those meetings designed for the presentation of diagnostic information. (Developmental disabilities include mental retardation, autism, attention deficit disorder, and other problems that are first manifested in early childhood.) In this field, those who present a diagnosis may be one of a variety of professionals, including pediatricians, psychologists, psychiatrists, social workers, or others. Those to whom news and information is given are not the patients themselves, but their parents. This situation, where news goes to a patient's representative, occurs in other clinical settings, as when a doctor tells news to a sick person's spouse, child (e.g. of an elderly parent), other relative, or even guardian. Therefore, while much of the literature on informing interviews concerns the doctor–patient relationship, more generic terms for participants in these meetings are *deliverers* and *recipients*. These terms, in fact, are generic enough to indicate that the situation where one party presents news (including bad news) to another is one that occurs in many contexts, and clinical interactants employ forms of talk that are arguably indigenous to everyday conversation (cf. Heritage, 1984, chap. 8). For purposes of this review, however, when the terms *deliverers* and *recipients* are used, they should be understood as referring to parties dealing with diagnostic news in clinical settings. Furthermore, I shall frequently resort to these terms to emphasize that clinicans may be persons from a variety of professions, recipients may be patients, their relatives, or guardians, and that deliverers and recipients are, probably foremost, members of society, in the sense of being competent practitioners of natural language (Garfinkel & Sacks, 1970).

Another preliminary matter regards the data excerpts that appear later in the paper. Except for the last example, which is from a television program, these fragments were collected in two diagnostic clinics for developmental disabilities.[1] Audiotapes or videotapes were made of the informing interview and then transcribed according to conventions developed by Gail Jefferson (cf. Atkinson & Heritage, 1984, pp. ix–xvi). For ease of presentation and reading, the fragments here are simplified and include only that detail which is necessary to an analytic point. Copies of original, finer transcriptions of these episodes can be requested from the author.

I. THE LITERATURE ON "BEARING BAD NEWS" IN CLINICAL SETTINGS

A. Disclosure in Historical Perspective

The present concern for delivering diagnostic news is part of a prominent debate in the history of medicine regarding whether and how clinicians should tell diagnostic information to patients. To put matters briefly, this debate[2] begins in the classical age of Greece, with Hippocrates cautioning physicians to conceal news from patients lest it upset them and have deleterious effects on their conditions. Through the ages, the weight of opinion has favored Hippocrates' position. Henri de Mondeville, a 14th-century French surgeon, Thomas Percivel, the early 19th-century English physician who wrote an influential book on medical ethics, and Oliver Wendell Holmes, the Harvard professor of anatomy who was active in the late 19th century, have all asserted that it is morally correct to withhold bad

[1] Data were collected under Grant No. HD 01799 from the National Institutes of Health, Stephan A. Richardson, principal investigator, and Grant No., HD 17803-02, Douglas W. Maynard, principal investigator. Bonnie Svarstad, who worked on the former grant with Helen Levens Lipton, with permission generously made the Richardson data available to the present author.

[2] The following synopsis depends heavily upon Reiser (1980) and Katz (1984, Chapter I).

news from patients. Most 19th and 20th century physicians, as evidenced in the American Medical Association's code of ethics and in various surveys of the profession, agreed that it was easiest to withhold bad news from patients. The belief was that the clinician should be a source of hope and strength, and should not do anything to upset the patient. Thus, according to the 1847 and first Code of Ethics of the AMA:

> The life of a sick person can be shortened not only by the acts, but also by the words or the manner of a physician. It is, therefore, a sacred duty to guard himself carefully in this respect, and to avoid all things which have a tendency to discourage the patient and to depress his spirits. (Katz, 1984, p. 20)

Over the years, the original Code of Ethics has been considerably reduced and now includes very few guides regarding doctor–patient relationships. However, Katz (1984, p. 22) suggests that the early sentiments lived on in spirit, because physicians developed no new or specific instructions about telling patients disagreeable information.

If the dominant stance in medicine has been to withhold bad news, dissidents, nevertheless, have not hesitated to take up the counterposition. During Hippocrates' time, some Greek physicians thought that it was best to present bad diagnoses to patients so that they could decide whether to let "nature take its course" or to commit suicide, which was an honorable way of ending life under certain conditions in Greek society. In 1769, Samuel Bond, an American doctor, suggested that "explaining the facts" was simply kinder and wiser than hiding them. It was not necessary to create unrealistic expectations to which the patient might adhere. Another American doctor, Worthington Hooker, argued in 1849 that concealment usually did not succeed in accomplishing anything and led to an undermining of confidence in the medical profession. Following Kant, Hooker even said that the sacrifice of truth for some higher end such as comforting the patient ultimately meant the greatest good—morality—itself was defeated. Then, in the early 20th century, Richard Cabot, challenged by his wife to be direct with his patients, experimented with disclosure and found that the truth was surprisingly innocuous; i.e., the expected harms failed to occur. Cabot went on to write an essay entitled "The Use of Truth and Falsehood in Medicine: An Experimental Study," in which he passionately indicted the use of any form of falsehood in the doctor–patient relationship, because it undermined the trust on which that relationship is based.

Until the 1960s, however, these dissidents were a minority within the medical profession. Since that time, for a variety of reasons, attitudes have changed both within the public and within the profession, so that currently there is much more pressure for physicians to be frank and to disclose the facts of illness and diagnosis to patients. Within the profession, for example, a 1961 study showed 90% of responding physicians preferred not to tell cancer patients their diagnosis

(Oken, 1961). A replication published in 1979 revealed a startling reversal of attitudes; 97% of 264 respondents would present the diagnosis to cancer patients (Novack et al., 1979). From written replies and comments, Novack et al. (1979, pp. 899–900) suggest that this change has several sources, including advances in therapy that offer patients more hope, increased public awareness of cancer as a disease and "death and dying" as discussable topics, and research which demonstrates (a) that patients wish to be told of their conditions and (b) that such news does not harm patients and their families. Furthermore, since the mid-1960s, the government has required research centers to disclose diagnoses to subjects as part of human subjects and informed consent protocols (Novack et al., 1979, p. 899; Reiser, 1980, p. 840). These changes also fit with "patients' rights" and "medical consumerism" movements (Novack et al., 1979, p. 899).

Despite the apparent attitude changes in both the medical profession and the public toward the importance of disclosing even bad news, studies in which patients are interviewed after discharge reveal their dissatisfaction with the adequacy of information they obtained while in the hospital (Reynolds, 1978, p. 1673; Fletcher, 1980, p. 281). Research on actual delivery of information shows that this delivery is inadequate in various ways. Clinicians often fail to perform simple tasks such as handing patients printed information regarding hospital routines and personnel (Reynolds, 1978). They may also neglect to give explanations about and results of diagnostic procedures (Dunkelman, 1979; Reynolds, 1978). Rather than blaming clinicians for some sort of failure, however, the literature on bearing bad news emphasizes how difficult it is for both deliverers and recipients.

B. Deliverers and Bad News

Why are clinicians so uncomfortable when delivering negative diagnostic news? A host of reasons can be suggested. First, doctors rarely receive any training in communication skills during medical school, particularly regarding the disclosure of bad news (Reiser, 1980). Partly this is due an explosion in knowledge and technology regarding diagnosis and treatment during the last 50 years which has utterly eclipsed the importance of interpersonal skills (Engel, 1977, p. 135; Fletcher, 1980, p. 846; Goldie, 1982, p. 130; Mishler, 1984). Thus, clinicians may simply be at a loss in deciding how to tell recipients of an incurable disease, life-threatening condition, or chronic malady (e.g., Buckman, 1984, p. 1598). Second, physicians and others who enter the medical or helping professions are often cure-oriented. Faced with a situation they cannot change, deliverers may feel powerless and ineffective (Kurtz, 1964; Kelly & Menolascino, 1975), and perhaps even that they have failed (Clark & LaBeff, 1982, p. 371). Related to this is the lack of knowledge regarding etiology and prognosis of many conditions, which undermines clinicans' confidence because they fear not knowing answers (Buckman, 1984, p. 1598; Zwerling, 1954) and expressing uncertainty (Fox,

1957; Katz, 1984, chap. 7). Third, deliverers may have to contend with the emotional reactions of recipients, which may require the employment of various *shoring* techniques (McLenahan & Lofland, 1976) that they may or may not know. Clinicans sometimes devalue displays of emotion on the part of recipients because of the anticipation that such displays disrupt clinic routine, or because the displays make them feel as if they failed to do the right thing to prevent them (Buckman, 1984, p. 1598). Finally, deliverers themselves are not immune to emotional reactivity (Rubin & Rubin, 1980; Solomons & Menolascino, 1968, p. 12). They have their own fears of illness and death (Buckman, 1984, p. 1598; Clark & LaBeff, 1982, p. 370) and have to contend with a role (bearer of bad news) that is inherently stressful no matter how effective one might be in that role (Anderson & Garner, 1973, p. 37). And while deliverers are expected to be sensitive to and understanding of recipients, the latter rarely return such empathy (Evans, 1983, p. 149).

These difficulties have consequences for how recipients perceive deliverers and the information they present. Clinicans can appear as disinterested (Rubin & Rubin, 1980; Solomons & Menolascino, 1968), may use circumlocutions or abstruse and jargonistic language, misemphasize elements of the condition, and play guessing games with recipients (Evans, 1983; Waskowitz, 1959; Anderson & Garner, 1973). Deliverers may soften the blow of bad news by reassuring recipients that basically all is well, which Buckman (1984, p. 1599) calls *shielding*. This may take the form of avoiding talk about the possibility of future relapse when a patient is in remission (Buckman, 1984) or disguising the reality of impending death (Katz, 1984, p. 219).

C. Recipients and Bad News

Investigators suggest that recipients react to bad news by becoming shocked and emotionally disorganized (Eden-Piercy, Blacker, & Eyman, 1986; Glaser & Strauss, 1965, p. 121). Still, while experiencing anger, shame, confusion, self-pity, and other emotions, patients may give off a variety of different and even contrastive displays, such as being "brave" or "going to pieces," and "losing all hope" or asking about the future, depending on where they are in the "response process," which includes such stages as "depression," "denial," "acceptance," and so on (Glaser & Strauss, 1965, p. 121). When the recipient of bad news is the patient's relative, guardian, or other caregiver, a clinician may have to contend with other feelings and reactions. Recipients may anticipate stigmatized social interaction (as when a child is retarded or a spouse has Alzheimer's disease), prolonged burden of care (when the patient's condition is chronic), and grief (if a patient is dying, or even undergoing a nonterminal change of status because of the condition) (Emde & Brown, 1978; Menolascino, 1977; Parks, 1977; Solnit & Stark, 1961; Wikler, 1981). An additional source of distress for recipients may be their disagreement with what the clinician has said. For example, in the area of developmental disabilities, one study found that 48% of families who came to a diagnostic clinic either doubted or were unaware of the possibility of mental retardation for their child. After the initial medical work-up, over half of this group still rejected the diagnosis. Such disagreements may have to do with conflicts between scientific and lay systems of categorizing and discussing behavior and symptoms (Kleinman, 1980; Mishler, 1984).

D. The Call for Research

Informing interviews are, then, difficult for both deliverers and recipients. Yet there is a surprising paucity of research on the process of bearing bad news. Articles that focus on deliverers are largely of an advisory nature (*The Lancet*, 1980; Michaels, 1983; Drayer & Schlesinger, 1960; Graliker, Parmelee, & Koch, 1959; Kirman, 1953; Matheny & Vernick, 1969; Wolfensberger, 1967; Wolfensberger & Menolascino, 1970; Zwerling, 1954), not based on empirical research, and often, as Goldie (1982), Hoy (1985), and others report, make recommendations that reflect physicians' own personal convictions, ethical considerations, or dogmas. Suggestions can therefore be contradictory (Evans, 1983). Thus, one author might argue that recipients be told of a condition immediately after its discovery (Kirman, 1953), while another proposes waiting until independent corroboration can occur (Parmelee, 1956). Or some will advise not to prognosticate, at least too far in the future (Drayer & Schlesinger, 1960, p. 365), because the shock of hearing the diagnosis is too great (Graliker et al., 1959, p. 821), while others will emphasize that discussing prognosis can provide recipients with realistic hopes (Solomons, 1970).

In probing recipients, researchers find dissatisfaction with the informing process (Anderson & Garner, 1973, p. 37; Caldwell, Manley, & Nissen, 1961; Evans, 1983; Reynolds, 1978; Turnbull & Turnbull, 1978; Waitzkin & Stoeckle, 1976). However, the literature is not clear on the source of this dissatisfaction, whether recipients express it in the interview, and to what extent the conduct of the interview is responsible for it (Svarstad & Lipton, 1977). That is, sometimes recipients may simply forget about or "not hear" the information they do receive. For example, after surveying clinicans and parents in a midwest city, Kelly and Menolascino (1975, pp. 10–11) found (a) that 81% of the physicians said they referred parents to a local developmental disabilities service, while only 3% of the parents agreed that they had been so referred; and (b) that 71% of physicians stated that they gave printed material about mental retardation to parents, while only 10% of parents reported receiving such material. Furthermore, most investigations of recipients' experience are retrospective in nature (Berg, Gilderdale, & Way, 1969; Gayton & Walker, 1974; Graliker et al., 1959; Matheny & Vernick, 1969; Svarstad & Lipton, 1977; Dunkelman, 1979; see the review in Reynolds, 1978) and thus contain no independent verification of how the interviews were actually conducted.

If the literature on bearing bad news demonstrates a lack of research, it also displays a further tendency, which is to focus on the communication practices of deliverers and to neglect those of recipients. Investigators, at least implicitly, regard recipients as passive targets whose anxiety and stress can be alleviated, or whose needs for information can be satisfied, through proper clinical conduct. As sources of knowledge, as having strategies for dealing with deliverers, and as influences on deliverers' own performances, patients are overlooked. This raises the possibility of too much emphasis on what deliverers can do when dealing with recipients who display varied desires, abilities, and levels of emotional readiness to handle diagnostic news (Appell, Williams, & Fishnell, 1964; Evans, 1983, p. 150; Hoy, 1985; McDonald, Carson, Palmer, & Slay, 1982; Novack et al., 1979; Svarstad & Lipton, 1977, p. 650; Waitzkin & Stoeckle, 1976; Waskowitz, 1959, p. 322). The very phrase *bearing bad news* is instructive. It suggests that bad news is a burden. If so, then, it is equally a burden for one who delivers it and for one who receives it. Surely, it is a different kind of burden for each, but what needs to be understood are the ways that both parties handle bad news and do so in interaction with one another.

Those who discuss the process uniformly recognize that communication is a key issue, and that research is needed that will shed light on how it can be made better. Interested clinicians desire to change the medical school curriculum to incorporate a greater emphasis on conversational skills, especially those involved in delivering diagnoses to patients (Buckman, 1984; Katz, 1984, p. 152; Novack et al., 1979). However, enormous complications surround the term *communication,* and literature regarding the sharing of information in clinical settings displays misconceptions that I will address under three headings: (a) the problem of communicative effectiveness, (b) the question of whether *intervention* is possible, and (c) what *disclosure* means. While these problems and questions are not capable of being completely answered or solved, they can at least be clarified in order to point the direction for further communication research.

II. ON COMMUNICATIVE EFFECTIVENESS

It is often thought that effectiveness is the key to unlocking the communication process, but deciding what constitutes effectiveness in conversation between physicians and patients is fraught with difficulty. For example, if the diagnosis is of a life-threatening, chronic, or disabling disease or condition, the informing interview is almost an inherently a perverse situation. Even the most competent communicators cannot do much to alleviate what may be a shocking, grievous experience for those on the receiving end of the news. While there may be devices for softening the blow, it is a blow nonetheless, and it is difficult to know how one would measure the force of various communication strategies on lessening its impact. Furthermore, even if we could gauge the effect on patients, it is worth repeating that they are not the only ones who must cope; doctors and clinicians themselves are subject to difficult emotional experiences during the interview.

Another difficulty in determining what would constitute effectiveness in the communication process is the problem of perspective. In the literature on doctor–patient interaction, the variable of effectiveness is usually stated from a clinical point of view; traditionally, researchers have regarded patient compliance as a measure of good medical care and communication. Even when patients' satisfaction is the dependent variable, it is translated into their performing physician-prescribed health regimens and their readiness to consult physicians and clinics. In part, this reflects the assumption of an "identity of interests" between doctors and patients, which translates into the belief that "patients needs are best served by following doctor's orders" (Katz, 1984, p. 86). A consequence of this assumption is that clinicians often are so certain of clients' needs and wants that they never ask the clients themselves what they are (Goldie, 1982, p. 132). And while patients are often reported as falling short of what physicians expect, researchers do not place physicians' behavior under the same rubric as the patients' and report their behavior as noncompliant (Mishler, 1984). In short, investigators have thought that communicative effectiveness occur when patients or clients are able to understand and accept what clinicians have to say, not vice versa.[3]

This problem in measuring communicative effectiveness is illustrated in the following segment from an informing interview that concerns a 5-year-old girl. Immediately before this, the psychologist (*psy* in the transcript) had reported to the mother that *Susan* was delayed in almost every area, that her rate of learning was slow, and that there were no identifiable, reversible causes for the disabilities. It was therefore a permanent condition.

1. *Psy:*	Now when a kid is delayed significantly, and when there's pretty
2.	good reason to believe that the delays are gonna be permanent,
3.	that's what we call mental retardation
4.	(2.6 second silence; psychologist nods)
5. *Psy:*	Slow learning with an indication that it's going to be a long term
6.	kind of problem. That's all that mental retardation means
7.	(22.5 second silence; mother sniffs audibly, then gets up and grabs Kleenex from table in front of her, sits down; psychologist nods head several times)
8. *Psy:*	Let me uhm not try to uh—I don't want to soft coat that because
9.	I mean that's a serious diagnosis and I don't wanna make a
10.	joke or make light of that. It's serious and you have a right to,
11.	and good reason to be real upset. Uh I think it's also tough, um

---

[3] See the review of literature regarding patient satisfaction and compliance in Mishler (1984, chap. 2).

12.		mental retardation does NOT mean uh that the child won't learn
13.		'cause the child WILL learn. Um it'll be a struggle and will take
14.		time and will be SLOwer but the child WILL continue to learn. It
15.		also doesn't mean that she can't live a happy uh and even
16.		proDUctive life
17.		(1.4 second silence)
18.	*Mrs. W:*	That's all I'm looking for, I just—I want her to talk
19.	*Psy:*	Yeah
20.	*Mrs. W:*	And I want her just to—I mean I know she'll be able to take care
21.		of herself, she's doing that quite well now
22.	*Psy:*	Mm hmm
23.	*Mrs. W:*	And— (sighs audibly)
24.	*Psy:*	Yeah I think um—
25.	*Mrs. W:*	If we can get over the speech problem, I think that's the basic
26.		problem
27.	*Psy:*	Would you be happy with that
28.	*Mrs. W:*	Yes I think definitely it's the basic—
29.	*Psy:*	Well it's not the basic problem
30.	*Mrs. W:*	Well to me it is.
31.	*Psy:*	It's a big one
32.	*Mrs. W:*	To me that is the problem. If she can communicate, with the words,
33.		you know we can take care of the rest
34.	*Psy:*	Okay yeah I think um I think that's a healthy way to look at it.
35.		To try to go with one problem at a time and to try to work at it.
36.		(6.5 seconds silence)
37.	*Psy:*	My own feeling would be since she's already using words I'm sure
38.		she'll learn more words
39.	*Mrs. W:*	Thank you eh heh heh heh that's all I wanted to hear

This episode is dramatic partly because of the huge silence (line 7) that occurs after the psychologist twice delivers the diagnostic term *mental retardation* (lines 3, 6). But it is also dramatic because of the disagreement between parent and psychologist regarding what the "basic problem" is. To Mrs. W, Susan's difficulty is only with language and communication (lines 25–26). To the psychologist (and to the other clinicians who evaluated the girl), the problem is more severe than that. If we were to take the traditional approach, the question now would be, How can we get the parent to better understand and accept the clinical findings and recommendations?

That question contains two assumptions. One is the correctness of the clinical perspective, and the other is the appropriateness of convincing the parent to take it. Stepping out of those assumptions momentarily would allow us to at least ask whether the parent has a legitimate position and how she could get the clinician to understand and accept it. I do not want to argue that this a better approach than the other, but to illustrate that stating the issue of communicative effectiveness in terms of recipient compliance with the clinical perspective covers only half of the the equation. If we are truly interested in communicative effectiveness, it has to be examined as a two-sided phenomenon. At the very least, as the above example shows, the recipient's perspective will affect the actual course of talk when a diagnosis is delivered (the mother does, after all, get the clinician to say what she "wanted to hear"; see lines 37–39).

However, the ways in which the recipient's perspective influences communication during the informing interview are often less dramatic than the out-and-out disagreement exhibited in the prior segment. It must be emphasized that the problem is not who is right and who is wrong, but rather one of understanding communication effectiveness as an interactional phenomenon. If this approach is taken, it has consequences for how one views the process, whether as researcher or as practitioner. Consider the following segment, which is from an interview in which a bilingual (Spanish- and English-speaking) mother and a pediatrician participate.

1.	*Dr. L:*	Okay. Well, Now uh since you've been here and through this
2.		thing, how do you see Ricardo now
3.	*Mrs. A:*	I guess I see him better since he here
4.	*Dr. L:*	How do you think things are better.
5.	*Mrs. A:*	'Cause. Let's see how could I explain . . . I guess for me 'cause
6.		you know when I bring him here, for example if he don't know, you
7.		know sometimes they ask him a (call) and he don't know how to
8.		said it, you know, so good. They teach him you know how to say-
9.		to TRY you know
10.	*Dr. L:*	Uh huh
11.	*Mrs. A:*	for him to do it the right way
12.	*Dr. L:*	Mm hmm
13.	*Mrs. A:*	But I thinks how he's doing better because the teacher told me
14.	*Dr. L:*	Mm hmm
15.	*Mrs. A:*	I asked yesterday and she told me to continue to bring him here
16.		'cause he's doing better 'n better in speech
17.	*Dr. L:*	Mm hmm. Is he getting speech therapy here now? Or you just came
18.		in one time and saw the speech therapist
19.	*Mrs. A:*	No this is the third time that he comes here
20.	*Dr. L:*	Right. Okay, just wanted to make sure that something wasn't
21.		going on that I didn't know about
22.	*Mrs. A:*	Heh
23.	*Dr. L:*	Okay now. Basically uhm Ricardo is a BRIGHT, NICE little boy who
24.		um is from everything that I can see in my evaluation and from uh
25.		Miss Gregory's evaluation, is you know—has real intelligence
26.		that is normal. The—there aren't any real problems with his
27.		ability to USE words. The problem is that sometimes the words
28.		don't SOUND quite correct
29.		(1.0 second silence)
30.	*Dr. L:*	And this is a speech problem which CAN be corrected
31.		(0.8 second silence)
32.	*Dr. L:*	The thing is it takes a long time to correct, to correct the kind

33.		of speech problem that he has, it's not going to happen in a
34.		couple of months. It's probably is going to take a couple of
35.		years
36.	*Mrs. A:*	Yes, she told me, the last lady that I saw
37.	*Dr. L:*	All right, Miss Gregory
38.	*Mrs. A:*	She told me, yes
39.	*Dr. L:*	Fine. And this kind of therapy can be done in school. The
40.		speech therapist, ALL the schools have speech therapists
41.	*Mrs. A:*	Yes but they told me at school that I have to take a note so
42.		any doctor will see him if they put him into the speech class at
43.		school. But without the letter I can do nothing
44.	*Dr. L:*	Uh huh. With your permission I will send a copy of my report
45.		to the school

From a clinical point of view, it appears that presenting the information to the mother (in lines 23–35) may not have had the desired result. At points where Mrs. A might have responded to Dr. L's delivery, there are silences (lines 29 and 31).[4] And when the mother does take a turn at talk, she reports (line 36) that the "last lady" she saw has already "told" her something of what Dr. L has just stated. Thus, she marks at least the last bit of information as "no news." This appears to be an instance of a parent, whatever the state of her own attitude on the matter, letting the doctor have her say. Two questions now present themselves. First, why is this? Why does the mother respond in the way she does? Second, from the clinical standpoint, what could be done to elicit from the parent a stronger indication of her beliefs about Ricardo's condition and, in particular, whether she accepts the official findings?

While with the evidence we have, we cannot be definitive, a partial answer to these questions can be attempted. And it requires stepping out of the clinical perspective to consider the parent's position. At the beginning of the segment, Dr. L produces a question about how Mrs. A "sees" her son (lines 1–2). Mrs. A answers with an assessment; she believes he is "better." But notice that she also indirectly praises the clinic (the improvement has occurred "since he here," line 3). Then, the doctor asks for a specification (i.e., "how" Mrs. A thinks "things are better," line 4), and Mrs. A answers in a way that again describes the effectiveness of the clinic (lines 5–9). Subsequently, she quotes Ricardo's school teacher as telling her that the boy is "doing better" (line 13), thereby proposing further (and perhaps more authoritative) evidence for the effectiveness of the clinic. Finally, Mrs. A reports that the teacher told her to continue bringing Ricardo to the clinic. In rough terms, praising the clinic and reporting the teacher's urging to have Ricardo continue there may be appealing for an offer

---

[4] Heath (forthcoming) notes that recipients of diagnostic news regularly withhold responses to the delivered assessment as a way of providing an opportunity for the practitioner to move into a discussion of how the condition can be managed.

from the clinician to indeed let him return on a regular basis.[5] If it is an appeal, the occasioned next move for the clinician is to grant it (by, for example, making the offer) or to deny it (by, for example, noting a reason as to why Ricardo cannot continue visiting the clinic). Dr. L, however, does neither, at least explicitly, in the immediate next turn. Instead, she asks questions (lines 20–21) that appear designed to disambiguate the situation in terms of her knowledge of clinic operations. (It is likely that Mrs. A has misinterpreted diagnostic visits to the speech clinician as therapy, which may account for Dr. L's apparent puzzlement.) Next, Dr. L launches into the delivery of clinical findings and diagnoses. Only after this (lines 23–35), does Dr. L mention where therapy can be obtained.

In short, when Dr. L delivers her news, a request from Mrs. A remains unanswered. It is possible, then, that her silences (29, 31) and the "no news" quotes (36, 38) are not so much exhibiting lack of understanding or lack of agreement with the clinical perspective as they are devices that indicate her waiting for an answer to her own appeal or to the concern with getting therapy that it expresses. Notice that, when Dr. L does return to the issue of therapy by suggesting its necessity (lines 32–35), Mrs. A's "no news" agreement tokens (lines 36, 38) occur immediately and occasion further related talk. When Dr. L next proposes where the therapy can be obtained (lines 39–40), Mrs. A again produces an immediate agreement token ("Yes," line 41) and goes on to make a further request for a "note" (lines 41–3) that is required for Ricardo's placement in the special class. Dr. L answers this request by telling her that a report will go to the school (lines 44–45). Thus, after an exit is made from the delivery of diagnostic and prognostic news, and a discussion of therapy is re-entered, the transfer of turns between the two parties is more regular than during the news delivery segments.

As compared with the prior segment, no dispute occurs here over who is right in regard to Ricardo's condition. Rather, just as articulation of the clinical perspective appears ineffective in obtaining a demonstration of understanding from the parent, so does a voicing of the parental perspective appear unsuccessful in occasioning an immediate and clear clinical response. Thus, the issue need not be whether the parental or clinical perspective is correct and appropriate. The problem is how both positions will influence the actual course of talk during the informing interview. Here, a clinician's delivery of findings, diagnoses, and prognoses in the context of an unanswered appeal from the parent may have resulted in that parent withholding talk until her issue gets returned to the conversational floor.

---

[5] The basis for seeing Mrs. A's talk as an appeal need not be speculation about her motivation. Rather, her talk appears to constitute a "reporting" similar to the kind that Drew (1984) discusses, in which a speaker lists the details of his or her situation without stating its implications or officially taking a position. Such reportings are "cautious" ways of soliciting such things as invitations and offers.

III. ON INTERVENTION

Analysis of the last example suggests that communication might have been more "effective" had the delivery of diagnostic news been a component separate from consideration of the parental concern with getting speech therapy. An appropriate intervention would be to recommend to the deliverer that she indeed should treat the parental concern and objectives earlier on as a possibly different topic from clinical aims and interests. Recall the more general point, however, that communicative effectiveness must be assessed as an interactional phenomenon. For that very reason, it is difficult to design interventions; it is in the nature of the communication process, as an interactional arena, to contain an immense amount of contingency and unpredictability. When we study the process, it does not mean that we can remove the contingency and unpredictability, although that is clearly the aim of those research strategies which are dominant in the social sciences. What it does mean is that we can understand more fully just how that contingency and unpredictability operate, how they are built into the situation.

The idea that communicative effectiveness can be controlled through the introduction of specific methods of information delivery probably derives from the belief that speakers form some conception or intent in their heads before speaking, and that, subsequently, their actual talk expresses such intent (Schegloff, 1984, p. 266). For effective communication, in other words, the problem is to ensure that a given speaker's intent is properly translated into speech, and we often assume that teaching proper skills will solve this problem. Thus, investigators sometimes recommend using a checklist (Dunkelman, 1979) or other pre-established format for informing, even to the extent of not allowing questions that would interrupt it (Solomons, 1970, p. 463). What this approach misses is how the interactive situation in which communication is embedded renders the effectiveness of preordained strategies highly equivocal. One of the readiest illustrations of this is the lecture. One may start with a well-planned way of presenting material to students, but, once something is actually said, audience reactions will have profound consequences for the actual course of things (provided, of course, that speaker is attuned to these reactions and not just reading notes). As Schegloff (1981, p. 72) observes, the wrinkling of brows, a few smiles, or nods, or their absence, may influence the speaker to review a preceding point, to elaborate, to simplify, to move more quickly to the next point, or to articulate a subtlety that was not planned at all.

Thus, communication, or talk, or discourse is not the product of one single speaker or a speaker's mind but is thoroughly interactional, even in lecture situations, and most certainly in other arenas in which turn-taking procedures allow each party equal rights to talk. This leads Schegloff (1981) to argue for viewing discourse (by which he means multisentence units of talk) as interactional achievements. That is, such units are outcomes of various practices that both (or all) parties to an event utilize. Applied to the delivery of diagnostic news, this view makes us appreciate how the actual course of the delivery is not just a matter of the clinician planning what to say and then stringing together a series of diagnostic terms and explanations. This course reflects ways of talking and acting on the part of both clinician and parent. Let us reexamine just the portion of the last interview in which the pediatrician tells of the clinic's findings.

23. *Dr. L:*   Okay now. Basically uhm Ricardo is a BRIGHT, NICE little boy who
24.   um is from everything that I can see in my evaluation and from uh
25.   Miss Gregory's evaluation, is you know- has real intelligence
26.   that is normal. The- there aren't any real problems with his
27.   ability to USE words. The problem is that sometimes the words
28.   don't SOUND quite correct
29.   (1.0 second silence)
30. *Dr. L:*   And this is a speech problem which CAN be corrected
31.   (0.8 second silence)
32. *Dr. L:*   The thing is it takes a long time to correct, to correct the kind
33.   of speech problem that he has, it's not going to happen in a
34.   couple of months. It's probably is going to take a couple of
35.   years
36. *Mrs. A:*   Yes, she told me, the last lady that I saw
37. *Dr. L:*   All right, Miss Gregory
38. *Mrs. A:*   She told me, yes
39. *Dr. L:*   Fine. And this kind of therapy can be done in school. The
40.   speech therapist, ALL the schools have speech therapists
41. *Mrs. A:*   Yes but they told me at school that I have to take a note so
42.   any doctor will see him if they put him into the speech class at
43.   school. But without the letter I can do nothing
44. *Dr. L:*   Uh huh. With your permission I will send a copy of my report
45.   to the school

This telling can be broken into three main segments. The first one (lines 23–28) concerns the diagnosis. Here, the doctor places positive descriptions of the boy in the initial part of the turn (lines 23–26), and formulates his "problem" in the latter part (lines 24–28). Thus, there is a good news/bad news structure to the way that the diagnosis is told. The second segment (lines 30–35) is occupied with prognosis and suggesting the necessity of therapy, and the third (lines 39–45) is specifically concerned with where the therapy can be obtained.

    Why do these three segments appear here? An answer that examines only the clinician's style of news delivery might suggest that she had the diagnostic, prognostic, and therapeutic components of a single telling preformulated in her mind and then schematically and unilaterally injected them into the conversation. An answer that also deals with the parent's reactions would focus, as we did earlier, on the silences at lines 29 and 31, as well as her eventual talk at line 36. That there is a shift from diagnosis to prognosis is an interactional achievement. According to the turn-taking system described by Sacks, Schegloff, and Jefferson

(1974), when a speaker has arrived at turn completion (as at line 28), and a co-participant does not start his or her own (line 29), speaker may initiate another unit of talk (line 30). This phenomenon may occur more than once (see the silence at line 31 and the following talk by Dr. L at lines 32–35) before recipient takes a turn (as in line 36). In fact, given the absent talk from Mrs. A, Dr. L's shift from diagnosis to prognosis appears as a means of eliciting her response. That is, given that the "bad news" part of the diagnostic segment obtains no remark from recipient, speaker exits from the segment by returning to some "good news," which is that the "speech problem CAN be corrected," although it will take a "long time." In short, the silences after the diagnostic news delivery result in specific work by speaker before turn transition is achieved, and that work involves a shift of topic from diagnosis to prognosis and therapy. Thus, the manner in which these three segments (diagnosis, prognosis, therapy) occur is as much a product of recipient's (the parent) activities as it is of teller's (the doctor).

Let us now return to the issues of contingency and unpredictability. I believe it would be hard to fault this clinician in terms of her clarity, informativeness, and style. For example, while there is bad news to deliver, it is softened by the preceding good news, the complimentary assessments of Ricardo. And yet, something is lacking in terms of effective communication. As we noted earlier, Mrs. A's own position regarding diagnosis never becomes visible. Whether Mrs. A is awaiting the return of talk to her own concern, or whether her silences operate in other ways, it seems that even the best delivery strategy on the part of a clinician has to confront the contingency of parental devices for receiving news that make the effectiveness of any given strategy highly unpredictable. Thus, it is reasonable to suggest that Dr. L should have answered Mrs. A's appeal before entering into a discussion of diagnosis, but not because we can know beforehand how successful that would be in getting a clearer display of Mrs. A's view regarding the nature of Ricardo's disability. The more general strategy is for clinicians to be alive to how the talk is going, and thus alter what they might project as effective ways of accomplishing their own tasks (including the delivery of diagnostic news) in response to behavioral (verbal and nonverbal) cues of the recipient.

In other words, to say that preestablished formats are inappropriate is not to suggest that intervention with respect to making communication better is impossible. To the contrary, the proposal is to develop interventions that deal with the real nature of talk. Clinicians sometimes prescribe blanket strategies, such as adhering to a policy of complete truth or complete falsehood, which are notoriously inept (Waitzkin & Stoeckle, 1976). But there is a more subtle argument; clinicians should become as familiar as possible beforehand with any particular recipient's physical condition, emotional state, or desire for information (Dunkelman, 1979; Hoy, 1985; Waitzkin & Stoeckle, 1976). The problem here is that prior knowledge, especially when it is gleaned from second-hand sources such as charts, records, and informal social networks (cf. Cicourel & Kitsuse, 1963,

Meehan, 1986), can lead to assumptions that impede sensitivity to recipients' cues during the actual informing episode (cf. Steele, Jackson, & Gutmann, n.d., pp. 8–9). The approach to be urged on clinicians is to use their understanding of patients, parents, and others, to increase and not decrease their interactive responsiveness to such cues (Frankel & Beckman, 1989). As Saunders (1969) has stated it, "The real question is not 'What do you tell your patients?' but rather, 'What do you let your patients tell you?' " (quoted in Novack et al., 1979, p. 899). The fact is that clinicians can be taught speaking and listening skills (Beckman & Frankel, 1984; Frankel & Beckman, 1982) that, for example, maximize the potential for presenting clinical assessments as agreeing with what recipients already know and believe or in an affirmative and nonconflicting manner (Maynard, forthcoming-a, -b).

Thus, if communicative effectiveness is defined, not in terms of how well one party gets his or her view across to the other, but in terms of understanding the organization of talk (i.e., its patterns and structure), there are other kinds of benefits to be gained. Clinicians, already well aware of the importance of explaining their own perspective during the informing interview, may want to orient less to promoting it and more to the perspective of the patients or parents, because the latter will affect both the receipt and, ultimately, the actual delivery of diagnostic news. The task that the communications or conversation researcher faces is to describe and analyze how both parties put the interview together. That kind of approach on the part of clinicians means being cognizant of the contingencies of talk and again implies an increased sensitivity to the collaborative enterprise that communication is.

IV. ON DISCLOSURE

The thrust of recent opinion in the medical profession and the general public is toward the advocacy of disclosure. Although the evidence is mixed (*The Lancet*, 1980), it does seem this policy has benefits. Often patients or other recipients suspect the truth and are relieved when informed of it (Goldie, 1982, p. 132). And, sometimes, fear of the unknown is worse than dealing with something known, even if it is bad. Anxiety about an amorphous future can be an impediment to possible recovery (Reynolds, 1978, p. 1675).

However, something is still missing when the choice facing doctors is framed in dichotomies of withholding or disclosing information, concealing or revealing "facts," and lying or telling the "truth." Missing is consideration of how deliverers present information, facts, and truth. For example, as Goldie (1982, p. 129) observes, "Patients may be told without having to ask questions or they may told the truth in response to a question." Stated differently, if clinicians decide that disclosure is a good policy, it is also a matter of the methods by which that is done. Thus, attention is needed to the sociolinguistic context surrounding the bearing of bad news. This matter seems straightforward enough, but the di-chotomous terms of the debate regarding disclosure remain resilient for a deep-seated reason.

A. The Conduit Metaphor

The reason for lack of systematic attention to the sociolinguistic context of news deliveries is an attitude that language is a neutral and transparent medium of communication through which information is, or can be, transferred from one party to another. Reddy (1979) calls this the "conduit metaphor," a common-sense way of thinking about communication which suggests that one person delivers information to another by inserting thoughts and feelings into words and sending the words along the conduit. People receive the words at the other end and extract the encoded thoughts and feelings from the words. The phrase, "I can't seem to get these ideas into words," utilizes this metaphor and also conveys its bias, which is that it is a speaker's job to make communication successful. A hearer (or reader) has the relatively passive job of unpacking the thoughts or emotions from the words in which they are contained. The phrase displays a further presumption of the conduit metaphor, to the effect that the communica-tion process is ordinarily unproblematic. Once you succeed at getting your thoughts into words, communicative success is automatic (Reddy, 1979, p. 295). Failure to communicate only means that a person has not exerted the effort to pack thoughts into words.

Clinically, the conduit metaphor lends to the historic disinclination of medical schools to take communication between doctors and patients seriously. The at-titude seems to be that, when a disease or lesion has been discovered, the hard work is over. What remains is to simply encode the condition using relevant medical categories and then speak those categories to the patient. Social scien-tists have shared this view as well, as is evident, for instance, in research on staffing interviews that occur between clinicians and parents of developmentally disabled children. Svarstad and Lipton (1977) assessed the informativeness of such interviews by coding whether clinicians were

1. Frank—i.e., whether they used official diagnoses;
2. Explanatory—whether they discussed the meaning of these diagnoses; and
3. Specific—whether they provided the child's I.Q. score.

Coding interviews for frankness, explanatoriness, and specificity presumes that the communicational work of the clinician lies in simply putting findings into the correct words. Clearly, such a coding strategy partakes of the conduit metaphor.[6]

---

[6] Lipton and Svarstad (1977) discuss the importance of the manner in which a clinician presents a diagnosis, and further highlight the interactional effects of this manner. For example, if a clinician is

The advantage a metaphor offers is in allowing us to comprehend one concept (communication) in terms of another (conduits). The trouble is, the same metaphor hides other aspects of the concept. Specifically, the conduit metaphor suggests that words and sentences have meanings that are independent of any context (Lakoff & Johnson, 1980, pp. 10–11). It compels clinicians and social scientists to assume that one has communicated once the correct diagnostic words are sent along the conduit, because the denotational meaning of these words is carried along with them and nothing else is important. That the sociolinguistic context of information is significant, however, can be illustrated with respect to two phenomena: the style of the deliverer, and the audience to whom news may be presented.

B. Style of Diagnostic News Delivery

We might want all clinicians (in the field of developmental disabilities, for example) to be frank (to use official diagnoses), explanatory (to discuss the meaning of such diagnoses), and specific (to provide a child's I.Q. score), but the question is whether that is enough. The fact is that, even when being informative in these terms, clinicians present news in a variety of ways. The sheer observation that a pediatrician has provided a diagnosis or an I.Q. score tells nothing of the manner in which it was delivered. For instance, we have seen that a pediatrician, before telling her clinical findings, may ask parents for their view of the child.[7] In many cases, that enables the pediatrician to carefully fit technical diagnoses to the parents' own formulations. I call this an *aligning style,* an example of which occurs in an interview between a male pediatrician, Dr. R, and both parents of a child with the pseudonym of David.

Dr. R: Have you noticed any improvement since I saw him last, which was over three, four months ago

The parents, with the father doing most of the talking, reply that David appears more "controlled" now, and less "wild." But the mother says that "he won't

---

"vague" in communicating, that might elicit emotional reactions from parents that are discomfiting. This, in turn, would make the clinician less likely to be further informative about the child's disability. The point raised by Lipton and Svarstad is that such effects cannot be traced when simply coding interviews for whether or not a child's diagnosis or IQ is mentioned. For another example of the conduit metaphor affecting social science research on informing, see Waitzkin and Stoeckle (1976, p. 267), who discuss the "transition probabilities" of the words that clinicians use. Judges measure these probabilities as a function of the content of these words; the more the content, the less the probability that a word can be excised from a transcript without loss of meaning. For a review and critique of this and other "information exchange" approaches in studies of doctor–patient interaction, see West (1984, pp. 23, 32–33).

[7] For a systematic consideration of the phenomenon of clinicians asking parents their view of a child, see Maynard (forthcoming-a, -b).

listen," and the father adds that "you really have to yell at him, repeat, repeat, repeat." Then:

```
 1. Mr. H:    You know I think basically the problem is as I also said to
 2.           Ellen that uh when you reach the age of about four or four and
 3.           a half you more or less stop maturing right there
 4. Dr. R:    Okay. Well that kind of leads into what we found uh, essentially
 5.           what we have found in David is that at a certain point his
 6.           development HAS stopped
 7. Mr. H:    Right
 8. Dr. R:    and uh, when tested he then tends to look to us like a kid
 9.           with retarded development
10. Mrs. H:   Mm hmm
11. Mr. H:    Mmm
12. Dr. R:    This is a kid who's reached a certain point and then he stopped
13. Mr. H:    Right
```

Given that the parents have displayed their view of David, when Dr. R provides descriptions of the boy (beginning in lines 4–6), they can be tied to this view. That is, Dr. R suggests that what the father has said "leads into what we have found" (line 4). Furthermore, the characterization of David that "his development HAS stopped" (lines 5–6) is produced as an assessment agreeing with the father's (line 3). (The emphasis on "has" is a way of marking the agreement.) Only after Mr. H produces a further display of agreement ("right," line 7) does Dr. R introduce the more official diagnosis of David as a "kid with retarded development" (lines 8–9).[8] Thus, the clinician here proposes to align the clinical view to that of the parents.

This can be contrasted with the next example, in which the clinician makes no attempt to elicit from the parents their view of the child before launching the diagnostic news delivery.

```
 1. Dr. D:    I think—you know I'm sure you're anxious about today and I
 2.           know this has been a really hard year for you. And I think
 3.           you've really done an extraordinary job in dealing with something
 4.           that's very hard for any human being or any parent—and you
 5.           know Mrs. Roberts and I can talk as parents as well as
 6. Mrs. R:   True
 7. Dr. D:    uh my being a professional. It's HARD when there's something
 8.           not all right with a child, very hard. And I admire both of
 9.           you really and, and as hard as it is seeing that there IS
10.           something that IS the matter with Donald, he's NOT like other
```

---

[8] The "retarded development" characterization is met with ambiguous utterances by both Mr. and Mrs. Hamilton (lines 10–11). These appear to actually withhold their disagreement with the term "retarded." Their objection to the term emerges later in the interview. See Maynard (in press).

11.   kids, he IS slow, he is retarded
12. *Mrs. R:*   HE IS NOT RETARDED!
13. *Mr. R:*   Ellen
14. *Mrs. R:*   HE IS NOT RETARDED!
15. *Mr. R:*   Ellen. Uh please
16. *Mrs. R:*   NO!
17. *Mr. R:*   May—look—it's their way of—I don't know
18. *Mrs. R:*   HE'S NOT RETARDED ((sobbing))
19. *Dr. D:*   He can learn and he is learning

Dr. D, a female pediatrician, does begin the interview with an apparent attempt at identifying with and complimenting the parents. She congratulates them on the "extraordinary job" they had done in dealing with the problem (line 3), invokes her own status as a parent (lines 4–5; Dr. D also has a disabled child), states how "hard" it is (line 7), and expresses her admiration for the parents (lines 8–9).

Dr. R then proceeds, in a step-by-step fashion, to deliver the diagnosis (lines 9–11), whereupon Mrs. Roberts, in a series of subsequent turns (lines 12, 14, 16, and 18), loudly disagrees and ends up sobbing. Thus, the pediatrician produces the clinical characterizations as a first piece of business, and in this interview that strategy appears rather direct and blunt. In contrast, providing a diagnosis secondarily to eliciting parents' discussion of the problem allows the clinician to anticipate their receptivity, and/or to tailor descriptions to the parents' announced perspective. The point here is, not to advocate for one or the other approach in the delivery of diagnostic news, but to make explicit that the manner in which words are spoken is as crucial in the communication process as the words themselves. The sheer recommendation that a clinician tell parents an exact diagnosis or I.Q. score or any other bit of information says nothing about how they should present it. The conduit metaphor obscures this very basic matter.

C. The Audience for Delivery of News

Let us say that language is a straightforward communication channel or conduit for the transfer of information, and let us agree that it is better to tell what is known regarding the condition of a patient than not. How that skirts another aspect of the sociolinguistic context of news is vividly shown in a segment from a program that aired on public television entitled "The Brain." This was a series of broadcasts that covered everything from anatomy and physiology to mental illness, creativity, and other phenomena associated with mental activity.

In the first program, which dealt with brain diseases, a neurologist, Dr. Plum, with his resident colleagues, was shown visiting patients in their rooms at New York Hospital. As the physicians begin their rounds, the narrator says, it is "their object not only to provide patients with the best medical cure, but to advance knowledge of the healthy brain by understanding the diseased brain." The first patient they visit appears to have already been diagnosed as having Parkinson's disease. The neurologist queries her about her medication and comments on her postural rigidity. With the next patient, Dr. Plum performs a variety of sensory tests by touching him at various places on his hands, face, and legs, and asking him what he feels. The narrator informs us that, "even by now, Dr. Plum suspects a slight stroke near the brain stem," as the neurologist says, "Why don't we look at the pictures," which seems to suggest that they will confirm the diagnosis by some harder evidence than so far elicited.

Although in neither of these first two visits is the doctor seen delivering diagnostic news to the patients, in the last vignette, after asking about and assessing a woman's symptoms, he tells her she has multiple sclerosis:

1.	*Dr.:*	What's the main problem right this minute?
2.	*Pt.:*	The weakness in my arm in a line of pain
3.	*Dr.:*	How about your legs?
4.	*Pt.:*	No just only at night they ache a lot
5.	*Dr.:*	But you're having problems walking I understand?
6.	*Pt.:*	Yes
7.	*Dr.:*	Where wh— why is that? Can you tell?
8.	*Pt.:*	It seems like I drag my right leg
9.	*Dr.:*	Dragged your right leg and a weak right arm
10.	*Pt.:*	(Nods)
11.	*Dr.:*	(Hitting patient's right arm, then left, with mallet) Let me— let
12.		me look at a couple o' things. Best reflexes on the right.
13.		(lifting legs:) what about the reflexes in her legs, are they— are
14.		they the same way?
15.	*Res.:*	Sh— sh— this right predominates.
16.	*Dr.:*	(Moves legs) Relax, relax, let it go. Can we let her walk, Lenny?
17.	*Res.:*	Sure, sure.
		(Change of scene; patient is standing and facing camera, Dr. Plum's back is to camera.)
18.	*Dr.:*	I'm curious. She has so much power. I'm not quite clear yet as to
19.		what to— what— now just walk. I'm right here and Miss Marcus is
20.		right there so you won't fall. Come toward me. (Camera is on
21.		patient's feet). Now I really see three things. (Camera cuts to
22.		residents silently watching). One is that she circumducts that
23.		right leg and holds her right arm stiffly. (Camera shows doctor
24.		gazing at patient, then cuts to residents watching). This
25.		combination of cerebellar dysfunction in one arm and cortico-spinal
26.		tract dysfunction in the other— (Camera closes up on Dr.'s profile,
27.		he shakes his head, raises his eyebrows, and looks at patient.)
28.		I'm sorry you know it's stronger than any other laboratory test we
29.		have. (He moves forward and smiles; puts hand on her shoulder.)
30.		It's— there's no other disease but multiple sclerosis that will do

31.   it. And that's the way we have to treat you. Thank you.
32. *Pt.:*   (Smiles, mumbles something, including a possible "thank you.")

The imbalance between an emphasis on performing a diagnosis and presenting it to a patient is reflected in this segment in at least two ways. First, out of the
three doctor–patient interviews displayed, only one of them—the last—contains
a segment wherein the doctor informs the patient of his findings. In the other
two, it is the voiceover that tells the audience what diagnosis is implicated. To
some degree, that may reflect the filmmaker's choice about how to present the
story of "the brain." Recall, however, that, as these diagnostic interviews began,
the physicians' task is defined both as providing patients with the best medical
care and with advancing medical knowledge of the brain. The narrative structure,
nonetheless, emphasizes an advancement of knowledge that overshadows the
part of patient care which involves sharing medical information with those from
whom it is generated. That is, showing the doctor in his search for findings while
using the narrator to convey results to the television audience accentuates the
importance of the search and devalues that of the conveyance itself. This suggests that the stronger emphasis on making as opposed to presenting a diagnosis
is not endemic to the profession of medicine but belongs, in some manner, to the
wider culture.

A second way the imbalance shows up is that, when the doctor is shown
delivering a diagnosis to the patient, it occupies only a small portion of the
interview (in terms of the transcript, the last 3 out of 32 lines). Now we do not
know the relation between "what actually happened" and what the filmmaker
presents. On the one hand, the interview may have been organized that way and
the filmmaker merely captured it on videotape. On the other hand, if a resident
saw the patient beforehand (see lines 5 and 16, which seem to indicate so), it is
possible that she was already told a probable diagnosis and that Dr. Plum is here
merely confirming rather than initially delivering a diagnosis. Thus, once again,
the deemphasis of the informing process may partly reflect the filmmaker's
judgments.

But whether Dr. Plum telling the patient her diagnosis is a confirmation or
initial delivery, it displays important features that are utterly ignored if we were
to examine the segment through the prisms of the conduit metaphor or the debate
about disclosure. In the terms of that debate, the doctor is probably attune to his
historically specific mandate. He has told the patient, almost in the process of
discovering it, what he knows, he has revealed the "facts" of her condition, he
has told the truth. In terms of the Svarstad-Lipton (1977) criteria, he has been, at
least, (a) frank, in telling the patient her official diagnosis, and (b) specific, in
reporting the major symptoms by which the diagnosis is made. His informing
may have been lacking in (c) explanatoriness, but he nonetheless scores well on
two out of three criteria.

We do not have to look too closely to see that these frameworks miss much of what occurs. In reporting on the symptoms, for example, the doctor resorts to technical terminology or jargon (lines 22–26) which, though no doubt correct and true, must surely be as lost on the patient as it is on the television audience (or at least this member of it). In addition, the doctor delivers the diagnosis in rapid-fire fashion. Starting with a apology or remedial term ("I'm sorry," line 28), he characterizes her visible symptoms as "stronger than any other laboratory test" (line 28), reports the disease that matches the symptoms (lines 30–31), comments that treatment will follow from the diagnosis (line 31), and then produces a device ("Thank you," line 31) that proposes to terminate the interaction. In response, the patient appears to fumble for what to say (line 32). Perhaps that, and even the doctor's rapid-fire delivery, are due to being "on camera," but there is more to it. When the patient is walking towards the doctor, he talks about her symptoms in the third person: "she circumducts that right leg and holds her right hand stiffly . . . " While at least the symptoms appear in a "person-description" (Maynard, 1982), he next uses technical terms to characterize conditions that, although embodied, are depersonalized; i.e., the terms do not describe a person but parts of the body ("cerebellar dysfunction in one arm and corticospinal tract dysfunction in the other"). Finally, the diagnosis is exhibited as an account for these symptoms ("no other disease but multiple sclerosis that will do it"). There is no news delivery of the sort that, while dependent on preceding diagnostic activity, still forms a discrete and separate event wherein the doctor tells the news to the patient (Maynard, in press). Instead, Dr. Plum pronounces the diagnosis, for anyone who is present to hear, in a way that primarily appears to solve the puzzle the symptoms present.

Note that these features are not ones that can be explained by the lack of a proper bedside manner. His nonverbal behavior includes smiling and putting his hand on the patient's shoulder, which are ways of "keying" or overlaying his verbal production with "ritualistic mollifiers" (Goffman, 1976, p. 48) that soften the news. More important than omissions in the conduct of the doctor is the presence of a particular audience. That which links the use of jargon, the referencing procedures, and pronouncement of diagnosis is the didactic or teaching environment in which the doctor is acting. Clearly, his relationship is not just with the patient in each of these episodes but with the residents who accompany him. The patient, then, is not entirely a subject who possesses an illness experience and to whom the doctor must speak, but a repository of signs, symptoms, and conditions relevant to the medical discourse in which he and the residents are engaged. From the patient's perspective, this is no doubt a climactic interactional episode, while from the clinician's perspective it is merely part of a series of similar encounters that make up the day's work (Cicourel, 1987). To paraphrase Hughes (1951, p. 320), what is one person's crisis is another person's routine. That this problem is to some degree widespread can be inferred from a study by Reynolds (1978, p. 1674). Hospital patients express a dislike for "the way in which they were excluded from discussion by doctors who muttered at the end of the bed, using incomprehensible jargon." Patients were insulted by such behavior because they thought doctors underestimated their intelligence.

Thus, it is not enough to regard language as a medium of information transfer, or a resource for encoding conditions in the world so that, once spoken, it is the end of the matter. Telling a diagnosis, in other words, is not simply a matter of finding and naming a condition in the presence of a patient, or sending that name down the conduit. Hearing the diagnosis does not just involve listening carefully to what is said, or being a proper recipient at the end of the conduit. The historical debate about telling the truth or not to patients needs to be recast by first discarding the conduit metaphor. Participants bear diagnostic news as part of social context that includes the courses of action their talk partly constitutes. Quite simply, being part of rounds and participating in a teaching interview infuse "delivering and receiving a diagnosis" with a particular character that is different from what it would have in environments where the audience was different (limited, for example, to the patient or patient's relatives solely).

D. Summary

Not enough is known about how clinician styles and the audiences to which deliverers speak affect the course of diagnostic news delivery. Other aspects of sociolinguistic context also need investigation, including the manner in which recipients receive the news. Especially important may be comparisons of professional and lay modes of talk. For example, Wallat and Tannen (1982), studying interviews between 12 medical personnel and the parents of an 8-year-old child, describe a tendency of the parents to discuss the child's problems in narrative, storytelling fashion, whereas professionals utilized a more telegraphic and focused style of talk.[9] A related issue is how the pacing of talk, paralinguistic mannerisms, questioning strategies, uses of silence, and so on vary according to participants' cultural backgrounds (Tannen, 1985). Research by Labov (1972) suggests the importance of differences between Standard English and Black English Vernacular, and how the confrontation of these two styles can result in the practitioners of one radically misreading the capacities and intentions of practitioners of the other. Erickson (1975) discusses this phenomenon and its effects on the relation between counselors and students in the school environment. In medical settings, Cicourel (1985, p. 201) argues that a clinician's "limited knowledge of sociocultural and cognitive-linguistic issues" can mean a

---

[9] Existing research documents a tendency among professionals to overemphasize formal tests as evidence for diagnostic categories, when in fact they rely greatly on observation (Mehan, Hertweck, & Meihls, 1986, chap. 6; Pomerantz, Mastriano, & Halfond, forthcoming). Further research needs to compare such practices among deliverers with the ways in which recipients use evidence to support their positions regarding diagnosis.

failure to understand those "mental" or "folk models" through which patients deal with technical information about illness.

IV. CONCLUSION

The disclosure of medical information has always been, and still is, a controversial topic. Perhaps more than ever, clinicians now think that revealing information is crucial to the well-being of patients or clients (Reiser, 1980). The neglect of effective disclosure may be a major precipitant of patient dissatisfaction (Hoy, 1985; Turnbull & Turnbull, 1978; Watizkin & Stoeckle, 1976). But belief in the importance of disclosure provides no ultimate relief for the problems of bearing bad news in clinical settings. In a variety of ways, the burden of bad news weighs heavily on both deliverers and recipients. Thus, clinicians and other concerned parties call for research that can lead to improved communication. However, for that research to proceed, various misconceptions about the process must be laid aside. Effectiveness of communication often translates into the clinicians or professionals being able to put their views across to the patients or clients without regard to how the patients' or clients' perspectives influence their receptivity as well as the actual course of diagnostic news delivery. Attempts at intervention, at prescribing strategies that make for effective communication, often presume that the problem for the teller of bad news is simply one of having preformulated means for saying it and then utilizing those means in conversation. This ignores the contingencies of actual interaction, especially the kind of responses that the bad news recipient provides. Finally, communication is not a conduit or a vehicle for the transfer of information; if that were the case, then remedies to improve communication would be a simple matter of cleaning up the language, refining our referencing activities, and being frank, explanatory, and specific. The task that clinicians face would be similar to that with which social scientists have been preoccupied—developing proper coding procedures.

Each of these critiques of traditional concepts of communication has its positive implication. If the communication process can be approached as an interactional arena in which both deliverer and recipient are attempting to realize their practical interests, then clinicians may better appreciate how consequential the caretaker or patient perspective is in organizing the talk that occurs, including their own delivery of diagnostic news. If this delivery cannot be preplanned to guarantee that any particular method will obtain a desired display of understanding or acceptance from the client, deliverers may nonetheless increase their reflexive awareness of the contingencies of recipient response that in turn reflect the recipient's structure of knowledge and belief. That the communication process is a contingent one does not mean there is no virtue in considering the different strategies that do exist for the delivery of diagnostic news. To the contrary, if the communication of information is not performed through a conduit, one thing to be considered is the matter of style or manner (Beckman & Frankel, 1984). The suggestion is that different kinds of interactional work can be accomplished through the ways in which a clinician speaks the specialized terminology of the clinic. One can, for instance, display alignment with the recipient's perspective by relating that terminology to the formulations that clients employ, or can be relatively confrontive by laying out diagnostic categories without ascertaining the client's view. A further consequence of abandoning the conduit metaphor is to allow consideration of the social groupings in which delivery of diagnostic news occurs. When speaking the information they have, clinicians may want to ask who their audience is. These and other aspects of the sociolinguistic context that surround the bearing of bad news in clinical settings deserve further, systematic scrutiny.

REFERENCES

Anderson, K. A., & Garner, A. M. (1973). Mothers of retarded children: Satisfaction with visits to professional people. *Mental Retardation, 11,* 36–39.

Appell, M. J., Williams, C. M., & Fishnell, K. N. (1964). Changes in attitudes of parents of retarded children effected through group counseling. *American Journal of Mental Deficiency, 68,* 808.

Atkinson, J. A., & Heritage, J. (Eds.). (1984) *Structures of social action: Studies in conversation analysis.* Cambridge, England: Cambridge University Press.

Beckman, H. B., & Frankel, R. M. (1984). The effect of physician behavior on the collection of data. *Annals of Internal Medicine, 101,* 692–696.

Berg, J. M., Gilderdale, S., & Way, J. (1969). On telling parents of a diagnosis of mongolism. *British Journal of Psychiatry, 155,* 1195–6.

Buckman, R. (1984). Breaking bad news: Why is it still so difficult? *British Medical Journal, 288,* 1597–99.

Caldwell, B., Manley, E., & Nissen, Y. (1961). Reactions of community agencies and parents to services provided in a clinic for retarded children. *American Journal of Mental Deficiency, 65,* 582–589.

Cicourel, A. (1985). Doctor-patient discourse. In T. A. Van Dijk (Ed.), *Handbook of discourse analysis: Volume 4* (pp. 193–202). London: Academic Press.

Cicourel, A. (1987). The interpenetration of communicative contexts: examples from medical encounters. *Social Psychology Quarterly, 50,* 217–226.

Cicourel, A., & Kitsuse, J. (1963). *The educational decision makers.* Indianapolis, IN: Bobbs-Merrill.

Clark, R. E., & LaBeff, E. E. (1982). Death telling: managing the delivery of bad news. *Journal of Health and Social Behavior, 23,* 366–380.

Drayer, C., & Schlesinger, E. (1960). The informing interview. *American Journal of Mental Deficiency, 64,* 363–370.

Drew, P. (1984). Speakers' reportings in invitation sequences. In J. M. Atkinson & J. Heritage (Eds.), *Structures of social action: Studies in conversation analysis.* Cambridge, England: Cambridge University Press.

Dunkelman, H. (1979). Patient's knowledge of their condition and treatment: How it might be improved. *Medical Practice, 2,* 311–14.

Eden-Piercy, G. V. S., Blacher, J. B., & Eyman, R. K. (1986). Exploring parents' reactions to their young child with severe handicaps. *Mental Retardation, 5,* 285–291.

Emde, R., & Brown, C. (1978). Adaptation to the birth of a down's syndrome infant: grieving and maternal attachment. *American Academy of Child Psychiatry, 17,* 299–323.

Engel, G. L. (1977). The need for a new medical model: A challenge for bomedicine. *Science, 196,* 129–136.

Erickson, F. (1975). Gatekeeping and the melting pot: interaction in counseling encounters. *Harvard Educational Review, 45,* 44–70.

Evans, D. P. (1983). *The lives of mentally retarded people.* Boulder, CO: Westview Press.

Fletcher, C. (1980). Listening and talking to patients. *Medical Practice, 281,* 845–847.

Fox, R. (1957). Training for uncertainty. In R. Merton, G. Reader, & Kendall (Eds.), *The student-physician* (pp. 207–218). Cambridge, MA: Harvard University Press.

Frankel, R. M., & Beckman, H. B. (1982). IMPACT: An interaction-based method for preserving and analyzing clinical transactions. In L. Pettegrew (Ed.), *Explorations in provider and patient interaction* (pp. 71–85). Louisville, KY: Humana Press.

Frankel, R. M., & Beckman, H. B. (1989). Conversation and compliance with treatment recommendations: An application of microinteractional analysis in medicine. In B. Dervin, L. Grossberg, B. Okeefe, & E. Wartella (Eds.), *Rethinking communication, Vol. 2. Paradigm exemplars.* (pp. 60–74) Beverly Hills, CA: Sage Publications.

Garfinkel, H., & Sacks, H. (1970). On formal structures of practical actions. In J. C. McKinney & E. A. Tiryakian (Eds.), *Theoretical sociology* (pp. 338–66). New York: Appleton-Century-Crofts.

Gayton, W. F., & Walker, L. (1974). Down Syndrome: Informing the parent: A study of parental preference. *American Journal of the Disabled Child, 127,* 510–512.

Glaser, B. G., & Strauss, A. L. (1965). *Awareness of dying.* Chicago, IL: Aldine.

Goffman, E. (1961). *Asylums.* New York: Anchor.

Goffman, E. (1976). *Gender advertisements.* New York: Harper Colophon.

Goldie, L. (1982). The ethics of telling the patient. *Journal of Medical Ethics, 8,* 128–33.

Graliker, V. V., Parmelee, Sr., A. H., & Koch, R. (1959). Attitude study of parents of mentally retarded children II: Initial reactions and concerns of parents to a diagnosis of mental retardation. *Pediatrics, 24,* 819–821.

Heath, C. (forthcoming). Diagnosis and assessment in the medical consultation. In P. Drew & J. Heritage (Eds.), *Talk at work: Social interaction in institutional settings.* Cambridge, England: Cambridge University Press.

Heritage, J. (1984). *Garfinkel and ethnomethodology.* London: Polity Press.

Hoy, A. M. (1985). Breaking bad news to patients. *British Journal of Hospital Medicine, 34,* 96–99.

Hughes, E. (1951). Work and self. In J. H. Rohrer & M. Sherif (Eds.), *Social psychology at the crossroads.* New York: Harper and Row.

Katz, J. (1984). *The silent world of doctor and patient.* New York: Free Press.

Kelly, N., & Menolascino, F. (1975). Physician's awareness and attitudes toward the retarded. *Mental Retardation, 13,* 10–13.

Kirman, B. H. (1953). Mongolism: Diagnosis and management at home. *Medical World, 78,* 258–265.

Kleinman, A. (1980). *Patients and healers in the context of culture.* Berkeley, CA: University of California Press.

Kurtz, R. A. (1964). Implications of recent sociological research in mental retardation. *American Journal of Mental Deficiency, 69,* 16–20.

Labov, W. (1972). *Language in the inner city: Studies in the Black English vernacular.* Philadelphia, PA: University of Pennsylvania Press.

Lakoff, G., & Johnson, M. (1980). *Metaphors we live by.* Chicago, IL: University of Chicago Press.

Lipton, H. L., & Svarstad, B. L. (1977). Sources of variation in clinicians' communication to parents about mental retardation. *American Journal of Mental Deficiency, 82,* 155–61.

Matheny, A. P., Jr., & Vernick, J. (1969). Parents of the mentally retarded child: emotionally overwhelmed or informationally deprived. *Journal of Pediatrics, 74*, 953–959.

Maynard, D. W. (1982). Person-descriptions in plea bargaining. *Semiotica, 42*, 195–213.

Maynard, D. W. (1989). Notes on the delivery and reception of diagnostic news regarding mental disabilities. In T. Anderson, D. Helm, A. J. Meehan, & A. Rawls (Eds.), *New directions in sociology* (pp. 54–67). New York: Irvington.

Maynard, D. W. (forthcoming-a). Perspective-display sequences and the delivery of diagnostic news. In D. Boden & D. H. Zimmerman (Eds.), *Talk and social structure*. London: Polity Press.

Maynard, D. W. (forthcoming-b). On co-implicating recipients' perspective in the delivery of diagnostic news. In P. Drew & J. Heritage (Eds.), *Talk at work: Social interaction in institutional settings*. Cambridge, England: Cambridge University Press.

McDonald, A. C., Carson, K. P., Palmer, D. J., & Slay, T. (1982). Physicians' diagnostic information to parents of handicapped neonates. *Mental Retardation, 20*, 12–14.

McLenahan, L., & Lofland, J. (1976). Bearing bad news. *Sociology of Work and Occupations, 3*, 251–272.

Meehan, A. J. (1986). Recordkeeping practices and the policing of juveniles: *Urban Life, 15*, 70–102.

Mehan, H., Hertweck, A., & Meihls, J. L. (1986). Handicapping the *handicapped: Decision making in students' educational careers*. Palo Alto, CA: Stanford University Press.

Menolascino, F. J. (1977). *Challenges in mental retardation: Progressive ideology and services*. New York: Human Sciences Press.

Michaels, E. (1983). Deliver bad news tactfully. *Canadian Medical Association Journal, 129*, 1307–1308.

Mishler, E. G. (1984). *The discourse of medicine: Dialectics of medical interviews*. Norwood, NJ: Ablex Publishing Corp.

Novack, D. H., Plumer, R., Smith, R. L., Ochitill, H., Morrow, G. R., & Bennett, J. M. (1979). Changes in physicians' attitudes toward telling the cancer patient. *Journal of the American Medical Association, 241*, 897–900.

Oken, D. (1961). What to tell cancer patients: A study of medical attitudes. *Journal of the American Medical Association, 175*, 1120–1128.

Parks, R. M. (1977). Parental reactions to the birth of a handicapped child. *Health and Social Work, 2*, 52–66.

Parmelee, A. H. (1956). Management of mongolism in childhood. *International Record of Medicine, 169*, 358–361.

Pomerantz, A. M., Mastriano, B. P., & Halfond, M. M. (forthcoming). Student clinicians' difficulties while conducting the summary diagnostic interview. *Text*.

Reddy, M. J. (1979). The conduit metaphor. In A. Ortony (Ed.), *Metaphor and thought* (pp. 284–324). Cambridge, England: Cambridge University Press.

Reiser, S. J. (1980). Words as scalpels: transmitting evidence in the clinical dialogue. *Annals of Internal Medicine, 92*, 837–842.

Reynolds, M. (1978). No news is bad news: patients' views about communication in hospital. *British Medical Journal, 1*, 1673–76.

Rubin, A. L., & Rubin, R. L. (1980). The effects of physician counseling technique on parent reaction to mental retardation diagnosis. *Psychiatry and Human Development, 10*, 213–221.

Sacks, H., Schegloff, E. A., & Jefferson, G. (1974). A simplest systematics for the organization of turn-taking for conversation. *Language, 50*, 696–735.

Saunders, C. (1969). The moment of truth: Care of the dying person. In I. Pearson (Ed.), *Death and dying* (pp. 49–78). Cleveland, OH: Case Western Reserve University Press.

Schegloff, E. A. (1981). Discourse as an interactional achievement: Some uses of 'uh huh' and other things that come between sentences. In D. Tannen (Ed.), *Georgetown University Roundtable on Languages and Linguistics* (pp. 71–93). Washington, DC: Georgetown University Press.

Schegloff, E. A. (1984). On some questions and ambiguities in conversation. In J. M. Atkinson & J. Heritage (Eds.), *Structures of social action* (pp. 28–53). Cambridge, England: Cambridge University Press.

Solnit, A., & Stark, M. (1961). Mourning and the birth of a defective child. *Psychoanalytic Studies of the Child, 16,* 523–536.

Solomons, G. (1970). Counseling parents of the retarded: The interpretation interview. In F. J. Menolascino (Ed.), *Psychiatric approaches to mental retardation* (pp. 455–475). New York: Basic Books.

Solomons, G., & Menolascino, F. J. (1968). Medical counseling of parents of the retarded. *Clinical Pediatrics, 7,* 11–16.

Steele, D. J., Jackson, T. C., & Gutmann, M. C. (n.d.). *The compliance assessment sequence in hypertension treatment encounters.* Milwaukee, WI: Mt. Sinai Medical Center.

Svarstad, B. L., & Lipton, H. L. (1977). Informing parents about mental retardation: A study of professional communication and parent acceptance. *Social Science and Medicine, 11,* 645–751.

Tannen, D. (1985). Cross-cultural communication. In T. A. Van Dijk (Ed.), *Handbook of discourse analysis: Vol. 4* (pp. 203–215). London: Academic Press.

The Lancet. (1980). In cancer honesty is here to stay. *The Lancet, ii,* 245.

Turnbull, A., & Turnbull, H. R. (Eds.). (1978). *Parents speak out: Views from the other side of the mirror.* Columbus, OH: Charles E. Merrill.

Waitzkin, H., & Stoeckle, J. D. (1976). Information control and the micropolitics of health care: summary of an ongoing research project. *Social Science and Medicine, 10,* 263–276.

Wallat, C., & Tannen, D. (1982, August). *The dilemma of parent participation in medical settings: A linguistic analysis.* Paper presented at the annual meetings of the American Sociological Association, San Francisco.

Waskowitz, C. (1959). The parents of retarded children speak for themselves. *Journal of Pediatrics, 54,* 319–329.

West, C. (1984). *Routine complications: Troubles with talk between doctors and patients.* Bloomington, IN: Indiana University Press.

Wikler, L. (1981). Chronic stresses of families of mentally retarded children. *Family Relations, 30,* 281–288.

Wolfensberger, W. (1967). Counseling the parents of the retarded. In A. A. Baumeister (Ed.), *Mental retardation: Appraisal, education, and rehabilitation* (pp. 329–400). Chicago, IL: Aldine.

Wolfensberger, W., & Menolascino, F. J. (1970). A theoretical framework for the management of parents of the mentally retarded. In F. J. Menolascino (Ed.), *Psychiatric approaches to mental retardation* (pp. 475–493). New York: Basic Books.

Zwerling, I. (1954). Initial counseling of parents with mentally retarded children. *Journal of Pediatrics, 44,* 469–479.

6

Gender and Communication Behaviors: A Review of Research*

Mary-Jeanette Smythe
Department of Communication
University of Missouri-
Columbia

---

*Anita Taylor and Barbara Bate encouraged me to undertake this review. They and Cheris Kramerae provided valuable feedback and suggestions for organizing the literature.

I am especially grateful to Robert M. Arkin and Pamela J. Benoit of the University of Missouri for their thoughtful and incisive comments on earlier versions of this essay.

Feminist scholars, psychologists, and linguists frequently disagree concerning how the terms *sex* and *gender* should be used. While some behavioral researchers have proposed usage of *sex difference* to designate only biologically caused differences and of *gender difference* to describe environmentally caused differences, others have asserted that *gender difference* should be used only when individuals' gender orientations have been determined. Although communication behaviors are socially learned, my preference for the term *gender* does not reflect a judgment about causation. Rather, this term captures more fully the meanings our society and its members attribute to female and male categories.

If men are always more or less deceived on the subject of women, it is because they forget that they and women do not speak altogether the same language. (Amiel, Journal 1868)

Early research in the fields of communication, psychology, sociology, and linguistics uncovered powerful stereotypes regarding male and female behavior. Rarely questioned, much less empirically substantiated, such stereotypes nonetheless gained force through frequent application in popular and scholarly descriptions of feminine and masculine behavior. Strikingly distinct depictions characterized men as stoic, objective, independent, analytic, disciplined, authoritative, competitive, domineering, task-oriented, unsentimental, and aggressive; women were portrayed as passive, subjective, empathic, supportive, noncompetitive, sentimental, interpersonally oriented, submissive, nonaggressive, dependent, and emotional (Baird, 1976; Key, 1975). Familiar dichotomies ("task-oriented" males vs. "social emotional oriented" females; Strodtbeck & Mann, 1956; "instrumental" and "expressive"; Piliavin & Martin, 1978; "dominant" and "affiliative"; Hammen & Peplau, 1978) quickly emerged.

Predictably, early studies found an abundance of such differences (Gleser, Gottschalk, & Watkins, 1959; Eakins & Eakins, 1978). Yet, critics observed a number of flaws inherent in these research efforts, two of which were especially significant. Robin Lakoff was among the first to contend that the labeling of women's linguistic behaviors reinforced images of women as tentative, polite, submissive, and powerless individuals whose competence was not even remotely comparable to men's. Lakoff identified behaviors she felt distinguished between male/female speech as well as a number of broader language conventions that discriminated against women in systematic ways. Though anecdotal, Lakoff's (1973, 1975) seminal works galvanized researchers and provided a number of hypotheses that focused investigations of what she called "women's language."

Similarly, Cheris Kramer (1974) detected discrepancies in the evolving literature on linguistic sex differences. Among other problems, Kramer noted that sex role stereotypes pervaded the literature. She labeled these allegations of sex differences based entirely on stereotypes "folk-myths." Although their impact has been substantiated empirically (Berryman & Wilcox, 1980; Bradley, 1981), stubborn adherence to the idea that dichotomous labels like "instrumental vs. expressive" capture meaningful distinctions has continued to create confusion and contradictions within the literature.

These and other factors inspired Maccoby and Jacklin's (1974) classic work titled *The Psychology of Sex Differences*. They reviewed over 1,400 published investigations covering cognitive functioning, personality, and social behavior, concluding that few expected sex differences were actually substantiated. Although only four areas yielded clear sex differences (three in the intellectual skill domain and one from the domain of social behavior), Maccoby and Jacklin readily conceded that, in most instances, the research base was inadequate to establish the accuracy or inaccuracy of presumed sex differences. As Deaux (1984) observed, that concession lured researchers to explore the sex differences question with renewed enthusiasm, if not necessarily fresh insights or improved methodologies.

It is to this swiftly accumulating body of work that the current review is addressed. In the years since Maccoby and Jackson's work, studies of sex differences in communication behaviors have proliferated briskly, as witnessed by the appearance of new journals to accommodate research and numerous book-length treatments of the topic (e.g., Key, 1975; Thorne & Henley, 1975; Eakins & Eakins, 1978; Kramerae, 1981; McConnell-Ginet, Borker, & Furman, 1980; Smith, 1985; Berryman & Eman, 1980; Pearson, 1985). Integrating a literature that evolves from so many different disciplinary perspectives whose abundance is rivaled only by its diversity is a formidable undertaking. Given the limitations of space, this review is necessarily selective. Further, several factors inherent in the sex differences in communication literature which make synthesis difficult. First, distinctions among data drawn from actual behaviors, self-reported behaviors, and other-perceived behaviors are not always clearly drawn. Difficulties of interpretation are further exacerbated by the absence of cross-situational sampling of relevant behaviors. And the preponderance of samples composed of white, upper middle class university students in public, mixed-sex situations remains a perennial dilemma.

Additional problems accrue from the fragmentary character of this literature. Many studies report differences in communication behaviors, but these are frequently buried in studies of some other phenomenon such as self-disclosure, interpersonal attraction, and so forth. Because the findings are often tied to the goals of specific investigations, there is little continuity in the selection and measurement of variables or the reporting and discussion of results. As Philips (1980) noted, comparability across disciplinary perspectives is especially problematic, yielding a melange of variables and associated findings rather than a set of basic linguistic categories that could effectively explore relationships among key variables.

Problems notwithstanding, the accumulation of new findings and emergence of competing explanatory perspectives dictate a review. In the absence of a unified theoretical perspective, the organizational schema of this chapter is drawn from the characteristics of the literature itself. Findings are grouped thematically, and presented in four sections concerning (a) differences in language performance or production studies, (b) differences in the evaluation of speakers' language behavior, (c) differences in nonverbal behaviors, and (d) differences associated with communication style or self-presentation. Following these summaries, explanations for gender differences are identified, with particular emphasis upon the major issues and controversies addressed by each framework. Implications of the androgyny construct for study of the gender differences in communication are considered, and the chapter concludes with an assessment of current efforts and advances some recommendations for future investigations.

I. GENDER AND PERFORMANCE: SEX ASSOCIATED DIFFERENCES IN LANGUAGE PRODUCTION

Early studies of language focused on conversations. They revealed differences between men and women which generally reinforced stereotypic conceptions of masculine and feminine speech. Careful scrutiny, however, suggested that no language cues were the preserve of either sex. Rather, any sex differences reflected in these studies were sex-preferential rather than sex-exclusive (Bodine, 1975). In an earlier review, Haas (1979) suggested that the literature best could be summarized by examining findings related to form, topic, content, and use of spoken language. In the interest of comparability, a similar pattern will be used here.

A. Differences in Form and Use

Regarding form and use, the variables that have received the most empirical attention include tentativeness, linguistic correctness, talkativeness, questions, and interruptions. The most robust set of findings, have been those concerning linguistic correctness. Writing in 1975, Thorne and Henley asserted that these were the best documented of all linguistic differences research, and noted that the comparisons cut across race (Wolfram, 1969), class (Labov, 1972), and culture (Trudgill, 1972). The general finding, that women use more standard, prestige language forms than men, appeared well established.

While no new evidence in the past decade has emerged to suggest revision of this position, related notions that men's language is more coarse, expletive-laden, or vulgar than women's (Haas, 1979) have found less confirmation. A series of studies concerning use of profanity has challenged the prevailing stereotypes. Perceptions of speakers who use profanity, according to Mulac (1975), did not differ according to either speaker or listener sex. Cohen and Saine (1977) found that both men and women exhibited more tolerance for swearing by members of the opposite sex. In both instances, the authors explained their findings in terms of shifting perceptions of appropriate male/female behavior within society. More recently, Selnow (1985) reported that women claimed to incorporate profanity in their interactions less frequently than men and expressed relatively greater disapproval of profanity use in a variety of settings. Yet the differences in self-reported swearing among males and females in Selnow's study were remarkably small, and the level of tolerance for use of profane language was comparable, particularly in those instances of profanity use in mixed-sex company. Taken together, these profanity studies seemed to reveal some subtle but distinct changes.

Numerous researchers and writers have described women's speech as more tentative and uncertain than men's. Lakoff's (1973) early analysis of this phenomenon identified several specific cues which she felt created the impression of uncertainty associated with women's discourse. Tag questions at the ends of declarative sentences, thought to reflect speakers' lack of confidence, were allegedly used most by women. Hedges and qualifiers, expressions which blunted the definitiveness of assertions, were another form, as were intensifiers and empty adjectives. Lakoff's assertions, of course, were based on her intuitions and observations. Others have dismissed the tentativeness dimension of linguistic differences as dubious at best (Berryman, 1980; Berryman-Fink & Wilcox, 1983).

Studies of the tentativeness of womens' speech have yielded contradictory findings. Consider the research on tag questions. In a frequently cited study, Dubois and Crouch (1975) reported that males used tag questions (following formal presentations at professional meetings) more, rather than less often, than females. Other studies, less commonly cited (Newcombe & Arnkoff, 1979; Martin & Craig, 1982; Baumann, 1976), all found no significant gender differences in the use of tag questions.

Some studies of tentative speech forms, however, have yielded gender differences supporting the stereotype. Analysis of problem-solving group interactions (McMillan, Clifton, McGrath, & Gale, 1977) yielded differences between the speech of college men and women, with women employing more tag questions, more imperatives in query form and more intensifiers like *such* and *so*. In a study of family interactions, Gleason and Weintraub (1978) reported that mothers produced twice as many tag questions during conversations with preschoolers than did fathers. Fathers also phrased more simple requests than mothers, an observation corroborated by comparisons of requests generated by male day-care teachers and their female counterparts. Finally, Crosby and Nyquist (1977) coded use of the "female register," defined by use of tag questions, empty adjectives, and hedges or qualifiers in three different settings. In two of the three settings examined, they found that women used the female register significantly more than men.

The tendency to qualify one's remarks or speak less fluently contributes to judgments of tentativeness or uncertainty. Research on both of these topics has been sporadic. In a study examining the effects of sex and sex-role orientation on language behavior during initial interactions, Smythe, Arkin, Nickel, and Huddleston (1983) found that use of qualifiers varied more by sex role orientation than by sex *per se*. Consistent with the linguistic stereotype, Smythe and her colleagues discovered that sex-typed males were least likely to qualify their remarks, followed by androgynous women and sex-typed women. Individuals who used qualifiers most were androgynous males. In another study of initial interactions, Martin and Craig (1983) determined that, while men and women did not differ in use of qualifiers when talking to men, men used qualifiers least when paired with women, and women qualified most when paired with another woman. Schultz, Briere, and Sandler (1984), however, reported no differences in males' and females' use of qualifiers when describing a picture.

Studies of fluency typically focused on fillers and nonfluencies, based upon the presumption that women who used fillers, or exhibited false starts or unfinished sentences, appeared tentative and uncertain. Two studies reported by Hirschmann (1973, 1974) reported discrepant findings on women's use of fillers. Martin and Craig (1983), as well as Smythe et al. (1983), reported no significant differences between males' and females' use of fillers, and found no sex differences in any of the measures of nonfluencies. Given this pattern of findings, it becomes apparent that some elements of the tentativeness construct may be more situationally specific than previously thought. A range of topic, task, and situational influences need to be explored more precisely. The investigations reviewed here are too contradictory to resolve the relationship between gender and tentativeness.

Three other dimensions of linguistic form that have generated significant amounts of research include the use of questions, interruptions, and talkativeness. Stereotypic conceptions about the behavior of the sexes on these dimensions have appeared since Jespersen's (1922) time, yet have only recently received systematic, empirical attention. Regarding questions, the literature is characteristically inconsistent. In an ethnographic analysis of married couples interactions, Fishman (1978) found that wives asked many more questions than their husbands. Similarly, Hirschman (1973), and Smythe et al. (1983), have reported significantly higher frequency of question use by females during initial interactions. Two other studies of initial interactions, however, produced contradictory findings. Martin and Craig (1983) found no differences in questioning in same-sex or mixed-sex dyads, while Douglas (1988) found higher rates of questioning in same-sex dyads during first encounters.

Considerably more is known about the relative talkativeness of the sexes, and most of the evidence contradicts Jespersen's observation to the effect that "the superior readiness of speech in women is a concomitant of the fact that their vocabulary is smaller than men" (1922, p. 253). In fact, only two studies support this contention, and these were rather unusual. One focused exclusively on 4-year-olds (Brownell & Smith, 1973). The other required subjects to describe a stimulus picture and found that females used more words to do so than men (Schultz et al., 1984). A stronger case might be made that men are the more verbose, as evidenced by studies encompassing marital communication (Strodtbeck 1951), dyadic communication (Argyle, Lalljee, & Cook, 1968), jury deliberations (Strodtbeck & Mann, 1956), and responses to stimulus pictures (Wood, 1966). Finally, empirical evidence finding no differences between men and women on talkativeness include studies on initial interactions (Martin & Craig, 1983;

Smythe et al., 1983) and interaction styles (Hirschmann, 1973, 1974). These findings were corroborated within small group settings, where McMillan et al. (1977) found no significant differences between men and women. Brouwer, Gerritsen, and DeHaann (1979) also reported no difference in amount of discourse. And in studies exploring total speaking time as an unobtrusive measure of dominance during dyadic interactions, neither Markel, nor Long and Saine (1976), nor Rogers and Jones (1975) found any sex differences in talkativeness.

Regarding this body of research, it seems apparent that the studies reporting no differences are more prevalent than those finding differences. Moreover, these more recent investigations are arguably more rigorous methodologically, inspiring greater confidence in the accuracy of their findings. Even so, considerable variance in findings remains. One somewhat speculative explanation for the discrepancies among findings on talkativeness is the diversity of measurements used in these studies, ranging from word counts to mean utterance length to average length of speaking turn. When these factors are considered, the presumed distinction between men and women seems small indeed.

A final element of linguistic form thought to distinguish one sex from the other is interruptions. Lakoff (1975), Bernard (1972), and other feminist analysts have long contended that men achieve and maintain conversational dominance by interrupting, particularly during mixed-sex interactions. Among the most commonly cited studies on this topic were Eakins and Eakins's (1976) analysis of interruptions during mixed-sex faculty meetings, and Zimmerman and West's (1975) investigation of interruptions during dyadic interactions. In both studies males interrupted females more frequently than females interrupted males. Similar results were reported by West (1979), Argyle et al. (1968), McMillan et al. (1977), and Natale, Entin, and Jaffe (1979). Kennedy and Camden (1983) examined mixed-sex groups, and their findings supported the trend to the extent that women were interrupted more often than men. The stereotypic pattern was disrupted, however, by their findings that women initiated interruptions more often than men. Studies reporting no significant differences between men and women during face-to-face interactions include Roger and Scumacher (1983), Rogers and Jones (1975), Martin and Craig (1983), and Smythe et al. (1983). Finally, studies exploring the relationship between interruptions and sex composition of dyads have failed to find consistent patterns of sex differences (LaFrance, 1981; Smythe et al., 1983; Trimboli & Walker, 1984; Dindia, 1987). Rather, the results of these studies revealed that, in all dyadic pairings, one interactant typically interrupts more frequently than his or her partner, but that behavior cannot be predicted by sex.

The contradictory findings suggest that some mediating variables may affect the likelihood of interruptions by either sex. For instance, the two studies of initial interactions reporting no differences (Martin & Craig, 1983; Smythe et al., 1983) might reflect a normative avoidance of any behavior that could be constructed as rude or disruptive. Individuals instructed to have a "get-acquainted" chat are likely to practice positive self-presentation. Similarly, competitive or problem-solving tasks like those used in the McMillan et al. (1977) or Kennedy and Camden (1981, 1983) investigations would probably enhance the likelihood of interruptive behaviors. Research which explores the incidence of interruptions relative to task or other context cues is required to clarify the matter.

An equally plausible alternative discussed by Dindia (1987) suggests that the inconsistent findings on interruptions spring from researchers' failure to isolate and test effects of subject sex, sex of their partner, and the interaction of these factors on the number of interruptions while controlling for between-partner correlation. By implication, therefore, a number of reported findings of differences may actually have been incorrectly attributed to sex when they were in fact the result of interaction effects or artifacts attributable to comparisons drawn from correlated data.

B. Gender Differences in Topic and Content

Early investigations of actual sex differences in speech focused on the topics of conversation chosen by men and women. In 1922, Moore eavesdropped on fellow pedestrians in New York City and reported that business dominated male–male talk, followed by amusements, other men, women, clothing, buildings, and decoration. Women spoke to one another most often about men, clothing, buildings, decorations, other women, amusement and business. Broadly similar findings were obtained by Landis and Burtt (1924). More recently, Haas (1981) has reported that, among children ages 4, 8, and 12, boys together talked most about sports while girls talked more about school. Finally, the stereotypic conception that men discuss sports and women discuss personal matters in same-sex conversations has been supported in self-report studies reported by Johnson and Aries (1983) and Haas and Sherman (1982).

Studies of speech content have yielded similarly distinct male and female patterns. When researchers ask subjects to recount a vivid personal experience or to describe a stimulus picture, women's language is characterized by more interpretive, evaluative, and emotional references (Haas, 1979). Men, by contrast, are likely to employ terms referring to spatial relations, quantity, and activity (Gleser et al., 1959). Similar findings demonstrating women's descriptions as more interpretive and men's as more precise have been reported by Wood (1966), Swacker (1975), and Schultz et al. (1984).

Taken together, the foregoing investigations seem to support a fairly stereotypic conception of male/female language. That appearance is somewhat misleading. For this series of studies, the arresting feature was the predominance of significant effects concerning male language and the comparative absence of predicted effects for so-called "women's" language. Gleser and associates (1959), for instance, reported no sex differences at all in linguistic categories presumed to be essential in a female register. In like fashion, Schultz et al.

(1984) were unable to find any support for the notion that children or women use "female" language.

The absence of large or consistent gender differences in spoken communication has gone largely unattended. An unhappy consequence of this oversight is that insupportable claims about the communication of men and women are made repeatedly. What is needed, therefore, is a systematic re-examination of the alleged "differences," using more precise operationalizations of variables, better research designs, and appropriate statistical analyses.

II. GENDER AND JUDGMENTS: SEX ASSOCIATED DIFFERENCES IN PERCEPTIONS OF LANGUAGE

Although the actual performance or production of specific linguistic cues may be quite variable across individuals, the perceptions of those cues are rarely as fluid or malleable. Listener evaluations of male and female speech invoke a wide array of cultural beliefs, norms, and stereotypes about sex and sex role behaviors embedded deep within our consciousness. Characterized by some authors as the *attributional* or *diagnostic* function of spoken communication, these impressions have a profound impact upon listeners' perceptions of and actions toward speakers (Berger & Bradac, 1982). For this reason, language scholars have examined the perceptions of speech with as much interest as was first directed toward speech performance.

Initial studies in this area revealed the enduring character of sex-based linguistic stereotypes. Jespersen's (1922) allegations that women's discourse was more hyperbolic, euphemistic, and refined while men's talk was more vivid, innovative, and slang-ridden were corroborated more than 50 years later in Kramer's (1977) study on perceptions of male and female speech. The college students in her sample made the following attributions concerning males' speech:

> demanding voice, deep voice, boastful, use swear words, dominating, show anger, straight to the point, militant, use slang, authoritative, forceful, aggressive, and sense of humor. (p. 157)

Females' speech evoked the following trait assignment:

> enunciate clearly, high pitch, use hands and face to express ideas, gossip, concern for the listener, gentle, tact, talk a lot, emotional, detailed, smooth, open, self-revealing, enthusiastic, good grammar, polite speech, and gibberish. (p. 157)

Based upon the listing provided by Kramer (1975), it is hardly surprising that authors repeatedly describe women's speech as weaker and less forceful than men's. Some studies provide general, albeit empirically flawed, support for this generalization. Siegler and Siegler (1976) examined male and female speech stereotypes and found that subjects could draw distinctions between male and female speech based on specific behaviors (e.g., tag questions) and make consistent attributions concerning a speaker's intelligence on these bases. Similarly, Edelsky (1976) selected 12 language variables thought to differentiate between the speech of men and women and systematically varied these elements in a stimulus composed of 25 statements. Respondents were instructed to determine the sex of the individual most likely to make each statement. Their accuracy, in terms of matching syntax to stereotype, approached 100%. Though interesting, both studies examined evaluations of small samples of written, rather than spoken, statements. Neither study provides direct evidence bearing on whether linguistic form affects listener judgments in actual speech contexts.

Research designed to address these concerns with greater precision explored the relationship between the sex-based linguistic content of messages and the attributions naive listeners make about speaker characteristics. Berryman and Wilcox (1980) reported a pair of studies in which subjects responded to source-anonymous messages that were allegedly the contributions of a participant in a group discussion. Messages were composed of either male or female sex-typed language. Results indicated that subjects distinguished male and female languages reasonably well and made sex role judgments consistent with linguistic stereotypes. That is, the use of questions and incomplete sentences in the "female" message, and the grammatical errors, slang, and obscenities in the "male" message, affected subjects' perceptions.

In an actual group discussion, Bradley (1981) investigated the impact of evidence, qualifying phrases, and sex upon naive group members' perceptions of a trained confederate's credibility, intelligence, and attractiveness. Male and female confederates systematically varied their use of tag questions, disclaimers, and statements supported by evidence during discussions. Results indicated that both males and females were perceived as more influential and likable when they used well-supported arguments, but on the issue of qualifying phrases a significant sex difference emerged. Tag questions and disclaimers did not appear to affect group members' judgments of men, but resulted in negative perceptions of knowledge, intelligence, and influence when used by women. Men could use stereotypically feminine language cues with little negative impact on their images, while the use of sex-stereotypic feminine cues by women results in lowered evaluations.

Devaluation associated with feminine language cues has not been a consistent finding. In a study of sex-appropriate and sex-inappropriate language use during a taped interaction Berryman-Fink and Wilcox (1983) found that feminine language features were associated with higher credibility ratings than masculine language, even when a male speaker used sex-inappropriate language. While this finding is quite consistent with Bradley's (1981) observation that males could use cross-sex language with impunity, there was no comparable negative effect on the perceptions of women who used feminine language features.

As evidenced by the foregoing studies, interest in identifying patterns of speech that are perceived as uniquely feminine or masculine, or in uncovering language cues that elicit differential judgments concerning the status of speakers, has dominated this research area. One perspective implies inherent differences associated with gender, while the other implies socially defined, external differences that are potentially gender-free. Following are brief syntheses of the research associated with powerful–powerless speech and gender-linked language effect constructs.

A. Powerful-Powerless Speech

Research on the social consequences of speech flowered during the an era when linguistic authorities became concerned with the racial implications of spoken language. Labov (1972) was among the first to articulate the difference and deficit hypotheses—two views of the discrepancies between black and white language. These hypotheses also find expression in recent research (e.g., Warfel, 1984) that explored whether women's speech constitutes a distinct, nongeneric style (difference hypothesis) or whether in addition to distinctiveness it possesses structural or substantive inferiorities (deficit hypothesis).

As a construct, powerful language style evolved from interest in the relationship between speech style and evaluations of speakers, spawned in large part by Howard Giles and his group at Bristol University (Giles & Powesland, 1975). Research since that time has been influenced as well by the works of O'Barr and his colleagues, whose initial observations of more than 150 hours of courtroom procedures refined the powerful–powerless speech construct. Using both ethnographic and experimental methods, O'Barr and his associates identified the following components as characteristic of powerless speakers. Those individuals with low social status tended to exhibit:

1. polite forms; *please, thank-you*
2. hesitation forms; *uh, well, you know*
3. questioning forms; rising inflections in declarative contexts
4. especially formal grammar; bookish grammatical forms
5. intensifiers; *so, very, surely*
6. hedges; *kinda, I think*

A powerful language, by contrast, was characterized by an absence of the cues associated with powerlessness.

Obvious parallels between "powerless" speech and Lakoff's (1975) concept of "women's" language generated new investigations. To test the relationship between sex and powerful/powerless language, Erickson, Lind, Johnson, and O'Barr (1978) prepared transcripts incorporating or avoiding powerless language. Testimony was presented either in written transcript form or on audio tape by a male or female witness. Measures of credibility, attractiveness, and acceptance of the "witnesses' " position were taken from listeners. Findings revealed a strong effect for powerful speech. Powerful speakers were perceived as more attractive and as more credible (especially when listener and speaker were the same sex), and they attained generally higher acceptance of the position advocated in their "testimony." Although tentative, Erickson et al. (1978) felt their data revealed no significant distinctions based on gender. Broadly similar results were reported by Lind and O'Barr (1979) and O'Barr and Atkins (1980). These studies suggested that gender and status cues were confounded in listeners' perceptions. While numerous writers (e.g., Kramerae, 1981; Smith, 1985) have argued that women's speech reflects their oppressed social status, these particular data provided a poor test of the assertion, since it was impossible to determine the extent to which listener expectations for courtroom speech behaviors affected the results.

The potentially critical role of listener expectations in this type of research has been demonstrated in several investigations. In two studies of linguistic forms (e.g., use of tag questions, hedges, and compound requests) Newcombe and Arnkoff (1979) prepared a series of statements, which were read by male and female speakers. Listeners were asked to evaluate speakers in terms of assertiveness, warmth, and politeness, and to estimate their use of tag questions, qualifiers, and compound requests. Results suggested positive ratings were associated with avoidance of these stereotypically feminine cues, but the only significant effect was that men were perceived as more assertive than women even when they used qualifiers. Listeners also overestimated use of linguistic forms in sex-stereotypic ways, suggesting that listeners' stereotypic expectations may be a stronger source of variation in judgments of individuals than their actual behaviors. Liska, Mechling, and Stathas (1981) documented a tendency for raters to associated deferential language style (compositionally and functionally equivalent to powerless languages) with femininity. Their finding suggested that language behaviors influenced respondents less than their own stereotypic expectations concerning women's or men's speech.

While some evidence (Bradac, Hemphill, & Tardy, 1981; Bradac & Mulac, 1984b) suggested that stereotypic judgments regarding the social consequences of powerful speech styles (i.e., higher credibility, competence, or attractiveness) were correct, other findings were less uniform. Wright and Hosman (1983) explored the use of hedges and intensifiers in simulated courtroom testimony. Using transcripts, respondents evaluated the credibility, attractiveness, and blameworthiness of male and female "witnesses" whose testimony varied systematically with regard to linguistic power cues. As Erickson et al. (1978) had found, both male and female speakers were perceived as less attractive when they used hedges and as more credible when they avoided hedges. Here, however, the sex of the speaker as well as his or her speech behaviors affected listener evaluations. Women who used intensifiers were perceived as especially attractive, though men were not, and women who used hedges were generally evaluated much lower than men who used that cue. These results not only suggested a differential, gender-linked standard of evaluation, but also contradicted the original powerless speech construct.

Various factors might affect the relationship between linguistic forms and the perceptions they evoke. The possibility that listeners' attitudes toward women color their perceptions of women's speech was a central part of Lakoff's (1973) first analysis. Warfel (1984) called this the "discrimination hypothesis" and reasoned that certain listener traits might predispose them to devalue women speakers because they are women rather than because women used powerless language. Using Bem's (1981) gender schema as a listener trait that could promote greater acceptance of a different (e.g., powerless) message style, Warfel presented subjects with transcripts of interpersonal exchanges designed to appear powerless or generic (free of powerless cues). Results revealed that listeners' gender schemas (sex-typed or non-sex-typed) did not affect their evaluations of speakers, but two findings clarified the powerful/powerless language construct. As anticipated, powerless speakers were perceived as less dominant than their powerful counterparts. Powerless speakers, however, were perceived as more credible than "generic" speakers, indicating that consequences of either speaking style are neither simple nor invariable.

Another factor suggested by Bradac and Mulac (1984b) concerned listeners' perceptions of speaker intentions. In a pair of studies respondents were provided with transcripts alleged to be responses of a male or female interviewee. Intent was manipulated through insertion of key words in the description of the interviewee suggesting either an authoritative or a sociable orientation. Results revealed a hierarchy of power levels in the transcripts defined by linguistic forms (i.e., tags, hesitations, polite forms, etc.). Messages characterized by powerful cues were deemed superior, followed by those with polite cues. Clearly powerless forms (i.e., hesitations and tags) were judged as relatively ineffective. Communicator intent affected perceptions of the interviewees in that less powerful language forms were more acceptable when the speaker appeared sociable rather than authoritative. Most interesting, however, was the finding that the relationship between power of style and gender was weak, even obscure. In both studies, sex of the interviewee had virtually no effect on respondents' judgments of his or her style.

Assessment of this cohort of studies revolves around methodological controversies. One concerns the explicit or implicit communication of experimenter expectations to respondents. It beggars the imagination to suppose that transcripts filled with tags or hedges do not alert judges that researchers are studying the impact of language variables. Moreover, to the extent that subjects perceived a connection between the language and the sex of the alleged communicator, their responses may have been influenced by social desirability. In the Bradac and Mulac (1984b) studies, for instance, subjects were instructed to rate "powerfulness" and "effectiveness" of statements attributed to "Susan Vivianson" or "John Jackson." And, although the authors noted that their female respondents were more sensitive to the "powerless" implications of tags and hedges than were males, they were unconcerned that the female subjects outnumbered males by two to one in both of their studies.

More important, however, are the objections concerning the external validity or generalizability of findings obtained through use of transcripts in which powerful or powerless language cues are inserted at will. Even assuming these insertions accurately depict "typical" language behavior, important reservations remain. Although most authorities agree that transcribed messages have relatively high internal validity, a serious question concerns how well the evaluation process subjects perform in these studies approximates the assessment processes involved in actual face-to-face communication. Do individuals scrutinize spoken language as closely as they are instructed to evaluate a transcript? The extensive literature on cognitive response models reviewed elsewhere (Petty & Caccioppo, 1981) would suggest not.

Finally, concerns voiced by Jackson and Jacobs (1983) regarding generation of message categories and measurement techniques in language perception studies are relevant here. The language-as-fixed-effect fallacy imposes severe limitations on the generalizability of results from these language judgment studies. Each of these objections represents a significant empirical issue which must be addressed before the relationship between language and power can be understood.

B. Gender-Linked Language Effect

Hopper (1982) argued that actions by themselves are neither powerful or powerless, but rather acquire their designation through association with individuals who are either powerful or powerless. In contrast to this position is research on the *gender-linked language effect,* a construct positing that men and women exhibit characteristic patterns of verbal expression quite apart from any consideration of linguistic stereotype. Most work on the gender-linked language effect has been produced by Mulac and his associates as an outgrowth of work with the Speaker Dialect Attitudinal Scale. Mulac and Rudd (1977) recorded male and female speakers during spontaneous descriptions of stimulus photographs. Somewhat serendipitiously, the authors discovered a major sex difference in raters' evaluations of the transcribed descriptions. Female speakers were perceived as significantly higher on aesthetic quality than their male counterparts, who were in turn perceived as higher in dynamism. In a follow-up study of four different age groups, using the same basic methodology, Mulac and Lundell (1980), reported identical findings.

To assess the generalizability of the effect, Mulac and Lundell (1982) used segments of public speeches made by male and female students. Two groups of raters, college students and older adults, evaluated the transcripts using the SDAS scales. Findings on aesthetic quality and dynamism were replicated. Additionally, females' speeches were judged higher in a factor labeled *socio intellectual status*. This factor was essentially described by negation; women's language avoided first-person pronouns, vocalized pauses, grammatical errors, and active-voice verbs. In the authors' view, this constituted a literate style.

To what extent are gender differences typical or detectable in male/female speech? Hall and Braunwald (1981) examined gender cues in same and cross-sex dyadic conversations by showing respondents clips from television programs. Each clip was rated on several dimensions and results indicated that subjects perceived both males and females as more dominant, condescending, business like, and unpleasant when they spoke to a man. The listeners' naive, stereotypic expectations had been that females would be most dominant when speaking to other women. In spite of their stereotypic expectations, however, raters evaluated the language cues "objectively." Another study, reported by Mulac, Bradac, and Mann (1985), focused on children's programs. Brief, random segments were transcribed and coded for 37 variables hypothesized to distinguish male and female speech. Results generally supported the gender-linked language effect. That is, children's TV programs were characterized by gender-differentiated language consistent with sex role stereotypes.

Discovery of the stereotypic language in TV programs led Mulac, Lundell, and Bradac (1985) to examine transcripts from the public speeches collected in an earlier study (Mulac & Lundell, 1982) with similar methods. Analysis revealed 13 language features which accounted for the between-gender variation and permitted virtually perfect accuracy in predicting speaker gender. The male predictors included syllables per word, first-person singular pronouns, present-tense verbs, vocalized pauses, grammatical errors, active-voice verbs, judgmental adjectives, and references to people. These factors constituted a style that was egocentric, nonstandard, active, and intense. Female predictors were adverbials beginning sentences, oppositions, rhetorical questions, references to emotion, and fillers. The authors felt this created a style that was complex, tentative, literate, and attentive to emotional concerns.

Taken together, the gender-linked language effect studies constitute some of the most ambitious gender and language research. It is equally true, however, that these investigations provoke at least as many questions as they answer. For instance, the relationship between the language features and gender styles is ambiguous. When it is recalled that female speakers in this study were considered higher in sociointellectual status and aesthetic quality, while males were perceived high in dynamism, it seems surprising that these specific language variables could relate to those particular judgments.

It is also interesting to note how well the stereotypic attributions reported by

Kramer (1975) for male speakers are reflected by the male predictors identified by Mulac et al. (1985). Does this suggest the coders were responding in line with gender stereotypes? Mulac and Lundell (1982) claimed individuals like the raters in their studies could not identify the gender of the individuals speaking in the transcripts, a finding corroborated in a study comparing perceptions of the gender-linked language effect and sex role stereotapes (Mulac, Incontro, & James, 1985). Hall and Braunwald (1981), however, found their naive subjects were quite accurate about such gender and topic distinctions. The absence of data relevant to the impact of raters' sex-role expectations on their evaluations of language cues makes meaningful interpretation of these studies difficult.

Similarly, the results produced by these studies introduce implications that at least appear inconsistent with other findings. Specifically, these studies seem to suggest that women are perceived as superior communicators, to the extent that the sociointellectual status and aesthetic quality factors signify what they appear to represent. Mulac and his associates do not address this matter at all, or even comment on the disparity between the positive evaluations of female writing and speech reported in their studies and the weight of evidence suggesting that women speakers and writers are negatively perceived (Maier, 1970; Kramerae, 1982). Do men and women really speak in ways consistent with sex-role stereotypes, or it is the case that respondents presensitized to those distinctions perceive it so? Are there reliable linguistic markers of gender? Only continued research can gauge the accuracy of these predictions.

III. GENDER GESTURES: SEX ASSOCIATED DIFFERENCES IN NONVERBAL COMMUNICATION

There is little doubt that women and men differ in nonverbal display (Knapp, 1979; Weitz, 1976; Mayo & Henley, 1981). Sex differences in nonverbal communication comprise a literature far too extensive for review here. Instead, this section is focused on the basic repertoires of gender gestures, comparisons of nonverbal skill levels, and accounts of sex associated patterns of nonverbal display.

A. Gender Gestures

Gender display, argued Ray Birdwhistell (1970), is fundamentally patterned, variable, and presentational. Specifically, he noted that human beings "and probably a number of other weakly dimorphic species necessarily organize much of gender display and recognition at the level of position, movement, and expression" (p. 42). Since biological and physiological similarities between men and women far outnumber differences, overt expressive displays are required to differentiate between the sexes. Thus, as LaFrance (1981) has stated, nonverbal cues ". . . carry important social information and they serve to regulate much social interaction" (p. 130).

Most nonverbal research has established pervasive differences in gender display, and these distinctions seem similar to some differences associated with language behavior. This is especially the case for those cues presumed to reflect dominance and power (Henley, 1977; Lamb, 1981). Gender gestures are not, however, sex exclusive. Rather, gender is defined nonverbally by factors including rate, variability, or patterning of behaviors.

Most early studies counted frequencies of various nonverbal behaviors, and significant differences in the display of men and women were reported. The following table, adapted from Henley (1977, p. 181), illustrates the array of differences thus far documented. Effects reported are generally at least moderate and often reflect replication across different subject populations. Cross-situational consistencies are, however, less well assessed than is desirable.

There has been a distinct readiness to universalize any findings of sex differences, which probably has obscured important issues, and impeded the development of more complex models or explanations of gender gestures. Deaux (1976), for instance, has reported that the objective elements of a social situation will sometimes obviate "established" sex effects. Still, research exploring the moderating effects of situational or personal variables has been slow to emerge.

Data reported in Table 1 are reviewed extensively elsewhere (see Henley, 1977; Knapp, 1979; Leathers, 1985) and generally echo the familiar theme that gender gestures are the result of societal sex-role expectations. Given that males are prescribed a proactive role, the behaviors listed support the contention. It is equally important to note several qualifications in regard to gender-linked nonverbal cues. An obvious issue is individual differences. To date, there is simply insufficient evidence to indicate what proportion of men or women display what proportion and/or combination of gender gestures.

Common experience suggests that gender displays are enacted differently by various individuals. Since sex or sex-role are but two of the unique factors shaping behavior at any time, variability is to be expected. Birdwhistell (1970) identifies a further complication in suggesting that gender gestures become increasingly pronounced as children move through puberty toward young adulthood and decline steadily thereafter. Research in other areas of expressive cues (Rosenthal, 1979; Prokasy & Raskin, 1973), is supportive at least for the prepubertal age groups. Since most research reports are accounts of the behaviors of young adults, the likely implication may be that current estimates of sex differences in the nonverbal domain are unduly inflated.

A related concern is framed in terms of the contextual nature of nonverbal behaviors. The gender gestures listed in Table 1 do not possess single, invariant meanings or function as consistently masculine or feminine displays. Eye behavior, for instance, embodies both poles of the affiliation/dominance continuum. High levels of eye contact may signify communion, sharing, and involvement, or

Table 1.   Gender Gestures Suggesting Power and Privilege: Examples of Nonverbal Behaviors Between People of Unequal Status and Between Men and Women

Type of Behavior	Used by Superiors and Men	Used by Subordinates and Women	Strength of Relationship
Address	Familiar forms	polite forms	moderate
Touching	Touching OK	Don't touch	weak
Demeanor	Informal	Guarded	unknown
Posture	Relaxed	Tense	moderate
Eye Contact	Stare/ ignore others	Avert eyes watch others	strong
Facial expression	Impassive/ don't smile	Expressive/ smile	moderate
Emotional expression	Suppress	Display	strong
Space	Closed to others/ less intrusion	Open to others/ less intrusion	strong

Note: Adapted from Nancy Henley, *Body Politics: Power, Sex and Nonverbal Communication* (p. 181). Englewood Cliffs, NJ: Prentice-Hall. Copyright © 1977 by Prentice-Hall. Reprinted by permission.

may reflect threat, hostility, and intimidation (Mehrabian, 1978). Context elements, in this case the relationship between the interactants, determine meaning. Moreover, well-entrenched claims about differences in nonverbal behaviors may be suspect. Recent meta-analytic research reported by Stier and Hall (1984) has questioned asymmetries in male–female touching behaviors. The relationship posited by Henley (1977) that male and female touching patterns conform to basic dominance and submission patterns was not supported, and the hypothesis that women were touched more than men achieved only tenuous support. Stier and Hall's admonition, "When male-female asymmetry is found . . . there is a great need to try to document when, where, and in what relationship it occurs" (1984, p. 456), applies to all studies of gender and nonverbal behaviors. The relationship between context-generated and gender-differentiated explanations for nonverbal behaviors has received virtually no attention in the literature. Until such a literature is developed, our understanding of gender gestures will remain shrouded in ambiguity.

B. Gender Differences in Nonverbal Skills

Viewing facility in nonverbal communication as a social skill is comparatively new, and thus research remains in the formative stages. Most studies have focused on skill in terms of display and/or recognition of nonverbal cues, especially those concerned with emotional expression. Common-sense explanations have long held that women are more expressive than men, and more sensitive to the displays of others as well. This stereotype finds support in surprising ways. LaFrance (1985) reports an analysis spanning 20 years and no less than 9,000 college yearbook photos with the consistent finding that women were more likely to smile in their photos than men.

Awash in stereotypes of "strong, silent men" and "women's intuition," researchers have tried to assess sex differences in nonverbal decoding (judging) and encoding (sending) abilities for over 50 years. Few definitive generalizations have emerged. Jeness (1932) reported it was "barely right" that women surpassed men in a task involving judgments of facial expressions. Maccoby and Jacklin's (1974) review of studies concerned with interpersonal responsiveness concluded that "neither sex has greater ability to judge the reactions and intentions of others in any generalized sense" (p. 214).

In contrast, a review of more than 75 studies by Hall (1978) determined a gender difference in decoding nonverbal cues favoring women. Across differences in task, such as listening to tape recorded voices, viewing slides, or even line drawings of facial expressions, women were found to be more accurate than men in 61 of the 75 studies (10 of the remaining 14 had reported no significant differences). Recent research has confirmed this trend (Blanck, Rosenthal, Snodgrass, DePaulo, & Zuckerman, 1981; Buck, 1983) Some intriguing qualifications to the gender effect have also been identified. Women's advantage in decoding nonverbal messages is enhanced when a message contains both visual and auditory cues rather than either alone (Hall, 1978), and women's superiority seems especially pronounced in decoding visual as opposed to vocal message (Leathers, 1985). Finally, some evidence suggests that source intentionality may mediate the gender effect, because women seem to lose some of their edge when asked to assess the implicit meanings of messages not intended for them (Rosenthal & DePaulo, 1979).

Is either sex superior in sending or encoding nonverbal messages? Studies reviewed by Hall (1978) suggest again that, when the task calls for expression through visual or vocal channels, women were superior to men. Studies included in this review indicated that the sex differences emerged early in life and were readily apparent by the elementary school years. Womens' advantage seems especially pronounced in the expression of negative affects (i.e., dislike, disgust) facially. To the extent that men demonstrate much skill, it is in the display of positive affects (i.e., happiness). According to LaFrance and Mayo (1979) this effect may be attributable to contrast—women smile so frequently and men so rarely that reversals of expected behavior are compelling. In a similar vein, other investigators have indicated that female superiority is exaggerated by the types of tasks used in the studies (simulating facial displays, etc.). When more specialized kinds of emotional meanings are involved, performance levels of men and women are more similar than different (Leathers & Emigh, 1980), and men may even be slightly superior in detecting deceptive displays (Siegal, 1980).

Based upon the foregoing review, is it legitimate to state that women are superior to men in the nonverbal domain? What implications are to be drawn relative to the broader concept of communication? A number of important factors were not addressed by the literature Hall (1979) reviewed. A variety of issues present serious qualifications to the reported gender effects. Their impact is not easily detected, however, due to inconsistent reporting across studies. Most damaging to the credibility of these effects are the metaanalytic findings reported by Eagly and Carli (1981) and Hall (1984) suggesting that experimenter sex unduly affected the outcomes of nonverbal decoding studies. Given this circumstance, further research is definitely needed to assess the gender/skill relationship.

C. Gender-Associated Accounts of Nonverbal Differences

Accounts of nonverbal differences invite speculation from both social and physiological perspectives. Rosenthal and DePaulo (1979) became interested in the social implications of nonverbal skill, specifically whether individuals skilled in encoding or decoding nonverbal cues experience greater success in their interpersonal relationships. Presumably, the relative excellence of women at nonverbal communication should promote smooth interpersonal functioning. Social relationships may suffer, however, if proficient decoders discern nonverbal cues they were not intended to receive (Rosenthal, Hall, Archer, DiMatteo, & Rogers, 1979). Therefore, Rosenthal and DePaulo reasoned that women might use their superior skills selectively, to affect positive relationships with others. Weitz's (1976) finding that women adjusted their nonverbal styles to adapt to the personality traits of male partners, as well as those language studies suggesting that women are more deferential and polite than men, lent support to Rosenthal and DePaulo's accommodation hypothesis.

Three series of studies were conducted to assess the hypothesized gender difference in accommodation. Generally, Rosenthal and DePaulo (1979) found support for their contention that women are overly polite in the nonverbal dimensions of their interactions. The pattern of behavioral accommodation displayed by women is consistent with and probably springs from the traditional sex role ascribed to women in this culture, a role emphasizing politeness to the exclusion of honesty. Similarly, Mulac et al. (1987) report that, in cross-sex dyads, women converged to male gaze/talk behavior patterns while men did not converge to female gaze/talk patterns. Whether female accommodation reflects their alleged lower status, more flexible repertoire of nonverbal skills, or some subtle complex of social motives remains to be determined by further research.

Although the foregoing cultural analysis has provided a popular perspective, scholars have observed that numerous gender-linked behaviors are not well explained within that framework (Burgoon, 1985). Physiologically based explanations offer alternative interpretations of male/female differences in nonverbal display. H. E. Jones (1935) formulated the mode of response patterning referred to as *externalizing* (overt expressiveness of emotion) and *internalizing* (less overt expressiveness of emotion) and noted that these modes were inversely related to physiological responses. The externalizer–internalizer phenomenon has been examined in terms of studies on facial and gestural cues. Ross Buck and his colleagues are among the leading researchers in this area, and their studies have revealed differences associated with gender. In studies of nonverbal encoding, Buck and his associated (Buck, 1977; Buck, Savin, Miller, & Caul, 1972; Buck, Miller, & Caul, 1974) found that women differentiate as externalizers and men as internalizers. That is, women are more nonverbally expressive and have smaller or less frequent electrodermal responses in affective situations. Men display the opposite tendency.

Differential brain functioning is another potential explanation which Restak (1979), among others, has argued accounts for expressive differences between the sexes. Hall (1979) has even suggested that women may be endowed with a greater innate capability for learning to communicate nonverbally. Safer (1978), however, favors hemispheric lateralization as an explanation, positing that the widely accepted sex differences in intellectual skills are associated with brain development and function in ways that favor females. Women's ability to access verbal codes and attach them to nonverbal stimuli (i.e., facial expressions) may even reflect more efficient communication between left and right hemispheres of the brain. Buck's (1979) anecdotal evidence that males express more spontaneous facial animation than women do while working on puzzles and spatial-relationship tasks suggests another instance of nonverbal display associated with brain function. Data relevant to this account of nonverbal communication behaviors are scant, but increasingly sophisticated research in the area may reveal much about the origins of sex differences in nonverbal behavior.

IV. A QUESTION OF STYLE: GENDER AND SELF-PRESENTATION

In her review of research on politeness, Brown (1980) complained that linguistic analyses have failed to reveal much about language use because linguists have been interested in establishing rules rather than regarding individuals as rational actors oriented toward communicative goals and employing strategies to achieve those goals. The perspective endorsed by Brown is essentially a self-presentational one, stressing the degree to which people organize their communication behaviors, sometimes quite self consciously, and enact these behaviors during interactions. According to Erving Goffman, whose *Presentation of Self in Everyday Life* (1959) framed many basic concepts, individuals may enact roles cynically or sincerely, but everyone is a performer. For this reason, a review of the communicative differences associated with gender would be incomplete without a perusal of the contributions from this developing literature. Two categories of studies seem most salient. One explores the concept of communicator style, and the other describes some dynamics and consequences of presentational differences. General findings related to each are summarized below.

A. Communicator Style

Describing the construct as "the way one verbally and paraverbally interacts to signal how literal meaning should be taken, interpreted, filtered, or understood," Norton (1978, p. 99) developed the initial construct and measures of communicator style. Research reported by Norton (1978), Miller (1977, 1980), Norton and Pettegrew, (1977, 1979), and Norton and Nussbaum (1980) extended the construct, conceptualized as a self-perceived phenomenon which manifested itself through consistently recurring patterns of behavior. Recurring patterns, in turn, provide form and structure to communication and influence the perceptions and expectancies of others.

Norton (1977, 1983) identified 10 style variables, including impression leaving, contentious, open, dramatic, dominant, precise, relaxed, friendly, attentive, and animated, which defined the domain of his construct. Montgomery and Norton (1981) reported two studies designed to explore sex differences in self-reports of communicator style. Two elements appear to distinguish men and women: men reported high levels of precise communicator style and women reported high levels of animated communicator style. The precise style, an adjunct of Norton's dominant–contentious–precise constellation, was characterized by behaviors communicating a concern for accuracy, documentation, and proof in both informative and persuasive interactions. Male subjects in the Montgomery and Norton (1981) study perceived themselves as possessing more of this attribute than their female peers. The animated style claimed more frequently by female subjects represented activity and expansive, overt behaviors that Norton (1983) suggests vivify and dramatize the content of a speaker's communication. Specifically, this style variable was characterized by the frequency, duration, and intensity of nonverbal presentational cues, including eye contact, gestures, facial expressions, and gross bodily movements.

Several implications seem relevant. As the authors noted, the parallels between subjects' self-descriptions and contemporary sex-role stereotypes were obvious and in some respects troublesome. Males have been expected to adopt a task-oriented perspective, so their self-described affinity for a precise style was consistent with traditional sex-role prescriptions, as was females' identification with high levels of animation. The issue that these data did not address was the degree to which knowledge of sex role stereotypes might have affected the subjects' self-reports. Although the absence of differences on other style dimensions associated with stereotypes, such as dominance or openness, would suggest a minimal impact, a related and less easily dispelled suspicion might argue bias in the specific descriptions used on the communicator style instrument. It seems possible that males would be less likely to endorse statements like "my eyes reflect exactly what I am feeling when I communicate."

A recent meta-analytic investigation reported by McDonald (1986) has suggested that male and female styles may differ on more than two of the style dimensions. On the other hand, Norton and Montgomery's finding that male and female subjects describe themselves so similarly on 8 of the 10 style dimensions was no less compelling than the discovery of differences. These findings might suggest that many alleged distinctions between the sexes' styles are principally "eye-of-the-beholder" phenomena and that women's self-reported efforts to present themselves as dominant, relaxed, or contentious (e.g., powerful) are frustrated by audiences who neither acknowledge nor endorse that performance style from a female. Indeed, Snodgrass's (1985) study of sex differences in interpersonal sensitivity suggests that women perceive themselves, and are perceived by their partners, as more sensitive to men than vice versa. Unfortunately, these are questions current findings cannot resolve.

B. Self-Presentation Strategies

Strategic communication implies that individuals make proactive decisions about how to achieve their communication goals. Impression management, scripts, and social accounting are but three familiar rubrics encompassing self-presentation strategies. Research to date has indicated that gender differences in self-presentation occur in relation to self-disclosure (Derlega & Chaikin, 1977; Hacker, 1981), humor (Coser, 1960), compliance gaining (Falbo & Peplau, 1980; McCormick, 1979), conflict resolution (Roloff & Greenberg, 1979) and assertiveness (Wilson & Gallois, 1985; Lewis & Gallois, 1984). In some instances (e.g., self-disclosure) the prevalence of inconsistencies has led researchers to conclude that gender interacts with task and context variables in ways that preclude detection of stable effects. In others, the literature is too sparse to yield meaningful generalizations. Two areas of perennial interest about which a modicum of information is available are assertiveness and persuasion.

Assertiveness, defined as the ability to communicate one's own feelings, beliefs, or desires directly and standing up for one's rights without violating the rights of others, has been stereotyped as a masculine characteristic. In part attributable to a research focus on negative assertion (aggression) in which gender differences have long been established (Maccoby & Jacklin, 1974), the stereotype is reinforced by findings that women present themselves in nonassertive ways. The phenomenon has been so consistently observed that nonassertiveness has been labeled a feminine trait by some authors, and females frequently label themselves as less assertive than men (Chandler, Cook, & Dugovics, 1978).

Available evidence suggests that assertiveness may vary according to sex, especially when both positive and negative types of assertion are considered. In a study of assertion in intimate relationships, Warren and Gilner (1978) reported that men had more difficulty expressing tender feelings than women; hence they did so with less facility and significantly less frequently. In negative assertion situations, however, Crassini, Law and Wilson (1979) reported that women described themselves as less capable. These results do not necessarily hold for situations in which only negative assertion (e.g., defending one's rights, expressing negative affect) is examined.

Two factors seem to moderate use of assertive self presentation strategies by both sexes. Leah, Law, and Snyder (1979) reveal that the difficulties subjects experienced in behaving assertively center on the relationship with the receiver of the messages and the type of message (positive or negative) of assertion that is involved. Males, predictably enough, have less difficulty with negative assertion than do females, although there is strong evidence that the type of message (e.g., refusal of requests vs. difference of opinion) may shift the effects (Lewis & Gallois, 1985). Both males and females seem to have difficulty with assertion in close or intimate relationships (Craighead, 1979).

In addition to closeness, gender of the recipient appears to affect assertiveness displays. Stebbins, Kelly, Tolor, and Power (1977) found that each sex was more assertive toward members of its own sex. Some inconsistencies emerge, however, when observer-rated assertion is compared with self reported assertion. Rose and Tryon (1979) and Wilson and Gallois (1985) report that perceptions of assertiveness vary according to the sex composition of dyads, with mixed sex dyads producing perceptions of the highest assertiveness. In that regard, Cowan and Koziej (1979) report that females are seen as more masculine than males when they behave in a dominant manner, while other findings suggest that assertive women are perceived as more negative than assertive men, especially when they are assertive toward men (Wilson & Gallois, 1984).

Equally intriguing are those data which recount gender differences in persuasive ploys. The prevalence of gender-based stereotypes attest that "getting one's own way" is one of the more enduring social motivations. Stereotypically, women are expected to exhibit less direct or forceful argumentation and to be more yielding to the persuasive attempts of others, while men are expected to demonstrate the opposite tendency. This popular notion of persuasibility may be suspect. Eagly and her colleagues' metaanalytic reviews (Eagly & Carli, 1981; Eagly & Wood, 1982) suggest that bias attributable to tasks used in the studies and, regrettably, the sex of the researcher may have accounted for these early findings.

Regarding specific strategy use, the evidence discloses similarities as well as differences along gender lines. A pair of studies involving compliance-gaining in intimate relationships illustrate the literature well. Falbo and Peplau (1980) asked students to describe "how I get (my romantic partner) to do what I want." The sample of men and women reported different presentational strategies. Women, in ways consistent with stereotypic predictions on politeness and subtlety, reported a higher use of indirect strategies such as hinting, pouting, or manipulative affectional displays. Men were similarly stereotypic in relying more on direct influence; stating needs, wants, and desires explicitly. Interestingly, subjects of both sexes reported higher levels of satisfaction with their relationships when they used direct influence strategies. In a similar vein, Andrews (1987) reported that in developing persuasive cases, men and women displayed different strategies and styles. Men tended to present arguments related to criteria presented within an experimental task, while women tended to invent arguments of their own, independent of information presented within the task.

In contrast to these findings suggesting basic gender differences are those reported by McCormick (1979) who asked both sexes to describe "come-ons" and "put-offs" they had used or observed. While both sexes seemed to expect sex differences (men expected to use more "come-ons", women more "put-offs"), the self-reports belied their own predictions. Specifically, both men and women reported using strategies such as seduction or provocative nonverbal displays for engaging in sex. Similarities in avoidance emerged strategies as well, including moralizing or outright coercion to avoid sex. The clear pattern of results, revealing use of indirect self presentation attempts by both sexes is fascinating and reflects the promise of these comparatively new venues in sex-role research well. Prospects for increased understanding of gender-associated differences in social behavior seem quite good.

V. EXPLANATORY FRAMEWORKS FOR GENDER DIFFERENCES IN COMMUNICATION BEHAVIORS

We turn now from recounting what differentiates male and female communication to inquire why such distinctions exist. A host of critics, writers, and researchers have grappled with the thorny questions of cause and effect as these bear upon gender and language literature. Is women's language inherently distinct from men's? How universal are language differences? How are such differences acquired and what structures maintain them? Of what significance are perceptions of male or female communication when compared to their actual communication performances? These are a few of the questions that an integrative framework for communication and gender must address. In this section, a brief review of the most relevant accounts for the gender and communication research is provided. It is critical to note, however, that there is a dearth of empirical evidence that bears directly on current explanations for gender display.

A. Sociocultural Accounts: Gender Display and Genderlects

Cheris Kramer (1974) defined the *genderlects* concept as "systems of co-occurring sex-linked linguistic signals in the United States" (p. 14). As an explanation, the genderlects construct presumes existence of pervasive, stable, and socially significant differences in the speech of men and women, although Kramer stipulates that "many differences appear to be a matter of context and frequency." On some levels, a genderlects explanation incorporates aspects of both the difference hypothesis and the deficit hypothesis (Labov, 1972) since women's speech is presumed to be, not only distinct from men's, but also evaluated in a manner that implies consistent discrimination (Kramer, Thorne, & Henley, 1978; Warfel, 1984).

For its time and place in social history, the genderlect construct was an ambitious thrust at a problem with broad academic, economic, and interpersonal implications. Some scholars, and most women, may have been aware of something more than slightly askew in the communication system as it affected their lives and perceptions, but there was no conceptual framework against which these experiences could be measured and understood, and a paucity of objective data on the topics of gender and communication behaviors. The political coloration of genderlects was inescapable, because the construct was implicitly about women's struggle against gender hierarchies (Kramerae, 1981; Thorne, Kramerae, & Henley, 1983) and as such emphasized the "separateness" of women's language. One unintended outcome was that, in attempting to document differences characterizing women's speech, the impression that male's speech was somehow "generic" or the normative language form was created.

The heuristic value of the genderlect concept has evolved more in critical and social analyses than in empirical research. The few studies completed focused on sex-typed language as a developmental phenomenon, following Lakoff's (1975) assertion that all children initially speak women's language. In an investigation comparing language of 4-, 8-, and 12-year-olds, Haas (1979) found no support for this hypothesis. Similarly, Schultz et al. (1984) reported no evidence of the genderlects construct in their comparisons of boys' and girls' descriptions of a stimulus picture.

Although the genderlects explanation remains unsubstantiated, sociocultural influences mark communication behaviors powerfully. In subtle yet indelible ways, role behaviors and status shape communication patterns. Bem (1981) contends that all human societies delineate adult roles on the basis of gender. Through implicit and explicit directives, individuals acquire knowledge of appropriate role behaviors. This socialization process doubtless entails modeling of sex-typed language, beginning in the home or day-care environments (Gleason & Weintraub, 1978; Ervin-Tripp, 1976) and continuing through myriad encounters with individuals and institutions. One particularly salient source of gender-role information is the mass-media, and the correspondence between sex role stereotypes and the behavior of television characters is striking (Goffman, 1979). Further, some evidence suggests that adolescents copy the conflict-management styles of their favorite television characters, leading to a predictable set of differences in their self-presentation (Roloff & Greenberg, 1979).

Taken together, the foregoing describe some of the more powerful sources of gender-role socialization. All behaviors used to communicate social roles are affected. As Hall and Braunwald (1981) have observed, one of the most important aspects of gender is that it prescribes roles and interpersonal behaviors. One popular example is the notion of gender-coded scripts or routines based on stereotypic sex role expectations. Scripts incorporate underlying social norms for male and female behavior, made explicit through language and nonverbal cues. Of course, the scripts reinforce the rule system as much as they reflect it. Thus, social sanctions permit women to display emotion and withhold the same privilege from men. Out-of-role behavior from either sex, on the other hand, typically provokes extreme or exaggerated responses from others (Deaux, 1984).

Society distributes status on the basis of gender and this allocation influences differences observed in the communication behaviors of men and women (Kramerae, 1981). Status implies power. The relative powerlessness of women's communication emerges because women are denied equal status in society. While Lakoff (1975) disagrees, observing that blacks are status-deprived and do not use powerless speech, there is solid support for the tension between sex and societally determined status. Briefly, the work of Berger and his associates (Berger, Cohen, & Zelditch, 1972) and Lockheed and Hall (1976) established that gender functions as a diffuse status characteristic like age, race, or physical attractiveness. Such cues provide a basis for others to evaluate one's capabilities or worth, and they tend to be transsituational. Merit is determined by how much of the characteristic one possesses. With gender, the scale is absolute, and masculinity is the valued "state."

Numerous social psychologists argue that status characteristics like gender have potent impact because people use these cues to form expectations for their own and others' behaviors, and then behave in ways that confirm their initial expectations (Darley & Fazio, 1980; Deaux, 1984). If one observes that men generally have higher status in society and interact with men in ways that are consistent with greater power and privilege, then the self-fulfilling prophecy effect will surely follow. One's original beliefs will be confirmed, and men will have gained an edge, at least in initial status judgments. Eagly (1983) and Deaux (1984) posit that sequences like this are played out constantly in interpersonal encounters.

For the gender and communication literature, the implications of status are especially acute, because, in virtually all the studies, sex and status are confounded. Communication behaviors are most often studied in settings that have no formal status inequities (i.e., dyadic interactions) associated with sex differences. Naive observers, however, are familiar with their daily world wherein hierarchial role discrepancies between men and women are ubiquitous. Moreover, subjects in these studies do not leave their life experiences outside the laboratory setting either. The probabilities that the results of these studies represent effects not solely attributable to gender is quite high, especially for the language evaluation studies.

Finally, two sets of findings that defy conventional wisdom regarding the gender and status relationship. Information about the comparative impact of sex and status comes from Locksley, Borgida, Brekke, and Hepburn (1980) and Deaux and Lewis (1984), whose studies suggest that, whenever specific status information about another is provided to respondents, the impact of gender as a determinant of their evaluations of that person is diminished. It is not clear whether these findings generalize to all behaviors in all settings. In one study high-status individuals exhibited dominance displays to express social power regardless of gender, and in another it was noted that, when two people of the same sex but unequal status meet, the behavior of the higher status persons resembles those labeled as stereotypically masculine (Ellyson & Dovidio, 1985). These studies suggest that status rather than gender affect the enactment of communication behaviors and the evaluations associated with them.

B. Language and Social Context: Gender Display as a Situationally Specific Response

Kramer et al. (1978) were among the first to appeal for investigations that integrated rather than ignored the social contexts in which language occurred. Descriptive accounts of sex differences in institutionalized contexts such as complex organizations (Fairhurst, 1986), and in marital settings (Burggraff & Sillars, 1987; Peplau, 1983; Fitzpatrick, 1984) have been reviewed extensively elsewhere. Most experimental studies continue to isolate language from situations despite recent evidence suggesting context effects influence communication behaviors significantly. In some instances (e.g., initial interactions) the context may well be the most powerful determinant of individuals' communication behaviors (Berger & Bradac, 1982; Smythe & Huddleston, 1987).

Situational cues are one significant element of every communication context. They are frequently structural in nature and thus communicate implicit rules for conduct. One of the most familiar situational cues in language research is the task variable, which affects every study greatly, but is rarely properly controlled or integrated into the overall research design. Instructing subjects to engage in problem solving elicits different behaviors from having a "get-acquainted" conversation (Newcombe & Arnkoff, 1979), and, in similar fashion, inductions emphasizing competition over cooperation affect participants' communication behaviors (Deaux, 1984). Generally speaking, the research suggests that certain tasks affect the likelihood that certain language forms will occur. If uncontrolled, this variable can mask or distort genuine differences.

Another important context variable is sex composition; whether on a dyadic or small group basis, the sex of the person with whom one interacts affects communication behaviors (Hacker, 1981; Dindia, 1987). There is ample evidence that women, for instance, exhibit far higher levels of task orientation in a group with men than in a group with women (Piliavin & Martin, 1978), that they speak louder to men than to women (Markel, Prebor, & Brandt, 1972), and that they display different interaction patterns in cross-sex as opposed to same-sex interactions (Hall & Braunwald, 1981; Martin & Craig, 1983; Mulac, Studley, Weimaunn, & Bradac, 1987). Other structural elements that appear to vary according to sex composition include interruptions (Roger & Schumacher, 1983), eye contact (Ickes & Barnes, 1978), and length of speaking turn (Martin & Craig, 1983).

Similarly, researchers have identified content differences that appear attributable to the sex of one's conversational partner. In a study of storytelling behaviors, McLaughlin and her associates (McLaughlin, Cody, Kane, & Robey, 1981) found no sex differences in numbers of stories told, but several differences related to the ways in which the stories were told, and to whom they were told. Women heard more stories than men did. Haas and Sherman's study (1982) of conversational topics reaffirmed the stability of sex differences in topic choice, and Pearson (1985) has summarized several studies suggesting that individuals tailor the content of their communication to the characteristics of their conversational partners.

Another context factor is the nature of the relationship between the interactants. The relational tone of an interaction affects aspects such as intimacy, formality, and ease of discourse (Berger & Bradac, 1982). Relational history is also important. Initial interactions are often characterized by high levels of reciprocity, positive self-presentations and uncertainty. As such, they differ from those interactions among friends of long standing. The impact of relationships on conversations is demonstrated by Haas and Sherman's (1982) study of conversational topics. For both sexes friends are most inclined to talk about members of the opposite sex, co-workers about their jobs, and kinfolk about family matters. Similar results on specific language and nonverbal behaviors suggest that absence of a relational history promotes the display of gender-typed cues, possibly because individuals rely on stereotypic role conceptions in situations where uncertainty is high (LaFrance, 1981; Smythe & Huddleston, 1987).

What all of these findings argue most persuasively is that many communication behaviors reflect an individual's interpretation of specific situational demands and constraints. The resultant constructions, and their likely influence on a speaker's actions, remain unknown. It seems that most of the studies reporting language and nonverbal differences reviewed earlier could be confounded by one or another of the context factors described here. Renewed efforts to design studies that incorporate and examine context elements in relation to gender-based behaviors are clearly required.

C. Self-Presentation: Gender Display as Strategic Response

Viewing communication behavior within a presentational framework has certain advantages. First, self-presentational approaches are not overburdened with excess conceptual and political baggage, as are sociocultural explanations. Presentational analyses also incorporate a proactive perspective on language and nonverbal behaviors which is consistent with contemporary communication theory. Finally, a self-presentation paradigm does not preclude consideration of any of the variables that research has suggested may have direct or moderating effects on gender-linked communication.

The fundamental tenet of the self-presentation explanation is that individuals make conscious choices about which behaviors they will use in specific settings. Further, it is assumed that men and women have behavioral repertoires that are quite similar. Performance differences arise from choices the individuals elect relative to personal goals, situational constraints, or target audience characteristics. In short, "enacted differences may derive from similar potentials" (Deaux, 1984, p. 1144).

A slender literature illustrates differences in self-presentational choices. In a series of studies, Zanna and his colleagues (Zanna & Pack, 1975; von Baeyer, Sherk, & Zanna, 1981) found that women vary their level of "feminine" behaviors according to the amount and type of information they have about a potential, attractive male partner. If led to believe such behavior was desirable, women altered their self-descriptions in the direction of greater sex-stereotypic self presentation. Similarly, Klein and Willerman (1979) have reported that women talk less with male group members during discussion tasks *until* they are informed that they will be evaluated on leadership skills. Then the women talk equally with the men and women in their groups. Alterations in the self-presentation of men have been documented by Schlueter and Smythe (1985), who report that selection of compliance-gaining strategies in a role-playing situation varied as a function of subjects' perceptions of their relationship to their co-interactant and whether their actions had long-term or short-term consequences.

The combination of personal motivations and situational constraints makes for variability in self-presentation choices, and many questions remain unanswered. It seems apparent, however, that individuals do self-present strategically, and for good reasons. Scotton (1976) reports that speakers respond to situations in which uncertainty levels are high by adopting strategies of neutrality to preclude negative evaluations from others. In later investigations, Scotton (1980) suggests that individuals use linguistic ploys (e.g., keeping quite or "playing dumb") to keep others from perceiving how they feel about situations. While manipulative in appearance, self-presentation strategies may also be viewed as appropriate responses to the subtly or explicitly expresses expectations of others. Securing social approval, and identity management, are but two familiar inducements to self present, and a number of studies have demonstrated why individuals do so. Lippa, Valdez, and Jolly (1979) found a positive correlation between perceptions of physical attractiveness in men and women and perceptions of their relative masculinity or femininity. In this instance, the better the gender display, the more positive the evaluations.

Regarding the selection of compliance gaining strategies, Schlueter and Smythe (1985) found that subjects made prudent choices between messages selected for use and those considered but not used. Analyses by naive judges revealed that the arguments chosen for use were significantly associated with judgments of communicator competence, credibility, and attractiveness. While tentative, their findings suggest the probity of self-presentational analyses of communication. It seems likely that further studies exploring the relationships among choice, interpersonal expectancies, and communication behaviors would illuminate current conceptions of gender.

D. Androgyny: Moderating Variable in Gender Display

While far from a full-blown explanation of gender linked behaviors, Bem's (1974) provocative and sometimes controversial construct bears upon gender-based differences in communication. In brief, Bem posited that *psychological androgyny,* a personality variable defined as a blending of masculine and feminine characteristics in roughly equal proportions, could account for some of the large variability seen in the behaviors displayed within male and female groups. Because androgynous individuals' self-concepts exclude neither femininity nor masculinity, they presumably exhibit greater behavioral flexibility than sex-typed (nonandrogynous) individuals, "engaging in situationally effective behaviors without regard for its stereotype as more appropriate to one sex of the other" (Bem, 1975, p. 634).

Behavioral flexibility is one reason that the androgyny construct becomes relevant to gender differences in communication. Gender often dictates roles, and since roles must be performed to have significance, it seems logical to infer that any differences attributable to gender would emerge in the domain of language and nonverbal display. The frequent disparities in these literatures have led researchers to propose broadening the definition of the sex variable to incorporate sex-role orientation (androgyny) to increase precision of measurement and interpretability of findings (Putnam & McCallister, 1980; Smythe et al., 1983).

Although androgyny became an immensely popular construct, research on the communicative implications of the construct is sparse. Extant studies indicate that androgyny may be a significant moderating variable in the gender/ communication behavior relationship, in sometimes unpredictable fashion (LaFrance, 1981). In a study investigating the effects of sex-typing on interpersonal attraction and interactional ease (defined as amount of speaking plus degree of self-reported effort) in mixed sex dyads, Ickes and Barnes (1978) found that both attraction and interactional ease were higher in dyads containing at least one androgynous member. The lowest levels on the two measures were observed in dyads composed of a sex-typed male and a sex-typed female. These findings on sex-typing differences were partially corroborated in studies of dominant/submissive self-presentation (Wiggins & Holzmuller, 1978), in studies of self disclosure and communication apprehension (Greenblatt, Hasenauer, & Freimuth, 1980), and in studies of nonverbal behaviors (Putnam & McCallister, 1980; LaFrance & Carmen, 1980; LaFrance & Ickes, 1981).

At least three studies have probed the relationship between selected language cues and androgyny. Renshaw and Johnson (1982), measuring language behaviors with the Syntactic Language Computer Analysis program, found that androgyny moderated the main effects of subject sex on a number of specific linguistic cues, leading the authors to conclude that biological sex and psychological sex role together are more efficient predictors of language behaviors than either taken alone. A less robust set of findings have been reported by Crosby, Jose, and Wong-McCarthy (1981) on the relationship between androgyny and assertiveness. Subjects were placed in dyads to decide the fate of fictional fellow travelers in a luxury liner catastrophe. Use of language cues characterized as the "female register" was measured. Only weak to moderate relationships were discovered between sex typing and language cues. Problems associated with the experimental task and the assignment of subjects to gender categories, however, might have suppressed the anticipated effects (Crosby, et al., 1981).

According to LaFrance (1981), evidence of androgyny's explanatory power depends in part on the identification of behavioral patterning in line with Bem's (1974) original conception. Thus, androgynous people would be expected to eschew certain sex-congruent behaviors and to exhibit cross-sex behaviors. Reporting results of a study on the nonverbal display of androgyny, LaFrance and Carmen (1980) found that both sex and sex type affected subjects' behaviors in this way.

Evidence supporting the androgynous "blend" of cross-sex-sex and sex-congruent language behaviors was described by Smythe et al. (1983). Dyads composed of every combination of sex and sex role had 12-minute initial interactions. Recordings of these conversations were coded for frequencies of eight specific language cues thought to be gender-linked. Results provided support for Bem's conception of androgynous people as situationally flexible, and in addition revealed some specific ways in which androgyny may qualify "typical" language and gender relationships. For instance, androgynous males used phrases that qualified their statements more than any group, followed by sex-typed females, androgynous females, and sex-typed males, respectively. In addition, findings of this study suggested that language behaviors cannot be adequately predicted without both personal and situational information about the interactants. A number of significant interactions among sex role, sex, and sex role of a conversational partner illustrated how individual and context variables affect spoken language. These findings, like LaFrance and Carmen's (1980), argued the efficacy of sex-role identification for research in the expressive domain. Even the sternest critics of androgyny concede that its place may be in prediction of what LaFrance (1981) calls "very local and very concrete behaviors" such as those described in these eight studies. Taken together, they rather clearly indicate the influence of personal characteristics on communication behaviors.

VII. SUMMARY

Gender-based differences in communication behaviors are an essential element in most scholarly depictions of social reality, and this review has attempted to capture some of the richness and diversity of that literature. In 1978, Kramer et al. commented on "how few expected sex differences have been firmly established by empirical studies of actual speech" (p. 640). In a later review, Haas (1979) pointed to the "need to know which sex-associated spoken language features are real and to document the conditions under which they occur" (p. 624). Philips (1980) concluded her review essay by stating that "differences in the language use of men and women are less evident than one would expect from gender stereotypes of speech" (p. 541). Each of these analyses documented a curious phenomenon that the present review has also detected. Stereotypes about the communication behaviors of men and women surpass actual differences in those behaviors in number, direction, and certainty.

The persistence of gender-based stereotypes is almost as striking as the absence of empirically documented differences in the communication of the sexes. Even though findings of similarities in behaviors rather than differences are now common, the stereotypic conceptions remain robust and it therefore seems appropriate to examine gender stereotypes more systematically. Three decades of deploring their existence has changed little. The gender-linked language effect (Mulac et al., 1985) is a strikingly faithful though empirically more respectable rendition of the familiar themes of forceful and assertive male speech in contrast to refined and aesthetic female speech. Research designed to refute these judgments, for all the positive values it embodies, is probably less productive at this point than research which attempts to understand attribution processes better as they relate to evaluations of the spoken language of men and women.

Several issues immediately suggest themselves. Can the circumstances in which language is the primary attributional source be identified? What factors facilitate/inhibit positive perceptions of powerless speech? Available data strongly suggest that context modifies evaluations of the appropriateness of such speech forms (Warfel, 1984), but little is known about the boundary conditions of the effect. Are communication behaviors themselves such powerful gender signals that they promote a stronger and more immediate coalescence of sex-related judgments (e.g., status, attractiveness) than other types of information? Answers to these and related questions are required if a coherent account of the gender–communication relationship is to be achieved.

Regarding the actual conduct of studies of women's and men's speech and nonverbal cues, several observations seem warranted. This is a strikingly diverse literature, a robust and colorful pastiche of theoretical and empirical perspectives that, despite large numbers of studies, has yet to generate a solid descriptive data base, without which theory development is impossible. As Brown (1980) has commented, decisions about which communication variables differentiate men's and women's behavior appear to have been chosen randomly and arbitrarily.

Researchers have made few attempts to build upon extant findings or, as Philips (1980) has urged, promoted use of the same basic linguistic categories in order to increase comparability across studies. As it is, linguists, and more empirically oriented researchers in communication and social psychology, appear to have few common interests, although both approaches contribute essential types of information to our understanding of gender differences.

A related issue involves the tendency to universalize specific, often unreplicated findings and elevate these to the status of organizing principles of human communication behavior. Through largely nonempirical outlets (e.g., textbooks, popular press articles) these statements acquire unwarranted force and lure investigators away from areas and research questions prematurely. At times, research halts just short of what would be truly interesting, compelling, or explanatory in available findings. One example of this tendency is the heavily cited study of interruptions during mixed-sex conversations reported by Zimmerman and West (1975). It is not uncommon to find this single citation produced as the support for general statements about male dominance during interactions, when in fact the empirical literature on interruptions is far from definitive. Largely ignored, however, were Zimmerman and West's findings about the conversational consequences of interruptive cues. Male speakers, it was found, dropped out (ceased speaking before completing their utterances) twice as often as females did when they were interrupted. Moreover, women contested the male-initiated interruptions significantly more frequently than was the case among men. Surely it is the case that this latter finding is most important, for it challenges the stereotypic explanation for masculine interruptions in terms of feminine submissiveness.

Two implications emerge at this juncture. Much early research sprang from an impulse to legitimize "women's language" and to identify and catalogue differences in speech associated with differential evaluations. The value of those theoretical and interpretive works by Lakoff (1975), Kramer (1974), and others can hardly be overstated, but they put in place an analytic framework that emphasizes differences rather than similarities between male and female communicators. To the extent that the framework encourages exaggerations of linguistic distinctions, its contribution is diminished.

Moreover, many of the basic questions posed in these seminal works remain unanswered. Kramerae (1981) has consistently argued that language differences are more associated with status discrepancies than with gender *per se*. Social psychologists (Deaux, 1984) and linguists (Lakoff, 1975) are less certain, conceding on the one hand that status has impact, but stipulating that, within roles, men and women differ in significant ways. This is a critical empirical question awaiting resolution.

A final implication concerns the need for a second wave of gender studies which go beyond simple frequency counts of discrete and easily observable phenomena toward analyses of broader patterns of form and usage. As the literature reviewed in earlier sections of this report illustrates, communication behaviors are too complex to be indexed and interpreted through single-variable analyses. Studies which explore the linkage between communication strategies and linguistic or nonverbal choices are a promising recent development. The reappearance of ethnographies and more sophisticated qualitative methodologies in language research is similarly encouraging. With a renewed emphasis on synthesis, the body of scholars committed to unraveling the gender and communication relationship may yet achieve its goal.

REFERENCES

Amiel, H-F. (1905). *Amiel's journal: The journal intime of Henri-Frederic Amiel*. (Mrs. H. Ward, trans.). New York: Macmillan.

Andrews, P. H. (1987). Gender differences in persuasive communication and attribution of success and failure. *Human Communication Research, 13*, 3722–3785.

Argyle, M., Lalljee, M., & Cook, M. (1968). The effects of visibility on interaction in a dyad. *Human Relations, 21*, 3–17.

Aries, E. J., & Johnson, F. L. (1983). Close friendship in adulthood: Conversational content between same-sex friends. *Sex Roles, 9*, 1183–1196.

Baird, J. E. (1976). Sex differences in group communication: A review of relevant research. *The Quarterly Journal of Speech, 62*, 619–627.

Baumann, M. (1976). Two features of "Women's speech?" In B. L. Dubois & I. Crouch (Eds.), *The sociology of the languages of American women*. San Antonio, TX: Trinity University Press.

Bem, S. L. (1974). The measurement of psychological androgyny. *Journal of Consulting and Clinical Psychology, 42*, 115–162.

Bem, S. L. (1975). Sex-role adaptability: One consequence of psychological androgyny. *Journal of Personality and Social Psychology, 31*, 634–643.

Bem, S. L. (1981). Gender schema theory: A cognitive account of sex-typing. *Psychological Review, 88*, 354–364.

Berger, C. R., & Bradac, J. J. (1982). *Language and social knowledge: Uncertainty in interpersonal relations*. London: Edward Arnold.

Berger, J., Cohen, B. P., & Zelditch, M., Jr. (1972). Status characteristics and social interaction. *American Sociological Review, 37*, 241–255.

Bernard, J. (1972). *The sex game*. New York: Atheneum.

Berryman, C. L. (1980). Attitudes toward male and female sex-appropriate and sex-inappropriate language. In C. Berryman & V. Eman (Eds.), *Communication, language, and sex* (pp. 195–216). Rowley, Mass: Newbury House.

Berryman, C. L., & Eman, V. A. (1980). *Communication, language and sex*. Rowley, MA: Newbury House.

Berryman, C. L., & Wilcox, J. R. (1980). Attitudes toward male and female speech: Experiments on the effects of sex-typical language. *The Western Journal of Speech Communication, 44*, 50–59.

Berryman-Fink, C. L., & Wilcox, J. R. (1983). A multivariate investigation of perceptual attributions concerning gender appropriateness in language. *Sex Roles, 9*, 663–680.

Birdwhistell, R. L. (1970). *Kinesics and context*. Philadelphia, PA: University of Pennsylvania.

Blanck, P. D., Rosenthal, R., Snodgrass, S., De Paulo, B., & Zuckerman, M. (1981). Sex differences in eavesdropping on nonverbal cues. Developmental changes. *Journal of Personality and Social Psychology, 41*, 391–396.

Bodine, A. (1975). Sex differentiation in language. In B. Thorne & N. Henley (Eds.), *Language and sex: Difference and dominance* (pp. 130–152). Rowley, MA: Newbury House.

Bradac, J. J., Hemphill, M. R., & Tardy, C. H. (1981). Language style on trial: Effects of "powerful" and "powerless" speeches on judgments of victims and villains." *Western Journal of Speech Communication, 45,* 327–341.

Bradac, J. J., & Mulac, A. (1984a). Attributional consequences of powerful and powerless speech styles in a crisis - intervention context. *Journal of Language and Social Psychology, 3,* 1–19.

Bradac, J. J., & Mulac, A. (1984b). A molecular view of powerful and powerless speech styles: Attributional consequences of specific language features and communicator intentions. *Communication Monographs, 51,* 307–319.

Bradley, P. H. (1981). The folk-linguistics of women's speech: An empirical examination. *Communication Monographs, 47,* 105–110.

Brouwer, D., Gerristen, M., & DeHaan, D. (1979). Speech differences between women and men: On the wrong track? *Language in Society, 8,* 33–49.

Brown, P. (1980). How and why are women more polite: Some evidence from a Mayan community. In S. McConnell-Ginet, R. Borker, & N. Furman (Eds.), *Women and language in literature and society* (pp. 111–135). New York: Praeger.

Brownell, W., & Smith, D. R. (1973). Communication patterns, sex, and length of verbalization in the speech of four-year-old children. *Speech Monographs, 40,* 310–316.

Buck, R. (1979). Individual differences in nonverbal sending accuracy and electrodermal responding: The externalizing-internalizing dimension. In R. Rosenthal (Ed.), *Skill in nonverbal communication: Individual differences.* Cambridge, MA: Oelgeschlager, Gunn, and Hain.

Buck, R. (1977). Nonverbal communication of affect in preschool children: Relationships with personality and skin conductance. *Journal of Personality and Social Psychology, 35,* 255–266.

Buck, R. (1983). Nonverbal receiving ability. In J. M. Weimann & R. P. Harrison (Eds.), *Nonverbal interaction.* Newbury Park, CA: Sage Publishing.

Buck, R., Miller, R., & Caul, W. F. (1974). Sex, personality and physiological variables in the communication of emotion via facial expression. *Journal of Personality and Social Psychology, 30,* 587–596.

Buck, R., Savin, V. J., Miller, R. E., & Caul, W. F. (1972). Nonverbal communication of affect in humans. *Journal of Personality and Social Psychology, 23,* 362–371.

Burggraf, C. S., & Sillars, A. L. (1987). A critical examination of sex differences in marital communication. *Communication Monographs, 54,* 276–294.

Burgoon, J. K. (1985). Nonverbal signals. In M. L. Knapp & G. R. Miller (Eds.), *Handbook of interpersonal communication* (pp. 344–390). Beverly Hills, CA: Sage Publications.

Chandler, T., Cook, B., & Dugovics, D. (1978) Sex differences in self-reported assertiveness. *Psychological Reports, 4,* 395–402.

Cohen, M., & Saine, T. (1977). The role of profanity and sex variables in interpersonal impression formation. *Journal of Applied Communication Research, 2,* 45–52.

Coser, R. (1960). Laughter among colleagues. *Psychiatry, 23,* 81–95.

Cowan, G., & Koziej, J. (1979). The perception of sex-inconsistent behavior. *Sex Roles, 5,* 1–9.

Craighead, L. (1979). Self-instructional training for assertive-refusal behavior. *Behavior Therapy, 10,* 529–542.

Crassini, B., Law, H., & Wilson, E. (1979). Sex differences in assertive behavior? *Australian Journal of Psychology, 31,* 15–19.

Crosby, F., & Nyquist, L. (1977). The female register: An empirical study of Lakoff's hypothesis. *Language in Society, 6,* 313–322.

Crosby, F., Jose, P., & Wong-McCarthy, W. (1981). Gender, androgyny, and conversational assertiveness. In C. Mayo & N. Henley (Eds.), *Gender and nonverbal behavior* (pp. 150–169). New York: Springer-Verlag.

Darley, J., & Fazio, R. (1980). Expectancy confirmation processes arising in the social interaction sequence. *American Psychologist, 35,* 867–881.

Deaux, K. (1976). *The behavior of men and women.* Monterey, CA: Brooks/Cole.

Deaux, K. (1984). From individual differences to social categories: Analysis of a decade's research on gender. *American Psychologist, 39,* 105–116.

Deaux, K., & Lewis, L. (1984). The structure of gender stereotypes: Interrelationships among components and gender labels. *Journal of Personality and Social Psychology, 46,* 991–1004.

Derlega, V., & Chaiken, A. (1977). Privacy and self-disclosure in social relationships. *Journal of Social Issues, 33,* 102–115.

Dindia, K. (1987). The effects of sex of subject and sex of partner on interruptions. *Human Communication Research, 13,* 345–371.

Douglas, W. (1988). Question-asking in same- and opposite-sex initial interactions: The effects of anticipated future interaction. *Human Communication Research, 14,* 230–245.

Dubois, B. L., & Crouch, I. (1975). The question of tag questions in women's speech: They don't really use more of the, do they? *Language in Society, 4,* 289–294.

Eagly, A. H. (1983). Gender and social influence: A social psychological analysis. *American Psychologist, 38,* 971–981.

Eagly, A. H., & Carli, L. L. (1981). Sex of researchers and sex-typed communications as determinants of sex differences in influenceability: A meta-analysis of social influence studies. *Psychological Bulletin, 90,* 1–20.

Eagly, A., & Wood, W. (1982). Inferred sex differences in status as a determinant of gender stereotypes about social influence. *Journal of Personality and Social Psychology, 43,* 915–928.

Eakins, B., & Eakins, G. (1976). Verbal turn-taking and exchanges in faculty dialogue. In B. L. DuBois & I. Crouch (Eds.), *The sociology of the languages of American women* (pp. 53–62). San Antonio, TX: Trinity University Press.

Eakins, B. W., & Eakins, R. G. (1978). *Sex differences in human communication.* Boston, MA: Houghton Mifflin Co.

Edelsky, C. (1976). Subjective reactions to sex-linked language. *Journal of Social Psychology, 99,* 97–104.

Ellyson, S. L., & Dovidio, J. F. (1985). *Power dominance and nonverbal behavior.* New York: Springer-Verlag.

Erickson, B., Lind, E. A., Johnson, B., & O'Barr, W. (1978). Speech style and impression formation in a court setting: The effects of "powerful" and "powerless" speech. *Journal of Experimental Social Psychology, 14,* 266–279.

Ervin-Tripp, S. (1976). Is Sybil there? The structure of some American English directives. *Language in Society, 5,* 25–66.

Fairhurst, G. T. (1986). Male-female communication on the job: Literature review and commentary. In M. McLaughlin (Ed.), *Communication yearbook 9* (pp. 57–82). Beverly Hills, CA: Sage Publications.

Falbo, T., & Peplau, L. (1980). Power strategies in intimate relationships. *Journal of Personality and Social Psychology, 38,* 618–628.

Fishman, P. M. (1978). Interaction: The work women do. *Social Problems, 25,* 397–406.

FitzPatrick, M. A. (1984). A typological approach to marital interaction. Recent theory and research. In L. Berkowitz (Ed.), *Advances in Experimental Social Psychology, Vol. 18* (pp. 1–14). New York: Academic Press.

Giles, H., & Powesland, P. (1975). *Speech style and social evaluation.* London: Academic Press.

Gleason, J. B., & Weintraub, S. (1978). Input language and the acquisition of communicative competence. In K. E. Nelson (Ed.), *Children's language* (Vol. 1). New York: Gardner Press.

Gleser, G. C., Gottschalk, L. A., & Watkins, J. (1959). The relationship of sex and intelligence to choice of words: A normative study of verbal behavior. *Journal of Clinical Psychology, 15,* 182–191.

Goffman, E. (1959). *The presentation of self in everyday life.* Garden City, NY: Doubleday Books.

Goffman, E. (1979). *Gender advertisements.* New York: Harper Colophon.

Greenblatt, L., Hasenaur, J., & Freimuth, V. (1980). Psychological sex type and androgyny in the study of communication variables: Self disclosure and communication apprehension. *Human Communication Research, 6,* 117–130.

Haas, A. (1979). Male and female spoken language differences: Stereotypes and evidence. *Psychological Bulletin, 86,* 616–626.

Haas, A. (1981). Partner influence on sex-associated spoken language of children. *Sex Roles, 7,* 225–234.

Haas, A., & Sherman, M. (1982). Reported topics of conversation among same-sex adults. *Communication Quarterly, 30,* 332–342.

Hacker, H. M. (1981). Blabbermouths and clams: Sex differences in self disclosure in same-sex and cross-sex friendship dyads. *Psychology of Women Quarterly, 5,* 385–401.

Hall, J. A. (1978). Gender effects in decoding nonverbal cues. *Psychological Bulletin, 85,* 845–857.

Hall, J. A. (1979). Gender, gender roles, and nonverbal communication skills. In R. Rosenthal (Ed.), *Skill in nonverbal communication: Individual differences.* Cambridge, MA: Oelgeschlager, Gunn, and Hain.

Hall, J. A. (1984). *Nonverbal sex differences: Communication accuracy and expressive style.* Baltimore, MD: The John Hopkins University Press.

Hall, J., & Braunwald, K. (1981). Gender cues in conversations. *Journal of Personality and Social Psychology, 40,* 99–110.

Hammen, C. L., & Peplau, L. A. (1978). Brief encounters: Impact of gender, sex-role attitudes, and partners gender on interaction and cognition. *Sex Roles, 4,* 75–90.

Henley, N. (1977). *Body politics: Power, sex, and nonverbal communication.* Englewood Cliffs, NJ: Prentice-Hall.

Hirschman, L. (1973). *Analysis of supportive and assertive behavior in conversation.* Paper presented at the Linguistic Society of American Summer meeting, Amherst, MA.

Hirschman, L. (1974). *Female-male differences in conversational interaction.* Paper presented at the Linguistic Society of America, San Diego, CA.

Hopper, R. (1982). Power is as power speaks: Linguistic sex differences reconsidered. In L. Larner & M. Badani (Eds.), *Proceedings of the 2nd and 3rd conferences on communication, language, and gender* (pp. 162–170). Madison, WI: University of Wisconsin Press.

Ickes, W., & Barnes, R. (1978). Boys and girls together and alienated: On enacting stereotyped sex roles in mixed-sex dyads. *Journal of Personality and Social Psychology, 36,* 669–683.

Jackson, S., & Jacobs, S. (1983). Generalizing about messages: Suggestions for design and analysis of experiments. *Human Communication Research, 9,* 169–181.

Jeness, A. (1932). The recognition of facial expressions of emotion. *Psychological Bulletin, 29,* 324–350.

Jespersen, O. (1922). *Language: Its nature, development and origin.* London: Allen and Unwin.

Jones, H. E. (1935). The galvanic skin response as related to overt emotional expression. *American Journal of Psychology, 47,* 241–251.

Kennedy, C. W., & Camden, C. T. (1981). Gender differences in interruption behavior: A dominance perspective. *International Journal of Womens Studies, 4,* 135–142.

Kennedy, C. W., & Camden, C. T. (1983). A new look at interruptions. *Western Journal of Speech Communication, 47,* 45–58.

Key, M. R. (1975). *Male/female language.* Metuchin, NJ: The Scarecrow Press, Inc.

Klein, H. M., & Willerman, L. (1979). Psychological masculinity and femininity and typical and maximal dominance expression in women. *Journal of Personality and Social Psychology, 37,* 2054–2070.

Knapp, M. L. (1979). *Essentials of nonverbal communication.* New York: Holt, Rinehart and Winston.

Kramer, C. R. (1974). Women's speech: Separate but unequal? *Quarterly Journal of Speech 60*, 14–24.

Kramer, C. R. (1977). *Language and Speech, 20*, 151–161.

Kramer, C., Thorne, B., & Henley, N. (1978). Perspectives on language and communication. *Signs: Journal of Women in Culture and Society, 3*, 638–651.

Kramerae, C. (1981). *Women and men speaking:* Frameworks for analysis. Rowley, MA: Newberry House.

Kramerae, C. (1982). Gender: How she speaks. In E. B. Ryan & H. Giles (Eds.), *Attitudes toward language variation: Social and applied contexts* (pp. 84–98) London: Edward Arnold.

Labov, W. (1972). *Sociolinguistic patterns*. Philadelphia, PA: University of Pennsylvania Press.

LaFrance, M. (1981). Gender gestures: Sex, sex-role, and nonverbal communication. In C. Mayo & N. Henley (Eds.), *Gender and nonverbal behavior* (pp. 129–150). New York: Springer-Verlag.

LaFrance, M. (1985, Spring). Does your smile reveal your status? *Social Science News Letter, 70*, 15–18.

LaFrance, M., & Carmen, B. (1980). The nonverbal display of psychological androgyny. *Journal of Personality and Social Psychology, 38*, 36–49.

LaFrance, M., & Ickes, W. (1981). Postural mirroring and interactional involvement: Sex and sex-typing effects. *Journal of Nonverbal Behavior, 5*, 139–153.

LaFrance, M., & Mayo, C. (1979). A review of the nonverbal behaviors of women and men. *Western Journal of Speech Communication, 43*, 96–107.

Lakoff, R. (1973). Language and woman's place. *Language in Society, 2*(45), 47–48.

Lakoff, R. (1975). *Language and women's place*. New York: Harper and Row.

Lamb, T. A. (1981). Nonverbal and paraverbal control in dyads and triads: Sex or power differences? *Social Psychology Quarterly, 44*, 49–52.

Landis, M. H., & Burtt, H. E. (1924). A study of conversations. *Journal of Comparative Psychology, 4*, 81–89.

Leah, J., Law, H., & Snyder, C. (1979). The structure of self-reported difficulty in assertiveness: An application of three-mode common factor analysis. *Multivariate Behavior Research, 14*, 443–462.

Leathers, D. (1985). *Successful nonverbal communication: Principles and applications*. New York: Macmillan Publishers.

Leathers, D., & Emigh, T. (1980). Decoding facial expressions: A new test with decoding norms. *Quarterly Journal of Speech, 66*, 418–436.

Lewis, P., & Gallois, C. (1984). Disagreements, refusals, or negative feelings: Perception of negatively assertive messages from friends and strangers. *Behavior Therapy, 15*, 353–368.

Lind, E. A., & O'Barr, W. M. (1979). The social significance of speech in the courtroom. In H. Giles & R. St. Clair (Eds.), *Language and Social Psychology* (pp. 145–157). Baltimore, MD: University Park Press.

Lippa, R., Valdez, E., & Jolly, A. (1979). *The effect of self monitoring on the expressive display of masculinity-femininity*. Paper presented at the American Psychological Association, New York.

Liska, J., Mechling, E. W., & Stathas, S. (1981). Differences in subjects' perceptions of gender and believability between users of deferential and undeferential language. *Communication Quarterly, 29*, 40–48.

Lockheed, M., & Hall, K. (1976). Conceptualizing sex as a status characteristic: Applications to leadership training strategies. *Journal of Social Issues, 32*, 111–124.

Lacksley, A., Borgida, E., Brekke, N., & Hepburn, C. (1980). Sex Stereotypes and social judgment. *Journal of Personality and and Social Psychology, 39*, 821–831.

Maccoby, E. E., & Jacklin, C. N. (1974). *The psychology of sex differences*. Stanford, CA: Stanford University Press.

Maier, N. R. (1970). Male versus female discussion leaders. *Personnel Psychology, 23*, 455–461.

Markel, N., Prebor, L., & Brandt, J. (1972). Bio-social factors in dyadic communication: Sex and speaking intensity. *Journal of Personality and Social Psychology, 23*, 11–13.

Markel,' N. N., Long, J. F., & Saine, T. J. (1976). Sex effects in conversational interaction: Another look at male dominance. *Human Communication Research, 2*, 356–364.

Martin, J. N., & Craig, R. T. (1983). Selected linguistic sex differences during initial social interactions of same-sex and mixed sex student dyads. *Western Journal of Speech Communication, 47*, 16–28.

Mayo, C., & Henley, N. (1981). *Gender and nonverbal behavior.* New York: Springer-Verlag.

McConnell-Ginet, S., Borker, R., & Furman, N. (1980). *Women and language in literature and society.* New York: Praeger Publishers.

McCormick, N. B. (1979). Come-ons and put-offs: Unmarried students' strategies for having and avoiding sexual intercourse. *Psychology of Women Quarterly, 4*, 194–211.

McDonald, B. F. (1986). *Male and female communicator style differences: A meta-analysis.* Paper presented at the annual conference of the Organization for the study of Communication, Language, and Gender, Fairfax, VA.

McLaughlin, M., Cody, W., Kane, M., & Robey, C. (1981). Sex differences in story receipt and story sequencing behaviors in dyadic conversations. *Human Communication Research, 7*, 99–116.

McMillan, J. R., Clifton, A. K. Mcgrath, D., & Gale, W. S. (1977). Women's language: Uncertainty or interpersonal sensitivity and emotionality? *Sex Roles, 3*, 545–559.

Mehrabian, A. (1978). *Silent messages.* Belmont, CA: Wadsworth.

Miller, L. (1977). Dyadic perception of a communicator style: Replication and conformation. *Communication Research, 4*, 87–112.

Miller, L. (1980). Correspondence between self and other perceptions of communicator dominance. *Western Journal of Speech Communication, 44*, 120–131.

Montgomery, B., & Norton, R. (1981). Sex differences and similarities in communicator style. *Communication Monographs, 48*, 121-132.

Moore, H. T. (1922). Further data concerning sex differences. *Journal of Abnormal and Social Psychology, 4*, 81–89.

Mulac, A. (1975). Effects of obscene language upon three dimensions of listener attitudes. *Communication Monographs, 43*, 330–307.

Mulac, A., Bradac, J., & Mann, S. (1985). Male/female language differences and attributional consequences in children's television. *Human Communication Research, 11*, 481–506.

Mulac, A., Incontro, C., & James, M. (1985). Comparison of the gender-linked language effect and sex role stereotypes. *Journal of Personality and Social Psychology, 49*, 1098–1109.

Mulac, A., & Rudd, M. (1977). Effects of selected American regional dialects upon regional audience numbers. *Communication Monographs, 44*, 185–195.

Mulac, A., & Lundell, T. (1980). Differences in perceptions created by syntactic-semantic productions of male and female speakers. *Communication Monographs, 47*, 111–118.

Mulac, H., & Lundell, T. (1982). An empirical test of the gender-linked language effect in a public speaking setting. *Language and Speech, 25*, 243–256.

Mulac, A., Lundell, T., & Bradac, J. (1985, November). *Male/female language differences and attributional consequences in a public speaking setting: Toward an explanation of the gender-linked language effect.* Paper presented at Speech Communication Association, Denver, CO.

Mulac, A., Studley, L. B., Weimann, J. M., & Bradac, J. J. (1987). Male/female gaze in same-sex and mixed-sex dyads: Gender-linked differences and mutual influence. *Human Communication Research, 13*, 323–343.

Natale, M., Entin, E., & Jaffe, J. (1979). Vocal interruptions in dyadic communication as a function of speech and social anxiety. *Journal of Personality and Social Psychology, 37*, 865–878.

Newcombe, N., & Arnkoff, D. (1979). Effects of speech style and sex of speaker on person perception. *Journal of Personality and Social Psychology, 37*, 1293–1303.

Norton, R. (1978). Foundation of a communicator style construct. *Human Communication Research, 4*, 99–112.

Norton, R. (1983). *Communicator style*. Beverly Hills, CA: Sage.

Norton, R., & Pettegrew, L. (1977). Communication style as an effect determinant of attraction. *Communication Research, 4*, 257–282.

Norton, R., & Pettegrew, L. (1979). Attentiveness as a style variable. *Communication Monographs, 46*, 12–27.

Norton, R., & Nussbaum, J. (1980). Dramatic behaviors of the effective teacher. In D. Nimmo (Ed.), *Communication Yearbook 4* (pp. 565–579). New Brunswick, NJ: Transaction Press.

O'Barr, W. K., & Atkins, B. K. (1980). Women's language" or "powerless language. In S. McConnell-Ginet, R. Borker, & N. Furman (Eds.), *Women and language in literature and society* (pp. 93–110). New York: Praeger Publishers.

Pearson, J. (1985). *Gender and communication*. Dubuque, IO: Wm. C. Brown.

Peplau, L. A. (1983). Roles and gender. In H. Kelley, E. Berscheid, A. Christensen, J. Harvey, T. Huston, G. Levinger, E. McClintock, L. Peplau, & D. Peterson (Eds.), *Close relationships* (pp. 220–264) New York: W. H. Freeman.

Petty, R., & Caccioppo, J. (1981). *Attitudes and persuasion: Classic and contemporary approaches*. Dubuque, IO: Wm C. Brown Company.

Philips, S. U. (1980). Sex differences and language. *Annual Review of Anthropology, 9*, 523–544.

Piliavin, J. A., & Martin, R. R. (1978). The effects of the sex composition of groups on style of social interaction. *Sex Roles, 4*, 281–296.

Prokasy, W., & Raskin, D. (1973). *Electrodermal activity in psychological research*. New York: Academic Press.

Putnam, L., & McCallister (1980). Situational effects of task and gender on nonverbal display. In D. Nimmo (Ed.), *Communication Yearbook 4* (pp. 679–699). New Brunswick, NJ: Transaction Press.

Renshaw, S., & Johnson, M. (1982, April). *Functional language indices in biological and psychological sex types*. Paper presented at the Southern Speech Communication Association, Hot Springs, AR.

Restak, R. M. (1979). *The brain: The last frontier*. New York: The Free Press.

Roger, D. B., & Schumacher, A. (1983). Effects of individual differences on dyadic conversational strategies. *Journal of Personality and Social Psychology, 45*, 700–705.

Rogers, W. T., & Jones, S. E. (1975). Effects of dominance tendencies on floor holding and interruption behavior in dyadic interaction. *Human Communication Research, 1*, 113–122.

Roloff, M., & Greenberg, B. (1979). Sex differences in choice of modes of conflict resolution in real-life and television. *Communication Quarterly, 27*, 3–12.

Rosenthal, R. (1979). *Skill in nonverbal communication: Individual differences*. Cambridge, MA: Oelgeschlager, Gunn, and Hain.

Rosenthal, R., & DePaulo, B. (1979). Sex differences in accommodation in nonverbal communication. In R. Rosenthal (Ed.), *Skill in nonverbal communication: Individual differences* (pp. 68–103). Cambridge, MA: Oelgeschlager, Gunn and Hain, Publisher.

Rosenthal, R., Hall, J., Archer, D., DiMatteo, R., & Rogers, P. (1979). The PONS test: Measuring sensitivity to nonverbal cues. In S. Weitz (Ed.), *Nonverbal communication* (pp. 357–370). New York: Oxford University Press.

Rose, Y., & Tryon, W. (1979). Judgments of assertive behavior as a function of speech loudness, latency, content, gestures, inflection and sex. *Behavior Modification, 3*, 113–123.

Safer, M. A. (1978). *Sex differences in hemisphere specialization for recognizing facial expressions of emotion*. Unpublished doctoral dissertation, University of Wisconsin.

Schlueter, D., & Smythe, M. J. (1985, May). *An interpersonal costs analysis of compliance-gaining behaviors*. Paper presented at the International Communication Association, Honolulu, HI.

Schultz, K., Briere, J., & Sandler, L. (1984). The use and development of sex-typed language. *Psychology of Women Quarterly, 8*, 327–336.

Scotton, C. M. (1976). Strategies of neutrality: Language choice in uncertain situations. *Language, 52*, 919–941.

Scotton, C. M. (1980). Explaining linguistic choices as identity negotiations. In H. Giles, W. Robinson, & P. Smith (Eds.), *Language: Social psychological perspectives* (pp. 359–366). Oxford, England: Pergamon Press.

Selnow, G. W. (1985). Sex differences in uses and perceptions of profanity. *Sex Roles, 12*, 303–312.

Siegel, (1980). Effects of objective evidence of expertness, nonverbal behavior, and subject sex on client-perceived expertness. *Journal of Consulting Psychology, 27*, 117–121.

Siegler, D., & Siegler, R. (1976). Stereotypes of males' and females' speech. *Psychological Reports, 39*, 167–170.

Smith, P. M. (1985). *Language, the sexes, and society*. Oxford, England: Basil Blackwell.

Smythe, M. J., Arkin, R. M., Nickel, S., & Huddleston, B. (1983, May). *Sex differences in conversation: The stereotype revisited and revised*. Paper presented at the International Communication Association, Dallas, Texas.

Smythe, M. J., & Huddleston, B. H. (1987, October). *Competition and collaboration: Male and female communication patterns in initial interactions*. Paper presented at the annual conference of the Organization for the study of Language, Gender and Communication, Milwaukee, WI.

Snodgrass, S. E. (1985). Women's intuition: The effect of subordinate role on interpersonal sensitivity. *Journal of Personality and Social Psychology, 49*, 146–155.

Stebbins, C., Kelly, B., Tolor, A., & Power, M. (1977). Sex differences in assertiveness in college students. *Journal of Psychology, 95*, 309–315.

Stier, D., & Hall, J. (1984). Gender differences in touch: An empirical and theoretical review. *Journal of Personality and Social Psychology, 47*, 440–459.

Strodtbeck, F. (1951). Husband–wife interaction over revealed differences. *American Sociological Review, 16*, 468–473.

Strodtbeck, F., & Mann, R. (1956). Sex role differentiation in jury deliberations. *Sociometry, 19*, 3–11.

Swacker, M. (1975). The sex of the speaker as a sociolinguistic variable. In B. Thorne & N. Henley (Eds.), *Language and sex: Difference and dominance* (pp. 76–83). Rowley, MA: Newbury House.

Thorne, B., & Henley, N. (1975). Difference and dominance: An overview of language, gender, and society. In B. Thorne & N. Henley (Eds.), *Language and sex: Difference and dominance* (pp. 5–42). Rowley, MA: Newbury House.

Thorne, B., Kramerae, C., & Henley, N. (1983). Language, gender, and society: Opening a second decade of research. In B. Thorne, C. Kramerae, & N. Henley (Eds.), *Language, gender and society* (pp. 7–24). Rowley, MA: Newbury House.

Trimboli, C., & Walker, M. B. (1984). Switching pauses in cooperative and competitive conversations. *Journal of Experimental Social Psychology, 20*, 297–311.

Trugdill, P. (1972). Sex, covert prestige, and linguistic change in urban British English of Norwich. *Language in Society, 1*, 179–195.

von Baeyer, C., Sherk, D., & Zanna, M. (1981). Impression management in the job interview: When the female applicant meets the male "chauvinist" interviewer. *Personality and Social Psychology Bulletin, 7*, 45–51.

Warfel, K. A. (1984). Gender schemas and perceptions of speech style. *Communication Monographs, 51*, 253–267.

Warren, N., & Gilner, F. (1978). Measurement of positive assertive behaviors: The Behavioral Test of Tenderness Expression. *Behavior Therapy, 9,* 178–184.

Weitz, S. (1976). Sex differences in nonverbal communication. *Sex Roles, 2,* 175–184.

West, C. (1979). Against our will: Male interruptions of females in cross-sex conversation. In J. Orsanu, M. Slater, & L. Adler (Eds.), *Language, sex and gender: Does 'la difference' make a difference?* (pp. 81–100). New York: New York Academy of Sciences.

Wiggins, J., & Holzmuller, A. (1978). Psychological androgyny and interpersonal behavior. *Journal of Consulting and Clinical Psychology, 46,* 40–52.

Wilson, L., & Gallois, C. (1985). Perceptions of assertive behavior: Sex combination, role appropriateness, and message type. *Sex Roles, 12,* 125–141.

Wolfram, W. A. (1969). *A sociolinguistic description of Detroit Negro speech.* Washington, DC: Center for Applied Linguistics.

Wood, M. M. (1966). The influence of sex and knowledge effectiveness on spontaneous speech. *Word, 22,* 117–137.

Wright, J. W., & Hosman, L. A. (1983). Language style and sex bias in the courtroom: The effects of male and female use of hedges and intensifiers on impression formation. *Southern Speech Communication Journal, 48,* 137–152.

Zanna, M., & Pack, S. (1975) On the self-fulfilling nature of apparent sex differences in behaviors. *Journal of Experimental Social Psychology, 11,* 583–591.

Zimmerman, D. H., & West, C. (1975) Sex roles, interruptions and silences in conversation. In B. Thorne & N. Henley (Eds.), *Language and sex: Difference and dominance* (pp. 105–129). Rowley, MA: Newbury House.

7 Information Use Environments

Robert S. Taylor
School of Information Studies
Syracuse University

I. INTRODUCTION

In the information field there are essentially three approaches to the study of information transfer. First is the *technological* approach, which basically prescribes the size, shape, function, dynamism, and even the content of information systems. That is to say, what is and can be stored in a book (report, paper, or other formal retrievable message) or in a computer memory defines what is accepted as knowledge or information. In this context, information systems, in Dervin's words, tend to protect whatever functional unit in which that system has a vested interest (Dervin, 1975, p. 13). The second is the *content-driven* approach, which stems from the human concern with the subject classification and ordering of knowledge and information, especially as reflected in library classification schemes, indexing constructs, and such mechanisms as thesauri and data dictionaries. In the beginning such constructs are recognized as tentative and subjective; but they soon take on a life and validity of their own. They tend to become reality rather than human representations developed to provide ways of organizing, by subject matter, information about *reality*.

These conventional approaches need to be tempered and informed by a third approach that looks at the *user and the uses of information,* and the contexts within which those users make choices about what information is useful to them at particular times. These choices are based, not only on subject matter, but on other elements of the context within which a user lives and works. The explication of this statement is a major focus of this chapter.

These contexts are what the author has called *information use environments* (IUE): the set of those elements that (a) affect the flow and use of information messages into, within, and out of any definable entity; and (b) determine the criteria by which the value of information messages will be judged (Taylor, 1986, pp. 25–26). This chapter has been, in part, informed by Dervin's observation that "systems personnel and researchers have been looking at something they call information rather than at something users call information" (Dervin, 1983a, p. 158). Papers by Paisley (1980), Wilson (1981), Roberts (1982), and Wersig and Windel (1985) influenced a good deal of the underlying assumptions and direction of this chapter.

The intent in this chapter is not a complete survey of the literature. Rather it is concerned with the delineation of a structure and a description of a particular area of concern in the information sciences. The author comes from the operating and professional side of the information field. Hence the essay should be perceived as a bridge between (a) users and their environments, and (b) the world of the system designer, information manager, and those who really make the system work—from reference librarians to information analysts. The chapter has three objectives:

- to provide a structure for the study of IUEs, thereby defining what those environments are;

- to describe, using this structure, what it is we know about three specific IUEs;
- to examine some of the problems of this approach

There is, of course, an assumption underlying all of these concerns. That is that people, settings, and problems and their resolution can be described, at least in preliminary fashion, in information terms.

This chapter is in six parts. First is a discussion of some of the limits of the chapter: what it does and does not cover, and some terminological questions. Second, ways of structuring and organizing the data are described and discussed. This might be construed as a model, albeit tentative and descriptive. It provides a vehicle for illustrating different types of information users in context and a means of comparing one user class with another. Sections III, IV, and V describe three sets of information users: engineers, physicians, and legislators. Section VI deals with some of the problems, weaknesses, and strengths of the suggested structure.

This chapter then is an early attempt to organize what we seem to know about the environments within which different types of users seek information and make choices about the utility of the information available to them. It is not graven in stone; indeed the author hopes that it will spur discussion and improvement as a means of organizing what it is we know, and that it will stimulate further research.

A. Limits

The area of concern is obviously vast. There are, consequently, two specific limitations. First, the *user population* is limited to those groups or classes of people who are active, experienced, and critical users of information. That is to say, they are aware of their problems; they know, at least in approximate terms, where they can find useful information; and they have a critical sensitivity to what constitutes a solution, or, better said, a resolution of a problem in their context. This population includes, for example, managers, scholars, scientists, teachers, social workers, engineers, farmers, physicians, small business people, etc. It might be more logical to discuss information users in terms of similar types of problems; we are, however, concerned with eventual input to systems design, and thus we will categorize users as managers, teachers, etc. That is to say, at this time, we believe that problems and their resolution in a management context are different from those in an engineering context, those in a teaching context from those in a physician's context, etc. The qualifier *at this time* in the last sentence implies that we may indeed find similarities useful to system design and operation among different professions and occupations in the process of defining specific IUEs. This is one of the intents of this chapter: to begin to isolate similarities *and* differences among varying populations in specific contexts.

We are also dealing with groups rather than with individuals. This says that, though individuals have specific idiosyncracies, there are real similarities among, for example, managers, whether they are in Seattle, Miami, or Boston. It is the argument of this chapter that each of these groups has different kinds of problems over varying time frames, different ways of resolving those problems, and consequently differing information seeking behaviors. The chapter excludes consideration of the general public, the elderly, consumers, the information-poor. It is not that these groups are not important but rather that they pose quite different sets of problems, experience, and information need which, in this brief essay, cannot be dealt with effectively. However, it is hoped that the structure presented here can also be used in organizing data about these groups.

It should also be noted that the chapter focuses especially on the American experience in the broader context of American culture. We suspect, without investigation, that there may be differences between European and American experience, education, and hence information behavior. There are, for example, certainly differences between the American practice of medicine and the Chinese practice (Eisenberg & Wright, 1985).

The second limitation concerns use of the term *information*. Discussion here is limited to formal information—both oral and recorded—which is sought in the context of recognized problems or concerns. That is to say, information is defined as formal, *not* because of its physical format, e.g., book, image, computer print-out, but rather because it responds, and is perceived as—and is intended to be—relevant to a particular problem. A consultant's oral report to a client, for example, or a discussion among engineers concerned with a particular device or physicians concerned with a particular patient, is perceived here as formal information. In fact, because such activities are interactive, in information terms they may be far more relevant to a problem than a written report. An understanding of this is crucial to the user-driven approach. It is the recognition of problems and the processes of seeking resolution to these problems which defines the information process. This chapter is not necessarily concerned with nonverbal information, though we will see, in the case of practicing physicians, that nonverbal information may become important in a defined context.

B. Use(s) of Information

The term in the title phrase—*use*—requires mutual understanding and agreement. Generally—and somewhat cavalierly—we can say that use is whatever the particular population says it is. In a way, that is really what we mean: that is what the user-directed approach is all about. There are some caveats, however.

Use of an information store—library, management information system, consultant, analysis center, etc.—has widely differing interpretations (Bookstein, 1982). It is the argument here, however, that such studies usually ask the wrong set of questions, start from the wrong end of the stick, from system-determined definitions rather than user's perceptions of information.

Dervin and Nilan (1986) argue that a paradigmatic shift is taking place in the study of information needs and uses. The 'alternative' paradigm, in contrast to the 'traditional,'

> posits information as something constructed by human beings. It sees users as beings who are constantly constructing, as beings who are free (within system constraints) to create from systems and situations whatever they choose. It focuses on how people construct sense, searching for universal dimensions of sense-making. It focuses on understanding information use in particular situations and is concerned with what leads up to and what follows intersections with systems. It focuses on the user. It examines the system only as seen by the user. It asks many 'how questions' e.g., how do people define needs in different situations, how do they present these needs to the system, and how do they make use of what systems offer them. (Dervin & Nilan, 1986, p. 16)

It is critical at this time to begin to provide some structure on the uses of information: what information does to or for the recipient *and for his or her problem or situation.*

II. STRUCTURING THE DATA

As a first pass, data about information use environments can be broken down into four categories: sets of people, typical structure and thrust of problems of those sets of people, typical settings, and what constitutes resolution of problems. This essay is about the *information behavior* of different sets of people. Information behavior is briefly defined here as the sum of activities through which information becomes useful. This essay is an attempt to put flesh on this bare-boned definition. We have already discussed what we mean by information. Two additional comments are necessary: (a) *activities* imply active search resulting from an area of doubt or more specifically a recognized problem; (b) *useful* implies ways of resolving a problem through clarification, alteration, or actual solution as a result of information gained. Following the pattern of the four categories noted above, information behavior is the product of the following elements of the information use environment.

- The assumptions, formally learned or not, made by a defined set of people concerning the nature of their work.
- The kinds and structure of the problems deemed important and typical by this set of people.
- The constraints and opportunities of typical environments within which any group or subgroup of this set of people operates and works.
- The conscious, and perhaps unconscious, assumptions made as to what constitutes a solution, or, better said, a resolution of problems, and what makes information useful and valuable in their contexts.

In these terms, the author believes that, generally speaking, the information behavior of engineers is different from that of practicing physicians, that of lawyers from that of farmers, etc. This essay is intended to explore and, it is hoped, to clarify some of these assertions.

A. Sets of People

What constitutes *a set of people* in terms of information behavior? What are the demographic and nondemographic characteristics of these sets of people? Are there differences within each set? Can those differences be seen in terms of information behavior?

In answering the question of what constitutes a set of people, there are two possibilities. First, is a set of people established on the basis of some set of variables and then labelled A, B, or C? Or is a set of people established a priori in a historical or social sense, i.e., doctors, engineers, farmers, etc., and then these groups examined to determine their information behavior? In a sense, society has already answered the question, and we already provide information services based on these societal distinctions. We call certain people physicians or engineers or managers because, in the first two cases, of their professional education, and because of their occupation in the case of managers. Their training, occupation, and usual activities are made up in part of sets of information behavior unique to the group under consideration.

For purposes of this essay, there seems to be a useful division into four classes of people. This division is based on an intuitive interpretation of information behavior, and will be argued in the chapter.

- *the professions:* engineers, lawyers, social workers, scientists, teachers, managers, physicians, etc.
- *the entrepreneur:* farmers, small business men, etc.
- *special interest groups:* consumers, citizen groups, hobbyists, political action groups, ethnic cultural groups, etc.
- *special socioeconomic groups:* information-poor, the disabled, minorities, the elderly, etc.

We are concerned principally with the first two classes. Each of us, of course, may be in several classes simultaneously. An engineer may also be a consumer activist, a teacher active in a political action group, a business person an amateur birdwatcher, a farmer active in a black minority group. Our concern, however, is only with the engineer acting as an engineer, the manager acting as a manager, etc.

In describing a set of people in *demographic terms* it is necessary to remember that, for this essay, we are concerned with those variables that help to define the information environment and behavior of a restricted population: professional and entrepreneurs. In general terms, *age, sex,* or *marital status* probably have little to do with the definition of the IUE, though they may have an effect on individual information behavior. Even with innovation and risk taking, age does not seem to play a role, though there is some inconsistency reported in the studies on the relationship of age to innovation (Rogers, 1983, p. 251). It is the assumption here—though not proven—that education for a particular profession, including its reflection as information style, will be the same regardless of sex or marital status. An interesting question to examine may be to ask what the effect on information behavior is when a profession is principally female, e.g., teaching, nursing, etc. *Race* may make a difference in restricting the options, and hence, changing the nature of required information, for a black farmer or business person. These four demographic variables, however, do not really affect in significant ways the basic hypothesis that certain predefined categories of people have different information behaviors one from another. It also appears unlikely—although there is no evidence one way or another—that the *socioeconomic status* of a profession has any appreciable effect on information behavior, though it may influence the entrepreneur, affecting his or her access to information. These are factors which need further investigation. The author does not intend to pursue this here.

Of all the demographic variables, *education* appears to be the most significant. It is necessary to note two aspects of education here. On the one hand, there are those activities, called professions, that are significantly affected, indeed controlled, by their formal education: physicians, lawyers, teachers, social workers, scientists, engineers.[1] On the other hand, there are activities, sometimes called professions, that are less dependent on formal education, and are more defined by context and the kinds of problems faced: farmers, managers, legislators, small business persons. With business persons, however, level of education may have some bearing because of certain needed skills: accounting, marketing, specific technological know-how, etc. There is, however, no formal certifying process for practitioners of these activities. Hence, formal recognition of problems, and resultant information behaviors, are not necessarily learned through formal education, as in the formal professions. In all of these cases, it is the organization and conceptual structure that these different sets of people bring to a particular context that give value to information, makes it useful (Knott & Wildavsky, 1980, p. 558).

Among the *nondemographic characteristics,* the more important in the context of this chapter seem to be *media use, social networks,* and *attitudes toward new technology, education, risk taking,* and *innovation.*

Concerning *media use,* extensive and long-standing studies have been made

---

[1] During the sixties, when the author was doing research on question negotiation, a law librarian in Washington made a most perceptive remark: "I can usually tell from which law school a person comes by the way he asks a question."

of the use of different media and channels by the populations under consideration here (Fabisoff & Ely, 1974; Lowry, 1979; Dervin & Nilan, 1986). Such studies tell us, for example, that scientists are print-oriented (Price, 1965; Allen, 1977) and regular readers of their periodical literature (Garvey, Tomita, & Woolf, 1979); that engineers use trade journals and textbooks much more than they use professional engineering journals (Allen, 1977); that managers prefer face-to-face meetings or the telephone over any other channels for information seeking (Mintzberg, 1975).

In *networks,* doctors find the social network of colleagues important for the confirmation of new drug information which they probably heard first from drug detailmen (Coleman, Katz, & Menzel, 1966). Productive scientists use the invisible college of colleagues throughout the world who are working on a particular research problem as the principle network for information transfer (Crane, 1972). Engineers, on the other hand, are able "to communicate better with their organization colleagues than with outsiders because of shared knowledge" (Allen, 1977, p. 139).

Attitudes toward education, new technology, risk taking, and *innovation* may be more individually idiosyncratic than collective, although the specific setting and attitudes toward rewards and penalties in that setting may well affect these attitudes, and hence their information behavior. Such a blanket statement, however, belies certain differences or gradations. Though in Section II-D below we will go into more detail in the context of problem resolution, generally knowledge is seen by a user as either enlightenment, *know-what,* or as instrumental, *know-how* (Boulding, 1978). Scholars and policy makers who seek context and background, and those for whom curiosity and its satisfaction are primary drives, seek enlightenment. Those concerned with the design, development, and management of an operation find instrumental knowledge more useful.

Those concerned with the development and production of pharmaceutical drugs or space shuttles, or with renal biopsies, will have different attitudes toward *risk* than those concerned with the manufactures of diapers, steel ingots, or carburetors. Degree of perceived risk has an effect on the amount and quality of information required for decision (Slovic, 1987).

B. Problems

What are the characteristics of typical problems that this particular set of people is concerned about? Do these problems change over time? If so, how? It should be noted here that our concern is not only with the subject matter as a definer of problems. It is rather with the nature of the problems themselves which are endemic or deemed important, and hence faced by a particular set of people.

Clients or users are perceived as a set of problems generated by a particular environment: problem types which can be described in information terms, and which have an effect on the kinds and nature of anticipated or appropriate response.

The term *problem* is used in a generic sense in this essay. Formalists tend to separate the concern into three parts: questions which specify, problems which connect, and sense making which orients (MacMullin & Taylor, 1984). However, the user does not separate these into nice neat categories. There may indeed be gradations (Taylor, 1962). The approach here, however, is that these differences may be more easily examined in the kinds of information sought and in the uses made of that information, than in a statement of the problem itself. What is conjectured here is that a problem and its resolution cannot readily be separated. We pose this as an interesting conjecture, one that needs further examination and analysis.

A user is concerned with establishing some degree of clarity in an area of doubt (a) by recalling previous experience for analogy; (b) through new knowledge or by confirming knowledge that illuminates, resolves, or alters the problem; or (c) with the discovery that there may be no resolution.

There are generally three concerns in discussing problems. The first is the tendency to think of them as static and immutable. Problems are not static. They change all the time in response to new information and in relation to the actor's position and perceptions. Frischmuth and Allen, in the context of engineering design, call this the 'concept of the variable problem,' which in large part goes unrecognized because engineering education focuses "almost exclusively on closed-form problems in which there is only one correct solution" (Frischmuth & Allen, 1969, p. 63). This is not exclusive to engineering. Sometimes the change is partly formalized, as in the engineering design process, where recognizable steps are assumed each of which may require entirely different information responses. Related to this is that, in the beginning, problems are often not well articulated, and indeed may exist only as a vague dissatisfaction with things as they are (Taylor, 1962, 1968). Responses, though that may be too formal a term, are apt at this stage to be highly informal and serendipitous.

A second concern is the recognition that each of the definable IUEs has a discrete class of problems, spawned by its particular setting and by the exigencies of its profession, occupation, or life style. Teachers in elementary or secondary school, for example, generally have problems that can be divided into five categories: subject matter and its organization, classroom control, discipline and aberrant behavior, presentation methods, and administration. It is from these contexts that a teacher's problems arise which define the shape of his or her information seeking and using. Because of the nature of the problems and the immediacy of the classroom, instrumental responses are apt to be most appropriate (Huberman, 1983).

A third concern is with problem dimensions, a more formal set of characteristics each of which illuminates the criteria for judging relevance of response.

MacMullin and Taylor (1984) discuss these dimensions at some length. Among the 11 dimensions noted, the more significant are:

- *Well structured/ill structured.* The former can be solved by the application of logical and algorithmic processes, and tend to require hard data. Ill-structured problems have variables that are not well understood and require more probabilistic information on how to proceed rather than hard data.
- *Complex/simple.* Complexity refers to the number and interaction of problem variables. Though they may be understood as single variables, their interactions with other variables are not known.
- *Assumptions agreed upon/not agreed upon.* In addition, assumptions may not be well understood or articulated. People tend to 'talk past each other' when they do not have some mutual understanding of assumptions which reflect their perceptions of the world or of that particular universe of discourse.
- *Familiar/new patterns.* Many problems are essentially procedural and rely on well-established method and techniques built up over centuries of practice. When this is not the case, trial and error become standard procedure.

Each of these dimensions would appear to have—though this has not been experimentally validated—an effect on the kinds of information deemed useful.

C. Setting

What is the nature and variety of settings these groups of people work in? What are the attributes of those settings? How does information generally move in those settings? What are the types and structures of information and means of dissemination in these settings?

We are concerned with physical context and with ways of describing the context in which a specific class of people usually works and lives, and which affects the way they seek and make use of information.

We tend to think of the bureaucratic organization as the only setting. Albeit important, the organization is but one setting. It has very little to do with, for example, practicing physicians, independent lawyers, farmers, or small business people, let alone consumers, the elderly, etc.

The rise of the service sector in the American economy is epitomized by the small organization (Fuchs, 1969). In many cases these services, together with the farmer and the small businessperson, are closer to information—must be closer for survival—than are larger and more formal organizations. *Closer* means more dependent on current information of high quality.

Within limits, information behavior essentially transcends the bureaucratic organization. This goes beyond the usual distinction between those who are organizationally oriented and those who are professionally oriented (March & Simon, 1958), which has to do with where one's loyalties are. Within a large corporation, the information behavior of, say lawyers, when acting as lawyers, is significantly different from that of engineers, when acting as engineers. School teachers, with minor variations due to the local setting, will have basically the same set of problems and seek the same kinds of information whether they teach in Peoria or Portland.

Having said all this—principally to break our organizational bias—we need to ask, then, what are the elements of setting that influence information behavior? There seem to be four general influences.

1. Importance of Organization.   Given different kinds of organizations, what effect does structure and style have upon the behavior of different classes of information users in the organization? Within a corporation management establishes, inadvertently or otherwise, an attitude toward information and consequently affects the information behavior of its employees. In research and development laboratories, for example, what executives emphasize and reward (useful products/processes *or* publishing a paper which adds significantly to the literature) has a great deal to say about the importance of different kinds of information services (Pelz & Andrews, 1966, pp. 297–299; Taylor, 1986, p. 38). For the entrepreneurial farmer, however, this will have little meaning except as he may be a member of a cooperative or other kind of marketing association. These organizations do not impinge on or affect the farmer's activities in the same way a corporation affects the information behavior of a financial manager or production foreman.

2. Domain of Interest.   Regardless of size or structure, what does the unit of concern do? (Unit of concern may be an organization of thousands of people, a part of that larger organization, or it may be a single practicing physician.) It may manufacture aircraft parts, educate adolescents, heal the sick, design skyscrapers, formulate policy and pass laws, sell and service automobiles, raise catfish, or test materials. Each of these domains, like thousands of others, will have certain attributes peculiar to that domain: availability of information, patterns of dissemination, and to some extent the level of reliability. In certain cases, information in the usual sense may in fact be unavailable. This is true especially in farming and engineering. For example, if, several years ago, a farmer wanted to get into the production of fuel alcohol from crops, there was basically an information vacuum. The farmer had to break new ground. In such a situation trial and error—learning by doing—becomes the principal mode of information gathering. As a result, that particular farmer becomes an information source in the future (Consumer Dynamics, Inc., 1981, pp. 17–20). Does the unit operate in the public or private sector? Research indicates that there are differing patterns of social science information use between public agency and private company. The major difference seems to be the high conceptual use (i.e., enlightenment) of research information in public organizations and high instrumental use of such information in private firms (Deshpande & Zaltman, 1983; Caplan, Morrison, & Stambaugh, 1975).

3. Access to Information.   What effect does the setting have on perceived ease of access to information? Accessibility appears in many studies to be the single most important variable governing use of information (Gerstenberger & Allen, 1968; O'Reilly, 1979, p. 16). In almost all studies of information use among various populations, dependence on personal sources far exceeds impersonal sources (Aguilar, 1967; Mintzberg, 1975; Matthews & Stinson, 1970; Chen & Hernon, 1982). That is to say, personal memory and friends, relatives, colleagues, and peers are perceived to be more accessible than more formal sources. Accessibility in this sense means somewhat more than just physical access. It seems to have something to do with the perceived validity and utility of information and, perhaps above all, with a sense that personal dialogue will help to clarify both need and response, and hence to provide more useful information. Formal gatherers of information, e.g., libraries, information centers, management information systems, tend to be too far—both physically and psychologically—from the users of information (Feldman & March, 1981; Taylor, 1986). The information packages stored and transmitted by the more formal channels seldom match the way people want or use information (Dervin, 1975).

This does not mean that formal text systems are not used. For scholars, scientists, policy report writers, decision formulators, and academicians generally such sources are important because these groups are paper centered, *papyrocentric* in the words of Derek Price (1965). Their output is paper, not devices, systems, decisions, or solutions.

4. History and Experience.   In an organization, the passage of time and increased specialization will tend to bureaucratize, to make complex tasks routine, and thus reduce the effect of new information (Kimberley et al., 1980). An organization may absorb a great deal of information with very little effect. On the other hand, the change in traditional institutions and in the professions as a result of the knowledge explosion has directly affected specialization and compartmentalization of knowledge, and hence the relevance and transfer of information and knowledge (Schon, 1983, pp. 3–20).

D. Resolution of Problems

What constitutes, for a given set of people, resolution of a typical problem? What kinds of information (amount, degree of relevance, quality, format, etc.) do people in a particular set anticipate? What filtering mechanisms exist? What are the attitudes towards the benefits and costs of information use? What are the criteria of information choice? What does information do for people in specific settings?

General attitudes toward information unconsciously assume the more information the better. Such an attitude, of course, leads to overload of irrelevant
information (Ackoff, 1967). Despite the burden of overload to managers, there is
still the feeling that "it is better from the decision maker's point of view to have
information that is not needed than not to have information that might be
needed" (Feldman & March, 1981, p. 176). We really do not know much about
information safety factors—so we tend to overload. People have developed a
whole variety of means for deflecting unwanted information. One can (a) throw
it away or (b) use colleagues, secretaries, assistants, or other staff to act as filters.
Public and private bureaucracies—legal, marketing, public relations, research
and development, strategic planning, budget departments—have grown during
the past half century in good part to filter information for decision making
(Taylor, 1986, pp. 136–140). We may well ask whether such methods lessen the
burden of overload or cause it. One can use a social network of peers or relatives
as a source for specific and reliable information.

More pertinent to our concerns here, however, is the way a given set of people
view their problems and what they anticipate as resolution. These perceptions
and anticipations are, in a way, a built-in but unconscious means of controlling
the amount of information used (Knott & Wildavsky, 1980). Engineers, for
example, in selecting among information channels,

> act in a manner which is intended not to maximize gain, but rather, to minimize
> loss. The loss to be minimized is the cost in terms of effort, either physical or
> psychological, which must be expended in order to gain access to an information
> channel. (Gerstenberger & Allen, 1968, p. 277)

Business decision makers act on a good deal less than total information; 70% is
considered high availability (Brinberg, 1980, p. 6). That is to say, they satisfice,
they "look for a course of action that is satisfactory or 'good enough' " (Simon,
1976, p. xxviii). And that is reflected in their information behavior.

Problems, in the larger sense of this essay, are not usually resolved by single
question and answer. Rather they pose different requirements on the type of
information perceived as necessary, and hence different uses to which information is put in the process of resolution. At the risk of premature classification, we
will tentatively set up eight classes of information use, generated by the need
perceived by users in particular situations. These are not mutually exclusive.
Indeed, answers to one class may operate on the needs and questions in another
class. These eight classes are listed with brief comment and a few typical questions and uses, which have been derived from a variety of sources and pertain to
many different user types. The work of Dervin, Nilan, and colleagues (Dervin
1983b; Nilan & Dervin, 1986) is highly relevant to this categorization, though
there are differences in number and interpretation.

1. *Enlightenment:* the desire for context information or ideas in order to make sense of a situation. Dervin[2] calls this "Got pictures/ideas/understandings." Are there similar situations? What are they? What is history and experience of Corporation X in making product Y, and how is this relevant to our intent to manufacture Y?

2. *Problem Understanding:* more specific than enlightenment; better comprehension of particular problems. This has to do with answerable questions. Blois (1984, pp. 189–190) points out that a medical question such as "Why does this injured patient have fever?" may be unanswerable at present, but answers to other questions may shed light: "Does the patient have an infection?" "Did the patient receive a blood transfusion?" The *why* question requires interpretation of data and judgment as to their relevance. Dervin calls this "Able to plan: this category includes being able to decide, prepare, plan ahead."

3. *Instrumental:* finding out what to do and how to do something; instructions; under certain conditions, instrumental information needs will define the need for other types of information. Dervin calls this "Got skills." How do I read this device? How do I interpret the readings?

4. *Factual:* the need for and consequent provision of precise data. There are two constraints to factual data: (a) the actual quality of the data, how well do they represent reality; and (b) related to the above, user perception of quality. We tend to accept data and information without qualification as valid because they are printed, computer generated, or in numerical form (Taylor, 1986, pp. 64–65, 165). What is the thermal conductivity of copper? (Lide, 1981, pp. 1345–1346). What can cause upper abdominal pain and blisters on the skin? (Blois, 1984, p. 152)

5. *Confirmational:* the need to verify a piece of information; in a medical context, to seek a second opinion. In Dervin's terms: "Got support, assurances, confirmation." Second opinions may not always confirm; indeed, they may confuse the situation. In such a case one may have to return to square one and reformulate the problem, or, in a very personal and intuitive way, decide which source to trust. Managers need to do this all the time (Kotter, 1982).

6. *Projective:* future oriented, but not related to political or personal situation (see 8 below); concerned with estimates and probabilities. What will be the effect of flush riveting on air speed, wing design, and wing stresses in airplanes? (Vincenti, 1984).

7. *Motivational:* has to do with personal involvement, of going on (or not going on). In Dervin's terms: "got started, got motivated"; "Kept going."

8. *Personal or Political:* has to do with relationships, status, reputation, personal fulfillment. In Dervin's terms: "Got control"; "Things got calmer, easier";

---

[2] In the eight categories, the statements preceded by "Dervin calls this . . . " are from Dervin, 1983b, p. 62.

"Got out of a bad situation"; "Avoided a bad situation"; "Took mind off things"; "Relaxed, rested"; "Got pleasure"; "Got connected to others." How will this decision affect my position with my boss? What effect will my negative vote on this piece of legislation have on my constituents? What situation am I in? What can I change? What conditions must I adjust to?

There is a strong need for more studies of differing populations working in varying contexts, and how individuals in those populations describe, in their own words, how specific information is used and how its use (or nonuse) affects their concerns.

The other side of this coin of problem resolution is content oriented. It asks basically if there are identifiable traits inherent in information, beyond subject matter, that can be related to the dimensions of problems and to the needs of people. MacMullin and Taylor have made a start by isolating and describing several such information traits (MacMullin & Taylor, 1984, pp. 98–102). Eight are very briefly described here.

1. *Quantitative continuum:* from quantitative data (phenomena that can be measured and represented numerically) to qualitative (descriptive).
2. *Data continuum:* from hard data (empirically derived and replicable) to soft data (not directly observable, must be inferred).
3. *Temporal continuum:* ranging from historical or precedence to forecasting and future modeling.
4. *Solution continuum:* ranging from single solution which meets resolution criteria to a range of options among which the receiver can choose on the basis of some internal, possibly inarticulate criteria or intuitions.
5. *Focus continuum:* from factual information of well-understood problems to diffuse information of idea generation and brainstorming.
6. *Specificity of use continuum:* ranging from applied (instrumental, immediately useful) to substantive (descriptive, know-what) to theoretical (explains and predicts why something works as it does).
7. *Aggregation continuum:* ranging from clinical information (a population of one) to census or aggregated information derived from large populations.
8. *Causal/diagnostic continuum:* causal information discusses why something happens; diagnostic describes what is happening.

E. Summary

For ease of scanning, the main points of this tentative IUE model are outlined here.

1. *Sets of People*
   • the professions

- defined by formal standards
- defined by problems and contexts
- the entrepreneurs
- special interest groups
- special socioeconomic groups
- Demographic variables
  - age, sex, marital status, race
  - socioeconomic status
  - education
- Nondemographic variables
  - media use
  - social networks
  - attitudes toward new technology, education, risk-taking, and innovation.

2. *Problems*
   - not static
   - each IUE has discrete classes of problems
   - problem dimensions (examples)
     - well structured/ill structured
     - complex/simple
     - assumptions agreed upon/not agreed upon
     - familiar/new patterns

3. *Settings*
   - importance of organization style and structure, if applicable
   - domain of interest
   - access to information
   - history and experience

4. *Resolution of problems*
   - information uses
     - enlightenment
     - problem understanding
     - instrumental
     - factual
     - confirmational
     - projective
     - motivational
     - personal or political
   - information traits
     - quantitative continuum
     - data continuum
     - temporal continuum
     - solution continuum
     - focus continuum

- specificity of use continuum
- aggregation continuum
- causal/diagnostic continuum

F. Three Information Environments

The following sections explore very briefly three information use environments in the context of the structure discussed above. The IUEs chosen illustrate different kinds of information needs and uses, varying types of problems, and significant differences between what each regards as information and accepts as problem resolution. All three are highly dependent on information, but the definition of *valid* information varies. The discussion on each of these follows roughly the structure developed above.

In at least one case—*engineers*—the approach taken by the author is one not shared by those who insist that engineering is "the art or science of making practical application of the knowledge of the pure sciences" (Florman, 1976, p. x). An all too brief explanation of the author's different point of view is argued below in section III.

The second IUE—*legislators*—represent a setting in which what is called information wears many faces, its value frequently dependent on how it is to be used. As one member of the U.S. Congress put it: "Information? What's information? Congressmen don't deal with 'information'. That's talk for political scientists. What I need to know is what people think" (quoted in Maisel, 1981, p. 264). Research concern with the legislature as an information-using organism is relatively recent.

The third IUE, that of the *practicing physician,* again poses a different set of information concerns. The emphasis, by the way, is on the practice of medicine, not on medical research. Medicine, over many centuries, has been a self-critical and self-aware profession. We know a good deal about clinical decision making. A fair amount of effort has gone into early prototypes of medical expert systems, even though they are not yet generally applicable for the practitioner. An indication of the interest may be seen in journals which have started in the past two decades, such as *Methods of Information in Medicine, Medical Decision Making,* and *Journal of Clinical Computing.*

III. ENGINEERS

A. Science, Applied Science, and Engineering

Since the Second World War we have linked science and technology (engineering) closely, with science, especially physics, assuming the dominant role and engineering merely applying the knowledge handed down to it. We have even coined the acronym STINFO to signify information for both. This has become part of our culture, with some unfortunate results, because it hides the fact that science and engineering are quite different intellectual systems. As Thomas Allen has pointed out, "empirical investigation has found little support for . . . the long held belief in a continuous progression from basic research through applied research to development." Allen further comments that "technology builds on itself and advances quite independently of any link with the scientific frontier, and often without any necessity for an understanding of the basic science which underlies it" (Allen, 1977, p. 48). This observation is borne out by the Department of Defense Project HINDSIGHT, which, in studying technological innovation in weapons research, found that basic science of the preceding 20 years did not play a significant role in the development of the innovation (Sherwin & Isensen, 1967; Utterback, 1971). Similar and partially supportive results were found in investigations on nonmilitary innovations (Mowery & Rosenberg, 1982). Indeed, as Rosenberg points out, "the normal situation in the past, and to a considerable degree in the present, is that technological knowledge has *preceded* scientific knowledge . . . workable technological knowledge is likely to be attained before the deeper level of scientific understanding" (Rosenberg, 1982, p. 144). Technological advances then cannot be explained by prior advances in basic science (Layton, 1978, p. 61).

Engineering has been thought of as applied science, which masks the long history of formal engineering thinking, know-how, technique, and design which preceded scientific thought by several millennia (Layton, 1974, 1978; Rosenberg, 1982; Vincenti, 1984, 1986; Price, 1965, 1984). There *is* an applied science, an intellectual product of the last century or so, but just where the borders are between it and engineering are hard to determine.

We have made these observations principally to emphasize the differences between the three modes (sciences, applied sciences, and engineering) of thinking, doing, learning, and, especially relevant to the concerns here, how each seeks and uses information.

B. Studies in Information Use

Much of the past work on the use of information by engineers is flawed for several reasons. First is the perceived linkage and its direction, already discussed, between science and engineering. Secondly, reflecting the biases of that linkage, is that most studies of possible relevance to the engineering IUE have been done within the research and development context, i.e., science and applied science. Such studies miss the production engineer, the manufacturing engineer, the highway engineer, the sanitary engineer, etc., who make up the bulk of the engineering profession (National Research Council, 1985). In speaking on manufacturing and engineering, MIT President Paul Grey was recently quoted as saying that "The highest prestige has been reserved for advanced research and development, and only casual attention has been paid to manufacturing." To which Professor of Engineering Arnold Kerr added: "Then we are surprised our cars don't work" (Rowe, 1987). A third reason why such work is flawed is that, in almost all cases, the studies have committed the sin that we have noted before: "Researchers have been looking at something they call information rather that at something users call information" (Dervin, 1983a, p. 158). Some of the studies, however, have useful insights into the information process, but they are in researcher's or system's terms, rather than in user's terms. We won't mention the number of downright poorly designed studies, and there are many of them.

C. The Engineering Process

Nonengineers tend to see engineering only as the process of developing new products/systems, of innovation derived from new information, when in reality most engineering work is "the steady accretion of innumerable minor improvements and modifications with only very infrequent major innovation" (Rosenberg, 1982, p. 7; see also Vincenti, 1984; Wolek, 1969).

Engineers not only learn by doing, but, perhaps more important, by using. The inability to predict with any precision how a large and complex system will operate under real conditions requires that very large safety factors be build into the original design.

> In science, what you don't know about is unlikely to hurt you (except possibly in some unfamiliar experimental situations). In engineering, however, bridges fall and airplanes crash, and what you don't know about can hurt you very much. (Vincenti, 1986, p. 751fn)

As engineers receive feedback from users and from repeated observation of actual operation, they are able to reduce the uncertainties (lack of information) concerning performance, and can, with confidence, generate changes that improve efficiency and operation substantially (Rosenberg, 1982, pp. 120–140).

D. Information Storage and Transfer

Part of our problem in dealing with engineering is how information is stored and transferred. It is not in the usual package of a paper, report, or book. Engineering consumes information, transforms it, and produces a product or a system which itself is information bearing. But it is not in verbal form. Thus, as Allen points out, the engineer obtains his or her information by analyzing and decoding physically encoded information, i.e., through artifacts, or by direct personal contact with other engineers (Allen, 1977, pp. 3–5). Very little work has been done directly on this form of information transfer, in part because it does not match the linguistic patterns of the sciences, nor is the physical artifact something controlled by traditional information agencies. The process is illuminated especially by studies of specific engineering developments, such as flush riveting for aircraft (Vincenti, 1984) and airfoil design (Vincenti, 1986). For information people trained to think in terms of recorded knowledge and the transfer of information in formal linguistic packages, this description of engineering may seem strange and inconsequential. However, as we stated early in this essay, we wish to describe information use environments in terms that approximate the reality of that context, and not description dictated by the information service or system. It is true that such a description may have little to do with present formal information systems and services. That is something information professionals will have to face and resolve. As Shuchman points out: "For at least 15 years researchers have demonstrated that there is serious discontinuity between the system producing technical and scientific information and the engineers to whom the information would be most useful" (Shuchman, 1981, p. 57).

Reliance on the written word appears to be useful only when the author is directly available to explain and to supplement the content (Allen, 1977). In extreme cases, engineers may be penalized for using the literature. Rosenbloom and Wolek report that an engineering manager highly respected by his peers and subordinates remarked that "when I see one of my men reading a professional journal I know he is wasting his time" (Rosenbloom & Wolek, 1970, p. 7). This may be partially the result of something Allen reports.

> Most professional engineering journals are utterly incomprehensible to the average engineer . . . rely heavily on mathematical presentation, which can be understood by only a limited audience. . . . Perhaps the most unfortunate circumstance that ever befell the engineering profession is that . . . it looked to the scientific so-cieties . . . to determine their form and function [i.e., of engineering societies]. (Allen, 1977, pp. 73–76)

As a result, the engineer has turned to the trade journal as his principal source, rather than to the professional literature.

E. Engineering Problems

The definition of an engineering problem is often more important and more difficult than is idea generation, and it has a critical impact on the quality of the solution. During the idea generation stage, which may run 5%–10% of the total project time (Wolek, 1969), it is usual to consider a large number of possible solutions. Of these types of messages, only a small percentage come through the literature (11%, according to Allen, 1977, p. 63), the remainder through personal contacts. Engineers, in contrast to scientists, tend to talk to colleagues before consulting the literature, if they do so at all. Generally, as Shuchman points out, "most engineers regard their technical assignments as problems to be worked out at the 'bench' and consider research into published sources seldom worth the effort since most engineering problems require original solutions" (Shuchman, 1981, pp. 27–28). It is worth noting that engineering problems are not fixed; in a sense, their solutions are dictated by specifications that may need to be altered, depending on properties of materials and design and time constraints. As Schon points out, "Engineering design is understandable as a reflective conversation with the materials of a situation" (Schon, 1983, p. 172). As a result the problem itself may be altered. One of the concerns of working engineers is that their professional education often fails to recognize the concept of the variable problem (Frischmuth & Allen, 1969) and the need to break away from fixed solutions.

F. Setting

Most engineers are employed by a bureaucratic organization and see it as the controller of the only reward system of importance. Many engineers work on products and/or systems of a proprietary nature. Thus, external information exchange is not encouraged. Engineers tend to communicate principally with their organizational colleagues, not only for this reason, but also because of shared knowledge, in which each knows what the other is referring to (Allen, 1977). This is especially true of those working on product and process development, in contrast to those working on research or technical services (Allen, Lee, & Tushman, 1980; Tushman, 1978; Allen, 1986).

The size of the firm may affect the acquisition of nontraditional information, especially under contingency conditions. The small firm is at a disadvantage because of the lack of external contacts (Fischer, 1979). In these studies of organizations most of the attention is focused on R & D operations, and, for reasons stated earlier, one is not sure if they pertain to engineers as we have described them in this chapter. This is one of the problems in the literature. A fair amount of work has been done on the 'gatekeeper' in R & D laboratories (Holland, 1974; Allen, 1977; Taylor & Utterback, 1975; Pelz & Andrews, 1966; Frost & Whiteley, 1971). Holland calls gatekeepers persons with high information potential, i.e., the information source value placed on an individual by his colleagues.

G. Information Support Technology

In studies in which new information services were initiated and controlled, Rubenstein and his colleagues found that there is a significant difference between what a technologist actually does about information and what he or she thinks he or she would do if certain constraints were not there (Rubenstein et al., 1970).

This observation, and that of Shuchman noted above, imply that superficial improvements in conventional information services will not have much impact on the use of engineering information nor on the quality of engineering work.

Modeling, simulation, and testing of small scale artifacts, e.g., airfoils in wind tunnels, has been a traditional way of deriving information for full scale design (Wolek, 1969). One of the difficulties with this form of information derivation is that a model may not behave in quite the same manner when brought up to full scale and tested under actual conditions. Today computer modeling and simulation, computer-aided drafting, computer-aided design (CAD) and computer-aided manufacturing (CAM) may in fact be major ways information technology aids the process of information transfer. Estimates of improvement of engineering productivity as a result of these systems range from 35% to 100% (National Research Council, 1985, p. 68).

H. Summary

- There appear to be fundamental differences between engineering and science which reflect on the processes of information transfer, relevance, and use.
- Engineering knowledge builds on the information carried in the device or system.
- Technical literature does not build on itself as does scientific literature: Published material in engineering will never be abreast of the state of the art.
- In searching for and using recorded information accessibility ranks first, and technical quality second (Goldhar, Bragaw, & Schwartz, 1976; Dewhirst, Avery, & Brown, 1978; Gerstenberger & Allen, 1968).
- Engineers rely almost wholly on personal contact for information (Allen, 1977; Shuchman, 1981).
- In selecting an information channel engineers act, not to maximize gain, but rather to minimize loss (Gerstenberger & Allen, 1968).
- There appears to be no relation between the quality of a solution and the use of literature (Allen, 1977).
- Such systems as computer-aided design and computer-aided manufacturing may be the major ways that information technology aids the process of information transfer.

IV. LEGISLATORS

I don't know if I have been eating magic mushrooms or wandering around Alice's Wonderland, but the more I learn about this field the bigger it gets. I'm always losing ground. I think I'm going to cry.

—Congressman Al Swift (Frantzich, 1982, p. 11)

A. The Setting

Legislatures in democratic societies are unique institutions in terms of information and its movement, power and influence, complexity and trade-offs, and problems and decision making. As Frantzich writes: "On the most basic level, the U.S. Congress . . . translates information on societal needs and desires into public policy by evaluating information on potential options" (Frantzich, 1982, p. 9). It is the legislative setting and the problems associated with that setting that are the principle definers of the IUE. This is in contrast to the doctor or engineer whose education, background, personal predilections are what define the environment, as do the kinds of problems they are trained to see as important.

In speaking of the U.S. Senate, Abrams has described the context vividly:

> detail is politics, and politics is one subject on which senators keep a very tight grip. The staff member may listen to all sides, boil down arguments, gather data, and recommend a course of action, but the ultimate choice is almost always political—who gets what—and that choice a politician carefully keeps to himself. No amount of reorganization of the Senate's committees or expansion of its staff, no amount of computerization, can ever lift the Senate from the slough of detail. . . . The Senate's problems do not stem from mismanagement and cannot be cured by efficiency experts, for the Senate is not a bureaucracy and can never become one. Its political organization is more akin to that at Runnymede than that of a modern corporation, and this is a condition which not even McKinsey & Co. can ever remedy. (Abrams, 1978)

This does not mean that we cannot describe a legislature. It means rather that such descriptions will be fuzzy and messy, because legislatures are indeed messy institutions where the same information can be both redundant and useful and where conventional objectivity may not be of particular value. What are some of the general observations that can be made about Congress and probably about most legislatures, that illuminate the description of context?

Congress is a verbal culture (Fox & Hammond, 1977, p. 103). Legislatures are almost invariably nonhierarchical (Mackenzie, 1981, pp. 19–20). Party is a major centralizing force (Fox & Hammond, 1977, p. 104). Time is one of the most valuable resources (O'Donnell, 1981, p. 148). The collegial character of the Congress, especially of the House, distinguishes it markedly from the executive branch of the government (Kieffer, 1981, p. 210) and, one might say, from traditional bureaucracies anywhere. The primary products are highly value-laden decisions. They constitute key outputs in the "decision-making processes of the state or political system and as such provide key determinations of the basic ends and means the society adopts when it acts as a collectivity" (Cooper & MacKenzie, 1981, p. 239).

The nature of the American legislature, local, state, or national, has changed significantly during the past two decades, making it more complex. The process is still going on. This is due to several major societal trends:

- the complexity of legislation and its impact resulting from the growing interdependence of economic, technological, and environmental concerns
- the need by constituents for assistance in dealing with large federal and state bureaucracies
- the number and especially the variety of bills considered in each session
- the necessity to maintain oversight of implementation of legislation

In response to these pressures, information support services for the U.S. Congress literally exploded during the 1970s. Though on a smaller scale this is true also for state legislatures (Chartrand & Bortnick, 1980). The figures below are from Malbin (1980, pp. 252–258) except where noted, and pertain to the 1970s.

- Support agencies (General Accounting Office, Congressional Research Service, Congress Budget Office, Office of Technological Assessment) increased personnel by 35%, to 6,500
- Committee staffs increased from 1,337 to 3,300
- Personal staffs of Members grew from 7,000 to 11,700, split between Washington and home districts or states
- Constituent cases handled by an individual congressman's office in 1976–1977 ranged from a low of 20 to a high of 95,000, with an average of 12,000 cases (Johannes, 1981, p. 79)
- Recorded votes increased from 1,110 to 2,700, though the number of public bills enacted declined from 695 to 634.

These figures are noted because they are a part of the information environment of the U.S. Congress, and are, to a lesser degree, reflected in state legislatures.

B. Problems

Basically, legislators have two concerns: (a) servicing of their individual constituencies, i.e., those who elect them; and (b) passing laws and, in some cases, overseeing their implementation. Because of the nature of the bicameral legislature, servicing the needs of individual constituents is more significant for the lower than for the upper house. Though we may depict these two concerns as separate, they are intertwined in a complex and intricate web which has a profound effect on the kinds of information needed and how that information may be used, and indeed on the structure of the legislatures themselves. Legislation must be considered a result of compromise among competing interests, ideologies, constituencies, and personalities. Information, then, is needed in response to six basic questions.

1. WHO is to be benefitted or burdened?
2. WHAT are to be the benefits or burdens?
3. WHEN are they to begin and terminate?
4. WHERE are they to be in effect?
5. HOW—organizationally and procedurally—are they to be effected?
6. WHY are these benefits or burdens and the methods for effecting them in the public interest? (Borchard, circa 1975, p. 13).

C. Types of Information

Careful reading of these concerns indicate the complex interplay of political and policy information. Indeed, there are four different kinds of information critical to the legislator (Sabatier & Whiteman, 1985, p. 397; Maisel, 1981, pp. 249–251).

- *Political Information*—about the position of other political actors on pending legislation, about the likely impact of the legislation on one's own constituency, and hence the effect on reelection or career prospects.
- *Policy Information*—on the actual content of proposed legislation, on alternatives and options, on the magnitude and causes of the problems they are designed to address, and on their probable effects on society.
- *Evaluative Information*—in their oversight function as evaluators of ongoing programs, legislators need to know how programs are functioning, how good the data are that they receive from the executive branch, and how they are to be interpreted.
- *Management Information*—procedural or operational information. Legislators, in order to manage their time, need to know what is happening on the floor, when bills are likely to come up for debate and vote, what is going on in their committees and in other committees, under what procedures certain pieces of legislation will be considered, when the legislature will adjourn for the day, week, session. The lack of this information in the past has been a frustrating part of a legislator's job. Current computer systems in Congress have done much to alleviate these problems.

D. Information Transfer

In legislative decision making every legislator plays two roles (Zweir, 1979). The first is as a *specialist,* a trusted colleague who is knowledgeable about a particular legislative issue, usually because of his or her experience on a specific committee, e.g., banking, science and technology, budget, defense, etc., and the knowledge built up over the years. The second is as a *nonspecialist*—and every legislator is a nonspecialist in some areas of concern. In each of these roles, they receive and process information in different ways. As specialists they are served by, and are dependent on, the considerable expertise of committee staffs who search for, listen to, filter, evaluate, and analyze information of concern. In their role as nonspecialists they are dependent on the party leadership, on input from specialist colleagues, and on voting cues from trusted colleagues who share their political outlook (Matthews & Stinson, 1970).

From this brief review we can infer that any policy information which does not recognize the importance of constituent and electoral factors in shaping legislative choice will probably be neglected (Webber, 1986, p. 287). In seeking scientific testimony, legislators and scientists tend to talk past each other. The scientist deals with probabilistic quantities and facts developed through consensus. The legislator, constrained by time and political pressures, cannot deal with probabilities, or with voluminous and detailed technical data, and hence must compromise (U.S. Congress, 1971, pp. 473–480). Research information is useful as enlightenment and context, but has little direct impact on legislation, because it is often seen as politically infeasible to base action on such research alone (Caplan et al., 1975; Mitchell, 1980).

E. Staff as Filters

Staff have become key elements in the information flow of Congress. To a large extent they are gatekeepers. This appears also to be the case in state legislatures (Sabatier & Whiteman, 1985; Bradley, 1980; Wissell, O'Connor, & King, 1976; Conniff, 1982; Porter, 1975).

In 1979, there were 17,275 staff in Congress itself to support 535 senators and representatives, or about 32 clerical and professional staff for every elected member of Congress. This does not include the separate support agencies, such as the General Accounting Office, Library of Congress, etc. (Malbin, 1980, p. 252). These committee and personal staff members are important in the flow of information throughout the legislature. They not only perform constituent service activities, but also undertake investigations, oversight, planning, and program evaluation. Personal legislative aides are, in many ways, decision formulators (Taylor, 1986, p. 173) for Congress, presenting options, alternatives, and, within the framework of their expertise, recommending decisions. They prepare testimony, write speeches, and coordinate legislative strategy (Fuerbringer, 1984; Nash, 1987; Fox & Hammond, 1977, pp. 1–2). In some cases committee staff mark up and design the final form of important bills for committee approval (Fox & Hammond, 1977, p. 143).

F. Computer Information Systems

Except for the management information systems, staff are the primary beneficiaries of computer information systems. Through the variety of systems available, for example, staff can research federal assistance programs, review current and historical budget data, search the U.S. Code and federal court cases, retrieve complete text of issue briefs developed by the Congressional Research Service, and search bibliographic and economic data bases throughout the country. There are problems associated with this automation. One of the more significant for the information environment is "the increasing fiscalization of legislative analysis." That is to say, because computers can only deal with definable and quantifiable aspects of legislation, financial implications become much more important than they were before the advent of the computer. In a way, however, computers represent the culmination of earlier societal concerns with data, in which quantification became the only valid representation of reality. Instead, as Goldberg points out, "of concerning themselves with the physical, cultural, and sociological implications of national programs, members' principal attention often focuses on how programs will affect tax rates, inflation, the value of the dollar, or on the prospect of a balanced budget" (Goldberg, 1981, pp. 287–288). This note harks back to an observation at the beginning of this chapter that information technology, be it book or computer, tends to prescribe the size, shape, function, dynamism, and *even the content of information systems*. It defines what is acceptable as knowledge or information. This is indeed something to worry about.

G. Summary

We have presented perhaps a more chaotic picture of a legislature than is in fact the case. Legislatures do function: they do form policy, pass laws, and perform oversight responsibilities. They may not do these things in very rational fashion; they are not bureaucracies. In summary we can say the following:

- A legislature is a verbal culture.
- Legislatures need four different kinds of information: political, policy, oversight, and managerial.
- Committee and personal staff are primary gatekeepers and analyzers of information, which comes from legislative support agencies, executive departments, lobbyists, external sources, and constituents.
- Computer systems, at present, perform much needed management information functions; computers, however, may have a deep and restrictive effect on the types of information perceived to be utilizable, and hence on the basis upon which judgments are made.

V. THE PRACTICING PHYSICIAN

A. Types of Practitioners

Practicing physicians, and the settings in which they work, differ from the previous two contexts. The physician is generally not part of an organization, or, if he or she is affiliated with an organization such as a hospital, the relationships are not those to be found in the usual bureaucratic organization. In contrast to large engineering projects or to the setting of policy in legislatures, the physician's concern is directed toward the well-being of a single human being, a patient. The practitioner faces a tremendous variety of medical situations every day which demand judgment and decision, often without recourse to any external information source.

We need to distinguish first between the basic medical scientist and the practicing physician. The latter takes care of patients, and must know what he or she is trying to cure, and indeed what constitutes a cure. The basic scientist has no concern for these questions (King, 1982, p. 136). In a sense these represent two contrasting views of disease. "One of these concepts views disease as an entity . . . as a thing existing by itself, whereas the other fixes attention upon a sick patient and contemplates the clinical attributes that are observed. . . . In the first a decision can be described completely in terms of attributes and without any reference to patients" (Blois, 1984, pp. 77–79). This dichotomy between a disease as (a) a thing described in texts, and (b) a set of dynamic symptoms which a physician observes in a patient poses some particular and peculiar (to medicine) problems in information and its utility.

Generally, students of medical information transfer have noted two types of practitioners. For the first, their patients are the only focus of their work: they are completely patient oriented. The second group "takes as their point of reference their professional colleagues, either those within the local community or those at the top of the profession" (Coleman et al., 1966, pp. 185–186). This should not be misinterpreted; they are both patient oriented, the former exclusively so, the latter, who may be medical specialists, within the larger framework of their special branch of medicine. For example, the latter may write and publish; the former almost never will. These orientations affect information behavior. The Coleman study, for example, found there were sharp differences in time of introduction of the drug gammanym between the two types. The profession-oriented doctors "were considerably ahead of the patient-oriented group, both in date of introduction and in the proportion who had used it by the end of the 16-month survey period" (Coleman et al., 1966, p. 186). The authors further note that both the lack of information, and, when they did know of the drug, a sensitivity to their patient's economic situation, predisposed the patient-oriented doctor against the use of the drug. Since this study was done in the early 1960s, one may wonder today what affect medical insurance and medical malpractice suits might have on the acceptance and use of a new drug.

B. Problems

Basically, the problems, the questions, a physician faces have, historically speaking, remained the same over the centuries. The answers to those questions, and the means of deriving information useful in diagnosis have changed dramatically—but not the questions. King (1982, pp. 9–10) suggests the following general questions as basic to the practitioner's frame of reference:

- What is the disease from which the patient suffers?
- How can we identify it?
- What can we do for it?
- How can we prevent it?
- What is the cause?
- How much confidence can we place in our assertions and our judgments?

King argues that these have been the fundamental questions of the medical profession for the past 2500 years.

C. Information Gathering

Several fundamental changes in 19th-century medicine had a profound effect on the gathering of information. First was a change in the approach to disease as something that always had to be treated to one in which "certain diseases were perceived to be self-limited, got better of themselves" (Thomas, 1979, p. 160). The second was the invention of the stethoscope, a means whereby a doctor could derive data about a patient without depending only on the patient's own description (King, 1982, pp. 82–84). This, of course, was the beginning of a whole line of technological aids to help acquire diagnostic information, from the microscope to computed tomography, biopsies, and nuclear imaging.

In order to approach answers to these problems—and the answers still remain judgmental, even with today's diagnostic aids (King, 1982, p. 308)—the doctor gains information and knowledge from several sources. First of all is the particular patient. "Many distinguished physicians," Blois writes, "have taught that history-taking is the most critical step in the entire diagnostic process, and that performance in this is what separates the exceptional physician from the less able" (Blois, 1984, p. 165). Even before a single word is spoken, however, a doctor will derive information from nonverbal clues: the gait, clothing, general appearance, handshake, age, gender (Cutler, 1985, p. 12). As the interview proceeds, the doctor begins to formulate hypotheses about the patient's ailments (Elstein, Shulman, & Sprafke, 1978, p. ix). In fact, as Cutler points out, "Two minutes of meaningful conversation directs you to the correct diagnosis nine times out of ten" (Cutler, 1985, p. 186). The ability to derive useful information through interview and to interpret that information seems to be based, not unnaturally, on "the possession of relevant bodies of information and a sufficiently broad experience with related problems" (Elstein et al., 1978, p. x). The patient not only provides data through verbal means, the interview, but also through tests and other means such as x-rays, cardiograms, etc. The doctor must still interpret these varied data. Where there is high consensus in the profession that, when, for example, symptoms A, B, C, and D occur together in a certain type of patient, then that patient has x and can be treated accordingly. These are text book cases and the information problems are relatively trivial. It is when the symptomatic data do not match any easy or known pattern, when there is low consensus, or where there are honest differences in data interpretation or treatment, that information seeking becomes critical (Brittain, 1985).

D. Transfer of Information

Mick's study of information behaviors in the Stanford Medical School indicates that, as one might expect, medical students generally were dependent on personal notes, plus colleagues (Mick, 1972). As one moved to practitioners, there was far less dependence on notes and more on colleagues and other external sources. Stinson and Mueller (1980) studied the information habits of health professionals in staying abreast of current advances in medicine. Physicians made up about 75% of the sample; consequently, it is difficult to interpret the results in terms of practitioners alone. Their results do seem to indicate that health professionals in urban settings used journals more than those in rural or semiurban settings, and that those in solo practice made less use of local medical libraries than did those in group or institutional practice. On the interpersonal level, Weinberg and his colleagues studied physician networks in a single county (population 66,000, with 79 physicians, at least 100 miles away from a major medical center). The study centered on questions concerning suspected or confirmed heart disease. As one might surmise, there were a small number of clusters, six in this case, around medical opinion leaders in the cardiovascular field in the county, with some significant links outside (Weinberg, Ullian, Richards, & Cooper, 1981).

The well-known work of Coleman and his colleagues in the early sixties concentrated on the introduction of the drug gammanym. One of the more frequently cited conclusions was that pharmaceutical representatives were the first source of information about the new drug (Coleman et al., 1966, p. 53). However, the study carefully distinguished between receiving the information and actual use of the drug, which was legitimated by professional colleagues and/or the professional literature (Coleman et al., 1966, p. 64). In contrast to the Coleman study, Manning and Denson (1980) found, in studying the introduction of cimetidine, that pharmaceutical representatives ranked considerably lower than medical journals, meetings, and colleague consultation as primary sources. Related to this, in the Scura study, several physicians responded that they had cut their use of representatives as sources, "since the representatives are now more likely to be trained in business and selling techniques than in the sciences, as had previously been the case" (Scura & Davidoff, 1981, p. 141). These are obviously but a very few of the many papers on the use of external medical information sources.

E. Effect of Information

In most studies of the physician's information behavior, little attention has been paid to the effect specific information has on physician behavior or on patient well-being. In most instances, such studies start from the service, for example, the library or continuing education unit, and hence tend to have the bias commented on before. In a study by Scura and Davidoff of the impact of clinical librarian service, they write that, "although we did not attempt measurement of the impact of clinical librarian services on outcome, we have obtained preliminary evidence that the services affected treatment in a substantial percentage, 20% of the cases" (Scura & Davidoff, 1981, p. 51). Similar work has been done by D. N. King (1986) at the University of Illinois. Worth noting here is that there was no attempt, in either case, to obtain in the physician's own words exactly what the effect of the information was.

F. Information Support Systems

Recent work in support of the use of medical information has taken two forms. The first is the development of means of tapping the vast body of recorded medical knowledge, through such traditional systems as MEDLINE. For the practitioner, however, they are too difficult to access and too undiscriminating, though clinical librarian intermediaries can be helpful. Recently we have seen the development of specific computer-based knowledge bases, e.g., the Hepatitis Knowledge Base, really dynamic equivalents of earlier handbooks and manuals on specific diseases. They are, however, costly forms of reorganizing, evaluating, and continually updating data on a specific medical subject matter (Siegel, 1982). These, or something like them, are probably necessary in the long run, though just how practitioners will tap them is moot at this time—in terms of both physical and intellectual accessibility. The second direction is that of decision analysis, the development of computer programs for the management of common medical problems, e.g., "criteria for diagnosing chest pain" or "optimal timing of repeated medical tests." As one might expect, there is controversy over such programs, which require, because the computer requires, precise quantification in areas thought to be dependent on the powers of intuition, judgment, and hunch. In his review of the pros and cons of decision analysis, Cutler states that "there is room and need for all tactics. The good physician must learn to intertwine hard facts with soft intellect" (Cutler, 1985, p. 45).

Both of these types of information support are attempts to provide easy access to external knowledge or to externally developed decision analysis. Blois points out that, in addition to specific patient information and the general corpus of medical knowledge, "the accumulation of the individual physician's own personal experience" is often overlooked in medical informatics. "We can thus visualize," Blois writes, "the physician's information environment as resulting from the merging of these [three] different information sources, and their flows converging at a single time and place" (Blois, 1985, p. 49).

Kochen, in a very preliminary study, points out that "clinicians rely primarily on their internal memories of personal experiences" (Kochen, 1983, p. 83). Physicians usually recall by patient's name. They also to a lesser extent rely on the recall of recent reading, meetings, and discussions with colleagues. Except for patient files there is little formal organization or linkage among remembered or physically stored information at present in the practitioner's office (Covell, Uman, & Manning, 1985).

If this picture is approximately valid, then one of the primary needs for the practitioner is memory augmentation and data management, which would (a) organize and link his or her patient records with references and notes of reading, meetings, and discussion, and (b) provide easy access to a highly filtered recall of knowledge bases or decision trees when necessary. Such a data base management system is, of course, the dream of all professionals who work with a variety of information inputs. The physician, however, has particular pressures: Time, variety, recall of personal experience, and the magnitude of potentially useful external information.

G. Summary

- Practicing physicians have as their primary objective the well-being of patients.
- There are many patients every day with widely varying states and symptoms.
- The following questions are basic to the practitioner's frame of reference: What is the disease? How identified? What can be done? How can it be prevented? What is the cause? How much confidence do we have in our assertions and judgments?
- Information is derived from three sources: from the patient by interview and by tests, from personal experience, and from other external sources.
- In perhaps as many as 90% of cases, an experienced physician can make a correct diagnosis after a few minutes of interview.
- In the remainder of the cases, the physician may (a) require extensive tests; (b) scan personal files, including personal memory for analogous cases; (c) discuss with colleagues; and/or (d) try to retrieve relevant literature.
- The primary technological need for the practitioner is memory augmentation and highly personalized data management systems.

VI. SUMMARY AND DISCUSSION

This chapter is an early attempt at structuring what it is we know about the information behavior of defined groups of people in their "natural settings." The author has covered a vast area. There are many points that need to be analyzed and hypotheses to be developed, and where possible, tested. The following comments are organized in three general areas.

A. Formalization of Listings

There are two specific areas where the author has abbreviated or listed without much discussion. Both occur in Section II-D on Resolution of Problems. The first is the list of information needs, or, better said, a list of uses to which information is put. In a way this difference in statement (needs and uses) signifies where one starts from: the problem which defines the need, or the resolution which defines the use. This needs clarification. The items in the list themselves require much fuller definition and possible expansion of categories, which can only come from more extensive studies of information use expressed in user terms.

The second is the listing of information traits and how these traits apply to or effect the resolution of problems. Not only does this relationship between information and problems need study, but, more fundamentally, the traits themselves need to be better explicated. Both analyses may need to be done in parallel, one informing the other.

B. Two New Categories

In the overall structure presented here—sets of people, problems, settings, resolutions—there may be a need for at least two additional categories of data which are important enough to be noted here. The first is how a given set of people perceive information. Because of the way they structure their universe, engineers, legislators, and physicians, for example, each see information differently. We hinted at this when we said that, for the engineer, the device or the system is a major carrier of information. In similar fashion, the physician must distinguish between what the patient describes or shows through testing as symptoms, and how he or she, the physician, interprets those symptoms. The former might be called raw information or *symptoms,* the latter interpreted information or *signs* (King, 1982, pp. 73–89). In this essay this concern was subsumed under *sets of people,* but it probably is critical and significant enough to be considered as a separate category.

The processes of decision represent a second possible new category. Generally, decision processes have been modelled on purely rational processes. Much financial support has gone into developing computer programs to make engineering or medical decisions or to assist the engineer or physician in making decisions. There has been a tendency in this work to perceive decision analysis as something formal, algorithmic, and thereby computable, excluding the importance of hunch and intuition based on experience and personal association. We need to have a better understanding of the nonrational (less rational?) environmental factors affecting these processes.

C. Requirements for Exploiting the Model

If the user-driven approach to information processes has promise, then there are several requirements beyond mere commitment to the user. In various ways these needs were threaded throughout the essay.

We need to free ourselves from the assumption that we can describe information behavior by starting from the system, the service, the knowledge base, or the information carrier. To use these as definers of useful information is misleading: only the recipient, the user, can define information in his or her context. This is not to say that this interface between information system/artifact and user is not complex and intellectually interesting, but the final determiner of information value is the user who sits in a particular context and develops criteria of information value from that context (Taylor, 1986).

We need to examine very carefully certain assumptions, carried over from the scientific frame of reference, that such professions as engineering and medical practice can be assumed scientific in the same way that physics, chemistry, and biology are. We have argued that, especially in the case of engineering, it is precisely the processes of information storage, transfer, and use that make up many of the elements that distinguish engineering from the basic sciences *and their application*. The assumption of direct connectivity has in this case resulted in poor information support for engineering work.

We need an understanding of basic definitions, a sort of rigorous flexibility with such terms as *information, use, media, decision, memory, experience,* etc. Flexibility is argued because we need to realize that, for example, *information* may have varied interpretations according to context and in the processes by which it becomes useful. In medicine the work done on decision analysis has illuminated some of these processes, and concomitantly the types of information which play a role in these processes.

We need descriptions of information use and effect in words of the user. The recent work of Dervin and Nilan (1986) and of Nilan and Fletcher (1987) have pointed the way.

We need long term and situation specific studies such as those done by Coleman et al. (1966), Allen (1977), Kotter (1982), and Blois (1984). We need studies of specific contexts, from which we can gradually build up a body of theories and testable hypotheses about particular IUEs. Such studies will of necessity be multidimensional, including such "unscientific" approaches as observation over long periods of time. Kotter, in his study of the general manager, discusses the necessity for and the difficulty of the multidimensional approach (Kotter, 1982, pp. 147–153).

If the presented structure is seen to be useful, then we need to ask if and how the results or insights of a particular study will contribute to the development of that structure. Perhaps more important, we need to ask if the structure as it develops can become a generalizable model, a fruitful means for organizing, describing, and predicting the information behavior of any given population in a variety of contexts.

REFERENCES

Abrams, E. (1978, February). The Senate since yesterday. *The American Spectator*, p. 13.

Ackoff, R. L. (1967). Management misinformation systems. *Management Science, 14* (4), BB147–BB156.

Aguilar, F. J. (1967). *Scanning the business environment.* New York: MacMillan.

Allen, T. J. (1977). *Managing the flow of technology.* Cambridge, MA: MIT Press.

Allen, T. J. (1986, May). Organizational structure, information technology, and R & D productivity. *IEEE Transactions on Engineering Management, EM-33,* 212–217.

Allen, T. J., Lee, D. M. S., & Tushman, M. L. (1980, February). R & D performance as a function of internal communication, project management, and the nature of the work. *IEEE Transactions on Engineering Management, EM-27,* 2–12.

Blois, M. S. (1984). *Information and medicine: The nature of medical descriptions.* Berkeley, CA: University of California Press.

Blois, M. S. (1985). The physician's information environment. *Journal of Clinical Computing, 14*(2), 48–51.

Bookstein, A. (1982, Spring). Sources of error in library questionnaires. *Library Research, 4,* 85–94.

Borchard, K. (1975). *Toward a theory of legislative compromise.* Paper presented at Faculty Seminar, Program on Information Technologies and Public Policy, Harvard University, Cambridge, MA.

Boulding, K. E. (1978). The future of the interaction of knowledge, energy, and materials. *Behavioral Science Research, 13*(3), 169–183.

Bradley, R. B. (1980, August). Motivations in legislative information use. *Legislative Studies Quarterly, 3,* 393–406.

Brinberg, H. R. (1980). *The contribution of information to economic growth and development.* Paper presented at the 40th Congress of the International Federation for Documentation, Copenhagen, Denmark.

Brittain, J. M. (Ed.). (1985). *Consensus and penalties for ignorance in the medical sciences: implications for information transfer* (British Library Research and Development Report No. 5842). London: Taylor Graham.

Caplan, N., Morrison, A., & Stambaugh, R. J. (1975). *The use of social science knowledge in policy decisions at the national level.* Ann Arbor, MI: Institute for Social Research.

Chartrand, R. L., & Bortnick, J. (1980). An overview of state legislative information processing. In B. Krevitt-Eres (Ed.), *Legal and legislative information processing* (pp. 49–73). Westport, CT: Greenwood Press.

Chen, C-C., & Hernon, P. (1982). *Information seeking: Assessing and anticipating user needs.* New York: Neal-Schumann.

Coleman, J. S., Katz, E., & Menzel, H. (1966). *Medical innovation: A diffusion study.* New York: Bobbs-Merrill.

Conniff, W. P. (1982). *Information patterns and needs of the New York state assembly staff.* Unpublished doctoral dissertation, Syracuse University.

Consumer Dynamics, Inc. (1981). *Development of a market research tool to support the design of information and education programs.* (Final Report, Phase III, Contract No. USDA53-KO6-9-76). Rockville, MD: Consumer Dynamics, Inc.

Cooper, J., & Mackenzie, G. C. (1981). *The House at work.* Austin, TX: University of Texas Press.

Covell, D. C., Uman, G. C., & Manning, P. R. (1985, October). Information needs of office practice: Are they being met? *Annals of Internal Medicine, 103,* 596–599.

Crane, D. (1972). *Invisible colleges: Diffusion of knowledge in scientific communities.* Chicago, IL: University of Chicago Press.

Cutler, P. (1985). *Problem solving in clinical medicine* (2nd ed.). Baltimore, MD: Williams and Wilkins.

Dervin, B. (1975). *Strategies for dealing with the information needs of urban residents: Information or communication.* Paper presented at the International Communication Meeting, Chicago.

Dervin, B. (1983a). Information as a user construct: The relevance of perceived information needs to synthesis and interpretation. In S. A. Ward & L. J. Reed (Eds.), *Knowledge structure and use: Implications for synthesis and interpretation* (pp. 153–183). Philadelphia, PA: University Press.

Dervin, B. (1983b). *An overview of sense-making research: Concepts, methods and results to date.* Paper presented at Annual Meeting of the International Communication Association, Dallas, TX.

Dervin, B., & Nilan, M. (1986). Information needs and uses. In M. E. Williams (Ed.), *Annual review of information science and technology* (vol. 21, pp. 3–33). White Plains, NY: Knowledge Industry Publications.

Deshpande, R., & Zaltman, G. (1983, June). Patterns of research use in private and public sectors. *Knowledge: Creation, Diffusion, Utilization, 4,* 561–575.

Dewhirst, H. D., Avery, R. D., & Brown, E. M. (1978, August). Satisfaction and performance in research and development tasks as related to information accessibility. *IEEE Transactions on Engineering Management, EM-25,* 58–63.

Eisenberg, D., & Wright, T. L. (1985). *Encounters with Qi: Exploring Chinese medicine.* New York: W.W. Norton & Company.

Elstein, A. S., Shulman, L. S., & Sprafka, S. A. (1978). *Medical problem solving: An analysis of clinical reasoning.* Cambridge, MA: Harvard University Press.

Fabisoff, S. G., & Ely, D. P. (1974). *Information and information needs.* Syracuse, NY: Syracuse University, Center for the Study of Information and Education.

Feldman, M. S., & March, J. G. (1981, June). Information in organizations as signal and symbol. *Administrative Science Quarterly, 26,* 171–186.

Fischer, W. A. (1979, February). The acquisition of technical information by R&D managers for problem solving in nonroutine contingency situations. *IEEE Transactions on Engineering Management, EM-26,* 8–14.

Florman, S. G. (1976). *The existential pleasures of engineering.* New York: St. Martins.

Fox, H. W., Jr., & Hammond, S. W. (1977). *Congressional staffs: The invisible force in American lawmaking.* New York: Free Press.

Frantzich, S. E. (1982). *Computers in Congress: The politics of information.* Beverly Hills, CA: Sage Publications.

Frischmuth, D. S., & Allen, T. J. (1969, May). A model for the description and evaluation of technical problem solving. *IEEE Transactions on Engineering Management, EM-16,* 58–63.

Frost, P., & Whitely, R. (1971, April). Communication patterns in a research laboratory. *R & D Management, 1,* 71–79.

Fuchs, V. R. (Ed.). (1969). *Production and productivity in the service industries* (Studies in Income and Wealth, Vol. 34). New York: National Bureau of Economic Research.

Fuerbringer, J. (1984, April 24). The men behind the men behind the budget. *New York Times*, p. 21.

Garvey, W. D., Tomita, K., & Woolf, P. (1979). The dynamic scientific information user. In W. D. Garvey (Ed.), *Communication: The essence of science* (pp. 256–279). Elmsford, NY: Pergamon Press.

Gerstenberger, P. G., & Allen, T. J. (1968). Criteria used in the selection of information channels by R & D engineers. *Journal of Applied Psychology, 52*(4), 272–279.

Goldberg, J. A. (1981). Computer usage in the House. In J. Cooper & G. C. Mackenzie (Eds.), *The House at work* (pp. 275–291). Austin, TX: University of Texas Press.

Goldhar, J. D., Bragaw, L. K., & Schwartz, J. J. (1976, February). Information flows, management style, and technological innovation. *IEEE Transactions on Engineering Management, EM-23*, 51–62.

Holland, W. E. (1974, December). The special communicator and his behavior in research organizations. *IEEE Transaction on Professional Communication, PC-17*, 48–53.

Huberman, M. (1983, June). Recipes for busy kitchens: A situational analysis of routine knowledge use in schools. *Knowledge: Creation, Diffusion, Utilization, 4*, 478–510.

Johannes, J. R. (1981). Casework in the House. In J. Cooper & G. C. Mackenzie (Eds.), *The House at work* (pp. 78–96). Austin, TX: The University of Texas Press.

Kieffer, J. A. (1981). Providing administrative support services to the House. In J. Cooper & G. C. Mackenzie (Eds.), *The House at work* (pp. 210–236). Austin, TX: University of Texas Press.

Kimberly, J. R., et al. (1980). *The organizational life cycle*. San Francisco, CA: Jossey-Bass Publishers.

King, D. N. (1986). The contribution of hospital library information services to clinical care: A study in eight hospitals (Draft copy).

King, L. S. (1982). *Medical thinking: A historical preface*. Princeton, NJ: Princeton University Press.

Knott, J., & Wildavsky, A. (1980, June). If dissemination is the solution, what is the problem? *Knowledge: Creation, Diffusion, Utilization, 1*, 537–578.

Kochen, M. (1983, April). How clinicians recall experience. *Methods of Information in Medicine, 22*, 83–86.

Kotter, J. P. (1982). *The general managers*. New York: Free Press.

Layton, E. T., Jr. (1974, January). Technology as knowledge. *Technology and Culture, 15*, 31–41.

Layton, E. T., Jr. (1978). Millwrights and engineers, science, social roles, and the evolution of the turbine in America. In W. Krohn, E. T. Layton, Jr., & P. Weingart (Eds.), *The dynamics of science and technology* (pp. 61–87). Dordrecht, Holland: D. Reidel.

Lide, D. R., Jr. (1981, June 19). Critical data for critical needs. *Science, 212*, 1343–1349.

Lowry, G. B. (1979). *Information use and transfer studies: An appraisal*. Washington, DC: U.S. Department of Education, Educational Resources Information Center (ERIC).

Mackenzie, G. C. (1981). Coping in a complex age: Challenge, response, and reform in the House of Representatives. In J. Cooper & G. C. Mackenzie (Eds.), *The House at work* (pp. 3–22). Austin, TX: University of Texas Press.

MacMullin, S. E., & Taylor, R. S. (1984). Problem dimensions and information traits. *The Information Society, 3*(1), 91–111.

Maisel, L. S. (1981). Congressional information sources. In J. Cooper & G. C. Mackenzie (Eds.), *The House at work* (pp. 247–274). Austin, TX: University of Texas Press.

Malbin, M. J. (1980). *Unelected representatives: Congressional staff and the future of representative government*. New York: Basic Books.

Manning, P. R., & Denson, T. A. (1980, May). How internists learned about Cimetidine. *Annals of Internal Medicine, 92*, 690–692.

March, J. G., & Simon, H. A. (1958). *Organizations*. New York: John Wiley & Sons.

Matthews, D. R., & Stinson, J. A. (1970). Decision-making by U.S. representatives: A preliminary mode. In S. Ulmer (Ed.), *Political decision-making* (pp. 14–43). New York: Van Nostrand Reinhold.

Mick, C. K. (1972). *Information seeking style in medicine.* Unpublished doctoral dissertation, Stanford University, Palo Alto, CA.

Mintzberg, H. (1975, July–August). The manager's job: Folklore and fact. *Harvard Business Review, 53*(4), 49–61.

Mitchell, D. (1980, November). Social science impact on legislative decision making: Process and substance. *Educational Researcher, 9*(10), 9–12, 17–19.

Mowery, D. C., & Rosenberg, N. (1982). The influence of market demand upon innovation: A critical review of some recent empirical studies. In N. Rosenberg (Ed.), *Inside the black box: Technology and economics* (pp. 193–241). New York: Cambridge University Press.

Nash, N. C. (1987, February 22). Power and the Congressional aide. *New York Times,* p. 48.

National Research Council. (1985). *Engineering education and practice in the United States: Engineering employment characteristics.* Washington, DC: National Academy Press.

Nilan, M., & Dervin, B. (1986). *Sense making and information seeking: A factor analysis of information seeking dimensions.* Unpublished manuscript.

Nilan, M., & Fletcher, P. (1987). Information behaviors in the preparation of research proposals. In C-C. Chen (Ed.), *Proceedings of the 50th ASIS Annual Meeting 24* (pp. 186–192). Medford, NJ: Learned Information.

O'Donnell, T. J. (1981). Controlling legislative time. In J. Cooper & G. C. Mackenzie (Eds.), *The House at work* (pp. 127–150). Austin, TX: University of Texas Press.

O'Reilly, C. A., III. (1979). *Variations in decision makers' use of information sources: The impact of quality and accessibility of information.* Berkeley, CA: School of Business Administration, University of California.

Paisley, W. J. (1980). Information and work. In B. Dervin & M. J. Voigt (Eds.), *Progress in communication sciences* (vol. 2, pp. 113–165). Norwood, NJ: Ablex Publishing Corp.

Pelz, D. C., & Andrews, F. M. (1966). *Scientists in Organizations: Productive climates for research and development.* New York: Wiley.

Porter, H. O. (1975). Legislative information needs and staff resources in the American states. In J. J. Heaphey & A. P. Bulutis (Eds.), *Legislative staffing: A comparative perspective* (pp. 39–59). New York: Sage Publications.

Price, D. (1965, Fall). Is technology historically independent of science? A study in statistical historiography. *Technology and Culture, 6,* 553–568.

Price, D. (1984, January). Of sealing wax and string. *Natural History, 93*(1), 49–56.

Roberts, N. (1982, April). A search for information man. *Social Science Information Studies, 2,* 93–104.

Rogers, E. M. (1983). *Diffusion of innovations* (3rd ed.). New York: The Free Press.

Rosenberg, N. (1982). *Inside the black box: Technology and economics.* New York: Cambridge University Press.

Rosenbloom, R. S., & Wolek, F. W. (1970). *Technology and information transfer.* Boston, MA: Harvard University, Graduate School of Business Administration.

Rowe, J. (1987, March 9). More engineers for factory floors. *Christian Science Monitor,* p. 25.

Rubenstein, A. H., et al. (1970). Explorations in the information seeking style of researchers. In C. E. Nelson & D. K. Pollock (Eds.), *Communication among scientists and engineers* (pp. 209–231). Lexington, MA: D.C. Heath.

Sabatier, P., & Whiteman, D. (1985, August). Legislative decision making and substantive policy information: Models of information flow. *Legislative Studies Quarterly, 10,* 395–421.

Schon, D. A. (1983). *The reflective practitioner: How professionals think in action.* New York: Basic Books.

Scura, G., & Davidoff, F. (1981, January 2). Case-related use of the medical literature: Clinical librarian services for improving patient care. *Journal of the American Medical Association, 245,* 50–52.

Sherwin, E. W., & Isenson, R. S. (1967, June 23). Project Hindsight. *Science, 156,* 1571–1577.

Shuchman, H. L. (1981). *Information transfer in engineering* (Report No. 461-46-27). Glastonbury, CT: The Futures Group.

Siegel, E. R. (1982). Transfer of information to health professionals. In B. Dervin & M. Voigt (Eds.), *Progress in communication sciences* (Vol. 3, pp. 311–334). Norwood, NJ: Ablex Publishing Corp.

Simon, H. A. (1976). *Administrative behavior: A study of decision-making processes in administrative organization* (3rd ed.). New York: Free Press.

Slovic, P. (1987, April 17). Perception of risk. *Science, 236,* 280–285.

Stinson, E. R., & Mueller, D. A. (1980, January 11). Survey of health professionals' information habits and needs. *Journal of the American Medical Association, 243,* 140–143.

Taylor, R. L., & Utterback, J. M. (1975, May). A longitudinal study of communication in research: Technical and managerial influences. *IEEE Transactions on Engineering Management, EM-22,* 80–87.

Taylor, R. S. (1962). The process of asking questions. *American Documentation, 13,* 391–396.

Taylor, R. S. (1968). Question negotiation and information seeking in libraries. *College & Research Libraries, 29,* 178–194.

Taylor, R. S. (1986). *Value-added processes in information systems.* Norwood, NJ: Ablex Publishing Corp.

Thomas, L. (1979). *The medusa and the snail.* New York: Viking Press.

Tushman, M. (1978, December). Technical communication in research and development laboratories: Impact of project work characteristics. *Academy of Management Journal, 21,* 624–645.

U.S. Congress. House of Representatives, 92nd. Committee on Science and Astronautics. (1971). *Technical information for Congress.* Washington, DC: Government Printing Office. (Originally issued in 1969.)

Utterback, J. M. (1971, November). The process of innovation: A study of the origination and development of ideas for new scientific instruments. *IEEE Transactions on Engineering Management, EM-18,* 124–131.

Vincenti, W. G. (1984, July). Technological knowledge without science: The innovation of flush riveting in American airplanes, ca. 1930—ca. 1950. *Technology and Culture, 25,* 540–576.

Vincenti, W. G. (1986, October). The Davis wing and the problems of airfoil design: Uncertainty and growth in engineering knowledge. *Technology and Culture, 27,* 717–758.

Webber, D. J. (1986, December). Explaining policymakers' use of policy information: The relative importance of the two-community theory versus decision-maker orientation. *Knowledge: Creation, Diffusion, Utilization, 7,* 249–290.

Weinberg, A. D., Ullian, L., Richards, W., & Cooper, P. (1981). Informal advice and information-seeking between physicians. *Journal of Medical Education, 56,* 174–180.

Wersig, G., & Windel, G. (1985, January). Information science needs a theory of 'information actions.' *Social Science Information Studies, 5,* 11–32.

Wilson, T. D. (1981, March). On user studies and information needs. *Journal of Documentation, 37,* 3–15.

Wissel, P., O'Connor, R., & King, M. (1976, May). The hunting of the legislative snark: Information searches and reforms in U.S. state legislatures. *Legislative Studies Quarterly, 1,* 251–267.

Wolek, F. W. (1969). The engineer: His work and needs for information. *Proceedings of the Annual Meeting of the American Society for Information Science, 6,* 471–476.

Zweir, R. (1979, February). The search for information: Specialists and nonspecialists in the U.S. House of Representatives. *Legislative Studies Quarterly, 4,* 31–42.

8 Bargaining Outcome, Bargaining Process, and the Role of Communication

Frank Tutzauer
Department of Communication
State University of New York at Buffalo

Negotiation is a pervasive phenomenon. Given the ubiquity of bargaining and negotiation, it is not surprising that an extensive research literature has developed. The largest bodies of work can be found in psychology and economics, although political science, management and industrial relations, sociology, and organizational behavior are also likely places to find significant bargaining research. More recently, communication and information scientists have begun contributing to the bargaining literature (Donohue, Diez, & Stahle, 1983), a development that seems quite natural given the importance of communication to negotiation and bargaining (Bednar & Curington, 1983).

A number of authors (Beisecker, 1970; Ikle, 1973; Putnam & Jones, 1982b; Tedeschi & Rosenfeld, 1980) have discussed the functions of communication in bargaining and negotiation. Basically, there seem to be four. First, communication serves as a vehicle for the transmission and acceptance of offers. Second, communication conveys information about the bargainers' preferences and expectations—either directly, through commitments and threats, or indirectly, through the manner and language in which the issues are described. Third, communication can shape the relationship between the bargainers—various types of argumentation and other persuasive strategies influence the way the bargainers view each other and, consequently, the course of the negotiations. Finally, communication holds the potential for uncovering new outcomes. The present chapter reviews recent literature relevant to these four functions of communication in bargaining settings. The dynamics of offers and counteroffers will be explored, as will the role that concessions play in shaping the opponent's behavior. Similarly, the process of discovering new outcomes, the role of argument, and the coding of communicative behavior will all be seen as important themes. In short, this chapter will highlight much of the current research in the study of bargaining and negotiation.

The negotiation literature, however, is vast, and constraints must be imposed to keep the review within manageable limits. First of all, I will focus on only the most recent research, primarily that reported during the last 10 or 12 years, stepping outside of this time span only to underscore a few significant works that have provided the impetus for current theorizing and research. Quite excellent reviews of older studies can be found in Chertkoff and Esser (1976), Morley and Stephenson (1977), and the encyclopedic Rubin and Brown (1975).

Second, I will avoid game-theoretic studies, not because they are unimportant, but because a discussion of the concepts necessary for a proper understanding of game theory would take us too far afield. Furthermore, experimental gaming research often deemphasizes communication (Hawes & Smith, 1973; but see Steinfatt, Seibold, & Frye, 1974, for a rebuttal) and is better suited to the study of conflict in general, rather than bargaining in particular. Thus, except where directly relevant, I will not discuss game-theoretic research. For an introduction to game theory and its application to the behavioral sciences, I recommend Luce and Raiffa (1957), a classic that has not been surpassed in 30 years.

For a briefer, but less technical introduction, see Rubin and Brown (1975). Regarding the research conducted on matrix games, Nemeth (1972), Oskamp (1971), Rapoport and Chammah (1965), and Tedeschi, Schlenker, and Bonoma (1973), are good sources, and Roth (1979) provides a fairly comprehensive treatment of axiomatic bargaining theory, a line of research begun by Nash (1950).

Finally, I will limit the discussion to two-party bargaining systems, ignoring (except where directly relevant) third-party intervention and the study of coalitions. Third-party intervention differs enough in form, and coalition formation differs enough processually, that they can be easily separated from standard two-party bargaining research. Good places to start on third-party intervention and coalitions are, respectively, Section III of Bazerman and Lewicki (1983), and Midgaard and Underdal (1977). Chapter 4 of Rubin and Brown (1975) covers both topics.

I. ORGANIZING THE BARGAINING LITERATURE

In an early work on labor negotiations, Walton and McKersie (1965) described four types of bargaining subprocesses: *distributive bargaining,* the traditional fixed-sum situation; *integrative bargaining,* where the parties search for mutually beneficial solutions; *attitudinal structuring,* or the process of altering attitudes and relationships; and *intraorganizational bargaining,* or the attempt to achieve consensus between the bargainer and the group he or she represents. These four subprocesses, although conceptually distinct, overlap quite extensively when used as descriptors of bargaining behavior. Distributive and integrative processes can happen simultaneously. Intraorganizational bargaining may influence a bargainer's attempts at attitudinal structuring, which may have different effects in distributive and integrative contexts.

The similarities and differences are especially apparent if one notes how communication operates in each of these types of bargaining. The transmission of offers is the hallmark of distributive bargaining and, to a lesser extent, integrative bargaining. The discovery of new alternatives, on the other hand, *is* integrative bargaining. Similarly, persuasion and the shaping of the opponent's expectations and preferences are intimately involved in attitudinal structuring, while the outcome of intraorganizational bargaining can influence all four functions of communication by constraining the negotiator's interactions with the opponent.

The Walton and McKersie framework is a useful starting place for researchers interested in bargaining communication. It also provides a convenient scheme for organizing the rather large corpus of bargaining research. Over the years, Walton and McKersie's book has been widely cited, and the various bargaining studies cluster quite naturally (despite the overlap) into the Walton and McKersie categories. It thus seems logical to maintain that system here. In the next four sections I review the research pertaining to each type of bargaining. Then, conclusions and suggestions for future research are offered.

II. DISTRIBUTIVE BARGAINING

Laypersons and practioners typically associate the term *bargaining* with competitive, win-lose negotiation interaction—what Walton and McKersie termed *distributive bargaining*. Distributive bargaining encompasses the classic fixed- or zero-sum context in which one bargainer's gain becomes the other bargainer's loss. Most bargaining situations that come readily to mind—a shopkeeper haggling with a customer, labor/management wage negotiations, dickering over the price of a house, and so forth—are usually treated within a distributive framework. Not surprisingly, a very large proportion of the negotiation research deals with such situations.

The term distributive bargaining can be used in three related, but distinct, senses. The first sense deals with the structure of possible outcomes. If two bargainers try to divide 10 dollars, for example, the situation is distributive. Every dollar one bargainer gets is a dollar the other one can't have. Here, distributiveness is built into the very structure of the situation. A second way in which the term can be used involves the bargaining process that occurs when the participants perceive the structure of the situation as distributive (independent of whether it actually is). This second sense treats bargaining as a cognitive framework in which the bargainers impose a win-lose orientation on the situation. Neale and Bazerman (Bazerman, 1983; Bazerman & Neale, 1983) call such a framework the bias of the mythical fixed pie. Finally, distributive bargaining can be characterized by "commitments, demands, arguments through repetition, threats, rejections, denials, and other forms of offensive or defensive communication. In distributive bargaining an individual seeks maximum information from his or her opponent while making minimal disclosures" (Putnam, 1985, p. 226). Thus, according to a third view, the use of competitive strategies and tactics (Lewicki & Litterer, 1985) marks bargaining as distributive.

Regardless of the use of the term, researchers interested in distributive bargaining have typically focused on the mechanisms by which bargainers obtain large individual payoffs. This section reviews the distributive bargaining literature, most of which has stemmed from Siegel and Fouraker's (1960) level-of-aspiration theory.

A. Aspirations, Information, and Outcome

In any bargaining situation, the participants enter the relationship with certain needs and expectations. Though the parties usually wish to reach an agreement, this desire is not so overwhelming as to dwarf all other concerns. A proposed settlement must be in a bargainer's best interests, or no settlement will be reached. It seems safe to posit the existence of a point below which, for whatever reason, a bargainer will concede no further. This value, called the bargainer's *resistance point* or *limit,* represents the point at which agreement becomes disadvantageous.

It should be obvious that a bargainer's resistance point, while representing the minimally acceptable settlement, represents neither the most desirable settlement nor (necessarily) the bargainer's expected settlement. At any point in the negotiation, the bargainer will have a certain goal in mind which may be quite different from his or her resistance point. This target point, or *level of aspiration,* characterizes the bargainer's immediate aims and thus potentially exerts an influence on the subsequent negotiations.

The first experimental findings dealing with level of aspiration in a bargaining context were obtained in the bilateral monopoly studies of Siegel and Fouraker (1960). Though they later expanded their efforts to include cases of unequal strength and oligopoly (Fouraker & Siegel, 1963), their earlier work has had the most profound impact. Siegel and Fouraker (1960) conducted a series of experiments where subjects tried to agree on the price and quantity of an imaginary good. After systematically varying such quantities as the amount of information available to each bargainer, various payoff parameters, and each bargainer's level of aspiration, Siegel and Fouraker concluded that bargainers with high levels of aspiration obtained better payoffs than bargainers with low levels of aspiration, and that the provision of information increased the tendency to negotiate *Pareto optimal contracts* (i.e., contracts in which it was impossible for both bargainers to improve their payoffs).

To provide a theoretical explanation for their observations, Siegel and Fouraker argued that the bargainers they observed had levels of aspiration that sometimes changed as the negotiations progressed. Bargainers who opened with high bids, and who conceded very little, communicated a message of firmness and resolution to their opponents. Their opponents, realizing that previous expectations were unrealistically high, subsequently lowered their levels of aspiration and, accordingly, demanded less. Conversely, those who began with soft strategies, communicated this softness to their opponents, causing the opponents to raise (or lower more slowly) their levels of aspiration, which resulted in lower earnings for soft strategists.

One line of research that emanated from level-of-aspiration theory deals with the effect of information on payoff. In an extension of Siegel and Fouraker's work, Hamner and Harnett (1975) proposed an "information-aspiration" model springing from two separate propositions (Church & Esser, 1980):

1. Information makes a bargainer's aspirations more realistic—that is, obtaining information will lower an aspiration that is excessively high and raise one that is excessively low.

2. An increase in level of aspiration will tend to increase the payoff from what it would have otherwise been, while a decrease in level of aspiration has the opposite effect.

Hamner and Harnett tested the latter of these two propositions in a 2×2 factorial design (high/low information by high/low aspirations). A significant interaction indicated that the receipt of information decreased the payoffs of bargainers with high levels of aspiration but increased the payoffs of bargainers with low aspirations. Hamner and Harnett also found that bargainers with high aspirations and bargainers with incomplete information tended to concede less and open with higher bids than other bargainers.

While the results of the Hamner and Harnett investigation tended to support the information-aspiration model, no direct test was made of the proposition that the provision of information makes one's aspirations more realistic. Such a test was made, however, in Church and Esser's (1980) study of the effect of information and initial aspiration on a bargainer's change in aspiration. These investigators found that initial level of aspiration was a good predictor of subsequent goals and expectations. However, the main effect of information and the interaction between information and initial aspiration, both in the predicted direction, were only marginally significant ($p < .10$ and $p < .11$, respectively). However, other research, although not testing aspirations directly, has shown the advantages of unilateral possession of information for both information about payoffs (Crott, Kayser, & Lamm, 1980) and information about resistance points (Yukl, 1976).

A second line of research stemming from level-of-aspiration theory deals with the impact of initial offers. The first offer sets the tone for subsequent rounds of bargaining and may contribute to images of firmness (Pruitt & Smith, 1981). Consistent with earlier research (e.g., Chertkoff & Conley, 1967; Liebert, Smith, Hill, & Keiffer, 1968; Yukl, 1974), current studies have indicated that a bargainer's opening bid exerts a strong influence on the course of the negotiations. For example, Bateman (1980), in a repeated measures design, looked at two levels of opening offers (moderate vs. extreme) and three levels of reward (low, medium, or high). The results showed that a high opening bid, though resulting in increased opponent concessions, also increased the number of deadlocks. Opening offer was positively related, and reward magnitude negatively related, to final payoff.

Slightly different findings were reported by Pruitt and Syna (1985). They had participants bargain against a programmed offer strategy that began with either a tough or soft initial offer, and assigned them to one of four different conditions regarding their knowledge of the opponent's resistance point. Bargainers deprived of information, when confronted with a soft initial offer, conceded less than bargainers in other conditions. These same bargainers also reached fewer agreements. Thus, although level-of-aspiration theory may be right about the beneficial effects of extreme initial offers, such effects may be moderated by information, and in any event may be offset by failure to reach an agreement at all.

B. Alternatives to Level-of-Aspiration Theory

Although, by and large, the research literature seems to support the predictions of level-of-aspiration theory, a number of alternative perspectives have emerged. The most serious challenge to level-of-aspiration theory comes from the assorted "reciprocity" theories. Reciprocal bargaining behavior has been observed in the laboratory (Benton, Kelley, & Liebling, 1972) as well as among real negotiators (Plovnick & Chaison, 1985), and it seems reasonable that bargaining outcomes should reflect this linking of behaviors. The unifying theme of the various reciprocity perspectives is that an individual's actions will, in some sense, be mirrored by the opponent, whose motives may be based on equity (Adams, 1965), norms of reciprocity (Gouldner, 1960), or justice (Homans, 1961). Osgood's (1962) proposal of graduated reciprocation in tension-reduction (GRIT) typifies this line of reasoning. The GRIT strategy holds that a bargainer should begin moderately tough in order to avoid exploitation, and then make a series of noncontingent concessions in order to reduce tensions and foster cooperative behavior. Other versions of the reciprocity notion vary slightly in their exact formulation, requiring, for example, a low initial offer coupled with a completely contingent, 100%-matching technique (Bateman, 1980). The variations tend to be minor, however, and Lawler and MacMurray (1980) have grouped all versions under the broader label *reciprocity theory* (Lawler & MacMurray, 1980).

Reinforcement theory closely parallels reciprocity theory, although it differs from reciprocity by using an operant conditioning explanation advocating rewards as a means of obtaining large opponent concessions. Bateman (1980) has distinguished between the two theories by arguing that reinforcement requires a higher opening bid than does reciprocity theory. The major distinction, of course, lies in the differing mechanisms—norms or conditioning—by which concessions achieve their purpose.

1. Support for Reciprocity Theory.   Combining predictions of Siegel and Fouraker (1960) and Osgood (1962), Hamner (1974) hypothesized that a tough or moderately tough strategy would be superior to a soft strategy only when there existed little or no pressure to reach agreement. By imposing a 5% penalty on each offer made in the later stages of the negotiation, Hamner was able to examine how bargaining costs modified the effects of a tough strategy. Not surprisingly, he found that subjects experiencing a high pressure to reach agreement took less time to settle, deadlocked less often, and conceded at a faster rate than subjects under low pressure to agree. A tough strategy resulted in more deadlocks and longer bargaining sessions. Contrary to predictions, however, a soft strategy yielded a high concession rate regardless of the pressure to reach agreement. Yet, despite these findings, the overall superiority of the soft strategy led Hamner to view Osgood's theory as the more plausible formulation.

Two similar experiments allowed subjects at each trial either to stand fast or concede $5.00 in attempting to agree on the price of a used appliance (Komorita & Esser, 1975). In one of the experiments, subjects' concessions and nonconcessions were reciprocated with a probability of 100%, 50%, or 0%, depending on their treatment condition. Those who received the most reciprocation reached significantly more agreements and took fewer trials to accomplish them. Reciprocity made no difference in predicting a subject's final offer, however. In a second experiment, Komorita and Esser manipulated the reciprocation of subjects' concessions and nonconcessions independently. Agreements increased when concessions were reciprocated, but were unaffected by the reciprocation of nonconcessions. On the basis of these two experiments, the investigators concluded that reciprocity provides a useful mechanism for obtaining opponent concessions, probably because of negotiator attributions about firmness and fairness. McGillicuddy, Pruitt, and Syna (1984) provided further support for Komorita and Esser's attributional explanation by having participants view the negotiation behavior of a confederate who followed one of three strategies: tough, soft, or matching. The participants then bargained with the confederates, all of whom followed a concession schedule designed to seem random to the subjects. Consistent with Komorita and Esser's (1975) speculations, participants perceived the soft strategy as weak but fair, the tough strategy as strong but fair, and the matching strategy as fair and midway in strength between toughness and softness. The matching strategy also elicited the largest subject concessions.

Lawler and MacMurray (1980) distinguished between two types of reciprocity: *naive reciprocity* (a soft approach in both the initial and later phases of negotiation) and *vigilant reciprocity* (derived from Osgood's GRIT and consisting of tough initial offers followed by later matching). In comparing these versions of reciprocity to level-of-aspiration theory's prescription of constant toughness, the experimenters found that a vigilant approach worked best in eliciting both a large concession magnitude and a high concession frequency, though a tough strategy was less likely to be exploited than a consistently soft strategy. Bargaining time, as well as the number of deadlocks, were both increased as a result of consistent toughness, but were unaffected by the other independent variables.

Finally, Seholm, Walker, and Esser (1985) generalized to oligopoly markets (many buyers and sellers, as opposed to just one of each, as in previous research). They examined three different strategies: *soft reciprocity* (similar to Lawler & MacMurray's naive reciprocity), *tough reciprocity* (similar to McGillicuddy et al.'s matching strategy), and *tough* (same as tough reciprocity, except that the concessions were only 50% as large). Overall, the soft reciprocity strategy elicited the most concessions and obtained the largest number of agreements. The soft strategy also realized a significantly higher profit per contact than the other strategies, although overall profits dropped. So, although matching has been shown to work in situations of bilateral monopoly, the soft strategy outperformed the matching strategy in an oligopoly market.

2. Support for Reinforcement Theory.   Among the studies examining reinforcement theory, the results are mixed. Even experiments supporting the theory do so only partially. Wall (1981) conducted three experiments in which subjects simulated a labor–management dispute. Though reinforcement and reciprocity theory both agree that large concessions are ultimately beneficial, they make different predictions when a negotiator's small concession is followed by a large opponent concession. Norms of reciprocity, of course, suggest that the large concession will be matched by an equally large concession from the subject. Reinforcement theory, however, predicts that, because the negotiator's small concession was rewarded with a large concession, the negotiator will respond with a second small concession. Wall examined situations where such differing concession patterns were expected, and found, contrary to the claims of reciprocity theory, that large concessions were not always matched. Expectations of opponent reciprocity ceased once the opponent failed to match concessions. However, the effect of opponent's reinforcement on the subject's behavior disappeared once a constituent entered the relationship.

Though Wall's experiments provide some support for reinforcement, the theory has not been completely confirmed. Other studies examining the question tend to support alternatives to reinforcement (see, e.g., Bateman, 1980; Wall, 1977).

C. Offer and Concession Dynamics

Both level-of-aspiration theory and the assorted reciprocity theories are in some sense normative. At their core, they attempt to answer the following question: What should a bargainer do to improve individual outcomes? The research reviewed in this section, although still limited to distributive contexts, has a fundamentally different goal. Rather than asking what bargainers *should* do, these studies seek to explain what bargainers *actually* do (cf. Luce & Raiffa's, 1957, distinction between normative and descriptive theories). This research is important for at least two reasons: First, the models are explicitly dynamical. Although level-of-aspiration and reciprocity theorists have occasionally addressed the over-time aspects of bargaining, these aspects have been subordinate to the larger concern of explaining individual outcomes. In contrast, the models in this section have explicit time-dependencies built into them. Second, these models may ultimately illuminate the normative aspects of bargaining as well. By knowing what bargainers actually do under a variety of circumstances, it becomes possible, as a corollary, to determine what strategies provide the most beneficial outcomes, and thus descriptive questions may, in the end, provide normative answers.

1. Noninteractive Dynamics. The first line of research begins, at least implicitly, from the premise that a bargainer's concessions are determined, not so much from the behavior of his or her opponent, but from external forces, primarily elapsed time and the bargainer's resistance point. Thus, rather than using communication to predict outcome, one uses external forces to predict the communication. The key theoretical development in this area is the Kelley, Beckman, and Fischer (1967) resistance model. These authors postulated the existence of a resistance force acting in opposition to concession making. The resistance force grows stronger as a bargainer approaches his or her limit. One implication of this assumption is that a bargainer's offers should exhibit exponential decay as a function of time, becoming asymptotic at the bargainer's resistance point. The data presented in Kelley et al. (1967) seemed to support such behavior.

Predictions about the effect of the resistance point on resistance forces, and thus on concession behavior, were confirmed by Holmes, Throop, and Strickland (1971), and theoretical extensions of the model—incorporating opponent toughness and time pressure (as distinct from elapsed time)—were made in Pruitt (1981) and Smith, Pruitt, and Carnevale (1982). This latter article presented data generally consistent with the resistance model, finding that concession rate was negatively related to one's resistance point, positively related to time pressure, and that time pressure enhanced the effect of resistance point on concession rate.

2. Interactive Models. Unlike the resistance model, other formulations of concession behavior have incorporated explicit dependencies between the bargainers into the models in an effort to describe the interactive nature of negotiation. Some of the most appealing interactive bargaining models are based on the Richardson arms race equations (Richardson, 1960).

The application of the Richardson equations to bargaining is a line of research initiated by Bartos (1966). In the simplest case of two antagonistic nations, X and Y, a Richardson process is defined by a pair of linear differential equations:

$$\frac{dx}{dt} = m_1 y - n_1 x + g_1$$

$$\frac{dy}{dt} = m_2 y - n_2 x + g_2$$

In the above equations, x and y represent the armaments levels of nations X and Y respectively; dx/dt and dy/dt are instantaneous rates of change with respect to time and describe the trajectory of armaments levels over the course of the race. The m and n coefficients (called the *reaction* and *fatigue* coefficients, respectively) represent each country's response to its opponent's arms modified by the burden of building arms. The constants g_1 and g_2 denote grievances between the countries which, if positive, act to speed up the race.

Because x and y both appear on the right hand sides of the equations, the Richardson model captures the action–reaction dynamic inherent in an arms race. Bartos, noting the similarity between this particular facet of an arms race and the pattern of interconnected concessions in negotiation, used a Richardson-type formulation to model the progress of a bargainer's level of demand over time. Naturally, the model had to be modified to account for the fact that bargaining is characterized by a series of discrete offers rather than a continuous buildup of arms. Bartos accomplished this modification by letting x_t denote the demand of Bargainer X at time t, and then substituting x_t for x in the above equations. He also substituted the change in demand for dx/dt—that is, he replaced dx/dt with $x_{t+1} - x_t$. Consequently, Bartos obtained

$$x_{t+1} - x_t = m_1 y_t - n_1 x_t + g_1$$

or

$$x_{t+1} = m_1 y_t + (1 - n_1)x_t + g_1. \tag{1}$$

Similarly, for Bargainer Y

$$y_{t+1} = m_2 x_t + (1 - n_2)y_t + g_2. \tag{2}$$

Equations 1 and 2 state that a bargainer's demand at time $t + 1$ is a function of the immediately previous demands of the bargainer and his or her opponent, and their respective levels of aspiration. The responses to the opponent's demands are still measured by the reaction coefficients, m_1 and m_2, and the levels of aspiration are measured by g_1 and g_2. It should be obvious from Equations 1 and 2 that when aspirations are high, x_{t+1} and y_{t+1} are greater than they would be when aspirations are low, indicating that increases in aspiration should increase a bargainer's demands.

The various m, n, and g coefficients in Equations 1 and 2 can be estimated using multiple regression, so Bartos expanded the analysis to the five-person case and used the model to derive contrasting predictions for GRIT and level-of-aspiration theory. If level-of-aspiration theory governed bargaining behavior, the reaction coefficients should have been predominantly positive. If, however, GRIT more accurately described the negotiation process, then the reaction coefficients should have been positive among allies and negative among enemies. (Since the task involved negotiation among a five-member group, some bargainers had very similar interests; thus, the distinction between allies and enemies.)

To see how these predictions were derived, let us focus on a hypothetical bargainer negotiating in a task that can be represented by a unidimensional scale (e.g., the price of a car). A negative reaction coefficient would imply that low offers were followed by high offers, and vice versa. A positive reaction coefficient would mean that low offers followed low offers and high offers followed high. Suppose our hypothetical bargainer preferred outcomes at the low end of the scale; allies of the bargainer would also prefer low outcomes, whereas enemies would prefer high outcomes. Clearly, allies' offers would always be at the same end of the scale, so we would expect positive reaction coefficients, regardless of the theory involved. For enemies, however, GRIT and level-of-aspiration theory would make contrasting predictions. In general, GRIT holds that toughness begets toughness, so, if our hypothetical bargainer made extremely low offers, the opponent would respond with extremely high offers, hence a negative reaction coefficient. In level-of-aspiration theory, however, toughness begets capitulation. Consequently, extremely low offers would be met with responses that were not very high, implying positive reaction coefficients.

Bartos tested these predictions by computing regression coefficients for 87 negotiation sessions, 73 of which allowed communication about offers only and 14 of which allowed relatively free communication. Unfortunately, the results were mixed. Among enemies, Bartos observed significantly more positive reaction coefficients than negative, suggesting the appropriateness of level-of-aspiration theory. When the data were divided by communication condition, however, a different pattern emerged. In the restricted communication condition, there were significantly more negative reaction coefficients than positive, whereas in the less restricted condition, negative and positive coefficients appeared in about equal numbers. Consequently, the results were somewhat inconclusive. Bartos suggested that, if more severe time restraints had been placed on the negotiators, GRIT would have faired better than it did.

More recent extensions have been concerned not so much with the differences between GRIT and level-of-aspiration theory, but with the appropriateness of the Richardson model, or modifications of it, to the negotiation process. For example, Bartos (1974) found reasonable support for a modification of Equations 1 and 2, which explicitly incorporated time (as a variable rather than a subscript) on the right hand side of the equations, and Druckman (1977) reviewed research suggesting that the Richardson formulation was at least a step in the right direction (although a more complicated model including bargainer expectations and adjustments also held promise).

Moving from the laboratory to the field, Hopmann and Smith (1977) content analyzed transcripts of the Soviet-American test ban negotiations in order to see which of four Richardson-like models was most appropriate. In general, Hopmann and Smith found that the most important factor in explaining negotiation behavior was the bargaining behavior of the opponent. Additionally, behavior of the opponent occurring outside of the negotiations seemed to alter the behavior of the United States, but not of the Soviet Union. Finally, with respect to grievances, the data, though not conclusive, suggested that the U.S. toughened whenever it perceived the Soviet Union in a positive manner, and softened when perceiving the Soviets as tough (cf. Zarefsky, Tutzauer, & Miller-Tutzauer, 1983).

Tutzauer (1986a) has advanced an alternative to the Richardson formulation. Rather than using differential or difference equations, one can define an *offer-response function*. Such a function accepts an input (offer) of one bargainer, and produces the output (response) of the other bargainer, which in turn becomes the input to predict the next offer. From the outset, three assumptions were made: first, the principle of alternation, which merely said that bargainers exchange offers; second, the principle of good faith bargaining, which essentially said that concessions would be toward rather than away from agreement; finally, the principle of weak reciprocity held that a bargainer's response to a tough offer would be tougher than his or her response to a soft offer. It was shown that portions of certain elementary ellipses satisfied the above assumptions. In particular, the relationship between offer and response was claimed to be

$$y = b \sqrt{(1 - x^2/a^2)}$$

where x and y represent offer and response, respectively, and a and b are the toughness parameters, termed *capitulation* and *resistance*. Capitulation deals with how much a bargainer yields, and resistance concerns the stubbornness of the opponent. The above model was estimated using laboratory data, and a reasonably good fit was obtained (Tutzauer, 1986a). Additionally, a number of predictions concerning the occurrence of deadlocks, bargaining success, the location of agreements, and the number of offers were confirmed. The major problem with the model appears to be theoretical; other offer-response functions, including the relatively simple $y = a + bx$, satisfy the three principles of bargaining behavior, and at present there seems to be no clear reason to prefer the elliptic function over various competitors.

D. Power in Bargaining

Although not addressing the matter directly, the studies reviewed in the previous sections have made tacit assumptions about the nature of bargaining power. Richardson models, for example, require one to accept the premise that the relative power of the two parties can be completely captured in the reaction and fatigue coefficients. Likewise, level-of-aspiration theory would probably treat an increase in power as an increase in aspirations, manifesting itself in tougher bargaining.

An alternative to making tacit assumptions about power would be to give power an explicit, perhaps even central, role. Bacharach and Lawler have done so in their power-dependence theory of bargaining. The basic theoretical ideas can be found in Bacharach and Lawler (1981a, 1986), and data relevant to the theory have been reported in Bacharach and Lawler (1981a,b) and Lawler and

Bacharach (1976, 1979). Before discussing power dependence, however, I should note that this theory is a good example of the overlap in Walton and McKersie's bargaining subprocesses. Bacharach and Lawler (1981a, pp. 101–102; 1986) have argued that certain power configurations may promote integrative bargaining. They also have used the theory to examine the effect of power on argumentation, a topic closely related to attitudinal structuring. Nonetheless, I have classified power-dependence theory as distributive bargaining research. I did so for two reasons. First, the emphasis on concession making and punitive tactics is closer to distributive bargaining than to any of Walton and McKersie's other subprocesses. Second, both theory and research have explicitly assumed that the bargaining issues could be represented on a unidimensional continuum (Bacharach & Lawler, 1981a, p. 207) making the theory structurally distributive, if not cognitively.

Bacharach and Lawler (1980, 1981a, 1986) viewed power in terms of dependence. Given two bargainers, A and B, A has power over B to the extent that B is dependent upon A. The dependence of one bargainer on another derives from two sources: the degree to which alternative sources of outcome are available to the bargainer, and how committed the bargainer is to bargaining outcomes (i.e., the importance of the outcomes to the bargainer). The important point is that a bargainer's power stems from the *other* party's alternatives and commitments. For example, in negotiations between a buyer and a seller, the seller gains power as the buyer's commitment to a particular outcome (like a certain model of car) increases. The seller loses power as more alternatives become available to the buyer (e.g., other car dealers who sell the desired model).

A major contribution of power-dependence theory has been the recognition of three distinct types of power. *Absolute power* refers to "the power of an individual party irrespective of the other party's power" (Bacharach & Lawler, 1981a, p. 65). Thus, the absolute power of A is determined by the alternatives and commitments of B. The *relative power* of a bargainer, on the other hand, can only be assessed in relation to the opponent. That is to say, the relative power of Bargainer A is the dependence of B on A compared to the dependence of A on B, a quantity that can be expressed as the ratio of absolute powers. Finally, *total power* is simply the sum of absolute powers.

Bacharach and Lawler have applied these conceptions of power to bargaining behavior. For example, they argued (Baracharch & Lawler, 1981a) that relative power can increase the likelihood of acceptance of a bargainer's definition of issues. They also presented data (Bacharach & Lawler, 1981a) showing that, as a bargainer's absolute power increased (via alternatives), the opponent's toughness declined, and that, as total power increased, a negative relationship between the existence of punitive capabilities and the carrying out of threats emerged. (For other research on threats, as well as promises, see Murdock, Bradac, & Bowers, 1984; and Rubin & Brown, 1975, pp. 278–288).

Power possesses very strong unifying capabilities as a theoretical construct. Bacharach and Lawler's power-dependence theory has the broadest theoretical scope of any of the theories discussed in this chapter so far. It may even be possible to embed bargaining theory within a larger theory of social conflict by using the concept of power. However, several difficulties prevent power-dependence theory from being completely successful. First, too much is omitted. Bacharach and Lawler have explicitly restricted themselves to unidimensional tasks. They also have decided to avoid addressing constituent–negotiator relationships (Bacharach & Lawler, 1981a, p. 207). As a later section will show, such relationships are vital to an understanding of bargaining processes. Until such time as multidimensional tasks and constitutent–representative relationships are brought within the confines of the theory, power will not be the unifying construct that Bacharach and Lawler foresee.

Second, and perhaps more critically, Bacharach and Lawler are entirely too cavalier in their derivation of power-dependence propositions, often deducing contradictory propositions from the theory (e.g., Bacharach & Lawler, 1981a, pp. 96–97, 142, 185, 198). Their "deductions," of course, are not really deductions at all, but just reasonable arguments using power-dependence terminology. The problem lies partly in the ambiguity inherent in any verbal theory, and partly in the imprecision with which power-dependence ideas have been presented; only greater formalism can remedy the situation.

E. Synthesis of Findings

Having now examined the various lines of research dealing with distributive bargaining, it becomes appropriate to try to merge the findings into a more coherent framework. The largest portion of studies, especially when coupled with other findings on initial offer and concession pattern (Komorita, Lapworth, & Tumonis, 1981; Liebert et al., 1968; Pruitt & Smith, 1981; Rubin & DiMatteo, 1972; Yukl, 1974), seem to support level-of-aspiration theory. Nonetheless, a sizable number reach contrary conclusions. Any of several explanations may account for the inconsistency.

First of all, the costs involved in bargaining may explain the discrepancies. If there are minimal costs, then a tough strategy is appropriate; if very high costs obtain, then a strategy similar to GRIT ensures better outcomes. Early experimental data (Komorita & Barnes, 1969) have suggested that concessions tend to be reciprocated when there are mutual pressures to agree. Thus, if one can afford protracted, possibly deadlocked negotiations, then the tough bargaining strategy of level-of-aspiration theory may be most appropriate. Otherwise, GRIT or a reciprocal strategy may be wisest.

Gray (1977) has posited a second explanation, one based on the bargaining interaction itself. She argued that the differing patterns of concession making could be attributed to differing initial offers. If bargainers had similar initial offers (both high or both soft), Gray predicted that, consistent with GRIT, a reciprocal concession pattern would emerge; when bargainers made dissimilar opening bids (one soft and one tough) she expected concession styles consistent with level-of-aspiration theory. In general, these predictions were confirmed. Concession patterns were positively correlated among tough/tough and soft/soft bargainers and negatively correlated among tough/soft bargainers. Gray concluded that the bargainers seemed to be responding to their own level of initial demand, rather than their opponents', and that GRIT's strategy of soft concessions "will only lead to a reciprocally conceded bargaining solution within a particular kind of bargaining situation: that which consists of participants with similar level initial demands" (p. 177).

Finally, the research on concession dynamics holds the potential of predicting exactly when level-of-aspiration theory or an alternative, such as GRIT, may be most appropriate. Although Bartos's (1966) study was inconclusive, it clearly showed that contrasting predictions could be derived from a dynamical framework. Not until we thoroughly understand the dynamics of concession making will definitive answers be provided. Consequently, future research efforts in distributive bargaining should be geared toward the introduction, extension, and modification of dynamical models of the offer process.

One way of contrasting the dynamical models with the other distributive bargaining theories is to examine the role that communication plays in each. Level-of-aspiration theory and the various reciprocity and reinforcement theories try to explain how communication (via different concession strategies) influences bargaining outcome. In particular, these theories posit various psychological mechanisms—aspirations, norms of reciprocity, conditioning—by which communication shapes the settlement. Power-dependence theory, on the other hand, uses a sociological force (power) to explain both the communication (strategic choice) and the outcome. In contrast, most of the dynamical theories seek models of the communicative interaction and attempt to explain bargaining outcome by looking strictly at the pattern of interaction rather than by appealing to intervening psychological mechanisms or external sociological forces.

The drawback of the dynamical approaches is that, to date, they have only modeled the communication of offers, ignoring other types of communication. (I will return to this point in the final section of the chapter, although it is worth observing that many nondynamical theories share the same flaw.) The great advantage of most dynamical theories is their high degree of formalism, often achieved using mathematical language. Although improvements can undoubtedly be made, the dynamical models allow a level of precision and predictive power unattainable by the other approaches discussed in this section.

It is instructive to note the difference between the mathematics I am advocating and earlier attempts at developing mathematical theories of bargaining. Earlier approaches, grounded as they were in utility theory, usually presented an extremely static view of bargaining behavior. For example, Nash's (1950) theory of bargaining began with a mathematical description of the preferences of the bargainers and then moved directly to the bargaining settlement, skipping the bargaining interaction itself. I suspect that earlier models fell into disfavor (at least in psychology, sociology, and communication science) primarily because they were static. But they were also mathematical, and researchers tended to blame the models' inadequacies on the mathematics rather than on, more appropriately, their static nature. This development is unfortunate. Mathematics is a powerful (perhaps even necessary) means of analyzing dynamical phenomena. Using mathematical formalisms, extremely complicated verbal sequences can be analyzed with a precision and explicitness unattainable by verbal constructions. Because of the complexity of bargaining behavior, precise and explicit theoretical languages are essential—especially if one wishes to treat interaction in any detail.

III. INTEGRATIVE BARGAINING

Just as with distributive bargaining, integrative bargaining can be viewed in three different ways: as a structure of possible outcomes, as a cognitive framework, and as a process of strategic and tactical choices. Structurally, integrative bargaining can be characterized by variable-sum models. In contrast to distributive bargaining, which represents outcomes on a unidimensional continuum, integrative bargaining structures require multidimensional outcome spaces in which one bargainer's gain needn't be at the other's expense. Cognitively, integrative bargaining involves the perceptions of the negotiators. By framing the situation positively and rejecting the mythical fixed pie, bargainers can develop win-win orientations. Finally, integrative bargaining can be viewed from the standpoint of the strategies and tactics used by the bargainers (Lewicki & Litterer, 1985). Information disclosure, problem solving, and logrolling are examples of integrative behaviors. All three integrative bargaining perspectives share a concern for the processes leading to high mutual benefit. This section reviews the current findings pertinent to the attainment integrative outcomes.

No discussion of integrative bargaining would be complete without recognizing the work of Dean Pruitt and his colleagues. These researchers are largely responsible for the current interest in integrative bargaining and extensive reviews of their work can be found in Pruitt (1981) and Pruitt and Lewis (1977). Rather than repeating these reviews here, I will proceed instead as follows. After introducing the basic concepts encountered in the study of integrative bargaining, I will very briefly summarize the findings up to 1980, concentrating instead on only the most recent developments.

A. Basic Concepts and Findings

Central to the concept of integrative bargaining is the notion that *both* bargainers may profit from negotiation; thus, any index of bargaining success should focus on joint, rather than individual, benefits. The most intuitive index of joint benefit, of course, is simply the sum of the bargainers' individual benefits, although this measure is sensitive to windfalls by one of the bargainers. Consequently, two other measures of joint benefit—the product of the bargainers' benefits, and the benefit of the least successful bargainer, based, respectively, on Nash (1950) and Sen (1970)—are sometimes employed in integrative bargaining studies.

Unlike distributive bargaining tasks, in which the bargainers are usually confronted with but a single issue, the dominant research scenario in integrative bargaining—developed by Lewis and Pruitt (1971)—involves three issues (see Pruitt, 1981, for a discussion). The issues are constructed so that the bargainers can fashion tradeoffs leading to high joint benefit. This scenario has been used to investigate a number of variables related to integrative outcomes. The first of these is motivational orientation. Integrative bargaining theorists have borrowed the concept of motivational orientation from gaming studies of conflict (e.g., Deutsch, 1958, 1973). The idea is that a bargainer's motives may be oriented in one of three possible ways. A bargainer with an individualistic orientation wishes to make as much as possible without regard to the opponent's earnings. In contrast, a bargainer with a competitive orientation tries to maximize the difference between his or her outcomes and those of the opponent. Finally, a bargainer might possess a cooperative orientation—that is, a motivation to seek high individual outcomes coupled with a sincere desire to see that the group, as a unit, does well. Those with a cooperative orientation engage in coordinative behavior and see the bargaining relationship in a problem-solving framework rather than a conflictual one. It is easy to see how a cooperative or problem-solving orientation might lead to more integrative outcomes, and the research seems to verify this idea (Pruitt & Lewis, 1975; Schulz & Pruitt, 1978; but see Roloff, Tutzauer, & Dailey, 1989).

Not only are the bargainers' motivational orientations important, but their goals and aspirations also influence the final agreement's integrativeness. As pointed out in the previous section, level of aspiration has a long history in the study of distributive bargaining and there seem to be sound reasons for including it in any explanation of integrative agreements (Pruitt, 1981). When aspirations have been manipulated by varying a bargainer's limit, those dyads with high aspirations have attained greater joint benefit than those with low aspirations (Kimmel, Pruitt, Magenau, Konar-Goldband, & Carnevale, 1980; Pruitt & Lewis, 1975; Roloff et al., 1989).

Two theoretical explanations of the results of the orientation and aspiration studies have been proposed. The first proposal was the *flexible-rigidity hypoth-*

esis (Pruitt & Lewis, 1977; Pruitt, 1981), which held that, by being flexible with respect to means, and rigid with respect to goals, bargainers could obtain integrative outcomes. Problem-solving orientations, of course, provided flexibility in means, whereas high aspirations functioned as rigid goals.

More recently, Pruitt (1983) has incorporated the flexible-rigidity hypothesis within a broader theoretical framework called the *dual-concern model*. Basically, Pruitt argued that negotiators choose from among four strategies: inaction, yielding, problem solving (where flexible-rigidity is most advantageous), and contending (i.e., contentious behavior). Levels of concern about one's own outcomes and about the other's outcome dictate strategy choice. A bargainer engages in problem solving when both concerns are high, and inaction when both concerns are low. The bargainer chooses yielding or contending depending on whether there is greater concern for the opponent's outcomes or for own outcomes.

In addition to orientation and aspiration, a number of communicative behaviors can lead to highly integrative outcomes. First of all, *incorporation* "entails adding to one's proposal or search model some element of a proposal made previously by the other party" (Pruitt, 1981, p. 169). Although small but significant positive correlations have occasionally been found, incorporation often has appeared unrelated to joint benefit (Pruitt, 1981). Second, Pruitt (1981) has suggested *information exchange*, reasoning that the exchange of information about profits and aspirations produces greater mutual insight into the priority structure of the issues and allows the bargainers to discover otherwise nonobvious solutions to their conflict. Positive relationships have been observed between joint benefit and the provision of a number of types of information (Pruitt, 1981). Similarly, the bargainers might engage in *heuristic trial and error*—that is, suggesting many different proposals, reducing the benefit being sought for oneself gradually and only when necessary. Heuristic trial and error has been found to be positively correlated to joint benefit, especially among high accountability dyads (Pruitt, 1981).

Finally, the bargainers might consider the issues either simultaneously or sequentially—that is, they may consider the issues all at once or, alternatively, they might discuss them one at a time. Simultaneous consideration of the issues allows the bargainers to develop tradeoffs, and a number of studies have confirmed the integrative aspects of simultaneous consideration (Erickson, Holmes, Frey, Walker, & Thibaut, 1974; Froman & Cohen, 1970; Walker & Thibaut, 1971; Yukl, Malone, Hayslip, & Pamin, 1976).

B. Recent Developments

Research on integrative bargaining reported during the last 5 to 7 years has taken one of two forms: either simple extensions and elaborations of the research conducted from 1971 to 1980, or relatively major departures that represent completely new directions in the study of integrative bargaining. Each will be discussed.

1. Simple Extensions.   A number of studies have continued earlier research by manipulating new variables, often in combination with previously studied factors such as limit or motivational orientation. By and large, these new studies corroborate earlier findings, though often in the context of statistical interaction. For example, King and Glidewell (1980) found that an individualistic orientation was superior to a competitive orientation when communication was face-to-face, but the reverse held when the bargainers were separated by a barrier. With respect to limit, Ben-Yoav and Pruitt (1984b) examined presence or absence of a limit in light of a bargainer's expectation of cooperative future interaction with the negotiation partner. They found that bargainers without resistance points (limits) who expected to engage in cooperative future interaction suffered an "aspiration collapse" and attained low joint benefit. On the other hand, when the limit was relatively high, aspirations could be maintained and expectation of cooperative future interaction led to increased joint benefit. In a similar study (Roloff & Tutzauer, 1985), high and low limits were combined with high and low levels of interpersonal orientation (Swap & Rubin, 1983). Although no interaction was found, the results indicated that high limits improved joint benefit. One difference between the two studies, however, is that, in the latter (Roloff & Tutzauer, 1985), only dyads reaching agreement were analyzed, whereas in the former (Ben-Yoav & Pruitt, 1984b) *all* dyads were analyzed. Ben-Yoav and Pruitt (1984b, p. 330) reported that, when deadlocked dyads were excluded from the analysis, the interaction remained but was not as strong statistically.

Other research explored the way that negotiation variables influence bargaining process and outcome. To Clopton (1984), the provision of clear and unambiguous information by one of the bargainers tended to increase systematic concession making (a measure of heuristic trial and error), though this finding was complicated by an interaction with accountability (a more in-depth discussion of accountability will be presented in a subsequent section). Another investigation (Tutzauer, 1986b) found only a marginal effect of information exchange on joint benefit ($p < .08$), but a main effect for the amount of integrative potential (a variable that indexed how much the structure of possible outcomes differed from a distributive task).

Information and aspiration may be affected by other factors, such as the relationship between the bargainers and the perceptions the bargainers have of each other. Fry, Firestone, and Williams (1983) found that, when compared to couples who were dating, strangers tended to use more distributive communication, exchange less truthful information, had higher aspirations, engaged in more heuristic trial and error, and obtained (marginally) greater joint benefit. Not only might the relationship between the bargainers be important, but the perceptions of the negotiators can influence the situation, too. Schurr and Ozane (1985) led bargainers to believe that their partners either were or were not trustworthy and typically adopted either a soft or tough stance. Those bargainers who perceived their opponents as either tougher or less trustworthy sent fewer distributive messages. There was also an interaction such that, when compared to those in the tough, low-trust cell, bargainers in the tough but high-trust cell made more concessions and resolved more issues. Thus, on the basis of both Fry et al. and Schurr and Ozane, it seems that relatively external factors, such as perceptions and prior relationships, alter communication patterns and, consequently, bargaining outcome.

2. New Directions. Recent innovations in the study of integrative bargaining include the development of dynamical frameworks and the application of behavioral-decision theory to integrative scenarios. The dynamics of integrative bargaining have been studied from two different perspectives: the internal dynamics of single negotiation sessions, and the market dynamics of a series of negotiation sessions. Both approaches have yielded valuable information about the time-dependent aspects of integrative bargaining.

Investigating the dynamics of a single-trial negotiation scenario like Pruitt's is in some ways analogous to the work done in distributive bargaining with elliptic and Richardson-type models. Basically, a mathematical description of offer trajectories over time is postulated and then examined for empirical and theoretical adequacy. But since integrative bargaining involves two individuals, and because the benefits of both must be simultaneously taken into account, matrix representations are more convenient than traditional differential or difference equations. The most recent work on the subject (Tutzauer, 1987) explored two possible functional forms. The first type of function—called a *simple concession function*—is analogous to the Kelley et al. (1967) resistance model in that it posits a pattern of exponential decay as the bargainer approaches a resistance point. On the other hand, an *oscillatory concession function* assumes that bargainers oscillate around and, in the limit, approach an equilibrium value. In essence, the simple model takes the type of communication patterns observed in distributive contexts and generalizes to the integrative case by allowing resistance points to be two-dimensional (self and other), whereas the oscillatory function more closely resembles Pruitt's (1981) heuristic trial and error, because it allows bargainers to search for integrative alternatives by systematically varying their offers.

Laboratory evidence showed that bargainers who engaged in information exchange exhibited a slight tendency to behave in a manner more consistent with the simple model. However, regardless of condition, the simple model fared well as a predictor of bargaining process and outcome. Future directions would include the investigation of other functions and, ideally, the discovery of a general model that includes the simple concession function as a special case. The advantage of these types of models is that, being mathematical, one can make unambiguous claims about bargaining behavior, such as whether or not behavior described by simple models can, in fact, be encompassed by a more general formulation.

An alternative to examining the dynamics of a single transaction involves tracking bargainers through a series of negotiation trials. In this way the effect of experience on the development of integrative solutions can be determined. Neale and Bazerman (1985a) adopted just such an approach. They employed the Pruitt scenario, but did so in a free market simulation that allowed participants to seek out new bargaining partners upon (perhaps unsuccessful) completion of a negotiation transaction. The experimenters also manipulated resistance point by creating four limit conditions: no goal (as in Ben-Yoav & Pruitt, 1984b), compromise and challenging goals (the standard low- and high-limit manipulations employed in other studies using the Pruitt scenario), and difficult goals (in which it was impossible for both negotiators to satisfy their limits). Results indicated that, over time, the market converged to the Nash equilibrium (the point of maximum joint benefit when indexed by the product of the bargainers' individual benefits). Furthermore, a series of regression analyses showed that bargainers with challenging and difficult goals earned higher *average* profit than compromise and no-goal bargainers, but difficult goals significantly lowered *total* profits and decreased the number of successful transactions completed.

Aside from bargaining dynamics, an exciting line of research involves the application of behavioral-decision theory to integrative bargaining. This approach takes a cognitive view of integrative bargaining by viewing it as a judgmental process. In contrast to a structural or strategic/tactical approach to integrative bargaining, a cognitive framework allows one to easily apply recent advances in the general psychology of human choice and decision making (e.g., Kahneman, Slovic, & Tversky, 1982; Tversky & Kahneman, 1974, 1981) to questions regarding the antecedents of integrative bargaining. The basic theoretical position was outlined by Bazerman (1983), Bazerman and Neale (1983), and Neale and Bazerman (1985c). Essentially they argued that normal biases of human judgment operate in negotiation settings much as they do in other areas of decision making. The two most important biases are negotiator *overconfidence* and the so-called *framing effect*. This latter phenomenon deals with the way messages or alternatives are presented (or framed). Tversky and Kahneman (1981) demonstrated that, when choices are framed positively (i.e., focusing on rewards, gains, etc.), people tend to be risk-averse, but when choices are framed negatively (focusing on costs, losses, etc.) risk-taking behavior results.

To examine the role of framing, Bazerman, Magliozzi, and Neale (1985) utilized the free-market simulation described above and altered the bargainers' profit tables and resistance points so that participants were confronted with either positively or negatively framed situations in combination with either high limits or no limits at all. Both limit and frame exerted an effect. Positive framing resulted in higher profits and a larger number of completed transactions, while high limits were associated with greater average and total profits. The study also replicated the over-time market convergence to the Nash solution found in Neale and Bazerman (1985a).

In a second study, Neale and Bazerman (1985b) combined framing with overconfidence. Although they used a union/management negotiation task instead of the standard Pruitt scenario, they obtained similar results. Both overconfident negotiators and negotiators presented with a negative frame showed decreases in concessionary behavior and obtained less successful outcomes.

C. Synthesis of Findings

Taken as a whole, the research on integrative bargaining presents a fairly consistent picture. Given the right combination of factors, it is possible to fashion agreements of high joint benefit. It seems that two ingredients are needed. First, the negotiators must be flexible with respect to the means of reaching an agreement. Simultaneous issue consideration, heuristic trial and error, information exchange, and cooperative orientation can facilitate flexibility, while negotiator overconfidence and negative framing hurt flexibility. However, flexibility by itself is not sufficient to assure high joint benefit; the negotiator must also have the incentive to search for integrative solutions. By and large, aspirations and limits can provide this incentive, although several qualifications are in order. First, the influence of a high limit is sometimes modified by other factors, for example expectations of cooperative future interaction. Second, aspirations seem to be primarily useful only in the short term. When viewed over lengthier time frames, a different picture emerges. As time progresses, bargainers gain experience in the market and aspirations become less important. In fact, aspirations, especially if too high, may even be detrimental to total profit, because bargainers complete fewer successful transactions. A useful parallel exists between integrative and distributive bargaining. As the last section demonstrated, in distributive contexts aspiration can improve individual payoffs, but only at the risk of a greater probability of deadlocking. So, too, with integrative bargaining, high aspirations can facilitate short-term gains but may have undesirable consequences over the long term.

IV. ATTITUDINAL STRUCTURING

Research on attitudinal structuring has dealt primarily with the formation of attitudes and expectations and their contribution to negotiated outcomes. The largest body of research on attitudinal structuring has involved the coding of communicative behavior into discrete categories, although more recently argumentation theory has been applied to bargaining. Both lines of research will be reviewed.

A. Coding Bargaining Interaction

There are a number of approaches to coding bargaining interaction, usually based on a set of exhaustive and mutually exclusive categories, although noncategorical methods have sometimes been employed. For example, Francis (1986) applied conversational analysis to transcripts of industrial negotiations in order to learn how negotiators structured their conversations and maintained topical coherence. In a somewhat different (although still noncategorical) fashion, Lindskold, Han, and Betz (1986) found that the GRIT strategy could be significantly improved by making a general announcement of intent prior to employing the strategy.

When categorical coding systems have been utilized, statements or turns are usually taken as the unit of analysis (e.g., Conference Process Analysis—see Morley & Stephenson, 1977), although Woodside and Taylor (1985) argued that blocks of two or more consecutive turns should be taken as the analytical unit in order to avoid "the violence done in uncoupling an exchange of turns between communicators" (p. 444). More traditional coding systems include Bales's (1950) well-known Interaction Process Analysis (IPA), which was developed for small group research but has also been applied to bargaining and negotiation (e.g., Theye & Seiler, 1979).

Similar to IPA is Bargaining Process Analysis (BPA) II (Hopmann & Walcott, 1976; excellent discussions can be fund in Putnam & Jones, 1982b, and Walker, 1984). The BPA system breaks the interaction into six types of behaviors: *substantive behaviors,* such as rejection and acceptance; *strategic behavior,* including commitments, threats, and promises; *persuasive behavior,* such as the use of evidence and arguments; *task behavior,* such as giving or requesting information, reactions, and so forth; *affective behavior,* or behavior dealing with feelings and emotions; and *procedural behavior,* or interaction concerning procedural aspects of the negotiation. A modified version of this category system has been applied to labor-management negotiations by Putnam and Jones (1982a). Lag-sequential analysis showed that the dominant behavior was a cycle of offensive-defensive acts, and that impasse dyads, in contrast to agreeing dyads, exhibited a symmetrical pattern of attack-attack or defend-defend (but see Putnam & Jones, 1984).

An interesting study, conducted by Bednar and Curington (1983), combined Bargaining Process Analysis with a variant of the Rogers and Farace (1975) relational coding system, which classifies messages as one-up ($\uparrow$), one-down ($\downarrow$), or one-across ($\rightarrow$). Examination of contiguous acts, called *interacts,* gives insight into the control-oriented aspects of the conversation. Bednar and Curington coded transcripts of a series of actual labor negotiation sessions and found that, overall, the dominant mode of interaction was competitive symmetry (i.e., interacts of the form $\uparrow\uparrow$). After dividing the sessions into three approximately equal phases, a Markov analysis revealed little change from phase to phase for the content codes (BPA), but significant changes from the first phase to the second phase for the relational codes (↑ , ↓ , and →), apparently caused by the increased probability of a one-up move being followed by a one-down move in the second two phases (see Table 4 of Bednar & Curington, 1983).

Another coding system designed for contiguous acts was developed by Donohue (1981a,b). Instead of interacts, however, Donohue coded each turn twice, once as a cue to the immediately subsequent act, and also as a response to the immediately prior act. Both cues and responses were classified as to whether or not they represented attacking tactics (designed to take the offensive and undermine the opponent's position), defending tactics (designed to stabilize the situation), and regressing tactics (tactics representing weakness or lack of confidence). Regressing, attacking, and defending cues/responses were then subdivided into still further categories.

Research utilizing this scheme showed that winners and losers (in a distributive bargaining context) used responding and cueing codes differently (Donohue, 1981b), and that a bargainer's relative advantage, when measured on the basis of weighted response and cue codes, could be used to predict negotiation success (Donohue, 1981a). In a later study, Donohue, Diez, and Hamilton (1984) modified the basic scheme and found that naturalistic bargainers differed from simulation bargainers, though this conclusion should be qualified somewhat, given that it was based on a comparison of only two simulation interactions and one naturalistic interaction (consisting of 24 sessions). Thus, any difference between naturalistic and simulated bargaining in general was inextricably confounded with the particular simulated and naturalistic negotiations used.

B. Argumentation

It is almost trivial to say that argumentation influences the course of negotiations; arguments can alter an opponent's expectations and aspirations. Although the importance of argument in bargaining has been noted before (e.g., Reiches & Harral, 1974), only recently has significant theorizing about bargaining argumentation been done (see, e.g., Keough, 1987, and Bacharach & Lawler, 1981a; Walker, 1986, provides a critique of the Bacharach & Lawler position). Earlier research on persuasion-related variables proved to be somewhat disappointing, never producing a completely clear picture. In research on bargainers of unequal power and status, for example, Tjosvold (1977b) found that a bargainer's self presentation exerted no effect on the likelihood of agreement, though it did alter the opponent's attitude of the negotiator. Similarly, neither affirmation of the opponent's personal effectiveness (Tjosvold, 1978a) nor type of justice rule (equity, need, self-advancement—Tjosvold, 1977a) altered the likelihood of agreement. On the other hand, sending control-based rather than collaborative messages (Tjosvold, 1978b), affirming the opponent's high status (Tjosvold, 1977b), and affirming the opponent's position and arguments (Tjosvold, 1978a) all decreased the likelihood of agreement. However, Tjosvold and Huston (1978) failed to replicate the effect of affirmation of position and arguments on the likelihood of agreement, although they did find that, when agreements occurred, they took much longer than when there was no such affirmation. Thus, the social-psychological study of persuasion variables failed to provide an adequate explanation.

More recent research has employed argument fields or rhetorical analyses, or has attempted to elucidate argument processes operating in distributive and integrative bargaining. Argument fields have been of interest independent of their application to negotiation (see, e.g., Willard, 1982). When applied to bargaining (e.g., Keough, 1986, 1987; Keough & Lake, 1986), the use of argument fields implies that factors such as the nature and evaluation of argumentation, the audience, and situational context all influence bargaining processes. Keough and Lake (1986, p. 1), in their defense of argument fields, claimed that such a perspective "would reject the view that negotiation is monolithic, and instead would legitimize the study of the differences between negotiation in, say, international relations and labor-management bargaining." Thus, in contrast to the usual goal of theory unification in which higher and higher levels of generality are sought, fields research is in some sense reductionistic, in that arguments used in negotiation are profoundly shaped by the fields appropriate to them. Furthermore, no one, as of yet, has conducted any empirical research whatsoever in support of the fields perspective as applied to bargaining and negotiation.

As an alternative to research on argument fields in bargaining, some have taken a more rhetorical approach (see, e.g., Alspach, 1986). In a case study of public sector bargaining, Putnam and Geist (1985) explicitly adopted a rhetorical stance. They found that most argumentative claims were evaluative and definitional, and that most reasoning was from analogy, cause, or hypothetical example, with very little "hard data" provided by the bargainers.

Also important to bargaining research, it seems, are the various functions of argument in negotiation. Wilson and Putnam (1986), beginning from the premise that bargaining is a goal-directed activity, claimed that arguments have multiple functions in a bargaining situation: to support and refute proposals, to establish the relationship between the bargainers, to obtain joint outcomes, and to protect the bargainers' identities. Wilson and Putnam further assumed that negotiators argue in order to accomplish their goals, and thus empirical regularities (in argumentation) can be explained by analyzing interaction goals and argument functions.

Finally, researchers have attempted to explicate the role of argumentation in integrative and distributive bargaining using both case-study (Putnam & Wilson, 1989; Putnam, Wilson, Waltman, & Turner, 1986) and experimental methods (Roloff et al., 1989). In a case study of teachers' bargaining, Putnam et al. (1986) examined case type (whether the arguments concerned needs, benefits, or goals) and case fit (whether the case faithfully portrayed perceptions of the status quo).

They found that distributive bargaining emerged when the negotiators disagreed over both case type and case fit, but problem-solving behavior resulted from an over-time shifting of case type and fit toward a redefinition of issues and alternatives.

Moving from a macrolevel (cases) to a microlevel (specific types of arguments), Putnam and Wilson (1989) analyzed the data from the above case study and found, surprisingly, that integrative bargaining resulted from arguments about harm, inherency, and plan workability. In contrast, laboratory evidence examining both distributive and integrative contexts (Roloff et al., 1987) has suggested that argumentation breeds contentiousness. In the distributive bargaining context, arguments about responsibility resulted in a significant increase in the number of deadlocks, and in the integrative context persuasive arguments were negatively related to joint benefit. After controlling for the effect of persuasive arguments on deadlocks, the negative relationship disappeared, although it was not replaced with a positive one. Thus, in opposition to Putnam and Wilson (1989), Roloff et al. (1989) concluded that vigorous argumentation does not promote integrative bargaining, and may in fact hinder it through the creation of conditions leading to deadlock.

Putnam (1989) has suggested a number of differences between Putnam and Wilson (1989) and Roloff et al. (1989) that might explain the contradictory results, including (respectively) the use of experts vs. students, bargaining by teams rather than individuals, and the use of caucus sessions vs. the absence of time outs, among other factors. Furthermore, because the Putnam and Wilson data were obtained from a case study, neither statistical nor experimental controls could be imposed, so it is difficult to say how bargaining behavior in the teachers' negotiations would have changed if argumentation strategies had been altered. At the very least, however, as Putnam (1989) has maintained, the two studies provide a strong justification for further research on argumentation in negotiation.

C. Synthesis of Findings

Unlike research on integrative and distributive bargaining, which has evolved into a highly developed literature, research on attitudinal structuring is much more tentative in nature. In the study of integrative and distributive bargaining, there are fairly well-defined research objectives (what strategies lead to agreement, how can joint benefit be improved), whereas with attitudinal structuring it is not at all clear what we should be studying. Nonetheless, a few general observations are possible.

First, the interdependent and interactional nature of bargaining seems clear. The actions of the negotiators are linked, sequences of coded behavior have been identified, and arguments appear to shape the bargainers' expectations and attitudes. Second, bargaining interaction certainly influences bargaining outcome, although we have not yet determined the relative contribution of offer strategies (studied in integrative and distributive bargaining), on the one hand, and other coded behaviors (such as argumentation), on the other. A related question deals with whether the nature, extent, or function of argumentation and other interactive behaviors differ between distributive contexts and integrative contexts. Finally, regarding argumentation in particular, we need more and better-controlled studies to yield further insight into the role that argumentation plays in the bargaining process.

V. INTRAORGANIZATIONAL BARGAINING

The research on intraorganizational bargaining differs somewhat from the previous three categories. Rather than examining the nature of the interaction between the bargainers themselves, the focus is on the bargainers' interactions with their constituents (or within bargaining teams) and how these interactions affect the process or outcome of the negotiations. Although not all bargaining situations involve constituents, a sizable portion—arms talks, labor–management negotiations, and so forth—do involve the negotiator as representative, so an understanding of intraorganizational bargaining is warranted.

The negotiator who represents a constituent must strike a balance between the desire to accommodate the opponent, on the one hand, and the allegiance to the constituent, on the other. As Walton and McKersie (1965) have claimed, the negotiator who represents a constituent is "the recipient of two sets of demands—one from across the table and one from his own organization" (p. 6). In fact, Colosi (1983) has argued that the communication taking place within the negotiation teams and between the teams and their constituents may be more important than communication between the representatives as they bargain.

In examining contituency and group pressure on negotiation behavior, experimenters have looked at a variety of manipulations in both distributive and integrative settings. Early research (e.g., Benton & Druckman, 1973; Druckman, 1967, 1971; Druckman, Solomon, & Zechmeister, 1972; Kahn & Kohls, 1972; Vidmar, 1971) compared negotiators who represented a constituent to those who did not. When effects were found at all, they tended to be small, and although group representatives often acted more competitively than nonrepresentatives, it made little difference in the final analysis whether one represented a group or not.

The argument to be made about this research, of course, is that rather than the mere presence or absence of constituents, we should be studying "the degree to which constituents can make representatives account for, justify, or defend the actions they took in negotiations" (Bacharach & Lawler, 1980, p. 133). Thus, it is not so much the existence of a constituent or group that is important, but, rather, the *accountability* of the negotiator that is critical.

Druckman (1977), in a stimulating discussion of boundary-role conflict, presented a model that helps to explain how accountability to group desires influences a representative's behavior. The group, as a collective, can (in principle) rank order all possible settlements on the basis of preference. This rank ordering may or may not be the same as the negotiator's own preferences. Thus, for any given settlement, we can distinguish between two utilities: U_g, or the settlement's utility to the group, and U_n, the corresponding utility for the negotiator. The utility which the negotiator attempts to maximize is given by

$$U = \alpha U_g + (1 - \alpha)U_n$$

where α is defined on the closed interval $[0,1]$ and denotes the degree to which the negotiator is accountable to his/her group. When $\alpha = 1$, the negotiator is completely accountable and attempts to maximize $U = U_g$. When $\alpha = 0$, the negotiator acts independently of the group and seeks to satisfy only his or her own preferences (i.e., $U = U_n$).

Most often, however, the level of accountability lies somewhere in between and the degree to which U tends toward the desires of the group or the representative depends on the size of the parameter α.

A number of factors might influence the magnitude of α, and thus, via accountability, alter negotiation process and outcome. For example, Knouse (1980) found that the adherence of the negotiator to the constituent's position was influenced by the quality of the constituent's position. A number of studies (Benton & Druckman, 1974; Peterson & Tracy, 1977; Slusher, 1978) have found that, when the constituent had a competitive orientation, or exerted pressure on the representative, competitive bargaining resulted, whereas Wall (1977) found that the constituent's stance interacted with locus of control so as to affect the *opposing* bargainer's behavior. (A cooperative stance resulted in cooperation from internals, but a competitive stance, or no stance at all, resulted in cooperation from externals.) More usually, however, accountability has been manipulated by varying either the power of the constituent or the type of constituent review. The remainder of this section discusses the research utilizing such approaches.

A. Constituent Power

As mentioned earlier, Bacharach and Lawler (1980, 1981a, 1986) have viewed power in terms of dependence—an individual has power over another in proportion to the degree of dependence between them. A bargainer's dependence on the constituent has been shown to alter bargaining behavior (Benton, 1972; but see Frey & Adams, 1972), although the most recent research shows a somewhat complicated pattern of findings.

Carnevale, Pruitt, and Seilheimer (1981) manipulated accountability by varying the degree to which the negotiator depended on the constituent for a share of the postnegotiation payment. The investigators combined this manipulation with whether or not bargainers had visual access to each other. They found that a cooperative atmosphere was jeopardized by accountability, and that accountability, when coupled with visual access, tended to decrease insight into the opponent's preferences. They also found an interaction such that, in the visual access condition, high accountability decreased joint profit and the score of the loser. For winners' scores and for payoff difference, no effects were obtained. (Other studies on visual access in bargaining, although not dealing with accountability, include Carnevale & Isen, 1986; Lewis & Fry, 1977; and Fry, 1985.) Ben-Yoav and Pruitt (1984a) used a similar accountability manipulation and found that accountability decreased joint benefit when there was no expectation of cooperative future interaction, but *increased* joint benefit when the bargainers did expect cooperative future interaction.

Jackson and King (1983) also manipulated power by using division of money as a criterion of dependence, but in some cases, the representatives had *more* power than the constituents. The researchers found that negotiations between two powerful representatives took significantly less time than negotiations among mixed dyads or dyads where the constituents held the power. No effects for deadlocks, earnings, or satisfaction were observed, although these hypotheses were tested with low satistical power (.35 for moderate effect sizes).

Finally, Bartunek, Benton, and Keys (1975) had subjects simulate a contract dispute between a teachers' union and a school board. Low accountability was induced by telling subjects that their contract as a union/school board representative had just been renewed for a 3-year period and that their job tenure would be unaffected by the present negotiations. High accountability was induced by telling subjects that their contracts would be up for renewal in 1-month and depended, in large part, on the outcome of the present dispute. Combining these manipulations with various types of third-party intervention, the researchers found that accountability interacted with intervention style. Although no main effects were found for accountability, some indication that accountability created a competitive view of the situation can be gleaned from the investigators' observation that "the high accountability condition created a 'face saving' problem" (p. 552) for the negotiators.

The results of these four studies, when taken together, suggest that the power wielded by the constituent does affect the way bargainers view the situation and how they subsequently act. However, this effect is not as strong as previously expected, and the representative's dependence on the constituent must be quite high before behavior is altered significantly. Furthermore, in integrative settings at least, accountability may interact with other variables. Sometimes it is a debilitating force; other times, given the right combination of circumstances, accountability may actually improve benefits.

B. Constituent Review

Klimoski and Ash (1974) have distinguished between *terminal accountability* (postnegotiation constituent review) and *continuous accountability* (constituent observation throughout the entire negotiation session).

Early studies (e.g., Gruder, 1971; Gruder & Rosen, 1971; Klimoski, 1972) typically manipulated terminal accountability and found modest effects. Continuous review, however, apparently heightens the impact of accountability. Klimoski and Ash found that, among groups with randomly selected representatives, more deadlocks occurred in the continuous condition (33%) than in either the terminal condition (25%) or the no-accountability condition (8%). Similarly, Carnevale, Pruitt, and Britton (1979), when comparing continuous review to no review, discovered that continuous surveillance decreased joint and individual outcomes and led to more distributive behavior. As with constituency power, however, constituency review may interact with other variables. Pruitt, Carnevale, Forcey, and Van Slyck (1986) replicated the Carnevale et al. (1979) results for surveillance by males, but found that surveillance by females discouraged contentious behavior. Clopton (1984) compared continuous review to terminal review and found that, when clear information was made available, continuous review decreased systematic concession making but increased it when ambiguous information was provided.

Interactions of a different sort were discovered by Roloff and Campion (1987). These investigators crossed accountability (whether negotiators were subjected to terminal review or no review at all) with authority (whether or not constituent ratification of the agreement was required). Results showed that accountable bargainers deadlocked more often, took longer to agree, and were generally less satisfied with negotiated outcomes than nonaccountable bargainers. Accountability also interacted with authority such that, among accountable bargainers, authority increased the extremity of initial offers but resulted in fewer deadlocks. Overall, it seemed that authority could mitigate the effects of accountability, but not to the extent of eliminating accountability altogether.

C. Synthesis of Findings

On the basis of the accountability studies reviewed in this section, it appears that the effects of representational role, though present, are not as strong as had been assumed. The constituent must either have a significant amount of power over the representative, or must be in a position to review the work of the representative, before boundary-role conflict becomes important. Apparently, it is not *representation* of the group that causes the conflicting goals for the negotiator, but rather accountability to the group is most important.

When representational effects do obtain, the negotiator tends to view the negotiation in more competitive terms and acts accordingly: Tougher stances are taken and deadlocks often ensue. The beneficial outcomes sometimes obtained by accountable negotiators (see also Haccoun & Klimoski, 1975) suggest that accountability may function in much the same way as high aspirations. Although fewer agreements result overall, when they do result they tend to be more desirable from the highly accountable negotiator's point of view. Indeed, the negotiator may even be able to use the unyielding constituent to his or her advantage. Rubin, Brockner, Eckenrode, Enright, and Johnson-George (1980) tested this "my hands are tied" ploy in a factorial design. Subjects, whose constituents either evaluated each offer or merely observed, bargained against a programmed opponent who either justified offers by referring to his or her constituent or who was silent regarding the constituent. Contrary to predictions, subjects made greater concessions in the no-justification condition. On the basis of this finding and a variety of postexperimental data, Rubin et al. concluded that, in order to work, the "weakness as strength" ploy must be both credible and legitimate, and the opponent must want to reach agreement. However, Friedland (1983) demonstrated that the unexpected reversal of findings could be attributed to the extreme toughness of the (programmed) final offer. In a 2 × 2 design, Friedland replicated Rubin et al.'s reversal effect for final offers outside the bargaining range (the interval between resistance points), but discovered that, as originally predicted, the "my hands are tied" strategy significantly increased the opponent's conciliation when the last offer fell within the bargaining range.

VI. THE FUTURE OF BARGAINING RESEARCH

Over the last three decades, the negotiation literature has grown rapidly, extending across numerous academic disciplines. And although such growth signals the vitality of the field, it also threatens fragmentation as the proliferation of articles initiating new lines of research makes the larger corpus of bargaining scholarship unwieldy. Such fragmentation hampers theoretical synthesis because of differences in terminology, methods, and applications (Oliva & Leap, 1981). As a result, it is difficult to locate gaps in our knowledge; research tends to be ad hoc, with a consequent lack of theoretical scope and explanatory power.

Already there are signs of splintering. As Oliva and Leap (1981, p. 340) pointed out, "it appears that little progress has been made toward theory unification or meaningful classification" of bargaining research. The subfields of integrative and distributive bargaining have developed as essentially two separate literatures, with little cross-citation. Similarly, researchers interested in the role of initial and subsequent demands tend to ignore other types of communication, whereas investigators who code all of a negotiator's communicative behavior fail to appreciate the importance of offer strategies and concession making. Indeed, in the current review, I have dealt with the size of the bargaining and negotiation literature by largely ignoring such obviously relevant topics as coalitions, game

theory, and third-party intervention. Thus, unlike other reviewers, I will not end this chapter by calling for the study of new bargaining variables (Putnam & Jones, 1982b; Rubin & Brown, 1975), replacing college students with other samples (Morley & Stephenson, 1977; Rubin & Brown, 1975), or even moving from the lab to the field (Putnam & Jones, 1982b; Rubin & Brown, 1975). Instead, I believe we should begin cumulating the findings into a single, grand framework. Rather than initiating new research in whatever contexts and dealing with whatever variables happen to strike the researcher's fancy, we must design our research programs so as to answer questions that promote unification. That is, instead of designing research around relatively narrow theories of bargaining interaction (level-of-aspiration theory, argumentative fields, theories of accountability and role representation, and so forth), we should attempt to incorporate current and future research and theorizing into broad unified theories. As Kitcher (1982), in a different context, has argued, "A science should be *unified*. A thriving science is not a gerrymandered patchwork but a coherent whole" (p. 47).

I should note, however, that there have been at least a few attempts at broad theoretical claims. Walton and McKersie (1965) devoted a chapter to the relationships between the four subprocesses, and Morely and Stephenson's (1977) "quasiprescriptive model," by focusing on bargaining stages, emphasized the move from distributive bargaining to problem solving and from problem solving to decision making. But neither of these approaches quite represent the truly synthetic theorizing I am advocating. Walton and McKersie's comments were more speculative than explanatory, and it is difficult to see how Morley and Stephenson's stages can adequately account for the entire constellation of negotiation behaviors and outcomes. Perhaps the best attempt to date is Bacharach and Lawler's power-dependence theory, in which offers, commitments, outcomes, and so forth flow from the power relationship between the bargainers. However, I share with Nagel (1979) the view that "single factor" theories will ultimately prove inadequate as social scientific explanations; postulating power as the single, driving force underlying bargaining behavior seems to slight such obviously important concepts as problem solving, interpersonal relationships, and relational history. Furthermore, as I pointed out in the section on distributive bargaining, power-dependence theory is beset with a number of problems concerning formalization and theoretical scope, so it seems unlikely that the theory can adequately cumulate and integrate current research findings.

The inadequacy of current approaches and the need for further unification becomes especially clear when one examines the role of communication. Consider first the transmission and acceptance of offers. This type of communication has been extensively studied by distributive bargaining theorists, and, to a lesser extent, by integrative bargaining researchers as well. On the other hand, those interested in the manner in which attitudes are structured have typically coded bargaining communication into discrete categories. And although both offer and nonoffer communications are important, researchers rarely (if ever) assess the *relative* contribution of the two types of communication. My own speculation is that offers exert a more profound impact on bargaining outcome than do other types of communication, although I know of no study addressing the issue.

A related problem concerns the various coding schemes used to analyze bargaining interaction. These coding systems are rarely theory driven and, on balance, tend to be cumbersome, particularistic, and of questionable validity, given that widespread collapsing of categories often takes place. A unified theory would go a long way toward assisting in standardization and helping us determine which behaviors should be coded.

Unlike the study of other functions of bargaining communication, serious research on argumentation is still in its infancy. There is a desperate need for controlled, experimental research on the role that bargaining argumentation plays in changing the opponent's preferences and expectations. Perhaps certain offer strategies work only in the presence of particular kinds of arguments. Maybe some arguments are more effective when coupled with negotiator accountability. Perhaps argumentation operates differently in integrative and distributive settings. A unified theory holds the potential for answering such questions and integrating the study of bargaining argumentation into a broader theoretical framework.

The last function of communication—discovering new alternatives—deals, of course, with integrative bargaining. We have a fairly thorough understanding of the antecedents of integrative bargaining which, in a unified theory, would be merged with our knowledge of distributive bargaining, enriching both. Putnam and Jones (1982a) argued that, in some negotiation sessions, both integrative and distributive behaviors emerge, suggesting the desirability of combining the two literatures into a single theoretical schema. As an example of how research into the determinants of integrative outcomes can enhance our understanding of distributive bargaining, consider the relationship between initial offer and final outcome which I discussed in the section on distributive bargaining. Typical explanations of the relationship rely on level-of-aspiration theory and the way in which a high initial offer by one negotiator drives the opponent's aspirations downward, resulting in a more favorable outcome for the first negotiator. An alternative explanation, consistent with the view of negotiation as a judgmental task currently popular in the integrative bargaining literature (Bazerman, 1983; Bazerman & Neale, 1983; Neale & Bazerman, 1985c), can be generated using Tversky and Kahneman's (1974) anchoring and adjustment heuristic. It is possible that the initial offer serves as an anchor, or reference point, from which adjustments are made in order to arrive at a decision. The tendency of people to underadjust may be responsible for the observed relationship between initial offer and final outcome.[1] Although it is quite natural to view integrative bargaining as

---

[1] I am indebted to Carol Miller-Tutzauer for suggesting the anchoring and adjustment heuristic as a possible explanation for the findings regarding initial offer. She also believes that the heuristic may

a problem-solving or decision-making task, the study of distributive bargaining, dominated as it is by strategic considerations, allows a judgmental explanation only when one begins thinking in unified terms.

Not only is unification a theoretical necessity, but it would have a number of applied benefits as well. Because of the current piecemeal approach, it is difficult for the practioner engaged in, say, out-of-court negotiations to determine the relevance of research conducted on buyer–seller transactions. Consequently, negotiation practitioners typically rely on experience as a guide in real life negotiations. And although experience is undoubtedly important, a unified theory would help the practioner select those theoretical results relevant to the situation at hand, whether the negotiation situation involves labor–management grievances, plea bargaining, or international arms agreements.

Granting the need for a unified theory of bargaining, a number of problems must be overcome before unification can take place. In particular, I feel the following questions must be answered:

1. What is the best way to account for both toughness and cooperation? It is almost a cliche to claim that bargaining is a mixed-motive activity. The negotiator faces a contradictory set of demands: maximizing individual outcomes (via toughness) and engendering trust on the part of the opponent (via cooperation). Our theorizing, too, reflects the bargainer's dilemma. In distributive bargaining, both GRIT and level-of-aspiration theory have their adherents, and in integrative bargaining the flexible-rigidity hypothesis is a popular theoretical perspective.

Ideally, both coordination and intransigence can be blended into a coherent explanation of bargaining outcome. To do so, of course, requires a unified theory, one that contains GRIT-like and level-of-aspiration explanations as special cases of a larger phenomenon.

2. How can distributive and integrative bargaining be incorporated into a single framework? I have already alluded to the possibility of merging distributive and integrative bargaining into a unified perspective using the anchoring and adjustment heuristic. There are undoubtedly other ways, and alternatives to anchoring and adjustment need to be explored. It may be that answering question 1 above will suggest the appropriate means of simultaneously explaining both distributive and integrative bargaining. In any event, discovering the appropriate way to incorporate the two bargaining types into a single framework is critical to the development of a unified theory.

3. How can the dynamic nature of concession making best be captured? Bargaining is an inherently interactive phenomenon, and it seems to me that a unified theory *must* treat bargaining dynamics in some detail. Both temporal and sequential information should be considered, especially with respect to offer strategies. However, bargaining dynamics are so complex that I see little pos-

---

play a role in decisions made by arbitrators after hearing the negotiating parties' positions. If so, it may be possible to bring not only integrative and distributive bargaining under the same umbrella, but third-party intervention as well.

sibility of avoiding a mathematical description. Social scientists in general (Bender, 1978; Cobb & Thrall, 1981) and communication scientists in particular (see discussions by Cappella, 1977, and McPhee & Poole, 1982) are beginning to recognize the necessity of stating theories in mathematical terms. With respect to offer dynamics, some progress has been made, but the proper functional forms have yet to be determined. Further research along these lines is essential to a unified theory. (I am of course referring to research such as that conducted with Richardson-type models, not economic utility models such as Nash, 1950. Whereas the latter research ignores communication, the former explicitly incorporates it into the formalisms.) By forcing us to make our assumptions explicit and unambiguous, mathematics gives us a powerful language for deriving predictions and testing the internal consistency of theories about bargaining dynamics. Verbal explanations simply cannot handle a phenomenon as complex as bargaining interaction in any but the most rudimentary of fashions.

4. How should nonoffer data be modeled mathematically? Although it seems quite natural to treat the dynamics of numerical offers from a mathematical viewpoint, a unified theory requires that both offer and nonoffer data be incorporated into the same framework. How can this be done? A common misconception is that mathematical explanations are necessarily quantitative. While it is true that mathematics can handle quantitative propositions better than can verbal descriptions, it is also the case that mathematics provides a rich framework for expressing and evaluating *qualitative* propositions. Mathematics is neither simply computation nor "number crunching." It is, instead, a logical framework for the manipulation of symbols. There is nothing inherently quantitative about mathematics. As Starbuck (1965, p. 340) has noted, "mathematics is not necessarily numerical. . . . and there is every reason to believe that nonnumerical mathematics will be particularly useful in the social sciences." For example, recent work in differential topology (Chillingworth, 1976) and catastrophe theory (Thom, 1975) gives us the ability to study such concepts as stability, periodicity, and the qualitative behavior of dynamical systems. By incorporating such notions into a unified theory, it becomes possible to examine the relative behavior (and contributions) of both offers and nonoffer communications. Thus, the question of how nonoffer data should be modeled mathematically is critical for the development of a unified theory.

Significant progress has been made in our understanding of bargaining and negotiation. In the past few decades, literally thousands of empirical and theoretical studies have been published. In 1975, Rubin and Brown ended their massive review of bargaining research by claiming that "a review of the literature, no matter how extensive, is simply not equivalent to a theory" (p. 299). I agree. But reviews such as the present one can suggest the next theoretical steps that should be undertaken. Without a move toward theory unification, the bargaining and negotiation literature may well collapse under its own enormity.

REFERENCES

Adams, J. S. (1965). Inequity in social exchange. In L. Berkowitz (Ed.), *Advances in experimental social psychology* (Vol. 2, pp. 267–299). New York: Academic Press.

Alspach, S. L. (1986, November). *A rhetorical approach to the study of negotiations*. Paper presented at the annual meeting of the Speech Communication Association, Chicago.

Bacharach, S. B., & Lawler, E. J. (1980). *Power and politics in organizations: The social psychology of conflict, coalitions, and bargaining*. San Francisco, CA: Jossey-Bass.

Bacharach, S. B., & Lawler, E. J. (1981a). *Bargaining: Power, tactics, and outcomes*. San Francisco, CA: Jossey-Bass.

Bacharach, S. B., & Lawler, E. J. (1981b). Power and tactics in bargaining. *Industrial Labor Relations Review, 34*, 219–233.

Bacharach, S. B., & Lawler, E. J. (1986). Power dependence and power paradoxes in bargaining. *Negotiation Journal, 2*, 167–174.

Bales, R. F. (1950). *Interaction process analysis: A method for the study of small groups*. Reading, MA: Addison-Wesley.

Bartos, O. J. (1966). Concession-making in experimental negotiations. In J. Berger, M. Zelditch, Jr., & B. Anderson (Eds.), *Sociological theories in progress* (Vol. 1, pp. 3–28). Boston, MA: Houghton-Mifflin.

Bartos, O. J. (1974). *Process and outcome of negotiations*. New York: Columbia University Press.

Bartunek, J. M., Benton, A. A., & Keys, C. B. (1975). Third party intervention and the bargaining behavior of group representatives. *Journal of Conflict Resolution, 19*, 532–557.

Bateman, T. S. (1980). Contingent concession strategies in dyadic bargaining. *Organizational Behavior and Human Performance, 26*, 212–221.

Bazerman, M. H. (1983). Negotiator judgment: A critical look at the rationality assumption. *American Behavioral Scientist, 27*, 211–228.

Bazerman, M. H., & Lewicki, R. J. (Eds.). (1983). *Negotiating in organizations*. Beverly Hills, CA: Sage.

Bazerman, M. H., Magliozzi, T., & Neale, M. A. (1985). Integrative bargaining in a competitive market. *Organizational Behavior and Human Decision Processes, 35*, 294–313.

Bazerman, M. H., & Neale, M. A. (1983). Heuristic negotiation: Limitations to effective dispute resolution. In M. H. Bazerman & R. J. Lewicki (Eds.), *Negotiation in organizations* (pp. 51–67). Beverly Hills, CA: Sage.

Bednar, D. A., & Curington, W. P. (1983). Interaction analysis: A tool for understanding negotiations. *Industrial and Labor Relations Review, 36*, 389–401.

Beisecker, T. (1970). Verbal persuasive strategies in mixed-motive interactions. *Quarterly Journal of Speech, 56*, 149–160.

Bender, E. A. (1978). *An introduction to mathematical modeling*. New York: John Wiley.

Benton, A. A. (1972). Accountability and negotiations between group representatives [Summary]. *Proceedings of the 80th Annual Convention of the American Psychological Association, 7*, 227–228.

Benton, A. A., & Druckman, D. (1973). Salient solutions and the bargaining behavior of representatives and nonrepresentatives. *International Journal of Group Tensions, 3*(1–2), 28–39.

Benton, A. A., & Druckman, D. (1974). Constituent's bargaining orientation and intergroup negotiations. *Journal of Applied Social Psychology, 4*, 141–150.

Benton, A. A., Kelley, H. H., & Liebling, B. (1972). Effects of extremity of offers and concession rate on the outcomes of bargainers. *Journal of Personality and Social Psychology, 24*, 73–83.

Ben-Yoav, O., & Pruitt, D. G. (1984a). Accountability to constituents: A two-edged sword. *Organizational Behavior and Human Performance, 34*, 283–295.

Ben-Yoav, O., & Pruitt, D. G. (1984b). Resistance to yielding and the expectation of cooperative future interaction in negotiation. *Journal of Experimental Social Psychology, 20*, 323–335.

Cappella, J. J. (1977). Research methodology in communication: Review and commentary. In B. D. Ruben (Ed.), *Communication yearbook 1* (pp. 11–27). New Brunswick, NJ: Transaction/ICA.

Carnevale, P. J. D., & Isen, A. M. (1986). The influence of positive affect and visual access on the discovery of integrative solutions in bilateral negotiation. *Organizational Behavior and Human Decision Processes, 37,* 1–13.

Carnevale, P. J. D., Pruitt, D. G., & Britton, S. D. (1979). Looking tough: The negotiator under constituent surveillance. *Personality and Social Psychology Bulletin, 5,* 118–121.

Carnevale, P. J. D., Pruitt, D. G., & Seilheimer, S. D. (1981). Looking and competing: Accountability and visual access in integrative bargaining. *Journal of Personality and Social Psychology, 40,* 111–120.

Chertkoff, J. M., & Conley, M. (1967). Opening offer and frequency of concession as bargaining strategies. *Journal of Personality and Social Psychology, 7,* 181–185.

Chertkoff, J. M., & Esser, J. K. (1976). A review of experiments in explicit bargaining. *Journal of Experimental Social Psychology, 12,* 487–503.

Chillingworth, D. R. J. (1976). *Differential topology with a view to applications.* London: Pitman.

Church, R. J., Jr., & Esser, J. K. (1980). Effects of information on level of aspiration in bargaining. *Representative Research in Social Psychology, 11,* 38–43.

Clopton, S. W. (1984). Seller and buying firm factors affecting industrial buyers' negotiation behavior and outcomes. *Journal of Marketing Research, 21,* 39–53.

Cobb, L., & Thrall, R. M. (Eds.). (1981). *Mathematical frontiers of the social and policy sciences.* Boulder, CO: Westview Press.

Colosi, T. (1983). Negotiation in the public and private sectors: A core model. *American Behavioral Scientist, 27,* 229–253.

Crott, H., Kayser, E., & Lamm, H. (1980). The effects of information exchange and communication in an asymmetrical negotiation situation. *European Journal of Social Psychology, 10,* 149–163.

Deutsch, M. (1958). Trust and suspicion. *Journal of Conflict Resolution, 2,* 265–279.

Deutsch, M. (1973). *The resolution of conflict: Constructive and destructive processes.* New Haven, CT: Yale University Press.

Donohue, W. A. (1981a). Analyzing negotiation tactics: Development of a negotiation interact system. *Human Communication Research, 7,* 273–287.

Donohue, W. A. (1981b). Development of a model of rule use in negotiation interaction. *Communication Monographs, 48,* 106–120.

Donohue, W. A., Diez, M. E., & Hamilton, M. (1984). Coding naturalistic negotiation interaction. *Human Communication Research, 10,* 403–425.

Donohue, W. A., Diez, M. E., & Stahle, R. B. (1983). New directions in negotiation research. In R. N. Bostrom (Ed.), *Communication yearbook 7* (pp. 249–279). Beverly Hills, CA: Sage.

Druckman, D. (1967). Dogmatism, prenegotiation experience, and simulated group representation as determinants of dyadic behavior in a bargaining situation. *Journal of Personality and Social Psychology, 6,* 279–290.

Druckman, D. (1971). On the effects of group representation. *Journal of Personality and Social Psychology, 18,* 273–274.

Druckman, D. (1977). Boundary role conflict: Negotiation as dual responsiveness. *Journal of Conflict Resolution, 21,* 639–662.

Druckman, D., Solomon, D., & Zechmeister, K. (1972). Effects of representational role obligations on the process of children's distribution of resources. *Sociometry, 35,* 387–410.

Erickson, B., Holmes, J. G., Frey, R., Walker, L., & Thibaut, J. (1974). Functions of a third party in the resolution of conflict: The role of a judge in pretrial conferences. *Journal of Personality and Social Psychology, 30,* 293–306.

Fouraker, L. E., & Siegel, S. (1963). *Bargaining behavior.* New York: McGraw-Hill.

Francis, D. W. (1986). Some structures of negotiation talk. *Language in Society, 15,* 53–79.

Frey, R. L., Jr., & Adams, J. S. (1972). The negotiator's dilemma: Simultaneous in-group and out-group conflict. *Journal of Experimental Social Psychology, 8,* 331–346.

Friedland, N. (1983). Weakness as strength: The use and misuse of a "my hands are tied" ploy in bargaining. *Journal of Applied Social Psychology, 13,* 422–426.

Froman, L. A., Jr., & Cohen, M. D. (1970). Compromise and logroll: Comparing the efficiency of two bargaining processes. *Behavioral Science, 15,* 180–183.

Fry, W. R. (1985). The effect of dyad Machiavellianism and visual access on integrative bargaining outcomes. *Personality and Social Psychology Bulletin, 11,* 51–62.

Fry, W. R., Firestone, I. J., & Williams, D. L. (1983). Negotiation process and outcome of stranger dyads and dating couples: Do lovers lose? *Basic and Applied Social Psychology, 4,* 1–16.

Gouldner, A. W. (1960). The norm of reciprocity: A preliminary statement. *American Sociological Review, 25,* 161–178.

Gray, S. H. (1977). Model predictability in bargaining. *Journal of Psychology, 97,* 171–178.

Gruder, C. L. (1971). Relationships with opponent and partner in mixed-motive bargaining. *Journal of Conflict Resolution, 15,* 403–416.

Gruder, C. L., & Rosen, N. A. (1971). Effects of intragroup relations on intergroup bargaining. *International Journal of Group Tensions, 1,* 301–317.

Haccoun, R. R., & Klimoski, R. J. (1975). Negotiator status and accountability source: A study of negotiator behavior. *Organizational Behavior and Human Performance, 14,* 342–359.

Hamner, W. C. (1974). Effects of bargaining strategy and pressure to reach agreement in a stalemated negotiation. *Journal of Personality and Social Psychology, 30,* 458–467.

Hamner, W. C., & Harnett, D. L. (1975). The effects of information and aspiration level on bargaining behavior. *Journal of Experimental Social Psychology, 11,* 329–342.

Hawes, L. C., & Smith, D. H. (1973). A critique of assumptions underlying the study of communication in conflict. *Quarterly Journal of Speech, 59,* 423–435.

Holmes, J. G., Throop, W. F., & Strickland, L. H. (1971). The effects of prenegotiation expectations on the distributive bargaining process. *Journal of Experimental Social Psychology, 7,* 582–599.

Homans, G. C. (1961). *Social behavior: Its elementary forms.* New York: Harcourt Brace.

Hopmann, P. T., & Smith, T. C. (1977). An application of a Richardson process model: Soviet-American interactions in the test ban negotiations 1962–1963. *Journal of Conflict Resolution, 21,* 701–726.

Hopmann, P. T., & Walcott, C. (1976). The impact of international conflict and detente on bargaining in arms control negotiations: An experimental analysis. *International Interactions, 2,* 189–206.

Ikle, F. C. (1973). Bargaining and communication. In I. de Sola Pool, W. Schramm, F. W. Frey, N. Maccoby, & E. B. Parker (Eds.), *Handbook of communication* (pp. 836–843). Chicago, IL: Rand McNally.

Jackson, C. N., & King, D. C. (1983). The effects of representatives' power within their own organizations on the outcome of a negotiation. *Academy of Management Journal, 26,* 178–185.

Kahn, A. S., & Kohls, J. W. (1972). Determinants of toughness in dyadic bargaining. *Sociometry, 35,* 305–315.

Kahneman, D., Slovic, P., & Tversky, A. (Eds.). (1982). *Judgment under uncertainty: Heuristics and biases.* New York: Cambridge University Press.

Kelley, H. H., Beckman, L. L., & Fischer, C. S. (1967). Negotiating the division of a reward under incomplete information. *Journal of Experimental Social Psychology, 3,* 361–398.

Keough, C. M. (1986, May). *The nature and function of argument in organizational bargaining research.* Paper presented at the annual meeting of the International Communication Association, Chicago.

Keough, C. M. (1987). The nature and functions of argument in organizational bargaining research. *Southern Speech Communication Journal, 53*, 1–17.

Keough, C. M., & Lake, R. A. (1986, November). *Argument fields and the study of negotiations.* Paper presented at the annual meeting of the Speech Communication Association, Chicago.

Kimmel, M. J., Pruitt, D. J., Magenau, J. M., Konar-Goldband, E., & Carnevale, P. J. D. (1980). Effects of trust, aspiration, and gender on negotiation tactics. *Journal of Personality and Social Psychology, 38*, 19–22.

King, D. C., & Glidewell, J. C. (1980). Dyadic bargaining outcomes under individualistic and competitive orientations. *Human Relations, 33*, 781–803.

Kitcher, P. (1982). *Abusing Science: The case against creationism.* Cambridge, MA: MIT Press.

Klimoski, R. J. (1972). The effects of intragroup forces on intergroup conflict resolution. *Organizational Behavior and Human Performance, 8*, 363–383.

Klimoski, R. J., & Ash, R. A. (1974). Accountability and negotiator behavior. *Organizational Behavior and Human Performance, 11*, 409–425.

Knouse, S. B. (1980). Effects of sex of representative and quality of constituency's position on a technical negotiating task. *Perceptual and Motor Skills, 51*, 19–22.

Komorita, S. S., & Barnes, M. (1969). Effects of pressure to reach agreement in bargaining. *Journal of Personality and Social Psychology, 13*, 245–252.

Komorita, S. S., & Esser, J. K. (1975). Frequency of reciprocated concessions in bargaining. *Journal of Personality and Social Psychology, 32*, 699–705.

Komorita, S. S., Lapworth, C. W., & Tumonis, T. M. (1981). The effects of certain vs. risky alternatives in bargaining. *Journal of Experimental Social Psychology, 17*, 525–544.

Lawler, E. J., & Bacharach, S. B. (1976). Outcome alternatives and value as criteria for multi-strategy evaluations. *Journal of Personality and Social Psychology, 34*, 885–894.

Lawler, E. J., & Bacharach, S. B. (1979). Power dependence in individual bargaining: The expected utility of influence. *Industrial and Labor Relations Review, 32*, 196–204.

Lawler, E. J., & MacMurray, B. K. (1980). Bargaining toughness: A qualification of level-of-aspiration and reciprocity hypotheses. *Journal of Applied Social Psychology, 10*, 416–430.

Lewicki, R. J., & Litterer, J. A. (Eds.). (1985). *Negotiation: Readings, exercises, and cases.* Homewood, IL: Richard D. Irwin.

Lewis, S. A., & Fry, W. R. (1977). Effects of visual access and orientation on the discovery of integrative bargaining alternatives. *Organizational Behavior and Human Performance, 20*, 75–92.

Lewis, S. A., & Pruitt, D. G. (1971). Orientation, aspiration level, and communication freedom in integrative bargaining [Summary]. *Proceedings of the 79th Annual Convention of the American Psychological Association, 6*, 221–222.

Liebert, R. M., Smith, W. P., Hill, J. H., & Keiffer, M. (1968). The effects of information and magnitude of initial offer on interpersonal negotiation. *Journal of Experimental Social Psychology, 4*, 431–441.

Lindskold, S., Han, G., & Betz, B. (1986). The essential elements of communication in the GRIT strategy. *Personality and Social Psychology Bulletin, 12*, 179–186.

Luce, R. D., & Raiffa, H. (1957). *Games and decisions: Introduction and critical survey.* New York: John Wiley.

McGillicuddy, N. B., Pruitt, D. G., & Syna, H. (1984). Perceptions of firmness and strength in negotiation. *Personality and Social Psychology Bulletin, 10*, 402–409.

McPhee, R. D., & Poole, M. S. (1982). Mathematical modeling in communication research: An overview. In M. Burgoon (Ed.), *Communication yearbook 5* (pp. 159–191). New Brunswick, NJ: Transaction/ICA.

Midgaard, K., & Underdal, A. (1977). Multiparty conferences. In D. Druckman (Ed.), *Negotiations: Social-psychological perspectives* (pp. 329–345). Beverly Hills, CA: Sage.

Morley, I. E., & Stephenson, G. M. (1977). *The social psychology of bargaining.* London: Allen & Unwin.

Murdock, J. I., Bradac, J. J., & Bowers, J. W. (1984). Effects of power on the perception of explicit and implicit threats, promises, and thromises: A rule-governed perspective. *Western Journal of Speech Communication, 48,* 344–361.

Nagel, E. (1979). *The structure of science: Problems in the logic of scientific explanation* (2nd ed.). Indianapolis, IN: Hackett.

Nash, J. F., Jr. (1950). The bargaining problem. *Econometrica, 18,* 155–162.

Neale, M. A., & Bazerman, M. H. (1985a). The effect of externally set goals on reaching integrative agreements in competitive markets. *Journal of Occupational Behavior, 6,* 19–32.

Neale, M. A., & Bazerman, M. H. (1985b). The effects of framing and negotiator overconfidence on bargaining behaviors and outcomes. *Academy of Management Journal, 28,* 34–49.

Neale, M. A., & Bazerman, M. H. (1985c). Perspectives for understanding negotiation: Viewing negotiation as a judgmental process. *Journal of Conflict Resolution, 29,* 33–35.

Nemeth, C. (1972). A critical analysis of research utilizing the prisoner's dilemma paradigm for the study of bargaining. In L. Berkowitz (Ed.), *Advances in experimental social psychology* (Vol. 6, pp. 203–234). New York: Academic Press.

Oliva, T. A., & Leap, T. L. (1981). A typology of metamodels in collective bargaining. *Behavioral Science, 26,* 337–345.

Osgood, C. (1962). *An alternative to war or surrender.* Urbana, IL: University of Illinois Press.

Oskamp, S. (1971). Effects of programmed strategies on cooperation in the Prisoner's Dilemma and other mixed-motive games. *Journal of Conflict Resolution, 15,* 225–259.

Peterson, R. B., & Tracy, L. (1977). Testing a behavioral theory model of labor negotiations. *Industrial Relations, 16,* 35–50.

Plovnick, M. S., & Chaison, G. N. (1985). Relationships between concession bargaining and labor-management cooperation. *Academy of Management Journal, 28,* 697–704.

Pruitt, D. G. (1981). *Negotiation behavior.* New York: Academic Press.

Pruitt, D. G. (1983). Strategic choice in negotiation. *American Behavioral Scientist, 27,* 167–194.

Pruitt, D. G., Carnevale, P. J. D., Forcey, B., & Van Slyck, M. (1986). Gender effects in negotiation: Constituent surveillance and contentious behavior. *Journal of Experimental Social Psychology, 22,* 264–275.

Pruitt, D. G., & Lewis, S. A. (1975). Development of integrative solutions in bilateral negotiations. *Journal of Personality and Social Psychology, 31,* 621–633.

Pruitt, D. G., & Lewis, S. A. (1977). The psychology of integrative bargaining. In D. Druckman (Ed.), *Negotiations: Social-psychological perspectives* (pp. 161–192). Beverly Hills, CA: Sage.

Pruitt, D. G., & Smith, L. D. (1981). Impression management in bargaining: Images of firmness and trustworthiness. In J. T. Tedeschi (Ed.), *Impression management theory and social psychological research* (pp. 247–267). New York: Academic Press.

Pruitt, D. G., & Syna, H. (1985). Mismatching the opponent's offers in negotiation. *Journal of Experimental Social Psychology, 21,* 103–113.

Putnam, L. L. (1985). Bargaining as task and process: Multiple functions of interaction sequences. In R. L. Street, Jr. & J. N. Cappella (Eds.), *Sequence and pattern in communicative behavior* (pp. 225–242). London: Edward Arnold.

Putnam, L. L. (1989). In A. Rahim (Ed.), *Managing conflict: An interdisciplinary perspective* (pp. 67–70). New York: Praeger.

Putnam, L. L., & Geist, P. (1985). Argument in bargaining: An analysis of the reasoning process. *Southern Speech Communication Journal, 50,* 225–245.

Putnam, L. L., & Jones, T. S. (1982a). Reciprocity in negotiations: An analysis of bargaining interaction. *Communication Monographs, 49,* 171–191.

Putnam, L. L., & Jones, T. S. (1982b). The role of communication in bargaining. *Human Communication Research, 8,* 262–280.

Putnam, L. L., & Jones, T. S. (1984). Corrections to lag sequential results in communication research: Responses. *Human Communication Research, 11,* 124–134. [A correction to Putnam & Jones, 1982a; see pp. 132–134 of the present citation.]

Putnam, L. L., & Wilson, S. R. (1989). Argumentation and bargaining strategies as discriminators of integrative outcomes. In M. A. Rahim (Ed.), *Managing conflict: An interdisciplinary approach* (pp. 109–119). New York: Praeger.

Putnam, L. L., Wilson, S. R., Waltman, M. S., & Turner, D. (1986). The evolution of case arguments in teachers' bargaining. *Journal of the American Forensic Association, 23,* 63–81.

Rapaport, A., & Chammah, A. M. (1965). *Prisoner's dilemma: A study in conflict and cooperation.* Ann Arbor, MI: University of Michigan Press.

Reiches, N. A., & Harral, H. B. (1974). Argument in negotiation: A theoretical and empirical approach. *Speech Monographs, 41,* 36–48.

Richardson, L. F. (1960). *Arms and insecurity: A mathematical study of the causes and origins of war.* Pittsburgh, PA: Boxwood Press.

Rogers, L. E., & Farace, R. V. (1975). Analysis of relational communication in dyads: New measurement procedures. *Human Communication Research, 1,* 222–239.

Roloff, M. E., & Campion, D. E. (1987). On alleviating the debilitating effects of accountability on bargaining: Authority and self-monitoring. *Communication Monographs, 54,* 145–164.

Roloff, M. E., & Tutzauer, F. (1985, May). *Looking for the golden needle in the haystack: Two tests of competing theories in integrative bargaining.* Paper presented at the annual meeting of the International Communication Association, Honolulu, HI.

Roloff, M. E., Tutzauer, F., & Dailey, W. O. (1989). The role of argumentation in distributive and integrative bargaining contexts: Seeking relative advantage but at what cost? In M. A. Rahim (Ed.), *Managing conflict: An interdisciplinary approach* (pp. 121–141). New York: Praeger.

Roth, A. E. (1979). *Axiomatic models of bargaining.* Berlin: Springer-Verlag.

Rubin, J. Z., Brockner, J., Eckenrode, J., Enright, M. A., & Johnson-George, C. (1980). Weakness as strength: Test of a "my hands are tied" ploy in bargaining. *Personality and Social Psychology Bulletin, 6,* 216–221.

Rubin, J. Z., & Brown, B. R. (1975). *The social psychology of bargaining and negotiation.* New York: Academic Press.

Rubin, J. Z., & DiMatteo, M. R. (1972). Factors affecting the magnitude of subjective utility parameters in a tacit bargaining game. *Journal of Experimental Social Psychology, 8,* 412–426.

Schulz, J. W., & Pruitt, D. G. (1978). The effects of mutual concern on joint welfare. *Journal of Experimental Social Psychology, 14,* 480–492.

Schurr, P. H., & Ozane, J. L. (1985). Influences on exchange processes: Buyers' preconceptions of a seller's trustworthiness and bargaining toughness. *Journal of Consumer Research, 11,* 939–953.

Seholm, K. J., Walker, J. L., & Esser, J. K. (1985). A choice of alternative strategies in oligopoly bargaining. *Journal of Applied Social Psychology, 15,* 345–353.

Sen, A. K. (1970). *Collective choice and social welfare.* San Francisco, CA: Holden-Day.

Siegel, S., & Fouraker, L. E. (1960). *Bargaining and group decision making: Experiments in bilateral monopoly.* New York: McGraw-Hill.

Slusher, E. A. (1978). Counterpart strategy, prior relations, and constituent pressure in a bargaining simulation. *Behavioral Science, 23,* 470–477.

Smith, D. L., Pruitt, D. G., & Carnevale, P. J. D. (1982). Matching and mismatching: The effect of own limit, other's toughness, and time pressure on concession rate in negotiation. *Journal of Personality and Social Psychology, 42,* 876–883.

Starbuck, W. H. (1965). Mathematics and organization theory. In J. G. March (Ed.), *Handbook of organizations* (pp. 335–386). Chicago, IL: Rand McNally.

Steinfatt, T. M., Seiblold, D. R., & Frye, J. K. (1974). Communication in game simulated conflicts: Two experiments. *Speech Monographs, 41,* 24–35.

Swap, W. C., & Rubin, J. Z. (1983). Measurement of interpersonal orientation. *Journal of Personality and Social Psychology, 44,* 208–219.

Tedeschi, J. T., & Rosenfeld, P. (1980). Communication in bargaining and negotiation. In M. E. Roloff & G. R. Miller (Eds.), *Persuasion: New directions in theory and research* (pp. 225–248). Beverly Hills, CA: Sage.

Tedeschi, J. T., Schlenker, B. R., & Bonoma, T. V. (1973). *Conflict, power, and games: The experimental study of interpersonal relations.* Chicago, IL: Aldine.

Theye, L. D., & Seiler, W. J. (1979). Interaction analysis in collective bargaining: An alternative approach to the prediction of negotiated outcomes. In D. Nimmo (Ed.), *Communication yearbook 3* (pp. 375–392). New Brunswick, NJ: Transaction/ICA.

Thom, R. (1975). *Structural stability and morphogenesis: An outline of a general theory of models* (D. H. Fowler, trans.). Reading, MA: Benjamin/Cummings. (Original work published 1972)

Tjosvold, D. (1977a). Commitment to justice in conflict between unequal status persons. *Journal of Applied Social Psychology, 7,* 149–162.

Tjosvold, D. (1977b). The effects of the constituent's affirmation and the opposing negotiator's self-presentation in bargaining between unequal status groups. *Organizational Behavior and Human Performance, 18,* 146–157.

Tjosvold, D. (1978a). Affirmation of the high-power person and his position: Ingratiation in conflict. *Journal of Applied Social Psychology, 8,* 230–243.

Tjosvold, D. (1978b). Control strategies and own group evaluation in intergroup conflict. *Journal of Psychology, 100,* 305–314.

Tjosvold, D., & Huston, T. L. (1978). Social face and resistance to compromise in bargaining. *Journal of Social Psychology, 104,* 57–68.

Tutzauer, F. (1986a). Bargaining as a dynamical system. *Behavioral Science, 31,* 65–81.

Tutzauer, F. (1986b, November). *Integrative potential and information exchange as antecedents of joint benefit in negotiation dyads.* Paper presented at the annual meeting of the Speech Communication Association, Chicago.

Tutzauer, F. (1987). Exponential decay and damped harmonic oscillation as models of the bargaining process. In M. L. McLaughlin (Ed.), *Communication yearbook 10* (pp. 217–240). Newbury Park, CA: Sage.

Tversky, A., & Kahneman, D. (1974). Judgment under uncertainty: Heuristics and biases. *Science, 185,* 1124–1131.

Tversky, A., & Kahneman, D. (1981). The framing of decisions and the psychology of choice. *Science, 211,* 453–458.

Vidmar, N. (1971). Effects of representational roles and mediators on negotiation effectiveness. *Journal of Personality and Social Psychology, 17,* 48–58.

Walker, G. B. (1984, May). *Analyzing bargaining behavior in international negotiations.* Paper presented at the annual meeting of the International Communication Association, San Francisco.

Walker, G. B. (1986, November). *Bacharach and Lawler's theory of argument in bargaining: A critique.* Paper presented at the annual meeting of the Speech Communication Association, Chicago.

Walker, W. L., & Thibaut, J. W. (1971). An experimental examination of pre-trial conference techniques. *Minnesota Law Review, 55,* 1113–1137.

Wall, J. A., Jr. (1977). Intergroup bargaining: Effects of opposing constituent stances, opposing representative's bargaining, and representative's locus of control. *Journal of Conflict Resolution, 21,* 459–474.

Wall, J. A., Jr. (1981). An investigation of reciprocity and reinforcement theories of bargaining behavior. *Organizational Behavior and Human Performance, 27*, 367–385.

Walton, R. E., & McKersie, R. B. (1965). *A behavioral theory of labor negotiations: An analysis of a social interaction system*. New York: McGraw-Hill.

Willard, C. A. (Ed.). (1982). Review symposium on argument fields [Special issue]. *Journal of the American Forensic Association, 18*(4).

Wilson, S. R., & Putnam, L. L. (1986, November). *Interaction goals and argument functions as schemes for organizing research on argument in bargaining*. Paper presented at the annual meeting of the Speech Communication Association, Chicago.

Woodside, A. G., & Taylor, J. L. (1985). Identify [sic] negotiations in buyer-seller interactions. *Advances in Consumer Research, 12*, 444–449.

Yukl, G. [A.] (1974). Effects of the opponent's initial offer, concession magnitude, and concession frequency on bargaining behavior. *Journal of Personality and Social Psychology, 30*, 323–335.

Yukl, G. A. (1976). Effects of information, payoff magnitude, and favorability of alternative settlement on bargaining outcomes. *Journal of Social Psychology, 98*, 269–282.

Yukl, G. A., Malone, M. P., Hayslip, B., & Pamin, T. A. (1976). The effects of time pressure and issue settlement order on integrative bargaining. *Sociometry, 39*, 277–281.

Zarefsky, D., Tutzauer, F., & Miller-Tutzauer, C. (1983, November). *The self-sealing rhetoric of John Foster Dulles*. Paper presented at the annual meeting of the Speech Communication Association, Washington, DC.

Author Index

Italics indicate bibliographic citations.

A

Abbott, V., 27, *59*
Abelman, R., 107, *135*
Abelson, R.P., 12, *15*, 27, *65*
Abrams, E., 239, *251*
Ackoff, R.L., 229, *251*
Adams, J.S., 263, 285, *293*, *295*
Adelman, M.B., 25, *27*, 32, 53, *59*, *65*
Agostino, D., 115, 121, 125, *135*, *136*
Aguilar, F.J., 228, *251*
Ahmed, D., 106, 114, *138*
Aiken, P.A., 73, *94*
Albrecht, T.L., 25, *59*
Alexander, A., 43, *59*, 106, *135*
Allen, T.J., 224, 225, 228, 229, 234, 235, 236, 237, 238, 250, *251*, *252*
Allison, P.D., 92, *94*
Alspach, S.L., 282, *293*
Altman, I., 44, 47, 51, *59*, 75, *94*
Amiel, H.F., 174, *207*
Anderson, J.A., 115, *135*
Anderson, K.A., 2, 10, *15*, 148, 149, *169*
Andrews, F.M., 227, 237, *254*
Andrews, P.H., 197, *207*
Appell, M.J., 150, *169*
Archer, D., 192, *213*
Argyle, M., 178, 179, *207*
Aries, E.J., 180, *207*
Arkin, R.M., 177, 178, 179, 203, 204, *214*
Arnkoff, D., 177, 184, 200, *213*
Arnold, E., 118, *135*
Aronson, E., 12, 13, 14, *15*
Arrington, A., 82, *95*
Ash, R.A., 287, *296*
Atkin, C.K., 29, *59*, 107, *136*
Atkins, B.K., 184, *213*
Atkinson, J.A., 134, *135*, 145, *169*
Austin, J., 12, *16*
Avery, R.D., 238, *252*

B

Bacharach, S.B., 269, 270, 271, 281, 284, 285, *293*, *296*
Badzinski, D., 76, 77, 79, *97*
Baer, W.S., 108, 115, *135*
Baird, J.E., 174, *207*
Bakeman, R., 91, *94*
Baker, E.E., 11, *15*
Bales, R.F., 280, *293*
Ball-Rokeach, S.J., 52, *59*
Balswick, J., 75, *96*
Bandura, A., 106, *135*
Banks, J., 43, *59*
Bantz, C.R., 126, *140*
Baran, S.J., 106, 134, *138*, *141*
Barge, J.K., 25, *65*
Barnes, M., 73, *95*, 271, *296*
Barnes, R., 201, 203, *210*
Baron, R.S., 14, *18*
Barraclough, R., 45, *62*
Barrios, L., 106, 114, *138*
Barry, W.A., 85, 92, *100*
Bartos, O.J., 266, 268, 272, *293*
Bartunek, J.M., 286, *293*
Basehart, J., 10, *18*
Bateman, T.S., 262, 263, 265, *293*
Baucom, D.H., 73, 78, *93*, *96*
Bauman, I., 79, *97*
Baumann, M., 177, *207*
Bavelas, J.B., 92, *94*
Baxter, L.A., 25, 35, *59*, *61*, 68, 75, *94*, *96*
Bazerman, M.H., 259, 260, 278, 279, 290, *293*, *297*
Beach, S., 78, *96*
Bealer, R.J., 11, *18*
Beavin, J.H., 84, *101*
Beckman, H.B., 159, 169, *169*, *170*
Beckman, L.L., 266, 277, *295*
Bednar, D.A., 258, 280, 281, *293*

301

Snodgrass, S.E., 191, 195, *207, 214*
Snyder, C., 196, *211*
Snyder, D.K., 89, *101*
Snyder, M., 44, 45, *66*
Sobol, B.L., 106, *136*
Sodetani, L.L., 49, 51, 52, 53, *63, 66*
Solnit, A., 148, *172*
Solomon, D., 284, *294*
Solomons, G., 148, 149, 156, *172*
Sommers, A.A., 81, *98*
Sonoda, K., 49, 51, 53, *63*
Spanier, G.B., 68, 88, *99, 101*
Speicher, C.E., 71, *98*
Sprafka, S.A., 245, *252*
Stack, C.B., 74, *98*
Stahle, R.B., 258, *294*
Stambaugh, R.J., 228, 242, 244, *251*
Starbuck, W.H., 292, *299*
Stark, M., 148, *172*
Stathas, S., 184, *211*
Stebbins, C., 196, *214*
Steele, D.J., 159, *172*
Steinfatt, T.M., 258, *299*
Steinberg, M., 32, 47, *64*
Steinfield, C., 108, *136*
Steinmetz, S., 83, *101*
Stephan, C.W., 52, 53, *66*
Stephan, W.G., 52, 53, *66*
Stephens, T., 73, *101*
Stephenson, G.B., 47, *66*, 84, *98*, 258, 280, 289, *297*
Sternberg, D.P., 76, *94*
Sternberg, R.J., 36, 37, 57, *66*
Sternthal, B., 7, 8, 12, *19*
Stier, D., 190, *214*
Stiff, J.B., 3, *19*
Stinson, E.R., 242, 246, *255*
Stoeckle, J.D., 149, 150, 159, 168, *171, 172*
Stoops, J., 10, 13, *17*
Stout, J.C., 71, *98*
Strauss, A.L., 148, *170*
Strickland, L.H., 266, *295*
Strodtbeck, F., 174, 178, *214*
Studley, L.B., 192, 201, *212*
Sultan, F.E., 75, *98*
Suomi, S., 84, *98*
Sunnafrank, M., 44, 54, 56, *66*
Svarstad, B.L., 149, 150, 160, 165, *170, 172*
Svennevig, M., 109, *137*
Swacker, M., 180, *214*
Swain, M.A., 85, 92, *100*

Swanson, D.A., 104, *138*
Swap, W.C., 276, *299*
Syna, H., 262, 264, *296, 297*

T
Tajfel, H., 47, *66*
Talarzyk, 132, *140*
Tannen, D., 167, *172*
Tannenbaum, P.H., 8, 12, 13, *15, 16, 18, 19*
Tardy, C.H., 184, *208*
Taylor, D.A., 75, *94*
Taylor, D.M., 44, 47, 49, 51, *59, 64*
Taylor, J.L., 280, *300*
Taylor, R.L., 237, *255*
Taylor, R.S., 218, 225, 226, 227, 228, 229, 230, 231, 242, 250, *253, 255*
Tedeschi, J.T., 258, *299*
Terman, L.M., 88, *101*
Tessmer, M.A., 107, *139*
Theye, L.D., 280, *299*
Thibaut, J.W., 275, *294, 299*
Thom, R., 292, *299*
Thomas, L., *255*
Thomas, M.M., 71, *95*
Thompson, L., 88, *101*
Thompson, W., 2, 11, *19*
Thorne, B., 175, 198, 200, 205, *211, 214*
Thrall, R.M., 292, *294*
Throop, W.F., 266, *295*
Timmer, S.G., 125, 134, *140*
Tims, A.R., 107, 114, 124, *136, 140*
Ting-Toomey, S., 41, 43, *63*, 85, *101*
Tinnell, C.S., 118, 119, *140*
Tjosvold, D., 281, 282, *299*
Tolor, A., 196, *214*
Tomita, K., 224, *253*
Towne, J.P., 38, *63*
Tracy, L., 285, *297*
Traudt, P.J., 106, 131, *138, 140*
Triandis, H.C., 42, 43, *66*
Trimboli, C., 179, *214*
Trudgill, P., 176, *214*
Trujillo, N., 33, 36, *66*
Tryon, W., 196, *213*
Tsou, B., 43, *59*
Tumonis, T.M., 271, *296*
Turnbull, A., 149, 168, *172*
Turnbull, H.R., 149, 168, *172*
Turnbull, W., 4, *17*
Turkle, S., 115, 119, *140*
Turner, D., 282, *298*

Subject Index